# Language of Ruin and Consumption

# Language of Ruin and Consumption

## On Lamenting and Complaining

*Juliane Prade-Weiss*

BLOOMSBURY ACADEMIC
NEW YORK · LONDON · OXFORD · NEW DELHI · SYDNEY

BLOOMSBURY ACADEMIC
Bloomsbury Publishing Inc
1385 Broadway, New York, NY 10018, USA
50 Bedford Square, London, WC1B 3DP, UK
29 Earlsfort Terrace, Dublin 2, Ireland

BLOOMSBURY, BLOOMSBURY ACADEMIC and the Diana logo
are trademarks of Bloomsbury Publishing Plc

First published in the United States of America 2020
This paperback edition published in 2022

Copyright © Juliane Prade-Weiss, 2020

For legal purposes the Acknowledgments on p. vii constitute
an extension of this copyright page.

Cover design by Eleanor Rose
Cover image: *Breakfast Table with Blackberry Pie* (1631),
by Willem Claesz Heda (1593/1594 – c. 1680/1682) © BPK / State Art
Collections Dresden / Elke Estel / Hans-Peter Klut

All rights reserved. No part of this publication may be reproduced or transmitted
in any form or by any means, electronic or mechanical, including photocopying,
recording, or any information storage or retrieval system, without prior permission
in writing from the publishers.

Bloomsbury Publishing Inc does not have any control over, or responsibility for,
any third-party websites referred to or in this book. All internet addresses given
in this book were correct at the time of going to press. The author and publisher
regret any inconvenience caused if addresses have changed or sites have
ceased to exist, but can accept no responsibility for any such changes.

Library of Congress Cataloging-in-Publication Data
Names: Prade-Weiss, Juliane, author.
Title: Language of ruin and consumption : on lamenting and complaining/
Juliane Prade-Weiss.
Description: New York : Bloomsbury Academic, 2020. | Based on the author's
habilitation–Universität Frankfurt am Main, 2019, with
title: Anhaltender Verzehr: Zur Sprache des Klagens. | Includes
bibliographical references and index. | Summary: "Analyses linguistic
structures of complaint and lament in key works of the modern canon"–
Provided by publisher.
Identifiers: LCCN 2020003344 | ISBN 9781501344190
(hardback) | ISBN 9781501344213 (pdf) | ISBN 9781501344206 (ebook)
Subjects: LCSH: Discourse analysis. | Complaints (Rhetoric) | Laments.
Classification: LCC P302.23 .P73 2020 | DDC 401/.41–dc23
LC record available at https://lccn.loc.gov/2020003344

ISBN: HB: 978-1-5013-4419-0
PB: 978-1-5013-7231-5
ePDF: 978-1-5013-4421-3
eBook: 978-1-5013-4420-6

Typeset by Integra Software Services Pvt. Ltd.

To find out more about our authors and books visit www.bloomsbury.com
and sign up for our newsletters.

# CONTENTS

*Acknowledgments* vii
*List of Abbreviations* viii
*Permissions* x

Introduction: Getting a Hearing 1
Consuming Structures of Language 2
Lamenting in Theory 5
Terms of Plaint 16
The Coming Chapters 25

1  Understanding Plaintive Language: Freud 27
   Complaint without a Cause: Treating Hysteria and
   Forgetting Laments in Modernity 29
   Complaining and Wish-Fulfillment 39
   Idiom of Plaint: The "Wolf Man's" Speech 48
   Mourning, Melancholia, and Consumption 55
   Metabolism of Plaintive Language 64

2  Ritual and Modernity: On Silencing Plaints
   (with Aeschylus, Rilke, Veteranyi) 77
   Tale of Lament's Life and Death 81
   Patterns of Looking at Ritual Plaints 88
   "The Dead Are Hungry": Metaphor and Liminality 99
   Antiphony: Response and Dissent 114
   Ta(l)king Revenge: No End to Lamentation 127

3  Voicing Pain and Destruction: Wittgenstein and Scholem  141
   Naming and Claiming Pain  146
   Knowing and Doubting Pain  150
   Complaint by Response  155
   A Nasty Move: Silencing Plaints  161
   Relationality and Symbol  164
   Lamenting Tradition  173

4  Lament of Nature: Benjamin, with Herder  177
   *Trauerspiel* and Tragedy: "The ear for lament"  179
   Benjamin's "Nature"  184
   Language as Such, and Terminology: Looking Away  188
   Vanishing from History  194
   Lament and Theory, Once Again  200

5  (No Way) From Complaining to Legal Action: Kafka  209
   "With every complaint understanding [subsides]"  210
   Understanding, Comprehension, Sympathy, and Inconsolability  214
   Plaints, Vanishing into Juridical Action  223
   Representation and Betrayal  229
   Politics of Outcry: Claiming Justice  239

Conclusion: Transgenerational Trauma and the Inability to Lament  243

*Bibliography*  261
*Index*  278

# ACKNOWLEDGMENTS

The book comprises the main parts of my *Habilitation* thesis in the field of Comparative Literature, accepted by Goethe University Frankfurt am Main in July 2019 under the title *Anhaltender Verzehr: Zur Sprache des Klagens* (Ceaseless Consumption: On Lamenting and Complaining). The topics, questions, and theses expounded in the book have been presented and discussed, challenged and supported, between 2012 and 2019, on many more occasions than I can possibly recall.

I am deeply indebted to Achim Geisenhanslüke of Frankfurt University, who hosted me while working on the first half of the project, 2014–17, and has generously supported me all along the way. I thank Heinz Drügh of Frankfurt University who encouraged me to take on and finish this comprehensive project, and Nikolaus Müller-Schöll, also of Frankfurt University, whose support made sure that I could in fact pursue the project. The book would not be what it is without the questions, comments, and inspiration, brought to me ever since a class on elegy and lament I taught in summer 2012, by the Bachelor, Master, and Graduate students of Frankfurt University's Comparative Literature program.

Working on the second half of the project, 2017–19, was generously sponsored by a German Federal Research Council (*Deutsche Forschungsgemeinschaft*) postdoc research fellowship (Forschungsstipendium, PR 1661/2-1). The grant was kindly hosted by the Department of Germanic Literatures and Languages at Yale University. I extend my thanks for their comprehensive scholarly, administrative, and personal support during this invigorating time to my host Paul North as well as to Kirk Wetters, Rüdiger Campe, and Katrin Trüstedt.

I have innumerable people to thank for their support, more than I can possibly name. I owe particular thanks to Eva Geulen (ZfL Berlin), Henry Sussman (Yale), Ilit Ferber (Tel Aviv), Dominic Angeloch (Frankfurt), Dominik Markl (Rome), and Nicole Sütterlin (Harvard). Errors, misjudgments, and infelicities are all my own.

# ABBREVIATIONS

| | |
|---|---|
| A | Kafka, Franz. *Amerika*. |
| AL | Bernhard, Thomas. *Auslöschung: Ein Zerfall*. |
| AV | *The Bible. Authorized King James Version with Apocrypha*. |
| CEV | *Holy Bible: Contemporary English Version*. |
| CS | Kafka, Franz. *Complete Stories*. |
| DL | Kafka, Franz. *Drucke zu Lebzeiten*. |
| DRB | *Douay-Rheims Bible*. |
| DW | Grimm, Jacob, and Wilhelm Grimm. *Deutsches Wörterbuch*. |
| E | Bernhard, Thomas. *Extinction*. |
| EA | *Der Neue Pauly. Enzyklopädie der Antike*. |
| GS | Benjamin, Walter. *Gesammelte Schriften*. |
| GW | Freud, Sigmund. *Gesammelte Werke: Chronologisch geordnet*. |
| HThKAT | *Herders Theologischer Kommentar zum Alten Testament*. |
| HWRH | *Historisches Wörterbuch der Rhetorik*. |
| IT | Kafka, Franz. "An Introductory Talk on the Yiddish Language." |
| KSA | Nietzsche, Friedrich. *Kritische Studienausgabe*. |
| LL | Scholem, Gershom. "On Lament and Lamentation." |
| LSJ | *A Greek-English Lexicon*. |
| LSPP | Wittgenstein, Ludwig. *Letzte Schriften über die Philosophie der Psychologie*. |
| LW | Wittgenstein, Ludwig. *Last Writings on the Philosophy of Psychology*. |
| LXX | *Septuaginta*. |
| MM | Abraham, Nicolas, and Maria Torok. "Mourning *or* Melancholia: Introjection *versus* Incorporation." |
| NRSV | *The New Oxford Annotated Bible. New Revised Standard Version with the Apocrypha*. |
| NSF | Kafka, Franz. *Nachgelassene Schriften und Fragmente*. |
| O | Benjamin, Walter. *The Origin of German Tragic Drama*. |
| OED | *Oxford English Dictionary*. 2nd ed. |
| OJB | *The Orthodox Jewish Bible*. |
| PI | Wittgenstein, Ludwig. *Philosophical Investigations*. |
| PR | Wittgenstein, Ludwig. *Philosophical Remarks*. |
| PU | Wittgenstein, Ludwig. *Philosophische Untersuchungen* |

| | |
|---|---|
| RSW | Rilke, Rainer Maria. *Sämtliche Werke.* |
| SE | Freud, Sigmund. *The Standard Edition of the Complete Psychological Works of Sigmund Freud.* |
| SW | Benjamin, Walter. *Selected Writings.* |
| TLP | Wittgenstein, Ludwig. *Tractatus Logico-Philosophicus.* |

# PERMISSIONS

Permission to reprint the following texts and image is gratefully acknowledged:

Excerpts from Rainald Goetz, *Klage*. (c) Suhrkamp Verlag Frankfurt am Main 2008. All rights reserved and controlled through Suhrkamp Verlag Berlin.

Excerpts from Aglaja Veteranyi, *Das Regal der letzten Atemzüge*. (c) 2002 Deutsche Verlags-Anstalt München, in der Verlagsgruppe Random House GmbH.

Cover image taken from Willem Claesz Heda, *Ein Frühstück mit Brombeerpastete*. (c) bpk | Staatliche Kunstsammlungen Dresden | Elke Estel | Hans-Peter Klut.

# Introduction: Getting a Hearing

> "... I keep no account with lamentation,
> (What have I to do with lamentation?)"
> WALT WHITMAN, SONG OF MYSELF 44.13–14.

Laments and complaints are pervasive among ancient texts, dominant in political discourse, and ubiquitous in everyday speech. Still, understanding plaintive language regularly fails because neither dirges, laments of love, neurotic complaints nor outcries against injustice are satisfied by a discourse on their particular claim—they all seem to want more. Plaintive cries, wailing, and sobbing make the hermeneutic difficulty apparent that all lamenting and complaining raise in claiming attention without presenting an object that could be discussed. This book assumes that the diverse forms of lamenting for, and complaining about, something all communicate a profound doubt in the possibility of verbal exchange and communication. A fundamental doubt in language is what makes very heterogonous utterances appear as variations of plaintive language. What all forms of lamenting and complaining fundamentally have in common is that they want to be heard. Getting a hearing is, time and again, what the paradigmatic lamenter Job insists on.[1]

The language of lamenting and complaining foregrounds a principle of language that is usually either taken for granted or relegated to mere rhetoric: Speech is not only *by* someone and *on* something, but also addressed *to* someone. Complaints and laments take special linguistic forms which focus on the hearing and attention of others, and reading these forms grants insight into how, in general, the structure of address is organized in language. Lamenting and complaining differ from other ways of speaking insofar as they make

---

[1] Job 13:17: "Listen carefully to my words, and let my declaration be in your ears." 19:7: "Even when I cry out, 'Violence!' I am not answered [heard]; I call aloud, but *there is* no justice." (NRSV, brackets AV)

apparent what the other modes elide, or conceal, to wit, that speaking wants to be heard, and some very important speech situations, the most important perhaps, show a desire to be heard when it is impossible that the speaker will be heard: One complains when the complainer cannot resolve things herself; one laments when this seems like the last thing on earth that can be done. These existential situations—brought about by death, catastrophes, bad news, neuroses, loneliness, cruelty, or something else—give rise to a mode of speech caught in a double bind: Being heard and responded to is urgently necessary and, at the same time, highly unlikely. Foregrounding the intention to being heard makes plaintive language irreconcilable and violent: Laments and complaints keep claiming attention while refusing symbolic substitution in order to insist that they cannot be answered, satisfied, or appeased by political, metaphysical, or therapeutic concepts. On a structural level, the violence of plaintive language appears in the disorganization of the principle of symbolic substitution. Lamenting and complaining communicate not by following linguistic conventions, but by decomposing and consuming the linguistic structures that usually enable comprehension—be it reference, address, and authorship that are undermined in ritual and in neurotic repetition, or be it articulation that is effaced in wailing and sobbing. Far from dysfunctional, this ruin of conventional structures of language in lamenting and complaining testifies to experiences of being overwhelmed which cannot be just named and seized in statements. Laments and complaints insist that the cause of distress is not to be re-presented by a sign, that such substitution would counteract the sense of lamenting over someone who has passed away, or complaining about something (like pain) that should pass. Lamenting and complaining thus communicate by way of consuming structures of language. This hypothesis certainly requires some explanation.

## Consuming Structures of Language

*Consumption* is no mere metaphor for the disorganization of language in lamenting and complaining but, rather, a theoretical vantage point for understanding symbolization that I, turning to psychoanalytical works, outline in Chapter 1. Freud sees a correlation between, on the one hand, various patients' incomprehensible laments and complaints (as he calls them) and, on the other hand, their refusal to mourn, to accept loss. In Freud, the disorganization of structures such as articulation and reference appears as a metabolic process. Abraham and Torok have further expounded the symbolic aspect of mourning as a cycle of internalization, fragmentation, appropriation, and excretion that forms the "I" in eluding the distinction between mental versus corporeal. In each of the following chapters, the terminology of consumption allows this study to describe the specific disorganization of language as well as a particular link of the expressed loss and pain to its psychological, social, juridical, or other negotiation. *Consuming* refers to both destroying, corroding, wearing away—in the sense that laments and complaints destroy comprehensibility—and the "the use or exploitation of resources"[2]—so as to denote the processual nature of the destruction of linguistic structures by way of repetition, slurring, and similar techniques. Describing the disorganization of language as a *consumption* of its structures alludes as much to the orality of many ritual laments (discussed below) as to the analysis of modern consumer culture, where consumption denotes the acquisition and usage or ingestion of goods that follows a set of rituals and fixed practices by which consumers define and identify themselves.[3] The consumption of linguistic structures in lamenting and complaining is a historically as well as culturally conditioned practice that aims at forming the everyday world, too, by giving voice to experiences (such as death or loss) and emotions (such as mourning or pain) in order to redefine and re-identify lamenters after experiences that profoundly alter life. These practices may be codified rites of passage or individual mourning; Chapter 2 will elaborate on the conflict between ritual and Modernity. What is pivotal as much to consumer culture as to the consumption of structures of language in lamenting and complaining is the lack of distance: The practices and rituals in question are not picked up, and later put aside, by sovereign subjects but, rather, generate those who perform them.[4]

The notion that plaintive languages causes a consumption of linguistic structures is far older than psychoanalysis and the critique of consumer culture, and it implies no naïve phonocentrism. Ezekiel, the mute prophet, is instructed by his god:

Ezek. 2:8 But you, mortal, hear what I say unto you; do not be rebellious like that rebellious house; open thy mouth and eat that I give you.

9 I looked, and a hand *was* stretched out to me, and a written scroll was in it.

10 And he spread it before me; it had writing on the front and on the back, and *written on it were words of* lamentation and mourning and woe.

---

[2] *Oxford English Dictionary* [*OED*] 3:801, s.v. "consume, v.1."
[3] Heinz Drügh, *Warenästhetik*, 21; my translation.
[4] Ibid., 34 with reference to Walter Benjamin, *One Way Street*, 89: "Fools lament the decay of criticism. For its day is long past. Criticism is a matter of correct distancing. It was at home in a world where perspectives and prospects counted and where it was still possible to take a standpoint. ... Today the most real, the mercantile gaze into the heart of things is the advertisement. It abolishes the space where contemplation moved and all but hits us between the eyes with things as a car, growing to gigantic proportions, careens at us out of a film screen." The vanishing of distance causes Benjamin to not only analyze but also lament the change himself.

> 3:1 He said to me, O mortal, eat what is offered to you; eat this scroll, and go, speak to the house of Israel.
> 2 So I opened my mouth, and he gave me the scroll to eat. (NRSV)

This vocation carries out the otherwise implicit assumption that God puts words into the prophet's mouth,[5] it makes Ezekiel incorporate the symbolic order so that his words shall henceforth follow scripture by the letter. The point of consuming the text is not that it spares from the arduous act of reading but that it addresses the issue of getting a hearing: God appears to Ezekiel as a speaker: "I heard a voice of someone speaking" (Ezek. 1:28, NRSV), elects him by saying "I will speak with you" (2:1), and Ezekiel obeys: "I heard him speaking to me" (2:2)—unlike the "rebellious house" of Israel, about whose lacking hearing God complains (2:4, 2:7). In order to create an efficient mouthpiece, God skips the very issue of lacking hearing that the prospective prophet shall denounce. This produces a prophet, and defers the crucial issue onto him. For the change of media from spoken to written word does not provide a remedy for the original dilemma that not even God is able to guarantee a fundamental aspect of all speech: the hearing that receives the spoken word, the attention for the written word in reading, and the reciprocity thus established with somebody.

Jakobson's differentiation of "six basic functions of verbal communication" provides one option for approaching this fundamental aspect of language: Lamenting and complaining emphasize the "appellative" or "conative" function of language concerned with address.[6] Yet these attributes do not clarify *how* the appeal, the direction at the hearing of others, forms speech—namely, by anticipation, as Bakhtin points out:

> Every word is directed toward an answer and cannot escape the profound influence of the answering word that it anticipates.
> 
> The word in living conversation is directly, blatantly, oriented toward a future answer-word: it provokes an answer, anticipates it and structures itself in the answer's direction.
> 
> All rhetorical forms, monologic in their compositional structure, are oriented toward the listener and his answer.[7]

Bakhtin's assumption that "primacy belongs to the answer, as the activating principle,"[8] insofar as the anticipation of a reception and a response forms utterances, permits a more accurate description of the problem presented in the book of Ezekiel. It points out that the utterance does not have all the

---

[5] Moshe Greenberg, *HThKAT: Ezek. 1–20*, 84.
[6] Roman Jakobson, "Linguistics and Poetics," 357–358.
[7] Mikhail Bakhtin, "Discourse in the Novel," 280.
[8] Ibid., 282.

"basic functions of verbal communication" at its disposal: In its dependence on the hearing of others that comes to the fore in the anticipation of possible answers (or, in plaintive language, of their lack), every form of speech is structurally unfinished and open toward relationality. Lacan calls the anticipation of hearing and response in speech "resonance" and, like Bakhtin, claims, "speech always subjectively includes its own reply." Lacan holds that this principle forms speech and, moreover, the speaker: "What I seek in speech is a response from the other. What constitutes me as a subject is my question."[9] Questions, however, indicate the kind of response they are after—much like requests, and unlike laments and complaints. Laments and complaints voice a profound doubt that there can be anyone to pay attention at and respond to them. Due to its lack of anticipation of a favorable answer, plaintive language is often reproached for being point- or aimless.[10] Insisting on getting a hearing while, simultaneously, failing to indicate a possible response, laments and complaints raise veritable affect and resentment that, in different contexts and with varying arguments, aim at silencing them. The rejection that laments and complaints often face is not merely a deplorable circumstance but part of the very structure of plaintive language.

To outline these assumptions, I will first continue to expound which insights into the structure of language and culture are gained by analyzing laments and complaints. Second, I will explain the mode of analysis, in particular the role of genre distinctions. Finally, a brief description will provide an overview of the chapters and main themes of this book. In spite of all my previous remarks, the subject still begs the question put straightforwardly in Rilke's tenth *Duino Elegy*:

*Was soll's? Sie ist eine Klage.*
(What's the point? It's a lament.)[11]

## Lamenting in Theory

The point of reading the language of lamenting and complaining is to provide deeper insight into structures of language and discourse. In theoretical approaches to language that require a stable relation between

---

[9]Jacques Lacan, "The Function and Field of Language in Psychoanalysis," 246–247.
[10]Popular culture takes on complaining find it to be dysfunctional; Cleo Wade, *Heart Talk*, 106: "Complaining is something that seems to come so easy and so naturally to us, but the problem is: complaints have no magic. They don't make anyone's day better, and they don't help any situation. Try going on a complaining cleanse." Julian Baggini, *Complaint: From Minor Moans to Principled Protests*, 19: "To complain is not only to be fully human: it is to defy the divine. ... At least, that is complaint at its best. At its worst it is a useless waste of energy, a futile cry against the inevitable, a refusal to accept reality for what it is."
[11]Rainer Maria Rilke, *Duineser Elegien* X. *Sämtliche Werke* [RSW] 1, 723; my translation.

signifier and signified in order to form terms and concepts, lamenting and complaining do not feature prominently but, rather, as an irritation, as this section will outline. Massumi, in his analysis of capitalism in terms of affect theory as "a global usurpation of belonging," underlines twice: "This is not merely a lament."[12] Why defend the apparently necessary remark as "not merely" a lament? Because lamenting profoundly doubts what Massumi seeks to discuss: relationality. Lament's fundamental doubt in reciprocity is the starting point for many rejections of utterances that do not deny to be laments. Religious and personal laments as well as poetic complaints are often reproached for following recognizable rhetorical patterns which are said to make the underlying individual affect of the speaker unrecognizable.[13] Such criticism projects the modern paradigm of the inwardness of sensation and emotion[14] onto texts from epochs and contexts that function under very different paradigms. Moreover, while in discussions of genre distinctions and rhetorical forms, following conventions is considered to vouch for comprehensibility, this principle tends to be neglected in readings of laments and complaints, where conventionality is often understood as testifying against the authenticity of the utterance and for its purely manipulative nature. Plaintive language may, of course, be a means of manipulation, yet the generalized skepticism about what any lament or complaint communicates testifies to a deeper, disquieting concern caused by this kind of language. As laments and complaints are unsure about the possibility of attaining someone's hearing and establishing reciprocity, it is easy to regard them as unproductive and self-absorbed. The language of lamenting and complaining articulates what might be called a "representational paradox":[15] On the one hand, it seeks to portray who- or whatever is lost in such a way that the pain caused by its loss is comprehensible without, on the other hand, accepting the portrayal as a compensation for the loss—which is no less understandable, but undermines the principle of symbolic substitution that the portrayal of the lost relies on. Yet laments and complaints do not enter into discussions of justification and coherence, because they arise precisely at those moments when it seems impossible to establish any kind of communication and exchange. Plaintive language highlights hearing, answer, and reciprocity because it finds them highly unlikely, even impossible.

The manifestation of a fundamental trait of all speech in the language of plaints, complaints, and laments tends to escape the grasp of theoretical approaches to language. This is true for both the Aristotelian paradigm,

---

[12]Brian Massumi, *Parables for the Virtual*, 88. Ibid: "Neither a celebration nor a lament: a challenge to rethink and reexperience the individual and the collective."
[13]Irmgard Scheitler, "Klagerede, Klagegesang," *HWRH* 4:958.
[14]Rüdiger Campe and Julia Weber, "Rethinking Emotion: Moving Beyond Interiority," 1–3.
[15]Burkhard Hasebrink, "Überlegungen zur Ästhetik der Klage," 105; my translation.

which regards language primarily as a means for making judgments about the state of things, and the paradigm of performativity, which sees language as a medium for realizing intentions. Both views presuppose that there is someone to listen and respond, yet this is not at all a given as plaintive language stubbornly points out. I will discuss the classic approach first. Ever since Aristotle's canonical description of speech, the structure of statements has come to be, as Heidegger puts it, "a normal form of human discourse, a form which, since the first reflections of the philosophy of antiquity, determined not only the theory of discourse, namely, logic, but also the study of grammar."[16] This approach to language refers back to Aristotle's description of speech as *logos apophantikos*, as "presenting speech," that is to say as proposition: While single words have meaning in the sense that they refer to something by convention (*sēmainein*), only compositions of noun and verb are able to present something (*apophainesthai*), which means, for Aristotle: attributing or denying something to the effect that the sentence is either true or false.[17] A single word may, of course, be appropriate or inappropriate to the thing it is supposed to name; yet articulating such a judgment requires the compound utterance of a proposition. Aristotle does concede in this description that there are forms of speech (*logoi*) which are neither true nor false, but mentions only one example: *euchē*, the "prayer, vow," or "curse," that is to say a "wish" for something good or bad to happen.[18] Heidegger explains the differentiation:

> By propositional statement we mean only the λόγος ἀποφαντικός, discourse that points out. Requesting, εὐχή, for example, is a non-apophantic λόγος. If my discourse is a requesting, then it is not attempting to inform the other person about something in the sense of increasing his or her knowledge. Nor, however, is the request a communication of the fact that I desire something or am filled with a desire. Nor is this discourse a mere desiring, but rather the concrete act of "requesting of another."[19]

Laments and complaints are likewise no information about what is lacking or disturbing but, rather, a "concrete act." Aristotle, however, relegates the analysis of non-propositional sentences like wishes from his consideration (*theōria*) into "the province of rhetoric or poetry."[20] Yet the *description* of language in terms of rhetoric or poetry is governed by the propositional structure of statements no less. Just like the discourses on grammar and

---

[16] Martin Heidegger, *Fundamental Concepts of Metaphysics* §72, 311.
[17] Aristotle, *On Interpretation* 16b.26–17a.3; affirmation and negation see 17a.8–9, 23–26.
[18] *A Greek-English Lexicon* Online [LSJ], s.v. "*euchē*," http://www.perseus.tufts.edu/hopper/text?doc=Perseus%3Atext%3A1999.04.0057%3Aentry%3Deu)xh%2F, accessed March 15, 2019.
[19] Heidegger, *Fundamental Concepts* §72b, 309.
[20] Aristotle, *On Interpretation* 17a.3–7.

logic, the examination of rhetoric and poetry forms predications in order to articulate judgments. This means that in the gaze of theory, even non-propositional forms of speech like wishes, laments, or complaints are subsumed under the paradigm of the statement. And in terms of grammar, many laments and complaints are indeed statements—for instance a stanza from Rückert's *Kindertotenlieder* (Songs on the Death of Children), partly set to music by Mahler:

*Das ist meine Klage,*
*Daß vor dieser Plage*
*Selbst verstummt die Klage.*[21]

(This is my complaint
That such a plague
Even mutes the complaint.)

Describing this stanza as a statement is grammatically correct but misses the pain it communicates as well as the specific form of its communication: The verses voice the experience of being stuck, seeing no way to carry on, and falling silent by way of an identical rhyme in which the outcry receives no answer, just an echo. Lamenting and complaining testify to experiences of being overwhelmed which cannot be seized in proposition as they, vice versa, overwhelm conventional structures of language. Aristotle on the other hand, commenting on the lament songs in tragedy, notes only what can be seized in a proposition: "A *kommos* is a song of lament shared by the chorus and the actors on the stage."[22] Significantly, considering how lament songs constitute a central element of the tragic text and performance, Aristotle's approach cannot explain what is bewailed so regularly in tragedy, or why.

The assimilation of all forms of speech to the paradigm of the statement is a fundamental difficulty in the examination of poetry as well as any comprehensive notion of language. This difficulty marks the overall relevance of the interest in the peculiar structure of plaintive language: Lamenting and complaining provide an outlook onto conventional structures of language that transcends the propositional form of statements. Many laments and complaints do, of course, form attributions, statements, and judgments. Yet their point is not to settle an issue, or to negotiate a truth claim, but to stir up attention for how the presented issue affects the speaker—an issue that, like death or loss, casts massive doubt on the possibility of finding anyone's hearing or response. For this reason, Old Testament jeremiads as well as contemporary appeals to outrage like Hessel's *Indignez-vous!*[23]

---

[21]Friedrich Rückert, *Kindertodtenlieder* 148.1–3, 178; my translation.
[22]Aristotle, *Poetics* 1452b.24–25.
[23]Stéphane Hessel, *Time for Outrage: Indignez-vous!*

tend to be accused of being meaningless. The complication is that the language of lamenting and complaining communicates "meaning" in a non-propositional way, that is to say otherwise than in statements which are either true or false. Rather, plaintive language communicates meaning by disorganizing and consuming linguistic structures in order to foreground the appeal to someone's hearing and response.

Although Aristotle does not follow up on his hint at the form of speech that is like a *euchē* (prayer, vow, curse, wish), it is instructive for reading the language of lamenting and complaining. Plaints are an important form of prayer, as many psalms prove,[24] and the Roman *nenia*, besides referring to the ritual dirge, also denotes a curse.[25] Like prayers, vows, curses, and wishes, laments and complaints, too, aim at being heard. All these forms of speech intend, primarily, not to portray something, but to speak to others, and to move them. A notion of language based on the paradigm of the statement is unsuited for describing such forms of speech dominated by the intention to be heard because a statement pays heed to a certain subject matter, silently assuming that there is someone to hear, or read, the words. Addressing the hearing is, however, crucial in poetry, to which Aristotle refers in passing. Aesthetics *is* the consideration of a text or other work with regard to how it appears to the senses. Poetic and literary texts transcend the propositional structure of the statement and are heavily informed by different genres of laments and dirges as well as by subjects like the complaint of love. This book will, therefore, read texts from the critical and philosophical canon next to works of literature, anthropology, and religious studies in order to examine structures of language in those "provinces" that the Aristotelian paradigm of language-as-proposition excludes from the field of theory.

The intention to being heard is crucial to rhetoric at which Aristotle hints, too. What matters to rhetoric, however—especially since it had come to focus on juridical speech after the abolishment of political deliberation in the late Roman Empire—are accusations and judgments, both of which correspond to the paradigm of propositional speech: They attribute or deny, thus stating what is either right or wrong. Still, plaintive speech is anything but foreign to juridical discourse, given that it is evoked by nothing else than a complaint, an "outcry against or because of injury."[26] And there is no complaint without a cause for a lament of, or a plaint for, some loss or harm; no attempt at compensating a pain or violation by means of attribution and judgment.

---

[24]Nancy Lee, *Lyrics of Lament*, 32: "The *dirge* and the *lament prayer to the deity* are the two primary forms of lament across cultures and religions." Otto Fuchs calls laments "a stepchild of Christian reflection on prayer" even though roughly 40 percent of the psalms lament (*Die Klage als Gebet*, 13; my translation).
[25]Dorota Dutsch, "Nenia: Gender, Genre, and Lament in Ancient Rome," 258.
[26]*OED* 3:608, s.v. "complaint, n.3."

Menke seeks to reconstruct the transition from an outcry of complaint to juridical action in terms of the philosophy of law, with allusion to Nietzsche's *Genealogy of Morals*: "The right to say no, and to criticism ... implies a self-empowerment of the subject. The subject who says no is the subject of complaint—prosecuting that things ought to change."[27] In this scenario, the complaint is structured as a proposition: It is a negation that calls for a remedy. Yet it is not actually the plaint that emancipates the subject, as Menke outlines: "The slave has always suffered and complained about it. A rebellion is the first time he asserts the right to not only express his suffering but to judge that, because he suffers, it is wrong."[28] Complaining appears as mere expression in this scenario; what is supposed to bring about emancipation is the judgment about the suffering. Menke's take on complaining represents a notion common in philosophical approaches to language: Who communicates his, or her, emotion is subject to suffering, not subject of a discourse that masters objects by way of statements and judgments. The "self-empowerment of the subject," Menke holds, springs from the judgment about one's own suffering as it "asserts and, at the same time, produces everyone's right to consideration," which is to say it institutes the rule by which it judges itself. "In the very complaint," Menke concludes, "the subject defines its relation to the Other is such a way that is being treated in a certain manner"—so that the subject who appears in active control over the judgment renders itself the passive aim of an Other's action, or non-action.[29] Yet neither a plaintive cry nor a juridical complaint *defines* the relation to the Other in such a way that the form of the successful response was predetermined. What Menke expounds as passivity is relationality: Complaints and laments depend on being heard in order to move others. The link between complaining about suffering and a juridical complaint cannot be explained in terms of subject and object (or master and slave) of propositional structures because they ignore the search for hearing and response that is the common trait of all plaints. Filing a complaint in order to assert the right to consideration does not define a relation between subjects, neither does it distinguish an active subject from its suffering as a

---

[27]Christoph Menke, "Sklavenaufstand oder Warum Rechte?," 115; my translation here and in the following.

[28]Ibid., 115–116. In Nietzsche, however, the point is that the slave does not complain: "This ancient mighty sorcerer in his struggle with displeasure, the ascetic priest—he had obviously won, *his* kingdom had come: one no longer protested *against* pain, one *thirsted* for pain; '*more* pain! *more* pain!' the desire of his disciples and initiates has cried for centuries" (*On the Genealogy of Morals* III.20, 141). It is, according to Nietzsche, rather the Greeks who complain—"so as to ward off the 'bad conscience'" but make "things too easy for themselves," as Zeus complains in Homer: "Strange how these mortals so loudly complain of the gods!" (ibid., II.23, 93–94; cf. *Odyssey* I.32).

[29]Menke, "Sklavenaufstand," 116.

mere object of consideration. The complaints shall, rather, point out that whoever complains is equal, capable of speaking and of responding to mistreatment. If the complaint remains unheard or unanswered—that is to say if it is not considered by anyone—then it fails to institute a sovereign, self-empowered subject.

Hamacher criticizes Menke's emphasis on the propositional structure by alluding to Arendt's notion that "the right to have rights" is the sole human right:[30] "This right," Hamacher writes, "consists in the minimal and not further reducible *claim* of the ability to be connected with others—and thus it does not consist in a judgement as to whether such a connection does or does not exist." Lodging a complaint in order to prosecute this claim, Hamacher continues, is not based on an established legal right, but aims—just like a prayer, vow, curse, or wish (*echē*)—at something "that is not yet given." Therefore, this complaint is "devoid of all predicative content."[31] Complaints and laments do not define a relation to the Other. Who makes a complaint in order to be considered "merely raises the claim to determination, pleading for it, desiring it."[32] In other words, the language of laments and complaints is not thetic but projective: it does not determine subjects but seeks to attain the attention, hearing, and response of others. Plaintive languages requires, therefore, a reading not as a discourse of the subject, but as a discourse negotiating the communication with others.

Since laments and complaints are no statements about loss or pain but addresses that seek a hearing and a response, understanding their particular form requires focusing on the course of their utterance or articulation. Speech act theory and the modern paradigm of performativity might seem more appropriate than the Aristotelian paradigm to grasping the structure of plaintive language. They seem promising with regard to describing the ritual character of many laments and complaints, such as the strong orality of many lament texts that resembles sound and music or the highly artificial written form of laments like the acrostics of the *Eicha*, the biblical book of Lamentations. Studies of different provenance indeed describe various forms of laments and complaints as (performative) speech acts.[33] Still, speech act theory contributes little to understanding the structure of lamenting and complaining: Austin does not mention them, Searle does not count them

---

[30]Hannah Arendt, *Origins of Totalitarianism*, 196–198.
[31]Werner Hamacher, "The Right to Have Rights," 355.
[32]Ibid.
[33]Cf. Linda Austin, "The Lament and the Rhetoric of the Sublime," 280; Hasebrink, "Überlegungen," 105; Gail Holst-Warhaft, *Dangerous Voices: Women's Laments and Greek Literature*, 10; Rebecca Saunders, *Lamentation and Modernity*, 47; James Wilce, *Crying Shame: Metaculture, Modernity, and the Exaggerated Death of Lament*, 49. The "speech act" of lament in Johannes Anderegg, "Zum Ort der Klage," 192; Jochen Schmidt, *Klage: Überlegungen zur Linderung reflexiven Leidens*, 133; Fuchs, *Klage*, 15.

among the performative utterances but states: "to lament that P is to assert P while expressing dissatisfaction and sadness that P."[34] But what does it mean to express sadness, and to express as opposed to assert something? While crucial to Searle's notion of complaints, he describes the differentiation as negligible:

> When one complains, one expresses discontent. ... complaining can be either an assertive or an expressive. One can complain by asserting that something is bad or one can simply express one's discontent. One can say, for example, "That was a terrible thing to do" (assertive), or one can complain by saying "How awful!" (expressive).[35]

Statements and interjections are indeed equally pervasive in laments and complaints; however, these grammatical descriptions hardly grasp what is peculiar about lamenting and complaining. Searle's differentiation between "assertives" and "expressives," still, follows the grammatical distinction, thus subsuming these speech acts under a paradigm that has great similarity to the statement.[36] The assertion that is absent in the interjection is effectively added in the theoretical account that does not care to outline what constitutes complaining besides its defining statement.[37] Speech act theory thus faces the same complication as any approach to language under the Aristotelian paradigm: Descriptors of language reduce even those utterances to attributions (affirmations or denials) that seem to be formed in a very different manner, for instance as an interjection. Confirming that this complication marks the focal interest of reading the language of lamenting and complaining, Wittgenstein's notes on utterances of pain revolve around the issue of attributions: "We surely do not always say someone is *complaining*, because he says he is in pain."[38] He, or she, might as well speak in a different mode. Wittgenstein continues: "Think of the expression 'I hear a plaintive melody'. ... 'Does he *hear* the plaint?'"[39] Calling an utterance "plaintive" or

---

[34] John Searle and Daniel Vanderveken, *Foundations of Illocutionary Logic*, 191; cf. 68 and 213.
[35] Ibid., 213; cf. 191.
[36] Searle describes assertives as statements with a surplus, as "a large number of performative verbs that denote illocutions that seem to be assessable in the True-False dimension and yet are not just 'statements' ... Thus, for example, consider 'boast' and 'complain'. They both denote assertives with the added feature that they have something to do with the interest of the speaker" (*Expression and Meaning*, 13).
[37] Searle's reduction of utterances to the paradigm of assertives does not distinguish between linguistic and psychic structures: "Lamenting, unlike complaining, need not be a speech act. One can simply feel sorrow for something and therefore be said to be lamenting it" (*Foundations of Illocutionary Logic*, 213). Here, too, the assertion that forms the paradigm of the speech act is added by the description while the role it plays in feeling remains completely unclear.
[38] Ludwig Wittgenstein, *Philosophical Investigations* [PI], 512.
[39] Ibid., 545.

"a lament" means forming an attribution, a statement; no analysis can avoid that. Yet what is at stake in reading laments and complaints is not avoiding statements but expounding the peculiar form of communication that works by way of consuming linguistic structures. This form comprises attributions and statements to portray the cause for distress, but eminently transcends them by not letting them stand as substitutes for what is lost or harmed.

Unlike Austin and Searle, Butler assumes that "performativity must be understood not as a singular or deliberate 'act,' but, rather, as the reiterative and citational practice by which discourse produces the effects that it names."[40] This discursive concept of performativity is well suited to describe how pain, loss, and mourning are formed and negotiated in ritual, neurotic, poetic, juridical, and other plaints that cite and vary historically and culturally specific patterns. The seminal aspect of the language of lamenting and complaining, however, escapes Butler's concept of performativity: The hearing, attention, and answer that lamenting and complaining are concerned about cannot be produced by the utterance. This impossibility is, in fact, an essential cause of distress in complaints and laments. This is why the God of the "rebellious house" of Israel that does not listen turns to Ezekiel. In its seminal feature, the language of lamenting and complaining is as little performative as it is thetic, but, rather, is projective and relational.

Butler, sure enough, does not claim that plaintive language is performative. Indeed she hardly mentions lamenting or complaining on the many occasions she analyzes the link between discursive violence, (lacking) public mourning, and political responsibility.[41] This might be due to the disappearance of ritual lamenting from the mourning culture of modernity, yet it also marks a problematic point in the concept of performativity. For even in reading Sophocles's *Antigone*, Butler merely touches upon lament: "the language becomes the event of the grievance, where, emerging from the unspeakable, language carries a violence that brings it to the limits of speakability."[42] The violence in lamenting and complaining that reduces the articulate tragic text to a sequence of vowels and moans is often, particularly in calls for revenge, aimed at individuals and social institutions.[43] This is the point where

---

[40] Judith Butler, *Bodies That Matter*, 2.
[41] Judith Butler, *Precarious Life* does not mention laments but solely the lacking "public 'act' of grieving"; she does quote Freud's *Mourning and Melancholia*, yet not on lamenting (20; *The Psychic Life of Power*, 144). *Frames of War* uses "lamentable" (41, 69, 95) without reflecting on the implied linguistic form.
[42] Judith Butler, *Antigone's Claim*, 80.
[43] Butler, *Frames of War*, 39 explains this link in terms of affects: "Open grieving is bound up with outrage, and outrage in the face of injustice or indeed of unbearable loss has enormous political potential. It is, after all, one of the reasons Plato wanted to ban the poets from the Republic. He thought that if the citizens went too often to watch tragedy, they would weep over the losses they saw, and that such open and public mourning, in disrupting the order and hierarchy of the soul, would disrupt the order and hierarchy of political authority as well."

numerous political sanctions against ritual wailing and public lamenting start, which often administer equally violent gender discourses (such as analyzed by Butler) to shut the language of lamenting and complaining out of politics; Chapter 2 will elaborate on this link. However, this is not the only form rejecting laments and complaints takes.

The rejection of laments and complaints can be understood as a response to the particular structure of plaintive language which—as an expression of what seems overwhelming and unbearable—often appears overwhelming and hard to bear itself. Studies of divergent lament texts and complaint genres thus often do not stick to reading but proceed to responding, as if to counter and silence the plaint. Rigorous distinctions of laments and complaints from elegy,[44] from outcries,[45] or from "our reality"[46] serve the purpose not of understanding plaintive language, but of containing it, and keeping it at bay. Old Testament scholar Plöger even draws a dividing line between lament songs and laments, maintaining that the latter were "without an independent meaning" and are merely "part of a prayer that starts and ends with a plea."[47] Linafelt cites this paradoxical differentiation as an example of a "common strategy of interpreters: valuing lament only insofar as it leads to something that is less strident and mournful, and more conciliatory and hopeful."[48] Theological readings of the book of Lamentations (*Eicha*), for instance, often endeavor to outline an original blame, an eschatological purpose, or a sublime hope in the lamented ruin of the city of Jerusalem and its people (discussed in Chapter 3).[49] The same strategy is employed when a reading of the book of Job presupposes: "the complaint shall not have the last word."[50]

Such readings refute rather than read the laments or complaints they address, which makes them questionable analyses, and yet they do correspond to the pivotal concern of plaintive language for hearing and response in a certain way: Refuting readings do recognize the plaint but counter it rather than suffering the fundamental doubt in the possibility of finding hearing, attention, and an answer. New Testament scholar Schmidt thus holds that insofar as it is an expression, every lament or complaint already provides a solution for the suffering it voices since it produces the "salutary distance from one's suffering" prerequisite to overcoming it.[51] From this point of

---

[44]Holst-Warhaft, *Dangerous Voices*, 125; Saunders, *Lamentations and Modernity*, 50.
[45]Schmidt, *Klage*, 126–127.
[46]Anderegg, "Zum Ort," 204; my translation.
[47]Otto Plöger, *Klagelieder*, 162; my translation.
[48]Tod Linafelt, *Surviving Lamentations: Catastrophe, Lament, and Protest in the Afterlife of a Biblical Book*, 11.
[49]Ibid., 1–18.
[50]Claudia Welz, *Vertrauen und Versuchung*, 27; my translation.
[51]Schmidt, *Klage*, 158, 16, 153; my translation.

view, plaintive language does not voice pain and loss, but has already stilled it, which means that nobody needs to listen to complaining and lamenting. The same conclusion is suggested in Kowalski's psychological inquiry into the "annoying behavior" of complainers:

> It's sometimes unclear whether they really want a solution or simply want to complain. Many of those who really do want to be heard seek out a professional therapist to whom they can complain nonstop for fifty minutes a time.[52]

Annoying as complaining can certainly be, it is nothing short of devastating to accept that, as Kowalski purports, hearing may be the very "solution" complaining seeks and to see no other legitimate option for finding a hearing, in a society organized as a system of interpersonal relations, other than a therapist paid to listen, yet apparently not to respond. In spite of their cynicism, these approaches still point at a crucial trait of plaintive language: In order to be heard, laments and complaints seek to diminish the distance from others, wherefore they may seem intimidating and annoying—a distance that theory, *theōria* (viewing, beholding), indispensably requires between the viewer and the viewed in order to be able to look at, and into, something. Refuting readings of laments and complaints point out that the disorganization and consumption of linguistic structures in plaintive language include even the distance between observer and observed, so that readings might be incited to join the plaint. Baggini's survey of complaints is structured by a "meta-complaint: that people tend to complain about the wrong things for the wrong reasons."[53] Quite a few studies on plaintive texts or genres set out by lamenting a suspended ritual, or vanished form, of lament.[54] Here, historical analysis faces a discursive effect from the peculiar structure of plaintive language: Lamenting and complaining communicate by way of consuming linguistic structures and tend to appear to historical investigations as vanishing—be it from the psalms,[55] from the Greek polis,[56] from church history,[57] from the Modern notion of death,[58] from non-Western

---

[52] Robin Kowalski, *Complaining, Teasing, and Other Annoying Behaviors*, 41.
[53] Baggini, *Complaint*, 5.
[54] Walter Brueggemann, "The Costly Loss of Lament"; Ottmar Fuchs and Bernd Janowski, "Vorwort"; Holst-Warhaft, *Dangerous Voices*, 6–7; Richard Hughes, *Lament, Death, and Destiny*, 1.
[55] Claus Westermann, *Lob und Klage in den Psalmen*, 155–164.
[56] Margaret Alexiou, *The Ritual Lament in Greek Tradition*, 4–23; Nicole Loraux, *Les mères en deuil*; Holst-Warhaft, *Dangerous Voices*, 98–170.
[57] Ernst Dassmann, "Die verstummte Klage bei den Kirchenvätern."
[58] Philipp Ariès, *The Hour of Our Death*, 559–601.

cultures,[59] or from the vocabulary of psychiatry.[60] Benjamin is one of the few authors who addresses this curious relation of plaintive language to theory, as the fourth chapter will outline. Before proceeding to the chapter outline, however, the role genre distinctions play in the book requires explanation since they are usually the form in which the structural and the historical analysis of speech are coordinated.

## Terms of Plaint

... —*Wir waren,*
*sagt sie, ein Großes Geschlecht, einmal, wir Klagen.*

(... —We were,
she said, a Great Lineage once, we Laments.)[61]

This passage from the tenth and last of Rilke's 1922 *Duino Elegies* harps on an equivocation of the German term *Geschlecht*, which means both "lineage" and "gender." A personification of elegy herself elucidates how the notion of decline is foundational to the construction of the history of the elegiac form: Elegy is the vanishing poem that laments a passing. Rilke's use of elegy personified reflects modernity's nostalgia for abolished ritual forms as much as it continues the history of the poetic form, traditionally depicted as female, while transferring Ovid's imagery of *flebilis ... elegia* (lamenting ... elegy) into a modern setting.[62] Rilke's lines seem to include a tautology, for what other than a lament might the elegy—a lament song genre—utter? Yet it is only within elegiac genre conventions that the implication of a lamenting tone in the title "elegy" seems evident. And these conventions, in turn, rely heavily on the construction of a history of the form within the text. For while Ovid's elegiac couplets are a conventional metric form that might speak of lament, or love, or anything else,[63] modern verse such as Rilke's have to do without the metric patterns of antiquity and rely, instead, on the definition of tone. What has vanished in modern elegy is thus, first, the metric pattern to which

---

[59]Wilce, *Crying Shame.*
[60]Hartmann Hinterhuber, "Die psychiatrische Dimension der Klage," 15–16.
[61]Rilke, *Duineser Elegien* X. RSW1:723; my translation.
[62]Ovid, *Amores* III.1.7–10; my translation.
[63]Maurice Cunningham, "Ovid's Poetics," 254.

the name elegy once referred.⁶⁴ *The* elegy is, therefore, anything but a stable persona. Rilke's personified lament wisely speaks in the plural form; still, it is unclear which kind of texts and utterances may claim kinship with "[us] Laments." And this is the very cue the following analysis of the language of lamenting and complaining takes from Rilke's evocation of the historicity of genre imaginations: The question of how laments and complaints communicate, and what it means to understand them, cannot be settled by way of following lines drawn by genre distinctions.

Distinctions between different genres of lamenting and complaining speech are, rather, an important part of determining the historically, culturally, and socially varying forms and functions of plaintive speech. In order to understand how these determinations correlate with the structure of plaintive speech, the comparative approach of this book will transcend distinctions between tragedy and elegy, drama and poetry, liturgy and everyday speech, in favor of understanding the politics of genre distinctions: The replacement of ritual Greek dirges by funerary orations and tragedy, discussed in Chapter 2 is a focal element of a sociopolitical modernization of the *polis* whose parameter still governs most readings of tragedy. The link Kafka's texts establish between complaints of love, political populism, and juridical action, discussed in Chapter 5, points out that genre delimitations serve as containments of the question of justice in modern societies. A further historical connection across genre distinctions beyond the scope of this book is the formation of the notoriously under-researched relational aspect of the modern "I": Autobiographical complaints are a seminal mode of speech that puts the world in relation to a self. The autobiographical mode of relationality via complaint has been paradigmatically shaped in Ovid's elegiac *Letters from Exile*, which are adapted in Rousseau's prose *Confessions*, which are, in turn, imitated in Roth's *Portnoy's Complaint*, a travesty of a psychotherapeutic dialogue. In order to take heed of such functional links, the subsequent chapters follow the question: What structure justifies calling such diverse utterances "laments, complaints," or "plaintive"? If laments and complaints are no literary or pragmatic genre, what, then, Chapter 3 inquires, do the texts have in common that may be classified as participating in the "language-game"⁶⁵ of plaints? In this book, I argue that the common trait in these texts is how, in quest of hearing and response, the language of lamenting and complaining consumes linguistic structures.

---

⁶⁴Cf. Eric Santner, *On Creaturely Life: Rilke, Benjamin, Sebald*, 49n6: "In the *Duino Elegies*, Rilke's resistance to the force of modernization is marshaled not as resistance against loss but rather as mournful resistance against the disappearance of the space and symbolic resources in which loss could still be experienced and worked through. The Duino Elegies are … second-order elegies: elegies for the passing of the space in which elegy is still possible."
⁶⁵Wittgenstein, PI §23, 127.

The heterogeneity of plaintive language evidently extends to the terminological level, comprising plaints, complaints, laments, dirges, wailing, and other terms in English. "Dirge" is the slurred first word of the antiphon in Psalm 5:8—*Dirige, Domine, Deus meus, in conspectu tuo viam meam* (Direct, O Lord, my God, my way in thy sight; AV)—that was used to introduce wakes and has since come to denote them, too.[66] In classic Hebrew, the language of the Psalms, dirges are called *kinah*,[67] but laments and complaints are also referred to as *mispêd*,[68] *nehî*,[69] and *śîḥî*,[70] and this list is far from comprehensive. Following Rilke's tenth *Duino Elegy*, this terminological heterogeneity could be called a *weite Landschaft der Klagen* (vast landscape of plaints).[71] The point of exploring this terminological range is to see that lamenting and complaining are not merely one among many poetic forms, literary genres, or rhetorical modes. Furthermore, as Feld emphasizes, lament is, "neither an ethnographically coherent or singular set of textual and vocal practices nor a unified downhill trope in diverse modernist discourses."[72] Plaintive language is, rather, a basic form of human speech such as the statement: Like statements, laments and complaints are articulated in different textual genres and forms that vary by historical, cultural, and functional context. I use the umbrella term "plaintive language" to highlight that this book analyzes the dynamics of a structure of speech that grants insight into how address, in general, is organized in human language while it takes very different forms. The book presents an ordered progression of seminal schemata under which plaintive language has been viewed and could be viewed, ordered according to regions of being: psyche, ritual, language, nature, and law.

The German language suggests a close relation between lamentation and dirge (*Klagelied*), plaintive cry (*Klagelaut*), complaint (*Klage*), and accusation (*Anklage*). Goetz's 2008 diary essay *Klage* enfolds a bilingual panorama of the "vast landscape of plaints" in a lexicological order that claims the heritage of the alphabetical acrostics in the biblical book of Lamentations (*Eicha*):

...
action—klage
case—klage
claim—klage
complaint—klage

---

[66]*OED* 4:708, s.v. "dirge," n.
[67]Gen. 50:10, Est. 4:3, Jer. 6:26, Ezek. 27:31.
[68]2 Sam. 1:17, Jer. 7:29, 9:19, Ezek. 19:1, 19:14, Amos 8:10.
[69]Jer. 9:19, 31:15, Amos 5:16.
[70]Ps. 55:2.
[71]Rilke, *Duineser Elegien X*. RSW1:724; my translation.
[72]Stephen Feld, "Comments," 904.

dirge—klage
grievance—klage
lament—klage
lamentation—klage
lawsuit—klage
legal action—klage
plaint—klage
suit—klage ...[73]

The collapse of a variety of English terms into one German word is relevant as most of the texts under consideration in this book fall in the same historical and cultural context as Rilke's *Duino Elegies*, representing German-language literature and thought from the late nineteenth until the mid-twentieth centuries, with some digressions to the eighteenth and the twenty-first centuries. The insights gathered from reading these texts, however, are not at all limited to German-language cultures. The comparative approach of reading them will, therefore, refer largely to works of literary criticism, anthropology, philosophy, classical, and religious studies written in English. The book thus provides tools for the interpretation of theoretical and literary texts from other languages and periods than those discussed by expounding crucial features of plaintive language. The late nineteenth- to the mid-twentieth-century German-language culture appears a suitable starting point for exploring the structure of plaintive language because it is an almost continual occasion for lamenting and complaining as well as a key moment in a renegotiation with both Jewish and Greco-Roman classical antiquity.

Insights provided by reading German laments and complaints can be transferred to texts from other languages in spite of terminological differences because the German language merely simplifies what appears as more complex lexicological textures in other languages, yet shares the same semantical implications. In many Western languages, three gestures[74]

---

[73]Rainald Goetz, *klage source code 5–16, Klage*, 278.
[74]Gesture and sound are interlinked even in scriptural culture, as Wickett points out with reference to Egyptian laments: "The multivalent nature of signs in the ancient Egyptian hieroglyphic system, and the use of 'stick-men' or other illustrative sketches (essentially, logograms and ideograms), to inflect the meanings of words or to denote what they depict suggests that there was some relationship between posture and sign. For example, the angle of the arms in some poses corresponds to the ideogram of 'pleading and complaint' ... and in some representations, the lamenters' fists are clenched as in the hieroglyph of exclamation that denotes paradoxically both 'jubilation', 'invocation' and 'mourning' ... The lifting of the arms above the head might also have had a literal function: to incarnate the protection and re-invigoration of the *ka* after death, since the hieroglyphic sign for *ka* is a pair of uplifted arms" (Elizabeth Wickett, *For the Living and the Dead*, 155).

dominate the semantic field of lamenting and complaining. As a first one, the classical Greek γόος (*goos*, wailing) and θρῆνος (*threnos*, tragic lament song), the Latin *quieri* and *lamentari*, to which English and most Romance languages relate, the German *klagen* as well as the Russian стенания (*stenaniya*) and рыдания (*rydaniya*) can all be traced back to denoting, and even imitating, inarticulate sounds of weeping, moaning, barking, or crying.[75] The Irish and Scottish word keening derives from Gaelic *caoin* (crying).[76] In the diverse Russian terminology of plaints, the noun жалоба (*zhaloba*: lament, complaint, legal action) is rooted in suffering pain, while *stenaniya* (lament, groaning) and *rydaniya* (lament, complaint, sobbing) are derived from descriptions of sobbing.[77]

A second notable gesture marking the Western vocabulary of plaints is the loud "beating" on the chest or head that used to accompany dirges and mourning. English *to complaint*, French *plaindre*, and Russian плач (*plach*) are all linked to the Latin *planctus*, which in turn refers to the Greek κόμμος (*kommos*), the aforementioned choral lament in tragedy, both of which denote a "beating."[78] Its ritual origin notwithstanding, *la plainte*, complaint and *Klage* span the same sematic aspects: the expression of pain and insult, the lament song, and the legal action in court.[79] These very different forms of speech seem to participate in one structure that allows their linkage. Etymology alone does not explain this link, but it provides a hint: the different forms of plaints are all related to inarticulate noises and, with the beating, even to non-oral sounds of pain.

Reading plaintive language as a basic form of human speech regards it as neither primarily an emotional sign (because legal complaints are none) nor as a specific poetic, ritual, or other form (because the genres of plaints vary), but in terms of its function. What classical studies and anthropology contribute to understanding laments and complaints is a functional approach to the analysis of language capable of finding links between utterances of different genres and contexts. Bachvarova thus explains the large "scope of the genre of 'lament/complaint'" in Sumerian texts that combine the seemingly contradictory modes of paean and accusation into a prayer with a precise

---

[75] Jacob and Wilhelm Grimm, *Deutsches Wörterbuch* [DW] 11:915, s.v. "klagen"; Alois Walde and Johann Baptist Hoffmann, *Lateinisches etymologisches Wörterbuch*, 754, s.v. "lamentum"; Pierre Chantraine, *Dictionnaire étymologique de la langue grecque*, s.v. "goaō," "threomai," "threnos"; Max Vasmer, *Russisches Etymologisches Wörterbuch*, 10, 554.
[76] Jenny Butler, "Symbolic and Social Roles of Women in Death Ritual in Traditional Irish Society," 114.
[77] Vasmer, *Wörterbuch*, 409–410, 10, 554.
[78] Émile Littré, *Dictionnaire de la langue française* 3:1962, s.v. "plaindre"; *OED* 3:607, s.v. "complain"; Vasmer, *Wörterbuch*, 364–365; *LSJ*, s.v. "*kommos*," http://www.perseus.tufts.edu/hopper/morph?l=kommos&la=greek#lexicon, accessed March 15, 2019.
[79] Littré, *Dictionnaire* 3:1963–64, s.v. "plainte"; *OED* 3:608, s.v. "complaint"; *DW* 11:907–924, s.v. "klage."

function: lamenting deities that cease with the season, and recalling them to renew their vegetative effect on crops. What made the ambivalent genre recognizable was its "mode of delivery, passionate and wailing."[80] As a basic form of human speech, the language of lamenting and complaining comprises different aspects of the concern for being heard and receiving an answer that are articulated in various contexts and different genres. What all of them have in common is that plaintive language casts doubt onto articulate speech.

A third trait informing the terms of plaintive language is highlighted in Holst-Warhafts explanation of Greek dirges: "The female lamenter articulates the inarticulate, forming a bridge between the living and the dead that is recognized by the community."[81] The language of lamenting and complaining marks a boundary, be it between life and death, between families and phases of life (in the case of the bridal laments),[82] between touch and injury, legality and illegality, or between genders. It is a worldwide phenomenon that lament appears, as Suter puts it, "as a particularly gendered genre":[83] gender codifications and genre conventions often interrelate, oftentimes to the effect that ritual laments are marked as female, irrational, and premodern, and abolished in favor of a sociopolitical modernization that is cast as male and rational. This logic informs the negotiation of ritual lamentation in the Attic polis and tragedy as much as the beginnings of psychoanalysis, and current discourses on sexism, where the genre of complaining tends to be marked as female. The logic of marking the plaint as a form of speech that disqualifies the speaker from participating in the negotiation (rather than listening to it) rules other discourses on discriminatory differentiations, too, as Chapter 5 points out. The way in which lamenting and complaining come to mark boundaries, however, is not sufficiently clear in Holst-Warhaft's characterization: All speech may claim to "articulat[e] the inarticulate" in one way or another, and many forms of plaintive language communicate by way of consuming articulation, thus undermining the distinction between articulate speech on the one hand and sound or noise on the other. Elements of self-mutilation in mourning rites such as beating the head or hitting the chest in *planctus/kommos* might give a hint at how the marking of boundaries in plaintive language can be approached: In religious studies, such practices are seen as rites of self-debasement that, in instances or mourning or capitulation, display the diminished status by performing the very act of being affected and depressed.[84] From an anthropological point of view,

---

[80]Mary Bachvarova, "Sumerian 'Gala' Priests and Eastern Mediterranean Returning Gods: Tragic Lamentation in Cross-Cultural Perspective," 28–33.
[81]Holst-Warhaft, *Dangerous Voices*, 9.
[82]Loring Danforth, *The Death Rituals of Rural Greece*, 71–115; Fred Blake, "The Feelings of Chinese Daughters towards Their Mothers as Revealed in Marriage Laments."
[83]Ann Suter, "Male Lament in Greek Tragedy," 156.
[84]Ernst Kutsch, "'Trauerbräuche' und 'Selbstminderungsriten' im Alten Testament," 36–37.

such practices appear as "ritual self-mortification"[85] and as a "corporeal mimesis of death, the transformation of ... bodies into a text of disorder."[86] Rather than portraying what has been lost or what causes distress, the beatings that are often part of laments as well as the crying in complaints make the painful strike of loss and affliction heard. The peculiarity of the two previously outlined gestures that inform the terminology of plaints—sobbing and beating—is somatic in method but concerns language in effect, enfolding the boundary between speech and noise into a spectrum of vocal and other bodily productions.

A common trait in the terms of plaint is the insistence on attaining attention that even names lamentations in English: dirge, *dirige*, that is to say "turn, direct" your ear, or eye, to me. The most distinctive common trait of the many forms of lamenting and complaining, however, is the hermeneutic and communicative difficulties they cause: Because the insistence of hearing and attention in plaintive language is unconditional, it is utterly unclear whether, or how, it is possible to answer it: the book of Job thoroughly discusses this feature. It is equally unclear whether there is in fact a community that, as Holst-Warhaft assumes, listens to and "recognizes" laments or complaints; the absence of a listener is a focal point of many complaints and laments. The following chapters will follow such difficulties as guideline for the analysis of different discourses that center around laments and complaints and allow to explain pivotal structures in the language of lamenting and complaining.

The language of lamenting and complaining manifests itself on all levels, and in all forms, of speech as a functional connection of a profound doubt in the possibility of finding a hearing and an answer with a disorganization of linguistic structures and the demarcation of a boundary. Such a functional description of plaintive language is necessary because the disorganizing structure of lamenting and complaining consumes every homogenous concept of *the* lament or *the* complaint. Because, as Adorno writes, "What is qualitatively contrary to the concept per se can only with difficulty be brought within the bounds of its concept; the form in which something may be thought is not indifferent to what is thought."[87] The book of Lamentations (*Eicha*), for instance, requests very different things of "daughter Zion," depending on the respective translation of the phrase in Lamentations 2:19a:

| | |
|---|---|
| Arise, *cry* out in the night | (AV, NRSV) |
| Arise, *cry* out balailah | (OJB) |
| Arise, give *praise* in the night | (DRB) |
| Get up and *pray* for help | (CEV)[88] |

---

[85] Wilce, *Crying Shame*, 119.
[86] Nadia Seremetakis, *The Last Word*, 74.
[87] Theodor Adorno, *Aesthetic Theory*, 111.
[88] All my italics.

The Hebrew verb in this phrase, *rānan*, denotes crying, sobbing, and lamenting just as well as cheering and rejoicing. The verb thus signifies two decisive forms of prayer in Israelite spirituality, polar opposites no less,[89] that are both expressed in shouting and yelling—no matter whether one shouts out of joy or distress.[90] Herder notes the same complication in the "moaning sound" of lament and other cries: "When they get articulated and get spelled out on paper as interjections, then the most opposed sensations have almost a single expression."[91] In the book of Lamentations (*Eicha*), the semantic collapse in the ambiguous verb does, however, correspond to the portrayed ruin of the structures. There is no stone left standing, neither in Jerusalem nor in language, as an earlier line of the same song notes:

Lam. 2:5 The Lord has become like an enemy;
he has destroyed [swallowed up] Israel.
He has destroyed [swallowed up] all her palaces,
laid in ruins its strongholds,
and multiplied in the daughter Judah
mourning and lamentation. (NRSV, parenthesis AV)

The consumption of a homogeneous concept of *the* plaint pertains to reading laments and complaints as much as to voicing them. Anthropological considerations of laments and complaints as cultural practices, psychological analyses as individual expressions, and theological, historical, or philosophical explanations of determinants of laments and complaints often appear as responses seeking to counter the consumption of linguistic structures in laments and complaints rather than as readings trying to understand them. Such responding readings are a symptom of a peculiarity in the language of lamenting and complaining: Undermining the principle of symbolic substitution by insisting on being inconsolable, and diminishing the distance from others in order to attain hearing and to elicit an answer, complaints and laments evade the hegemony of theory. This marks both the greater relevance and the great difficulty of pursuing the following readings of plaintive language.

The discussion of ritual forms is relevant beyond the scope or theology, religious studies, and anthropology, as it contributes eminently to

---

[89]Fuchs, *Klage*, 13.
[90]Ulrich Berges, *HThKAT: Klgl.*, 162–163; Wickett, *For the Living*, 155. Egyptian hieroglyphs display a similar proximity of "jubilation," 𓀁 , to "lamentation," 𓀁 (Erich Lüddeckens, *Untersuchungen über religiösen Gehalt, Sprache und Form der ägyptischen Totenklagen*, 27). Lüddeckens's 1943 study is one of a number of anthropological and classicist works testifying to a sudden interest of the German academia in plaints by the end of the 1940s. The suggestive association with the crimes of National Socialism and the losses of the Second World War corrupts their scholarly quality often, yet not in his case; see chapter 2, 86)
[91]Johann Gottfried Herder, "Treatise on the Origin of Language," 68–69.

understanding current structures in political and public discourse. Current responses to violence, terror, and war retrace ancient politics of mourning,[92] not least in that they are aimed against lamenting. Butler parallels the lacking "public act of grieving" for the victims on the other side of the so-called war on terror with the prohibition of a burial for the enemy of the state in *Antigone*—without mentioning laments or dirges as essential elements of the tragic text or media for mourning.[93] Didi-Huberman explains the flooding of the press with "images of lamenting" as a "worldwide medialization of wailing women" that removes them from their specific context to render them as an unchanging icon of all suffering, but effectively produces indifference to the image.[94] Weigel sees media coverage of "'public crying'" at sites of violence and disasters as a return of a set of pathos formulas[95] which are "almost automatically associated with the 'East' and the 'Orient'"; one is, she writes "reminded of wailing women," using the common yet derogatory German *Klageweiber*.[96] Such characterizations of ritual forms as Eastern, female or effeminate, and premodern already rule the discourse on dirges in the *Oresteia* and approximate to what Said calls "orientalism." He writes: "As early as Aeschylus's play *The Persians* the Orient is transformed from a very far distant and threatening Otherness into figures that are relatively familiar (in Aeschylus's case, grieving Asiatic women)."[97] Actually, *The Persians*, the oldest known tragic text, features only one female character, the Persian queen; it is a chorus of Persian men, the court council, who is lamenting in Aeschylus. Said's mistake illustrates how commonly ritual lament is associated with whatever is taken to be in an inferior, marginal position. The same is true for the classicist Holst-Warhaft, locating what she calls the "theatrical representation" of public mourning and lamenting "in the realm of ritual rather than logos"[98]—an opposition that, as portrayed in the *Oresteia*, already rules the classical Greek policy of excluding supposedly dangerous ritual laments from public discourse.

What is problematic about the reactivation of binary distinctions such as Eastern versus Western, modern versus archaic, rational versus emotional, male versus female—which are all meant to culminate in the distinction of democratic versus despotic—in current responses to violence, terror, and

---

[92] A striking instance are readings of the Sumerian and Hebrew Bible genre of City Laments with regard to 9/11 (Dereck Daschke, *City of Ruins*, 199–209; Randall Heskett, *Reading the Book of Isaiah*, 150–152) and the siege of Sarajevo (Lee, *Lamentations*).
[93] Butler, *Precarious Life*, 36. On the danger of mourning for democracy, comparing Attic tragedy and American policy, see Simon Stow, *American Mourning*, 1–56.
[94] Georges Didi-Huberman, "Klagebilder, beklagenswerte Bilder?," 29–30; my translation. Cf. Georges Didi-Huberman, *Peuples en larmes, peuples en armes*, 380–384.
[95] Sigrid Weigel, "Public Crying," 53; my translation.
[96] Ibid., 44; as opposed to the neutral *Klagefrauen* (wailing women).
[97] Edward Said, *Orientalism*, 21.
[98] Holst-Warhaft, "No Consolation: The Lamenting Voice and Public Memory," 212, 216.

war is that they are part of a cultural geopolitics that limits rationality and governmentality to the West, while locating emotionality and ritual forms on the European or global periphery that appears so remote it seems no problem to say factually incorrect things about it, or to use derogatory terms. A clear instance of complicity with the escalation of political discourses by fostering polarization, such stereotyping fuels the violence inherent to discourses of mourning and lamenting instead of contributing to their analysis. And analysis of the link between public lamenting and political polemics, which Greek authors deemed capable of causing civil war, is urgently necessary. This link and its potential for violence was realized, in 2018, in the eastern German city of Chemnitz, where "mourning marches" turned into riots over immigration. The link already seemed an imminent threat to French President Hollande in his 2015 funeral oration for the victims of the Paris terror attacks. Following the genre protocol set by Pericles in his speech for the first Attic casualties of the Peloponnesian War, commemorated by Thucydides, Hollande underlined: *La liberté demande pas à être vengée, mais à être servie.*[99] (Freedom demands not to be revenged, but to be served.) No private revenge, but (military) service for the state is deemed a responsible answer to the attacks. The difficulty is that while populisms of all kinds claim *responsiveness* to populations' complaints and oppose it to conventional political *responsibility* that seems to be ruled by globalized corporations,[100] condemning lamenting and complaining in general as dangerous and revanchist from the public sphere leaves the devastating gap of not being able to think a form of language capable of doing the work of mourning, of negotiating and accepting loss, that renders trauma communicable history—a narrative for understanding the present and enabling a future.

## The Coming Chapters

The first chapter, "Freud on Understanding Plaintive Language," outlines the profound change in Freud's responses to complaints and laments, from the early treatment of Emmy v. N., through the instructive complications of the Dora case, to the analysis of the "Wolf Man." Adopting conceptual work done by Abraham and Torok, the chapter shows that the consumption, disorganization, and ruin of linguistic structures in complaints and laments is no metaphor but, rather, part of an oral process at the basis of symbolization and mourning. The second chapter, "Ritual and Modernity:

---

[99]https://www.dailymotion.com/video/x3ft9pj; 0:00–0:06, accessed February 23, 2019.
[100]Christóbal Rovira Kaltwasser and Cas Mudde, *Populism*, 97–118.

On Silencing Laments," describes the structural similarities between neurotic complaints and ritual laments which give rise to recurrent efforts to silencing plaintive language in sociopolitical modernizations (as featured in the *Oresteia*), and the concurrent nostalgia for ritual forms (as articulated in Rilke). This reading parallels criticism with anthropology, religious, and classical studies. "Voicing Pain and Destruction," the third chapter, turns to theoretical approaches that directly focus on the language of complaints and laments, comparing Wittgenstein's *Philosophical Investigations* and the epilogue to Gershom Scholem's translation of the biblical book of Lamentations (*Eicha*). Both explore how experiences of pain and disaster can be communicated, highlight the crucial role of the hearer and the possibility of a response that opens up room for (rather than concludes) individual and communal communication and history. Chapter 4, "Lament of Nature," features Benjamin's recurrent notes on the ancient motif of nature lamenting, along with its precursors in Herder, all of which assume that complaints and laments do not only communicate particular, individual, or communal experiences of suffering, but are fundamental to all language, world-relation, and the notion of history itself. The fifth chapter, "(No Way) From Complaining to Legal Action," elaborates on Kafka's criticism of an important gesture of modernity in *The Stoker/America* and other stories: the public outcry against injustice that establishes a platform for advocates who speak out on behalf of the client, and in doing so take away their voice. Modernity, Kafka supposes, makes complaining the medium of individuality with the promise of justice, yet the institutional logic of juridical action cannot but betray this promise. The conclusion, "Transgenerational Silence" relates the discussions of the book to the lack of lamenting in the modern notion of history, as diagnosed by Benjamin, and to recent discourses on transgenerational trauma, outlining how literature is a medium capable of discovering possible new languages for lamenting and complaining, citing Bernhard's 1986 novel *Extinction* as one such instance. This discovery appears necessary as the gap left by the elimination of ritual forms of lament poses the difficulty that under the modern paradigm of the inwardness of emotion, only silence counts as authentic expression of mourning but is indistinguishable from the silence of repression and denial.

# 1

# Understanding Plaintive Language: Freud

*"But should one believe that Sergei Wolf Man keeps speaking endlessly to analysts in order not to be heard?"*[1]

Laments and complaints are at the heart of psychoanalysis. Patients complain before, during, and after analyses about pains, symptoms, or people; complaints about therapies are the impetus for revisions of psychoanalytic theory. Doctors complain about patients, Freud himself laments that this science will never be scientific enough.[2] "Plaint" is, nevertheless, not a primary concept in psychoanalysis,[3] and this is hardly surprising. Complaints and laments undermine the referential stability indispensable for concepts. Plaintive language holds a key operative position in Freud's writings exactly because of its resistance to terminological stability. While "The Function and Field of Speech and Language in Psychoanalysis," as Lacan headlined, has been analyzed broadly,[4] hardly any attention has been paid to the language of complaining and lamenting, and this might be due to its instability. Yet it is precisely because complaining and lamenting cannot be narrowed down to a term, a drive, a defense, or "royal road" to the unconscious—because plaintive language remains a phenomenon—that it is a driving force behind the constriction of psychoanalytic therapy and theory. The issue of comprehending complaints and laments, and of what comprehending means here anyway

---

[1] Nicolaus Abraham and Maria Torok, *The Wolf Man's Magic Word*, 30.
[2] Sigmund Freud, *Studies on Hysteria. Standard Edition* [SE] 2, 159: "It still strikes me myself as strange that the case histories I write should read like short stories ..."
[3] "Plaint" is not used as a mere descriptor throughout book; the reading follows Freud's language use.
[4] Since Freud is, as Foucault puts it, an "initiato[r] of discursive practice" ("What Is an Author?," 310), it is impossible to reference all major research on language and literature in psychoanalysis. Sources will, therefore, be given in context.

(understanding their occasion, their origin, their aim, or something else) gives rise to many concepts, such as "talking cure," transference, afterwardsness, and (notoriously) mourning. The endeavor to comprehend plaintive language inspires a multitude of concepts because it remains an unsettled question that, in turn, questions the functioning of theorization, which is to say: whether it suffices in a particular instance, and whether it can be done at all. Freud's work provides an ideal guide for insight into the structure of plaintive language because his inquiry into how to respond to complaints and laments is engaged in all the discourses any study of this form of language must draw from: literature, anthropology, law, classical, and religious studies.

Exploring the soul and understanding language had long been a domain of philosophy. Freud employs hermeneutic and aesthetic terminology from the philosophical tradition in order to enter into competition with philosophy as a discipline,[5] pinpointing two of the crucial blanks, which Stanley Cavell highlights: "psychoanalysis and cinema share an origin as responses to the suffering and knowledge of women."[6] Modern philosophy after Descartes, in its foundation onto rationality as the faculty of doubting everything and of finding everything uncertain except for its own undertaking[7] is, according to Cavell, a violent response to the experience of the mind's limitedness.[8] Assuring that everything short of the doubt is unsure is a way to immunize thinking against experiences that would otherwise seem lamentable: loss, suffering, death. Plaintive language voices such experiences, thus raising the issue of response emphasized by Cavell. As the following chapters will outline, plaintive language provides no symbolic compensation for damage, pain, or death, but claims hearing for the insufferable while finding every response insufficient. This irreconcilable, restless, and seemingly non-dialogic form of speech is often furnished with a genre or gender codification in order to delimit its apparent impertinence: Ritual laments as well as neurotic complaints have come to be considered female in many contexts while poetic complaints or religious laments are often considered male and part of tragedy, elegy, or prophecy—while, in fact, all, regardless of sex or gender, have always been lamenting and complaining everywhere. Freud's interdisciplinary approach to understanding plaintive language allows to make a cross-section through these discursive dynamics.

On the one hand, Freud sees the issue of response in complaints early on: The *Studies on Hysteria* is based on the assumption than an insult which remains unanswered becomes a trauma manifest in symptoms; as possible responses, Breuer and Freud list crying, acts of revenge, and "lamentations"

---

[5] Sigmund Freud, *The Interpretation of Dreams*. SE4:614: "It is not without intention that I speak of 'our' unconscious. For what I thus describe is not the same as the ... unconscious of the philosophers."
[6] Stanley Cavell, "Freud and Philosophy: A Fragment," 386.
[7] René Descartes, *La Lumiere Naturelle*. Œuvres 10:523: ›*dubito, ergo sum‹, vel, quod idem est: ›cogito, ergo sum‹*.
[8] Stanley Cavell, *Contesting Tears: The Hollywood Melodrama of the Unknown Woman*, 90.

(SE2:7). On the other hand, Freud's understanding of what plaintive language communicates, and of how to respond to it by way of therapy, changes fundamentally over time: In the early concept of theory, complaints and laments are means for discharging affects by way of naming the cause for distress. It seems, however, that a fissure disconnects the patients' words from their referents, which raises doubts as to who complains about (or laments) what (or whom) in whose words. Reconstructing Freud's changing understanding of plaintive language expounds fundamental, historical as well as systematic complications that any study of the language of lamenting and complaining faces: The uncovering of supposedly anachronistic, ritual forms in modern subjectivity, the yearning for a juridical, religious, therapeutic, or other compensation that silences plaints, and the undermining of any clear distinction between healthy and pathological organizations. These issues are seminal to the subsequent chapters.

This chapter will outline how the disorganization of linguistic structures in lamenting and complaining cannot be answered by therapeutic intervention or terminological stabilization, that is neither therapy nor theory succeeds in appeasing and silencing plaintive language. A tension marks Freud's inquiry into lamenting and complaining: He suggests a not at all metaphoric concept of the consumption of linguistic structures in lamenting and complaining that leaves no room for an answer even though it seeks nothing more than response. Yet in spite of these insights Freud, still, holds on to the juridical promise of compensation and restoration since the therapeutic endeavor is otherwise unthinkable. Lagache as well as Abraham and Torok further elaborate the dynamic of the consumption of linguistic structures in plaintive language. A restless center that stimulates theorization, the issue of understanding plaintive language evokes the whole scope of Freud's works; This chapter will do justice to it only as far as the outline of the structure of plaints requires.

## Complaint without a Cause: Treating Hysteria and Forgetting Laments in Modernity

In the 1895 *Studies on Hysteria*, Breuer and Freud examine "psychical trauma" (SE2:5) as a wound which is characterized by the patient being "genuinely unable to recollect" (2) what, or who, has caused it. Hysterical symptoms replace any recollection of pathological events: patients complain about pains without a cause,[9] about amnesias, anxiety,[10] hallucinations,[11]

---

[9] SE2:50, 55, 157; all lists non-exhaustive.
[10] SE2:59, 61–62, 66.
[11] SE2:49, 51, 73, 177.

and sensations without an apparent trigger.[12] At the onset of psychoanalytic therapy, Breuer's and Freud's inquiry does not target the sematic or semiotic relation between verbal complaining and physical complaint but the etiological relation between trauma and symptom. Unlike a physical wound, a psychological trauma does not appear as the lasting result of a single occurrence such as a blow, in fact, the cause of the trauma does not occur in the patients' memories at all and remains incessantly active. In order to eliminate symptoms, Breuer and Freud infer their cause has to be made apparent: "The psychical process which originally took place must be repeated as vividly as possible; it must be brought back to its *status nascendi* and then given verbal utterance" (SE2:5). In the *Studies on Hysteria*, the task of therapy is articulation; a verbal expression of the traumatic process is thought to make its symptoms disappear. According to this model, therapy is the substitution of a substitute, for hysterical symptoms are themselves alternative articulations insofar as they share dynamics fundamental to language: association and reproduction. A symptom, formed by associating an affect with a physical phenomenon as its expression, occurs like a word by way of reproducing associations in different contexts. Hence symptoms may even appear to be "'joining in the conversation'" between patient and analyst (SE2:295). However, a symptom does not, as a symbol does, refer to the trauma but replaces it entirely, even the knowledge of it. The purpose of therapy is to revoke this collapse by way of narrative reconstruction. Speech has two tasks in this process: on the one hand it repeats the events—the propositional part that makes use of conventional statements—on the other hand it expresses the accompanying affect in such a way that it is released and vanishes—the dynamic part and the reason why Breuer and Freud call this "the cathartic method" (SE2:107). The form of speech therapy seeks to attain is able to both show the traumatic events and erase the pathogenic affect they cause: "The patient is, as it were, getting rid of it by turning it into words" (SE2:279).

Thus, therapy is supposed to supplement the erasure of the affect usually brought about by retaliation or plaintive language. Because whether or not an event becomes a trauma depends not on the nature of the event but on the response, on

> *whether there has been an energetic reaction to the event that provokes an affect*. By "reaction" we here understand the whole class of voluntary and involuntary reflexes—from tears to acts of revenge—in which, as experience shows us, the affects are discharged. If this reaction takes place to a sufficient amount a large part of the affect disappears as a result. Linguistic usage bears witness to this fact of daily observation

---

[12]SE2:147, 54.

by such phrases as "to cry oneself out" ..., and to "blow off steam" ... If the reaction is suppressed, the affect remains attached to the memory. An injury that has been repaid, even if only in words, is recollected quite differently from one that has had to be accepted. Language recognizes this distinction, too, in its mental and physical consequences; it very characteristically describes an injury that has been suffered in silence as "a mortification" ... —The injured person's reaction to the trauma only exercises a completely "cathartic" effect if it is an *adequate* reaction—as, for instance, revenge. But language serves as a substitute [*Surrogat*] for action; by its help, an affect can be "abreacted" almost as effectively. In other cases speaking is itself the adequate reflex, when, for instance, it is a lamentation [*Klage*] or giving utterance to a tormenting secret, e.g. a confession.[13]

This negotiation of the response in traumatic pathology points out that the catharsis crucial to Breuer and Freud's approach to therapy has two dimensions: the aim of therapeutic catharsis is adopted from humoralism's notion of cleaning by way of purgation, the media of catharsis are adopted from Aristotle's theory of tragedy.[14] Therefore, Breuer and Freud consider revenge the regular affective response, and speech only its surrogate. This notion is by no means antiquated: in 2003, Kowalski lists "venting feelings (catharsis)" as the main purpose of the "annoying behavior" of complaining.[15] In Freud's terms, an event that causes an affect does not become traumatic if a response answers the blow intensely enough to equal the triggered affect, thus annihilating it. Without such a response, in passive or silent toleration, the affect is internalized and damages the organism "like a foreign body" causes "a reactive inflammation"—or, Freud corrects, "far more like an infiltrate," since the difficulty of psychic traumas is that the pathological structure is impossible to "cleanly" separate from the healthy ones (SE2:289). In order to form a regular recollection of events, it is crucial that its accompanying affect be expressed; internalization bars memory. "Linguistic usage" testifies to the necessity of externalization, Breuer and Freud remark, because it appears itself as linguistic process: "Hysterics suffer

---

[13]SE2:7/*Studien über Hysterie. Gesammelte Werke* [GW] 1, 87.
[14]Aristotle, *Poetics* 1449b:25–30. Freud adopted a reading of the concept by classicist Jacob Bernay, his wife Martha's uncle, which had been reissued in 1880; see Michael Kenney, "Trauma, Memory, and Catharsis," 487.
[15]Kowalski, *Complaining, Teasing, and Other Annoying Behaviors*, 28. Cf. Lee, *Lyrics of Lament*, 27: "Lament, in essence, provides a cathartic vehicle for human beings to express all aspects of suffering"; Alexiou, *Ritual Lament*, 124; Baggini, *Complaint*, 32–35. Disputed in Wilce, *Crying Shame*, 30: "We err in uncritically applying such Western notions as catharsis ... to lamenters whose cultural models of emotion, personhood, and communication are quite unlike Aristotle's."

mainly from reminiscences" (SE2:6), from an ever-present past, because psychical traumas are an exception to what Breuer and Freud call *Usur* (GW1:86), "the normal wearing-away processes by means of abreaction and reproduction" (SE2:10) that results in the "fading of a memory or the losing of its affect" (7). Traumas are, literally, useless; they do not connect to anything else in memory or speech and are thus inaccessible to "linguistic usage" (7). The "cathartic method" of psychotherapy seeks to generate a substitute for the missing original reaction, yet it suffers from an eminent shortcoming: Notwithstanding all emphasis on affect and response, the "cathartic method" centers on a reconstructive narrative in statements and misses the patients' complaints, the one element of hysterical symptoms analogous to a regular affective response by way of lamentations.

Breuer and Freud's early characterization of trauma as a lack of *Usur*—a term later dropped, conventionally denoting the abrasion by usage of bones or teeth—still provides useful orientation in current trauma theory debates: Unavailability to usage and wearing-away means that trauma is not, as such, unknowable, as Caruth's trauma paradigm would hold,[16] yet indeed an obstacle to verbalization resulting in the disorganization of speech, or text,[17] notably in plaintive language as a means to avert as much as to indicate traumatization. For while Breuer and Freud introduce lamenting and complaining as responses that prevent trauma, the discussion of plaintive language in this and later works is based on the ambiguity of "response" as deflecting and/or indicating a blow.

As regular ways of an affective response, Breuer and Freud list very different things: somatic expressions like crying, acts of revenge, lamentations, and confessions. What all of these have in common is an emphasis on address, reaching out, obtaining attention, and touching someone. In terms of semantics, lamentations, confessions, and insults say very different things, but what matters to all of them is that the expression is formed in order to obtain a hearing. Regular affective reactions, which prevent traumatization, do not comprise a truthful portray of the affecting events; they are not at all concerned with truth claims. Benchmark of the adequacy of the utterance is whether it equals the affect. The "cathartic cure," however, is based on a truthful reconstruction of the traumatizing events—something that can, even in regular cases, be articulated only after the events have been separated from the fear, anger, or other affect they raise. The separation of events from their accompanying affect is the aim of a regular response such as crying, revenge, or lamentations, but it is also the condition of the possibility of hysterical symptoms and a complication in the attempt to understand the patients' complaints. For

---

[16]Cathy Caruth, *Unclaimed Experience*, 2–3; cf. note 49 and Conclusion, 250; for criticism Ruth Leys, *Trauma: A Genealogy*, 266–297.
[17]Joshua Pederson, "Speak, Trauma," 338–340.

these, too, are utterances testifying to an affect rather than portraying their cause. The "cathartic method" takes this into account when the "'talking cure'" (SE2:39), as Breuer's patient Anna O. calls her treatment, seeks to articulate whatever had been traumatizing until "a symptom was being 'talked away'" (36), and even "her disturbances of speech" that made her talk only in English were "'talked away'" (34). The articulated trauma is supposed to replace the symptom because, in speech, the traumatizing event can enter into associations with different contexts and come into "linguistic usage," that is become subject to "the normal wearing-away processes by means of abreaction and reproduction" (10). Yet in order to enable this, the traumatizing event has to be identified, and the pathogenic affect it raised has to be named, which requires a reconstructive narrative formed in statements and truth claims—even though this propositional aspect of the reconstructive narrative is not supposed to be its psychologically operative part eradicating the pathogenic affect. The separation of events from their accompanying affect becomes a problem here. For how could one tell the cause of an affect from its expression if the separation between the two is so thorough that the ideas associated with the expression are a replacement of all knowledge of the cause, that is a symptom? How is it possible, under these circumstances, to understand what patients complain about? What, in fact, does it mean to understand complaints: to take them literally as statements or, rather, as symptoms and signs of something else than what is being said?

It is an, as it were, ambivalent ear that Breuer and Freud lend to their patients' complaints: In the *Studies on Hysteria*, Breuer and Freud understand complaining as indication that a therapeutic intervention is necessary, and they assume that this necessity has been met with adequate care as soon as the complaints fall silent. While this approach does speak to the dominant aspect of discourses on plaintive language—being heard—it does so by giving into the impulse to silence lamenting and complaining—an impulse that results from plaintive language's enervating insistence on being heard and also rules many discourses on ritual plaints. Breuer and Freud's understanding of particular complaints in the 1895 case histories largely contradicts their theoretical comprehension of complaints: Complaints are usually taken as statements about the physical state of the patient and *about* their symptoms, not *as* a symptom. Breuer and Freud implicitly assume a correlation between verbal and physical complaint, between an utterance and its cause, that they expect neither in regular affective responses nor in the relation between trauma and symptom. Freud explains, for instance, about the application of Breuer's initial therapeutic approach of suggestion while placing his hands onto the patient's head: "It is quite common for the patient to complain of a headache when we start on the pressure procedure ... The headache indicates her dislike of allowing herself to be influenced" (SE2:301). This clarification is as short as simple because it disregards the complaint as a verbal utterance: Freud sees a symbolic structure only in the pain, not in the complaining from which he learned about the headache.

Other instances question the assumption of a de facto identity of verbal complaining and physical complaint, for example when the verbal utterance explains the shift of reference in the symptom "astasia-abasia":

> The patient ended her description of a whole series of episodes by complaining that they had made the fact of her "standing alone" painful to her. In another series of episodes, which comprised her unsuccessful attempts to establish a new life for her family, she was never tired of repeating that what was painful about them had been ... the feeling that she could not "take a single step forward." ... I could not help thinking that the patient had done nothing more nor less than look for a symbolic expression of her painful thoughts. (SE2:151)

In Freud's reading of the symptoms, the "painful" feeling of being single, of "standing alone," finds "symbolic expression" in pain while standing (astasia), and the "painful" feeling of not being able to move on in the inability to walk (abasia). Yet Freud does not consider the complaining as "a symbolic expression of her painful thoughts," that is to say an expression in words. The verbal complaints are left aside as mere transitory tools for understanding the symptoms—yet these somatic manifestations of her complaints might, in turn, be an effect of the therapeutic gaze: It is only when paralleled with a physical symptom that the patient's complaints about standing alone, and not moving on in life, are being listened to—an attention that comes at a price: In a therapeutic discourse, the complaint is not heard as asking for a response with reference to what it names (the lack of a partner), but as explaining a symptom that cannot be "talked away" in complaints since it is not their actual cause. The *Studies on Hysteria* understands neurotic complaints as an index of symptoms, not as means for achieving a "wearing-away processes by means of abreaction" as in the case of regular lamentations. The difference between regular (healthy) and pathologic, however—often mirrored in the difference between "complaint" and "lament(ation)" in the English translation of Freud's writings—remains deeply problematic in psychoanalytic theory since it is not supported by any linguistic structure: Freud is confronted with *Klagen*, a German word that comprises complaints, laments, wailing, and even accusations. The chapter will continue to outline that the structure of plaintive language does not allow for a distinction between healthy as opposed to pathologic forms. Before this can be done, however, the hermeneutic difficulty presented by plaintive language and the parameter of its discussion have to be clarified further.

In 1917, Freud writes about "the commonest example" of a wife suffering from her marriage "that by escaping into a neurosis the ego obtains a certain internal 'gain from illness.'" The gain is that the symptoms make the suffering communicable: "To complain [*klagen*] of her illness is allowable, though to lament [*beklagen*] her marriage was probably not" (SE16:382/ GW11:397–398). The earlier *Studies on Hysteria* struggles to understand that neurotic complaints testify to suffering and provide comfort by obtaining not a remedy, but a surrogate: The "'gain from illness'" is the production of a referent that can be named in complaining in such a way that the plaint is heard and answered by way of therapy. This primary aim of getting a hearing, however, raises doubt about the assumption that symptom, complaint, and cause always match as neatly as "standing alone" and astasia do. It, rather, seems that neurotic complaints (i.e., those of people suffering from incomprehensible symptoms) are structured by the very same principle as regular affective responses to insults, by the intention to reach out, obtain hearing, and touch someone. The possible shift of reference from traumatic cause to lamented symptom this entails, however, is an eminent complication for the therapeutic endeavor to reconnect the pathogenic affect to the event(s) that raised it.

Well aware that he is facing considerable hermeneutic difficulties, Freud adopts heuristic approaches of disciplines other than medicine, most notably from the poetics of tragedy (as mentioned) and from archaeology, a tremendously popular field by the end of the nineteenth century. In 1896 Freud concedes that "it would be a good thing to have second method of arriving at the aetiology of hysteria, one in which we feel less dependent on the assertions of the patients themselves."[18] There is such a way, Freud suggests:

> Imagine that an explorer arrives in a little-known region where his interest is aroused by an expanse of ruins, with remains of walls, fragments of columns, and tablets with half effaced and unreadable inscriptions. He may content himself with inspecting what lies exposed to view, with questioning the inhabitants—perhaps semi-barbaric people—who live in the vicinity, about what tradition tells them of the history and meaning of these archaeological remains, and with noting down what they tell him—and he may then proceed on his journey. But he may act differently. He may have brought picks, shovels and spades with him, and he may set the inhabitants to work with these implements. Together with them he may start upon the ruins, clear away the rubbish, and, beginning from the visible remains, uncover what is buried. If his work is crowned with success, the discoveries are self-explanatory. (SE2:191)

What Freud suggests is that rather than handing their symptoms over to the therapist, patients should participate in the search for a cure. But

---

[18] Freud, "The Aetiology of Hysteria." SE3:187–221, 190.

the analogy also tells of the discursive context in which Freud seeks to understand complaints: Patients may appear as "semi-barbaric" insofar as they are unable to explain how they came into their present state—a historic amnesia contemporary archaeology attributed to non-European inhabitants of the world. Yet the analogy is telling mostly due to its inconsistencies: For both patients and "semi-barbaric people" do, in fact, account for past events, it is only that their account is often no chronology but, for instance, a symptom or a myth—"mnemic symbols," Freud says (SE2:192). Yet while incomprehension of mythic accounts and the assumption of a lack of history in non-European cultures assured nineteenth-century archaeology to better made locals dig then tell, psychotherapy cannot do without talking to patients. Pain is inaccessible without symbolization.[19] What is new about Freud's method is that it takes complaints about suffering by their word. But by which word exactly?

The therapeutic-archaeological analogy refers back to the 1895 diagnosis "Hysterics suffer mainly from reminiscences" (SE2:6), from remnants that do not pass. While connecting this insight to the interest in the long-past, Freud passes over a piece of the recently passed that is almost omnipresent in the *Studies on Hysteria*: dirges, laments for the dead, and mourning rites that have fallen out of fashion in the social context of Freud's urban bourgeois patients while still being practiced in other, particularly rural areas. The parallel between neurotic complaints and ritual forms of plaint is important because these, too, are voiced by changing speakers with reference to divergent situations, borrowing words from authors who remain latent. Given that many of Freud's female patients develop hysterical symptoms while nursing sick or dying relatives,[20] wakes, laments, and dirges linger mutely in the background of hysteria.[21]

"There are," Freud explains in the *Studies on Hysteria*, "good reasons for the fact that sick-nursing plays such a significant part in the prehistory of cases of hysteria" (SE2:160). During care, there is little occasion for the women to physically care for themselves and little time to ponder emotions. These retained impressions are reactivated if the sick person dies, only to be retained again because the conventions of mourning require prioritizing the

---

[19]See Chapter 3.
[20]This is true for Anna O. (SE2:23, 28, 37), Emmy v. N. (SE2:91), Elisabeth v. R. (SE2:135, 140, 147); furthermore Freud, "A Case of Successful Treatment by Hypnotism." SW1:115–128, 123–124; *Fragment of an Analysis of a Case of Hysteria*. SE7:57 (although Dora's father, whom she nurses, does not die).
[21]Emmy v. N. adopts the seminal ritual formula from the book of Lamentations, *eikhah* (how), that opens every line or stanza, just as otherwise dirges and epitaphs: "All the accounts she gave of traumas arranged like these in groups began with a 'how', the component traumas being separated by an 'and.'" Freud understands that her wording is a "protective formula … designed to safeguard her against a recurrence of such experiences" (SE2:56) but does not comment on its ritual origin.

deceased (161). Mourning does not become an explicit topic of psychoanalytic theory until the case of the so-called Wolf Man, whom Freud analyzes between 1910 and 1914; yet the subject of mourning anticipates important theorems already in 1895: the "subsequent[t]" (*nachträglich*) dealing with traumas (SE2:161; GW1:229) later called "deferred action" (SE17:45) or "afterwardsness"[22] (*Nachträglichkeit* [GW12:72]) and the intricate relation between healthy and pathological structures, for in mourning, "we get no general impression of illness but ... the mechanism of hysteria is nevertheless retained" (SE2:161). In a different 1895 text, Freud counts the "exhausting exertion—as, for instance, after night-watching, sick-nursing" among the pathogenic conditions independent from gender.[23] This night-watching, however, does not comprise wakes for the dead; Breuer and Freud do not mention dirges or ritual lamentations. Freud's discussion of mourning as a psychical issue makes Leader wonder: "What happened to the social dimension of mourning?"[24] It has been abolished by the modern paradigm of the inwardness of emotions, as the next chapter will outline, and left the problem of the transgenerational transmission of trauma due to a lack of mourning behind that is addressed in recent psychoanalytical works, as the conclusion to this book will discuss. It is precisely because Breuer and Freud never talk about the social dimension of mourning, which had once been negotiated in rites, that the disorganization of speech in neurotic complaining appears as manifestation not solely of individual "reminiscences," but just as much of the abandoned cultural practices of dirges, wakes, and ritual laments. This return of cultural practices that have just recently faded away as a pathology in the structure of individual subjectivity, in turn, appears as a symptom of Modernity discussed, for instance, in Rilke's elegies and anthropological studies.[25] On the one hand, laments for the dead are often portrayed as "semi-barbaric" in these discussions, that is to say archaic, incomprehensible, and dangerous—a characterization already established in Aeschylus's *Oresteia*. On the other hand, in not knowing anything about the history and meaning of highly conventionalized utterances such as ritual laments, Modernity is just as "semi-barbaric" by the standards of Freud's therapeutic-archaeological analogy. Psychoanalysis is part of this Modernity. The disorganization of articulate speech in dirges and wailing is an obligatory element of the poetics of tragedy, which the *Studies on Hysteria* evokes in the term "catharsis" and the emphasis of the reciprocity of revenge. Yet this is not the aspect of tragedy that Breuer and Freud have in

---

[22] Jean Laplanche, *Essays on Otherness*, 264–269.
[23] Freud, "On the Grounds for Detaching a Particular Syndrome from Neurasthenia under the Description 'Anxiety Neurosis.'" SE2:101.
[24] Darian Leader, *The New Black*, 71.
[25] Both discussed in Chapter 2.

mind, and Freud's adaption of archaeological imagery is about the removal of disorganized remnants, not about their presentation.

There is (at least) one more incoherence to Freud's analogy: "the discoveries are self-explanatory" he says (SE2:191), however, neither ruins nor symptoms explain themselves, both require interpretation. The imagery bypasses the difficulty "the cathartic method" is supposed to reconstruct and, at the same time, erases the recollection of the events that caused pathogenic affects. The project of reconstruction faces tremendous difficulties, as has been shown, yet the erasure is no less problematic. The case histories outlined in the *Studies on Hysteria* show neither a traceless removal of affects analogous to a catharsis of the intestines, nor an expression and negotiation of affects analogous to Aristotelian catharsis. The traumatic structure proves to be an irreversible "infiltrate" (SE2:289) in that the intervention—under hypnosis (Breuer's idea)—rather, seems to cause a proliferation of affect and complication familiar from early modern revenge tragedies, such as *Hamlet*. The hypnotic treatment of Emmy v. N., for instance, erases her initial cause for complaint, the expectation of misfortune. Yet rather than silencing her complaints, "removing her whole recollection" (SE2:60) of all-too-clear traumatic reminiscences appears as a trauma itself and only replaces the original cause for complaint: "I promised her that this would lead to her being freed from the expectation of misfortune which perpetually tormented her and from the pains all over her body, of which she had been complaining precisely during her narrative" (60). In a footnote to this sentence, Freud speaks of "the overwhelming success of the treatment," when what he describes might well be read as a grave complication: Rather than being relieved, the patient suffers from amnesia:

> On this occasion my energy seems to have carried me too far. When, as much as eighteen months later, I saw Frau Emmy again in a relatively good state of health, she complained that there were a number of most important moments in her life of which she had only the vaguest memory ... and I had to be careful not to tell her the cause of this particular instance of amnesia. (SE2:60)

As Torok has pointed out, Emmy v. N.'s treatment does not follow "the cathartic method" of talking away symptoms.[26] Freud, rather, replaces a pathologic amnesia with what he considers to be a healing one, and replaces her symptoms with his suggestions—yet the complaint stays in place and testifies to a lasting wound. Emmy v. N.'s treatment is singular; still, it corresponds to "the cathartic method" by adhering to the principle that complaints shall be silenced. What it points out—though not in the intended

---

[26]Maria Torok, "Restes d'effacement," 124–126.

manner—is that there are indeed no grounds for complaint: no grounds, that is, on which plaintive language firmly rests as a mere verbal utterance. Complaining and lamenting are suitable for erasing affects precisely because they are capable of becoming detached from their original cause, and of joining a different one. Understanding plaintive language requires comprehending that its cause is not the provoking event (causa efficiens) but the aim of being heard (causa finalis). Lamenting and complaining do not simply presuppose that there will be someone to listen and respond as a question presupposes an answer but doubt the possibility of reciprocity and has, therefore, no firm ground to rest on. Emmy v. N.'s continued complaining about painful events insists that it did not aim for a closure, solution, or erasure, but for an ear. Freud, however, does not listen yet, at least not to the right one, insofar as he notes: "I also met the family doctor, who had not many complaints to make about the lady" (SE2:82–83).

Freud quits hypnosis in the course of the treatments portrayed in the *Studies on Hysteria* in order to listen to the patients' discourses. Talking remains in focus, yet no longer as "talking away," but as "working-through of the resistances" against the comprehension of symptoms.[27] After the *Studies on Hysteria*, Freud's approach to understanding plaintive language shifts from the cause *for* complaint, from reconstructing the relation between trauma and symptom, to the cause *of* the complaints, to their intention. The imbalance of power in the doctor–patient relationship remains an important occasion for complaining that spurs revisions of psychoanalytic theory.

## Complaining and Wish-Fulfillment

Freud's 1900 *Interpretation of Dreams* serves the same purpose as the earlier interest in hysteria: understanding psychic structures and dynamics. The dream is relevant not as an aberration from reality but as indicating that "conscious life" accounts for only a small part of the psyche: "The unconscious is the true psychical reality" (SE4:612). Consciousness is, according to Freud, "a sense-organ for the perception of psychical qualities" (614). Its faculties are limited, what is mainly active in the psyche is the "Unconscious" ("*Ucs.*"), which is "inadmissible to consciousness" (614). The "Preconscious" ("*Pcs.*," 616) is not but may become conscious. Whenever an idea passes from the *Ucs.* to the *Pcs.*, and from the *Pcs.* to Consciousness ("*Cs.*," 541), it passes a "psychical censorship" (606) that transforms it. This is what forms dreams (159), but also other phenomena, as Freud explains with reference to the case history of a girl:

---

[27]Freud, "Remembering, Repeating, and Working-Through." SE12:145–156, 155.

> She complained of having pains in her leg and, without being asked, exposed her calf. But what she principally complained of was, to use her own words, that she had a feeling in her body as though there was something "stuck into it" which was "moving backwards and forwards" and was "shaking" her through and through: sometimes it made her whole body feel "stiff." My medical colleague, who was present at the examination, looked at me; he found no difficulty in understanding the meaning of her complaint. But what struck both of us as extraordinary was the fact that it meant nothing to the patient's mother ... —The girl herself had no notion of the bearing of her remarks; for if she had, she would never have given voice to them. In this case it had been possible to hoodwink the censorship into allowing a phantasy which would normally have been kept in the preconscious to emerge into consciousness under the innocent disguise of ... a complaint [*in der Maske einer Klage*]. (SE4:617/GW2/3:623)

Psychic censorship cannot fully bar ideas from consciousness, but it may change them to the effect that they are voiced not as a "phantasy" but as a complaint. As a complaint, the idea finds a hearing with the male doctors. There is no shift of reference between phantasy and complaint but, rather, a shift in the qualification of the idea: Censorship turns the unfulfilled erotic phantasy into a present suffering, the opposite. Unconscious phantasies, however, do not care about propositional logic, affirmations and negations serve the purpose of *naming* the right thing equally well.[28] The "disguise of ... a complaint" allows to present what should but (lamentably) does not happen. The dynamic that forms this complaint is the same as the one that forms dreams: both "replace thoughts by hallucinations" (SE4:59) in order to "represent a wish as fulfilled" (122). The aspect of representation is emphasized somewhat less in Freud's summary of one of the basic assumptions of *The Interpretation of Dreams*: "A dream is a (disguised) fulfilment of a (suppressed or repressed) wish" (159). There are "other forms of abnormal wish-fulfilments," Freud adds, such as "psychoneurotic symptoms" (567–568), one instance of which is certainly the girl's unmistakable complaint. In a footnote, Freud states more precisely: "One portion of the symptom corresponds to the unconscious wish-fulfilment and another portion to the mental structure reacting against the wish" (568). Articulating an unmistakable complaint instead of an unambivalent offer is an instance of the psychic censorship reacting against the wish. But can the

---

[28] SE4:317: "'No' seems not to exist so far as dreams are concerned." Freud, *The Unconscious*. SE14:186: "There are in this system no negation, no doubt, no degrees of certainty: all this is only introduced by the work of the censorship between the *Ucs.* and the *Pcs.* Negation is a substitute ... for repression." The subsequently developed concept of "negation" follows up on this observation that an idea is independent from its propositional frame; idem "Negation." SE19:234; Chapter 5, 214.

presentation of a wish in the "disguise of ... a complaint" be considered "a (disguised) fulfilment of a (suppressed or repressed) wish"? Is complaining an instance of wish-fulfillment?

As odd and even cynical as the question might seem, it is prompted not solely by Freud's *Interpretation of Dreams*, but also by recent works from other fields like New Testament scholar Schmidt's: He holds that as an expression, plaintive language already provides a solution to the problem it names in that it produces the "salutary distance from one's suffering" prerequisite to overcoming it.[29] The girl's unmistakable complaint thus deserves a closer look: She seems far from a fulfillment of what Freud identifies as her disguised wish because presenting it is possible only after a censoring compromise with her psychic censorship that the wish shall be cast as undesirable. While this presentation does find a hearing, the doctors' understanding of her wish contributes nothing to answering her sexual desires, it, rather, transfers them into the discourse of pathology. Still, there is no denying that "the bearing of her remarks" is the lamentable failure of a wish-fulfillment. A clarification of how Freud's theory of wish-fulfillment may elucidate the structure of plaintive language requires a more precise look at the involved terms: What is a wish, what does it mean to fulfill it, and for whom is it fulfilled?

Freud conceptualizes "the psychical nature of wishes" as the reproduction of a link: "the psychical apparatus" seeks to "kee[p] itself so far as possible free from stimuli" but is hindered in this endeavor by "major somatic needs," such as hunger (SE4:564). The "excitation" thus caused is discharged by movement: "A hungry baby screams or kicks helplessly," and relief is provided only by food and repletion. The "'experience of satisfaction'" consists of these sensations accompanied by "a particular perception (that of nourishment, in our example)" which is remembered due to its satisfying effect (564). As soon as the need reappears, the link is activated, the "mnemic image" (565) of food plus satisfaction is re-evoked in order to reestablish the satisfaction. Freud elaborates: "An impulse of this kind is what we call a wish; the reappearance of the perception is the fulfilment of the wish" (565). What equals the infantile, "primitive state of the psychical apparatus" to dreams and neuroses is the weakness of the borders erected by psychic censorship between the *Ucs.*, *Pcs.*, and *Cs.*, so that wishing may actually "en[d] in hallucinating" (565). Experience tells that hallucinating does not satisfy hunger, still, the link between the need and "mnemic image" is maintained and connected to movement, that is to acting and, later, speaking as "a roundabout path to wish-fulfilment." "Thought," Freud maintains, is "nothing but a substitute for a hallucinatory wish" (566); both hallucinations and thoughts imagine whatever is missing in order to attain it.

---

[29]Schmidt, *Klage*, 158, 16, 153; my translation.

In a roundabout path, in disguise, is also how the girl's unmistakable complaint pictures her wish. This wish-fulfillment is "abnormal" in Freud's terms because the path is not long enough, as it were, because her complaint shares her hallucination with others instead of leaving it in the *Pcs.*, and becoming conscious in terms more acceptable to 1900s bourgeois society, such as the demand to marry. "The girl herself," that is to say her consciousness, "had no notion of the bearing of her remarks" but only of the form of complaint, the reaction against the hallucination. Yet whose disguised wish-fulfillment can the complaining be called if "the 'experience of satisfaction'" (SE4:597) remains concealed even from the wisher? In 1913 Freud writes: "It is not difficult for a skilled analyst to read the patient's secret wishes plainly between the lines of his complaints and the story of his illness."[30] Patients might have "no notion of the bearing" of their complaints, of the wishes and hallucinations they articulate, even if they appear unmistakable to whoever listens to them—and this is hardly surprising, given that these complaints are formed in such a way that they may find a hearing. Unlike what he presupposes in 1895, Freud's 1913 remarks strictly distinguish the analyst's understanding from the patient's: In order for therapy to have any beneficial effect it is necessary for patients "to get hold of the explanation for himself" (SE12:139). Treatment thus becomes less of an archaeological endeavor; understanding why wishes are articulated as complaints is equally important as understanding which wishes are repressed or suppressed, and what (possible) trauma has formed them. Freud later calls this process "working-through ... resistances" (SE12:154), when "something that the patient wishes to discharge in action is disposed of through the work of remembering" (152).

While Freud has dropped "the cathartic method" outlined in 1895, he still conceptualizes therapy as a catharsis reconnecting complaints to their origin in the propositional order of statements. With the *Interpretation of Dreams*, however, it becomes clear that although complaints are not primarily statements about difficulties, they are far from chaotic but follow a different organizing principle: the attention and hearing they seek to attain simultaneously disguises what cannot be said verbatim. Patients' complaints often correspond neither to their symptoms nor to their supposed cause but to the addressee of their speech and to the aim of being heard. This intention of being heard determines the reference of the complainers' words, which means that listening to these words does in a certain way answer them—without achieving what is generally called comprehension. According to Freud's approach, what neurotic complaints seek to make heard is misunderstood (or not at all understood) suffering; and this form

---

[30]Freud, "On Beginning the Treatment." SE12:121–144, 139.

of speech is adequate since incomprehension (of an affect or wish) is the reason for the suffering. The incomprehension is no mere disguise put on a well-present thought; what is active in the *Ucs.* is not readily discernable. Its communication in complaining may, therefore, precede its comprehension. The "disguise of ... a complaint" (SE4:617) seeks to find an ear so that, in conversation with someone who listens, the mis- or not at all understood wish it communicates may be comprehended. This approach to interpreting plaintive language rests on insights into the dynamics of "the dream-work" (177) active in other instances of psychic censorship, too. It remains true that not every complaint voices a wish; some complaints, however, may be considered wish-fulfillment insofar as their articulation follows structural dynamics which, according to Freud, present wishes as fulfilled in dreams. What parallels dreams with plaintive language is not the aim to communicate (dream intelligibility is a defect more than an intended effect[31]) but that dreams are supposed to catch attention so that the sleeper does not awake.[32] Whatever the dream produces is informed by this purpose,[33] just like complaints are formed to find hearing. Not the identity of the addressee is what is relevant for complaints, however, but the direction of the utterance, its relationality.

Two processes are essential for what Freud calls "dream-work": condensation (SE4:278) and displacement (304). The "work of condensation" results in the peculiarity that "the elements of a dream" are "determined by the dream-thoughts many times over" and represented by several elements (283), therefore, there is no simple correspondence as there is between "standing alone" and astasia. The "work of displacement" makes sure that the dream focuses on "different elements as its central point" (304) than the ideas or needs that gives rise to the dream. This is "the essential portion of the dream-work" (307), concerned with the "transference and displacement of psychical intensities" (306). It creates the disguise in which the repressed and suppressed may be imagined in spite of psychic censorship. The dream is not the only scene where condensation and displacement are active, they transform all wishes psychic censorship deems to be harmful. Whenever this happens, the excitation that drives the wish is made "mobile and capable of discharge" (596) by way of condensation and shifts along associations such as homophones or rhymes; Freud calls this the (unconscious) "'primary

---

[31] SE15:230: "A dream does not want to say anything to anyone. It is not a vehicle for communication; on the contrary, it is meant to remain ununderstood."
[32] SE4:232: "All dreams ... serve the purpose of prolonging sleep instead of waking up. *Dreams are the guardians of sleep and not its disturbers.*"
[33] When traumatic neuroses manifest in recurring nightmares had became epidemic with the First World War, Freud will formulate an exception to this rule; cf. SE18:32; Conclusion, 247.

process'" (600).³⁴ Its evasion into the next best association is hindered by the (preconscious) "'secondary process'" (600) that follows logic. Together they result in the "transformation of affect," usually termed "'repression'" (603), the ill-reputed dynamic that makes sure most wishes are not pursued in waking life but presented as fulfilled in dreams—or in neurotic complaints. One of the most prominent means of "dream-work" is, according to Freud, "reversal, or turning a thing into its opposite" (326). It gives "expression to the fulfilment of a wish in reference to some particular element of the dream-thoughts. 'If only it had been the other way round!'" (326) Turning a wish into a complaint about undesirable symptoms also serves this purpose. Reading neurotic complaints with reference to the means of representation active in "dream-work" provides a better understanding of how plaintive language communicates than the assumption of a shift of reference alone: The dynamics of condensation and displacement point out that psychic censorship and the transformation of affect do not make use of just any accidentally available idea as a disguise. These dynamics actively form the referent of dream images: "new unities are formed (in the shape of collective figures and composite structures)" and "words and names" are handled as objects (294).

The close affinity between dreams and complaints is brought to the fore in Freud's discussion of one of his dreams, centered around the opposition "*Auf Geseres—auf Ungeseres*" (SE4:440–441). Incomprehensible as first glance, the pair is "determined ... many times over" and evocative, among others, of the German farewell *Auf Wiedersehen* (441), of the contrast "leavened—unleavened bread," the latter being a reminiscence of the Exodus from Egypt commemorated in the feast of Passover Seder (442), and of a Hebrew word imported into German: "'Geseres,'" Freud continues, "is a genuine Hebrew word derived from a verb 'goiser', and is best translated by 'imposed sufferings' or 'doom'. The use of the word in slang would incline one to suppose that it meant 'weeping and wailing'" (441). The antonym "*Ungeseres*" is a neologism formed in dream-work, probably expressing a wish like "'If only it had been the other way round!,'" if only there was no reason to complain.³⁵ The narration and the discussion of the dream ponder,

---

³⁴Freud, *The Unconscious*. SE14:199: "In schizophrenia *words* are subjected to the same process as that which makes the dream-images out of latent dream-thoughts—to what we have called the primary psychical process." 197–198: "A patient of Tausk's, a girl who was brought to the clinic after a quarrel with her lover, complained that *her eyes were not right, they were twisted*. This she herself explained by bringing forward a series of reproaches against her lover in coherent language. 'She could not understand him at all, he looked different every time; he was ... an eye-twister, he had twisted her eyes; now she had twisted eyes; ... now she saw the world with different eyes.'"

³⁵Earnest Rappaport, *The Ritual Murder Accusation*, 328: "A wordplay based on a slight distortion of the German *gesäuert*, i.e., leavened, to Geseres, Yiddish, meaning laments, and *ungesäuert*, i.e. unleavened, changed to a new word coined by Freud, *Ungeseres* meaning free from lamenting, i.e., rejoicing."

among other things, the anti-Semitism that hinders Freud from receiving full professorship at the university of Vienna, his brother's success in exile in Britain, the possible need to join him there, and the structural proximity of reversal and repetition that raises the question of whether his exile will duplicate the brother's success or be the reverse. What Freud's discussion does not spell out is that the word *Geseres* is present not only in Viennese slang but also in historic consciousness: *Wiener Gesera* (Vienna Gesera) is both the name of the extinction of the Jewish community in 1421 upon order of Albert V, archduke of Austria, and the title of a text that portrays the pogrom in German language and Hebrew script.[36] This text is the model for the word's shift of reference from "imposed sufferings, ... doom," the content of the text, to "weeping and wailing" (SE4:441), the mode of utterance. Freud's text, to be sure, is neither a dream nor a complaint but a conscious articulation that links the structures of the two, speaking in the same way as the girl's unmistakable complaint: it communicates in such a way that it may find hearing and can be brought to comprehension.[37] The distinction between "manifest" and "latent content" (134), in particular, is as essential to Freud's discussion as to the texture of the dream: Neurotic complaints name and portray a certain manifest ground for complaint which is formed by the intention to find a hearing while the pain or discomfort that aroused the complaint may remain latent. This assumption of a double text in neurotic complaints replaces that of a merely expressive function of plaintive language in the *Studies of Hysteria* that was unable to explain the contradiction between patients' symptoms and utterances.

The mechanisms of psychic censorship that form dreams also form neurotic complaints as necessary disguises to communicate suffering at the expense of causing a massive disorganization of linguistic structures that jeopardizes understanding—shifts in reference and interchanges between the positions of subject, addressee, and author. These dynamics, uncovered in dream-work, are active not solely in neurotic complaints but in all plaintive language. In the popular-interest study *Psychopathology of Everyday Life*, published in 1901, one year after *The Interpretation of Dreams*, Freud points out that condensation and displacement form complaints and laments of so-called healthy people, too, in cases when some idea or wish

---

[36]A transcription in Arthur Goldmann, *Das Judenbuch der Scheffstraße zu Wien*, 125–132; context in Samuel Krauss, *Die Wiener Geserah*.

[37]The parallel is supported by a remark: "In every epoch of history those who have had something to say but could not say it without peril have eagerly assumed a fool's cap. The audience at whom their forbidden speech was aimed tolerated it more easily if they could at the same time laugh and flatter themselves with the reflection that the unwelcome words were clearly nonsensical. The Prince in the play, who had to disguise himself as a madman, was behaving just as dreams do in reality; so that we can say of dreams what Hamlet said of himself, concealing the true circumstances under a cloak of wit and unintelligibility" (SE4:443).

shall not become manifest and appears as the latent content of slips of the tongue or "symptomatic acts" (SE6:31) instead. Shifts between author and addressee of a complaint are nothing trivial; they form ambiguous complaints and false accusations. It might seem surprising that a complaint should be inconclusive even to the extent of questioning its author, however, the author (or originator) of a complaint is not simply the person who utters it since the words may be borrowed, as later case histories show. This complication to psychotherapy is, in fact, a rule in ritual or literature, where plaintive language features just as prominently. In ritual and literature, the uncertainty of who complains about whom, or laments over what, in whose words, parallels the complaints of Freud's patients with ritual laments like dirges and poetic complaints like elegies. These, too, are voiced by changing speakers in divergent contexts, borrowing words from authors who remain latent. Freud's interpretation of the *Geseres-Ungeseres*-dream does so, for instance, in quoting Psalm 137:1: "'By the waters of Babylon we sat down and wept'" (SE4:441).

Yet even if the shifts that disorganize usually well-coordinated elements of speech such as word reference, author, and addressee seem less pathological with regard to other discourses they, still, bear grave consequences for the therapeutic attempt to reorganize neurotic complaints into a personal discourse free from misunderstood suffering. The gravest of these complications is the question: Whose authority is it to tell what is manifest and what is latent, and to identify a wish in the suffering? The 1905 case of the patient synonymously called Dora proves to be instructive for Freud's endeavor to understanding plaintive language because he fails to understand her, she stops the therapy, and he discovers the dynamics of transference.

Dora suffers from cough and the "incessant repetition of the same thoughts about her father's relations with Frau K" (SE7:53), an extramarital affair, a punishable offense at the time. Yet what concerns Freud is that while her words and symptoms seem to result from her father's affairs, it is hard to distinguish which are caused by him and which are borrowed from him: "As she kept on repeating her complaints against her father with a wearisome monotony, and as at the same time her cough continued, I was led to think that this symptom might have some meaning in connection with her father" (45). Coughing regularly serves her father as a pretext to leave his family for cures, and to see "Frau K" (33). Yet like every symptomatic utterance, Dora's cough is "determined ... many times over" (SE4:283). It accuses the father of deceitfulness by copying him, and latently testifies to a different set of repetitions as well: her accusation of the father also refers to the facts that due to his "loose life" (SE7:74), she is infected with hereditary syphilis, and that her father left his underage daughter to "Herr K.," his lover's husband, as a substitute for "Frau K.," thus forcing his daughter into his lifestyle. The repetition becomes pathogenic when it is articulated, when "Herr K." approaches Dora with the words: "'I get nothing out of my wife,'" the same line she knows he used with a servant. Freud sees Dora's reaction as "wounded pride" (105). It is only in footnote where he remarks: "It is not a matter of indifference, perhaps, that Dora may have heard her father make the same complaint about his wife, just as I myself did from his own lips" (105). The literal repetition of her father's complaint (about her mother) by "Herr K." (about "Frau K.") puts Dora into the position of "Frau K.," the woman with whom her father has intercourse. The complaint about the lacking sexual compliance of a woman seems like a ritual and works along the same lines as the infection: Starting from the father, it affects the daughter. Yet the full scope of the repetition structure implicates Freud, too, who fails to see the gravity of the abuse. He insists on a shift of addressee to the affect that "behind the ... open accusations against her father there lay concealed as usual a self-accusation" (75)—about masturbation, he infers, apparently the only reason he can imagine for her to refuse "Herr K.," about whom he writes in a footnote: "I happen to know Herr K., for he was the same person who had visited me with the patient's father, and he was still quite young and of prepossessing appearance" (28). In the fragment of Dora's analysis, psychotherapeutic interpretation of what may be disguised in complaints undermines the patient's emotional and hermeneutic independence, attributing to her the wishes these adult men wish the underage girl had.[38] Freud conceptualizes this as "the factor of 'transference'" (12) and takes into account, in later analyses, that in the disorganized discourse of neurosis, a good way to disguise something might be to just name it straight away.

The background of Dora's treatment at which Freud only hints in passing and which cannot but seem obscene to later readers—that two adult men hand an underage girl over for treatment to make sure she stops complaining and assumes the social and sexual position they have allotted her—is not only telling of the context that gives rise to hysteria and its theory, it is also paradigmatic in portraying plaintive language as a highly gendered phenomenon in Modernity. Chapter 2 will outline how divergent sociopolitical modernizations, from antiquity to the present day, go along with defining complaining as feminine, irreconcilable, dangerous, and, therefore, as an antisocial discourse best silenced.

"'I can think of nothing else', she complained again and again" (SE7:53), Freud notes of Dora. In a footnote, he adds: "A supervalent thought of this kind is often the only symptom, beyond deep depression, of a pathological condition which is usually described as 'melancholia', but which can be cleared up by psychoanalysis like a hysteria" (53). The 1910–14 analysis of

---

[38] Patrick Mahony, *Freud's Dora*, 63: "In therapy and in his writing he would continue to abuse Dora and effect acceptance of his version by his colleagues and later analysts. ... If the Dora case was truly a clinically organizing experience in Freud's relations with women, it was also an untoward organizing experience in the psychoanalytic movement."

the patient later called "Wolf Man"[39] (Sergei Constantinovitch Pankeiev[40]) will contradict this assumption of a parallelism, and while Dora's treatment already doubts the possibility of ascertaining who complains in whose words about what, the "Wolf Man" analysis adds a temporal factor. Moreover, it raises doubts about Freud's seminal assumption so far: that making the cause(s) for suffering understood to the patients is the common aim of neurotic complaining and the psychoanalytic endeavor. This entails a profound change of Freud's outlook onto complaining: He fully drops the paradigm of expression and, rather, wonders how the affection happens—how, in other words, is first internalized what lamenting and complaining supposedly purge, as Freud assumed in 1895. The texts that refer to the "Wolf Man" analysis portray an excess in plaintive language reminiscent of Job's discourse: an insistence on being heard that refutes every specific response and remains unsatisfied with every analytical explanation. The "Wolf Man" analysis points out that the therapist's response is not to be paralleled with that of God in the book of Job, complaining does not cease due to an all-comprising recompense. In the "Wolf Man" analysis, relationality appears as the most important feature of plaintive language; its prominence causes the disorganization of other structures of language—indeed their consumption.

## Idiom of Plaint: The "Wolf Man's" Speech

In 1918, after the end of the so-called Great War that will turn out to have been only the first one of its kind in the twentieth century, Freud publishes a case history already composed in 1914: *From the History of an Infantile Neurosis* (SE17:1–124), portraying the complaints of a Russian native suffering from phobias, obsessions, and depression since childhood. Freud parallels these complaints with hysteria, thus assuming that they are concerned with affects and purgation: "His principal subject of complaint was that for him the world was hidden in a veil ... This veil was torn only ... when, after an enema, the contents of the bowel left the intestinal canal" (74–75). As in the *Studies on Hysteria*, Freud first reads the symptom rather than the complaint in analogy to a linguistic utterance: "in the course of the work his bowel began, like a hysterically affected organ, to' join in the conversation'" (76) and made its history available: Initially, there was nightly incontinence without any shame which his Russian nanny understands to be an instance of "defiance" against the English governess (76). One year later, at four and a half years, the "Wolf Man" already suffers from the phobia to which he owes his alias, and the incontinence appears during daytime.

---

[39]Freud, *Inhibitions, Symptoms and Anxiety*. SE20:75–176, 106.
[40]Abraham and Torok, *Magic Word*, lii.

In the recollection of these events, the symptom gives precedence to the complaining. It is necessary to go into some metabolic detail in order to comprehend his discourse and the aftermath of lacking lament:

> He was terribly ashamed of himself, and as he was being cleaned he moaned that he could not go on living like that. So that in the meantime something had changed; and by following up his lament we came upon the traces of this something. It turned out that the words "he could not go on living like that" were repeated from someone else. His mother had once taken him with her when she was walking down to the station with the doctor who had come to visit her. During this walk she had lamented over her pains and haemorrhages and had broken out in the same words, "I cannot go on living like this," without imagining that the child whose hand she was holding would keep them in his memory. Thus his lament (which ... he was to repeat on innumerable occasions during his later illness) had the significance of an identification with his mother. (SE17:76–77)

The "Wolf Man" does not merely cite the mother's lament, as Freud's text does, but adopts his mother's discourse and substitutes himself for the "I" in it. She complains about "abdominal disorders" (SE17:13) from which the son cannot suffer. In order to apply her words to himself, the child needs to produce a different symptom. He finds an analogue in the explanation of a raging dysentery, "you find blood in your stool" (77), given by his mother

> whose haemorrhages he had heard about in the conversation with her doctor. In his later attempt at identification (when he was four and a half) he had dropped any mention of the blood; he no longer understood himself, for he imagined that he was ashamed of himself and was not aware that he was being shaken by a dread of death, though this was unmistakably revealed in his lament. (SE17:77)

The symptom is produced in such a way that it matches the complaint; the affect is misinterpreted (as shame) to be caused by the symptom while the words of the complaint ("'he could not go on living like that'") present it as fear for his life. This does not yet explain why a boy of four and a half fears for his life, and why his caregivers seem to care for the symptom more than for the words. Freud will need a sophisticated conceptual construct to even approach these questions, but first more of the complaint: Freud's "Wolf Man" analysis ends with the onset of the war in 1914; in 1916 the patient consults Ruth Mack Brunswick, recommended by Freud for the treatment of "a hypochondiacal *idée fixe*. He complained that he was the victim of a nasal injury." This complaint proves to be more important than the symptom, Brunswick notes: "He expressed the complaint voiced in all his earlier illness: as a child when he soiled his drawers and thought he had dysentery ... This complaint, containing the nucleus of his pathogenic mother-identification, was: 'I can't go on living like this any more.'"[41] As with the plaint, the assumed wart on the nose is borrowed from his mother.[42] His sister, two years his senior, "shortly before her suicide had voiced his won complaint that she was not beautiful enough."[43] Freud notes her complaint (SE17:21) but fails to see a parallel between the siblings. What is decisive, however, is not a particular symptom but the persistence of the lament—the wording of the plaint persists while already the boy of four and a half does not understand the utterance anymore, and the grown up patient does not comprehend the terror that is "unmistakably revealed in his lament." Similar to a ritual lament, the "Wolf Man's" complaint uses a fixed wording to talk about changing occasions (the bowels, the nose), and like in a ritual, the borrowed words communicate something even when the one uttering them lacks comprehension. Yet how could understanding be established, given the profoundly disorganized structure of this lament?

The "Wolf Man's" plaintive language communicates misunderstood suffering by way of uniformity. By 1914, the very "wearisome monotony" in which Dora "kept on repeating her complaints" (SE7:45) to Freud's irritation nine years prior appears as a key symptom itself, "'joining in the conversation'" (SE2:295; SE17:76) between patient and analyst as an insistence that the hearing, response, and understanding attained so far are not enough. Nothing will ever be enough, lamenting and complaining are the idioms he repeats from his mother throughout his life. Neither the Russian language of his infancy, the English of his upbringing, nor the German of his education operates as the "Wolf Man's" mother tongue, but the language of lamenting and complaining. This idiom of plaints can be articulated in different so-called natural languages[44] and casts doubt on the identity of the speaker: the "Wolf Man" is not only a native speaker of the language of lamenting and complaining, but speaks his mother tongue *as* his mother—in full "identification" with her, as Freud says, so that he *is* her, as Brunswick writes.[45]

The authorship of plaints is, however, not the only thing that the "Wolf Man's" idiom outlines as questionable. It also demonstrates the weight of the postulates that a trauma resists "the normal wearing-away processes" of abreaction and forgetting (SE2:10) and that the content of the *Ucs.* in general is "timeless[s]" (SE17:10):[46] In the timeless unconscious all those

---

[41]Muriel Gardiner, *The Wolf-Man by the Wolf-Man*, 264–265; cf. 273: "This was the end for him; thus mutilated he could not go on living." Brunswick also notes "the difference between the present psychotic mother-identification and the past hysterical one. ... He no longer plays the mother, he *is* the mother" (301).
[42]Ibid., 272: "His mother's wart had come and gone."
[43]Ibid., 272–273.
[44]Even Latin and French (SE17:40).
[45]Gardiner, *The Wolf-Man*, 301.
[46]"The processes of the system *Ucs.* are timeless; ... they have no reference to time at all" (SE14:187).

things correspond (by way of condensation and displacement) that work together in forming a complaint or lament, that is to say in attaining attention. The mother's lament about "not being able to live on like that" grasped a doctor's and, most notably, the child's attention, therefore, it is reproduced in the son's complaint about his suffering. Because of this timeless functional organization, a chronology of expressed or concealed wishes, anxieties, and plaints alone does not elucidate the trauma that drives them. In order to gain insight into its nature, Freud wonders "what can have been the meaning of this identification with his mother?" (SE17:77)

Freud reads it as testifying to a traumatic experience that happened in between the normal protest by way of nightly incontinence and the daily incontinence accompanied by the complaint he learned from the mother. The experience is "not an external trauma, but a dream" (SE17:28) that terrified him: Six wolfs sit motionless in a tree and look at him in his bed (29–30). Freud interprets the dream as testifying to an earlier "'primal scene'" (59) that was retained as a troubling impression but could be grasped *as* something only by the cognitive faculties of four year old. The scene is "primal" because it precedes all means of comprehension and representation, therefore, its character can only be inferred from the effects it brings about. Freud assumes that the primal scene consisted of the child watching his parents' "*coitus a tergo*," displaying the genitals (59), at about one and a half years old when he did not have the means for grasping what he saw. When he is later confronted with both fairy tale wolves who eat people (16) and genital sexuality from his sister (20), he acquires the means to present the event and translates the erect father's genitals into sitting wolfs. "The effects of the scene were deferred [*nachträglich*], but meanwhile it had lost none of its freshness in the interval between the ages of one and a half and four years" (SE17:44/GW12:43). The theory of "deferred action" (SE17:45) or "afterwardsness"[47] (*Nachträglichkeit* [GW12:72]) assumes that impressions may remain latent and become manifest only when the cognitive capability as well as the psychic need to realize them arrives, so that the difference between once and now, past and present, vanishes:

> At the age of one and a half the child receives an impression to which he is unable to react adequately; he is only able to understand it and to be moved by it when the impression is revived in him at the age of four; and only twenty years later, during the analysis, is he able to grasp with his conscious mental processes what was then going on in him. (SE17:45)

The theory of the "primal scene" and its deferred activation is relevant for understanding plaintive language because it highlights the structural disconnect between cause for complaint and cause of complaint: The

---

[47]Laplanche, *Essays on Otherness*, 264–269.

"conscious mental process" of analysis reconnects symptoms to the traumatizing wolf dream and outlines it as a deferred attempt to grasp the primal scene—the scene itself, however, is impossible to recall. It drives the "Wolf Man's" idiom of plaint which aims at finding a hearing and a response since the overwhelming early impression has cast doubt on the possibility of reciprocity. The primal scene is, as Nägele writes, "not only an epistemological presupposition, but also a *real* limit, and it appears only in the form of a limit."[48] With the cause for complaint unable to be attained, the language of lamenting and complaining takes center stage. Its monotony and repetition presents the character of the first impression that transcended all comprehension and insists that no analytic explanation of the wolf dream or other belated response can ever replace the original want of reaction. Like ritual laments for the dead, neurotic complaining forms what would otherwise be overwhelming, and thus impossible to represent, into a negotiable content by way of searching a hearing for it.

Both Freud's description of a belated full understanding of the primal events in therapy and his detailed depiction of the primal scene present a startling contrast to his description of the psychic structure as overwhelming impression that does not leave an organized image behind and is thus impossible to recall. The structural assumption of a primal scene resembles the *skēnē* in Greek theater: an empty stage-building in the background of plays to hide actors while they change costumes and masks.[49] The "Wolf Man's" primal scene spills out a series of representations—complaints, dreams, and symptoms—without ever exhausting its resources. From a therapeutic point of view, the contradiction between the elusive character of the primal scene and its elucidation in analysis cannot be dispelled. In order to interrupt the chain of presentation it produces—that is, to stop the repetition compulsion it drives[50]—the unknowable mark must be replaced

---

[48]Rainer Nägele, *Reading after Freud*, 178.
[49]*LSJ*, s.v. "*skēnē*," http://www.perseus.tufts.edu/hopper/morph?l=%CF%83%CE%BA%CE%B7%CE%BD%CE%AE&la=greek#lexicon, accessed March 15, 2019.
[50]In the 1920 *Beyond the Pleasure Principle*, Freud analyses the "'compulsion to repeat'" (SE18:19) in "neurotics" and well as "in the lives of some normal people" (21), "which overrides the pleasure principle" (22) that regulates, for instance, the wish-fulfillment in dreams. Repetitive nightmares in traumatic neuroses caused by war, accidents, and abuse call for an "exception" to the doctrine of wish-fulfilment (32). "The most moving poetic picture" of a painful compulsion to repeat "is given by Tasso in his romantic epic *Gerusalemme Liberata*. Its hero, Tancred, unwittingly kills his beloved Clorinda in a duel while she is disguised in the armor of an enemy knight. After her burial he ... slashes with his sword at a tall tree; but blood streams from the cut and the voice of Clorinda, whose soul is imprisoned in the tree, is heard complaining that he has wounded his beloved once again" (22). Caruth reads this passage as paradigm of the "language of trauma": "The voice of his beloved addresses him and, in this address, bears witness to the past he has unwittingly repeated. ... trauma ... is always the story of a wound that cries out, that addresses us in the attempt to tell us of a reality of a truth that is not otherwise available. This truth, its delayed appearance and its

by a concrete image even though, or exactly because, the relevance of the scene results from its lack of concretion. The replacement of the mark by a concrete hypothesis such as Freud's does not change the dubious ontological character of the scene fluctuating between being represented by signs and an appearance produced by signs in the same way as theatrical scenes do according to Plato.[51] From a critical point of view, however, it is worthwhile to distinguish between, on the one hand, Freud's structural assumption of the possibility of an impression that precedes all comprehension and becomes activated, and real, only with a delay and, on the other hand, his portrayal of the scene which is informed by the social taboos concerning sexuality prior to the First World War. Instead of parental intimacy, Abraham's and Torok's re-reading of the "Wolf Man" files (detailed in the next section) assumes a scene of sexual abuse of the sister by the father, witnessed by the son. Freud's summary of the "Wolf Man's" "family romance"[52] finds a disorganization in the son's sexual wishes:

"The analysis would be unsatisfactory," Freud writes, "if it failed to explain the phrase used by the patient for summing up the troubles of which he complained" (SE17:99), mainly the impression of a world veiled from him. Shortly before taking leave he recalls that he was told he had been born with a caul—*Glückshaube* (GW12:133), literally "lucky hood"—wherefore he saw himself "as a special child of fortune whom no ill could befall" (SE17:99), an estimation that was repeatedly proven wrong, first of all by the wolf phobia. "Thus the caul was the veil," Freud concludes, which makes the complaint appear as something very different: "The complaint

---

belated address, cannot be linked only to what is known, but also to what remains unknown in our very actions and our language" (Caruth, *Unclaimed Experience*, 3–4). Caruth elaborates neither on the theoretical context of repetition compulsion, nor on the fact that Freud calls Clorinda's speech "complaining" (2). The German *klagt ... an* (GW13:21), in fact, comprises both complaining and accusing—accusing him of having inflicted the wound upon her out of which she speaks as if it was a mouth. Pain, expression, and reference are curiously identical in this complaint, which is not at all the rule in traumatic speech. Still, Caruth reads the scene as paradigm the psychotherapeutic dialogue: "A parable of psychoanalytic theory itself as it listens to a voice that it cannot fully know but to which it nonetheless bears witness" (9). This figurative reading bears the grave consequence of casting the therapist in the role of Tancred, the killer, not least because, in spite of declaring literature as model for the psychoanalytic understanding of language (5), Caruth reads Freud but skips Tasso: In his epic, Clorinda's complaint/accusation is the deferred echo of Tancred's mute astonishment when he understands but cannot articulate whom he has killed in his enemy's armor: *e restò senza/voce e moto. Ahi vista! ahi conoscenza!* (Torquato Tasso, *Gerusalemme libertata* 12.67.7–8) Weigel reads the repeated slaying as aftermath of Tancred's failure to mourn, and Caruth's forgetfulness of the (double) killing as a repetition of this failure on the systematic level (Sigrid Weigel, "Télescopage im Unbewußten," 61).
[51]Plato, *Republic* 392c–395d. Nägele, *Reading after Freud*, 178: "But what about the supposed real event? It is essentially exactly that: supposed, i.e., a necessary supposition or presupposition."
[52]Freud, "Family Romances." SE9:235–242, 235.

that he made was in reality a fulfilled wishful phantasy: it exhibited him as back once more in the womb, and was, in fact, a wishful phantasy of flight from the world" (100), of being unborn and free from disappointment. Strange as it may seem, the wish to be un-born equals Job's first curse when all misfortunes have befallen him: "Let the day perish in which I was born, and the night that said, 'A man-child is conceived'" (Job 3:3; NRSV). However, the "Wolf Man's" wish of a revision of birth disguised as complaint cannot explain the necessity of an enema "administered to him by a man" (SE12:100), with himself serving only a replacement. Freud assumes that the primal scene, the later confrontation with genital sexuality by the sister, and the nanny's prohibition to masturbate caused the boy's sexual life to take on "a sadistic-anal character" (26) which gives the wish for a revision of birth a different spin: "It is easy to make a unified statement of what was expressed ... by the complaint he made ... : he wished he could be back in the womb, ... in order that he might be copulated with there by his father, might obtain sexual satisfaction from him, and might bear him a child" (101). The "Wolf Man's" main complaint, this interpretation suggests, reformulates the primal scene into a condition for recovery; it is hallucinated over and over again as the only thing that gives relief. The complaint may be considered a wish-fulfillment insofar as it puts him into the mother's position: The point of identifying with her, it seems, is not being close to her but replacing her in order to be close to the father.

One family member, however, is missing in this constellation: the sister. "She poisoned herself and died far away from her home" (SE17:21) in 1907. Her death elicits no lament at all, which irritates Freud:

> When the news of his sister's death arrived, so the patient told me, he felt hardly a trace of grief. He had to force himself to show *signs of sorrow*, and was able quite coolly to rejoice at having now become the sole heir to the property. ... I must confess that this one piece of information made me for a long time uncertain in my diagnostic judgement of the case. It was to be assumed, no doubt, that his grief over the loss of the most dearly loved member of his family would meet with an inhibition in its expression, as a result of the continued operation of his jealousy of her and of the added presence of his incestuous love for her which had now become unconscious. *But I could not do without some substitute for the missing outbursts of grief.* And this was at last found in another expression of feeling which had remained inexplicable to the patient. A few months after his sister's death he himself made a journey in the neighbourhood in which she had died. There he sought out the burial-place of a great poet, who was at that time his ideal, and shed bitter tears upon his grave. ... He only understood it when he remembered that his father had been in the habit of comparing his dead sister's works with the great poet's. (SE17:23; my italics)

Grief is conceptualized in modern terms, here, as an individual's feeling expressed and proved by "signs of sorrow" such as tears; in a ritual paradigm, it would be the other way around, and grief a social production brought about by conventional laments and tears so that individuals might feel it. And yet, Freud's concern focuses on the lacking "signs of sorrow," their displacement and deferral. The *History of an Infantile Neurosis* mentions the sister's death only in passing. While not explicitly naming the "Wolf Man," the essay "Mourning and Melancholia"—written in 1915, published in 1917—compares the two positions that collide in his analysis: Freud's, who "could not do without some" sign of mourning, with the "Wolf Man's," who had to force himself to display "signs of sorrow" when he did not feel them and produced them, actually their substitute, with sincerity at Lermontov's grave.[53] Just as assumed already in 1895, what initially seems pathological will prove to largely comprise the "normal affect of mourning" (SE14:243). Linking the "Wolf Man's" seemingly singular pathology to the general structure of grief, "Mourning and Melancholia" is all about substitutions for, and signs of, losses.[54] It seeks to answer not solely why signs of mourning might be missing in particular instances but also why Freud "could not do without" them, in other words: "In what ... does the work which mourning performs consist?" (SE14:244).

## Mourning, Melancholia, and Consumption

Mourning, Freud assumes in 1915, serves to withdraw "all libido ... from its attachment to" a lost loved object (SE4:244). The inner "opposition" and pain this evokes can be "so intense that a turning away from reality takes place," so that a mourner clings to the object in a "hallucinatory wishful psychosis" (244). This is only temporary, however, "when the work of mourning is completed the ego becomes free and uninhibited again" (245). This economy of the "normal affect of mourning" (243) has been criticized

---

[53] Gardiner, *The Wolf-Man*, 31–33.
[54] The approaches to loss discussed in "Mourning and Melancholia" have been adapted for discourses on historical loss and the constitution of subjectivity, notably the psychology of infants (Melanie Klein, *A Contribution to the Psychogenesis of Manic-Depressive States*), gender identity (Julia Kristeva, *Le Soleil Noir*; Butler, *The Psychic Life of Power*, 132–166), and postcolonialism (David Eng and Shinhee Han, "A Dialogue on Racial Melancholia"; Annie Cheng, *The Melancholy of Race*; Jermaine Singleton, *Cultural Melancholy*)—without considering the complaining prominent in Freud, therefore, these adaptions do not guide my reading.

as it leaves little room for the memory of the deceased,[55] a fundamental commandment even of modern piety. In 1915, Freud indeed characterizes mourning the same way he portrays therapeutic success in 1896 with analogy to archaeology: as complete clarification that erases even the traces of its own "work." In his short 1915 text "Transience," Freud sums up this notion in view of the war that has started in 1914:

> Mourning, as we know, however painful it may be, comes to a spontaneous end. When it has renounced everything that has been lost, then it has consumed itself, and our libido is once more free … to replace the lost objects by fresh ones equally or still more precious. (SE14:307)

In this early concept, Freud pictures mourning as a retreat of desire and attachment into a stable, unchanged "I" preparing for a replacement of the loved object. The expression of "signs of sorrow" that Freud cannot do without in the "Wolf Man" analysis appears as neither socially mandatory nor structurally necessary. It seems, rather, that Freud's 1915 notion of mourning spells out the very "revolt … against mourning" (SE14:306) he seeks to analyze in "Transience," which closes with an outlook onto universal replaceability: "We shall build up again all that war has destroyed, and perhaps on firmer ground and more lastingly than before" (307). It is crucial to keep in mind that Freud will revise his theory of mourning in 1923, after the experience of mass death and loss in the First World War, on the basis of what he considers, in 1915, to be the logic of pathological melancholia. This "work of melancholia" (257) is done mainly in lamenting and complaining:

> In mourning it is the world which has become poor and empty; in melancholia it is the ego itself. The patient represents his ego to us as worthless, incapable of any achievement and morally despicable; he reproaches himself, vilifies himself and expects to be cast out and punished. He abases himself before anyone and commiserates with his with his own relatives for being connected with someone so unworthy. …
> It would be equally fruitless from a scientific and a therapeutic point of view to contradict a patient who brings these accusations [*Anklagen*]

---

[55] Tammy Clewell, "Mourning beyond Melancholia," 47: "Freudian mourning involves less a lament for the passing of a unique other, and more a process geared toward restoring a certain economy of the subject." Nouri Gana, *Signifying Loss*, 24: "The reconciliatory work of mourning can be understood as nothing less than an incitement to and a normalization of the praxis of disloyalty." Paul Ricœur, *Freud and Philosophy*, 132: "A cruel but penetrating remark: the work of mourning is undertaken in order to survive the loss of the object … But that is not, perhaps, the sole function of narcissism in the work of mourning … Narcissism no longer pursues the every-man-for-himself attitude of the survivor, but the survival of the other in the ego."

against his ego. He must surely be right in some way ... He really is as lacking in interest and as incapable of love and achievement as he says. But that, as we know, is secondary; it is the effect of the *internal work which is consuming his ego—work which is unknown to us but which is comparable the work of mourning.* He also seems to us justified in certain other self-accusations [*Selbstanklagen*]; it is merely that he has a keener eye for the truth than other people who are not melancholic. ... he has come pretty near to understanding himself; we only wonder why a man has to be ill before he can be accessible to a truth of this kind. For there can be no doubt that if anyone holds and expresses to others an opinion of himself such as this (an opinion which Hamlet held both of himself and of everyone else[56]), he is ill, whether he is speaking the truth of whether he is being more or less unfair to himself. (SE14:246–247/ GW10:431–432; my italics)

Unlike neurotic complaints (*Klagen*), melancholic accusations (*Anklagen*) are neither mistakable nor hallucinatory but accurate enough to pass for self-knowledge. In these self-accusations (*Selbstanklagen*), melancholy enters the stage in her traditional robe of profound pensiveness.[57] What gives the accusations away as symptoms of a pathology (as such called melancholia) is that they are right—painfully right, so that nobody in their right mind would utter them. The work this speech testifies to is comparable to the work of mourning because it is busy "consuming"—not the attachment to a lost object of love, however, but the lover's ego. The sense of direction appears to be perverted in melancholic accusations, therefore, Freud's approach at understanding them does not target their propositional truth but the purpose of such self-destructive speech.

What appears striking about melancholia's main feature—"insistent communicativeness which finds satisfaction in self-exposure"—is that it lacks those "feelings of shame in front of other people" (SE14:247) that would normally follow from stating very unflattering self-knowledge. Melancholic accusations speak of the "I" as if it was an other, which hints at a shift—a displacement—between addressee and attribution:

> If one listens patiently to the melancholic's many and various self-accusations, one cannot ... avoid the impression that often the most violent of them are hardly ... applicable to the patient himself, but that with insignificant modifications they do fit someone else, someone whom the patient loves or has loved or should love. ...

---

[56]Freud's footnote (SE14:246): "'Use every man after his desert, and who should scape whipping?' (Act II, Scene 2)."
[57]Walter Benjamin, *The Origin of German Tragic Drama*, 231: "bottomless pit of contemplation."

> The woman who loudly pities her husband for being tied to such an incapable wife as herself is really accusing her *husband* for being incapable. (SE14:248)

Freud's question is not: "incapable" of what, but: why complain loudly? Because there is, even with the distorted attribution, a certain "'gain from illness'" analogous to that of the neurotic suffering from marriage: "To complain [*klagen*] of her illness is allowable, though to lament [*beklagen*] her marriage was probably not" (SE16:382/GW11:397–398). Melancholic laments and complaints address the one that cannot be both accused and loved. Ostentation is thus the very consolation, or sense, these self-reproaches seem to lack, as Freud explains:

> Their complaints [*Klagen*] are really 'plaints' [*Anklagen*] in the old sense of the word. They are not ashamed and do not hide themselves, since everything derogatory that they say about themselves is at bottom said about someone else. (SE14:248/GW10:434)

"Old" is not the inversion of self and other but the scene: The *Oxford English Dictionary* defines a plaint as a "(spoken or written) statement of grievance, submitted to a court of law for the purpose of obtaining redress; an accusation, a charge."[58] Grimms' German Dictionary, which would have been accessible to Freud, explains *Klage* in a similar way as shouting by which the wrongdoer is blamed so that everyone hears it, and the judge is appealed to.[59] Melancholic accusations are analogous to this primal scene of law since, in both, address precedes proposition: the accusation requires wailing in order to be conveyed. With regard to this foundation, accusations transcend propositional logic and disregard truth claims. Melancholic "self-accusations" are thus more than (false) attributions—they are plaints that insist on being heard. In these plaints melancholics "succeed, by the circuitous path of self-punishment, in taking revenge in ... their loved one through their illness" (SE14:251), while still maintaining the relationship with them. Shifting the attribution from the other onto the self is the way out of the dilemma of having to complain *and* wanting to love, that is to say: not wanting to suffer a loss. Yet nobody does. Giving up a loved object always raises "opposition" according to Freud (244), so what is pathological about melancholia?

While the notorious ostentation of melancholic accusations turns out to be an element of the technique of taking—via ta*l*king—revenge, the shift between addressee and attribution in the melancholic's discourse is more

---

[58] *OED* 11:956, s.v. "plaint, n."
[59] *DW* 11:908–910, s.v. "klage."

than a rhetorical stratagem: it is testimony of "the internal work which is consuming his ego" while disorganizing his[60] speech. Freud's description of the suspiciously correct self-knowledge in melancholic self-accusations would acutely contradict his latter claim that they are actually reproaches against the loved one if there were not "a few genuine self-reproaches ... scattered among those" (SE14:248) that mean someone else. This mixture stems, Freud assumes, "from the conflict of love that has led to the loss of love" (248). Rather than abandoning the conflicted relationship, it has been transferred into the ego. Ostentatious self-reproaches show how "one part of the ego sets itself ... against the other, judges it critically, ... takes it as its object." This structure, usually called "'conscience'" (247), destroys the melancholic instead of regulating him along social expectations because, Freud infers, he has become one with the object he refuses to let go: Due to a "slight or disappointment" (such as being left by the deceased), a loved object is lost. Rather than detaching the libido from that object and re-attaching it to someone else, as Freud assumes (in 1915) regular mourning does, the aetiology of melancholia is such that it maintains the love and only abandons the object: "the free libido ... was withdrawn into the ego" and established "an *identification* of the ego with the abandoned object" (249). The ego is turned into a replacement for the lost object so that the relationship does not have to be forsaken; yet this wish-fulfillment comes at a price: "Thus the shadow of the object fell upon the ego, and the latter could henceforth be judged ... as though it were an object," which means that an painful but common "object-loss was transformed into an ego-loss" (249), a pathological structure.[61] Driven by a conflict of wishes (to complain and to love), identifying with a lost love object does not result in unison but discord. The substitution of the "I" for the lost lover results in a decomposition of the self.

It is remarkable that Freud's inquiry into the "old sense of the word" plaint (*Klage*)—yet another reappearance of psychoanalysis's archaeological demeanor—gestures toward the scene of the law, where judges are institutionalized to listen to accusations and to compensate for injuries or losses by the propositional means of judgment and attribution, thus settling disputes. It is significant that Freud's reference to the scene of the law does not (also) gesture toward Greek tragedy—even though he evokes its poetics

---

[60] I adopt Freud's usage of the male form here because it is indicative of the "Wolf Man" as the background to the theory of mourning.
[61] It is misleading to correlate Freud's dichotomy of mourning and melancholia with an ethical one of right and wrong, as Ferber suggests: First proposing that "the work of mourning can be seen as an egotistic rather than a healthy response ... Melancholic stubbornness is fundamentally ethical in nature because it manifests pristine responsibility to the lost object," she immediately has to concede that "all-consuming melancholia" has an "alternative face, one of destruction and betrayal" (Ilit Ferber, *Philosophy and Melancholy*, 35).

already in the *Studies on Hysteria* to explain the cathartic economy of affects as following the reciprocal logic of revenge, and even though revenge is pointed out as the purpose of melancholic (self-)accusations—all the while mourning, revenge, and jurisdiction are tightly interlinked in plays like the *Oresteia*. Freud mentions only *Hamlet* in the context of mourning and melancholia—a modern revenge play without the lament songs seminal to Greek tragedy. What is more, Shakespeare's *Hamlet* negotiates the "conflict about muted lamentation" in reformation England, as Döring writes,[62] where "*ersatz* rituals performed on stage" substitute for abolished rites of mourning.[63] Yet the substitute marks the lost social space more than filling it, as Lacan suggests when he notes that *Hamlet* stages "insufficient mourning":

> In the accommodations worked out by modern society between use values and exchange values there is perhaps something that has been overlooked in the Marxian analysis of economy ... —something whose force and extent we feel at every moment: ritual values. ... Ritual introduces some mediation of the gap opened up by mourning. ... in all the instances of mourning in *Hamlet*, one element is always present: the rites have been cut short and performed in secret.[64]

In retracing melancholia's plaintive language to a call for jurisdiction, "Mourning and Melancholia" is one instance of the general dismissal of ritual forms from the structure of modern individual subjectivity, but it is also an adaption of the exclusion of ritual laments such as wailing and dirges already from the public of the ancient Greek *polis* as performed in the *Oresteia*.[65] Aeschylus's trilogy settles that kinship-based retaliation shall be replaced by a court of citizens in Athens, and that ritual lament—taken to arouse vindictiveness—shall be silenced. Freud knows the *Oresteia*.[66] A reference to Greek tragedy, its lament songs, and logic of revenge, however, would have pointed out that there is no clear link of complaints and accusations to compensation and restoration—a promise as seminal to jurisdiction as to psychotherapy. Therefore, when Freud understands plaintive language to be more than an expression of self-consuming affects, namely, a medium for reciprocity and revenge, he cannot but link it to the scene of the court and thus to the outlook onto justice—in order not to be, otherwise, left with nothing but the irreconcilability of plaintive language

---

[62]Tobias Döring, *Performances of Mourning*, 4.
[63]Ibid., 53.
[64]Jacques Lacan, "Desire and the Interpretation of Desire in Hamlet," 39–40.
[65]See Chapter 2, 130–140.
[66]Freud mentions the *Oresteia* in the 1939 *Moses and Monotheism*. SE23:114.

and the perpetuated destruction of revenge logic, which even the *Oresteia* manages to stop only with a sleight of hand.⁶⁷

Melancholic self-accusations are the irreconcilable, violent medium for a decomposition of the self as they allow for no grammatical distinction between the ego and the lost object identified with it. Just as the trauma forms an "infiltrate" impossible to "cleanly" isolate from the structure of the psyche (SE2:289), it is impossible to tell apart the object from the ego that has identified with it, and impossible to unite with it. Melancholic self-accusations are thus a medium of dispute between heterogeneous parts of the self which—unlike Freud's evocation of a primal scene of jurisdiction suggests—end neither in judgment nor in reconciliation. The accusations judge the object that is impossible to tell apart from the ego, loosen the attachments to it by "disparaging it, denigrating it and even as it were killing it" (SE14:257), thereby "emptying the ego until it is totally impoverished" (253). This work that results in "consuming" the melancholic's ego is exerted in plaints: "The laments which always sound the same and are wearisome in their monotony nevertheless take their rise each time in some different unconscious source" (256). Melancholic complaining seems to resemble Dora's neurotic/ritual complaints, which Freud also describes as monotonous, yet the process he ascribes to both plaints is very different: A melancholic identification with the other is no substitution of well-differentiated positions, no portrayal of a suffering by way of condensation and displacement that appears hardly mistakable to the audience it targets. Melancholic identification is a replacement of the "I" in the attempt not to suffer a loss. The complaints about the aftermath of this replacement work like a rumination, a process of chewing—not only because they are repetitive but because they form a metabolic cycle of incorporation (of the lost object), consumption (of the structures of the ego, including its differentiation from others), renovation (the object replaces the ego), and excretion (of the ego). The "Wolf Man" articulates this cycle in complaints about his metabolism and about the fear of being eaten by the wolf.

Before reconnecting the analysis of plaintive language in "Mourning and Melancholia" to his case history, however, one further structural assumption requires introduction in order to outline that "incorporation" is no metaphor here but part of an oral process at the basis of symbolization and representation, that is to say of speaking and wishing. Not every relationship allows for an identification with the object, Freud elaborates,

---

⁶⁷Pivotal issue of the *Oresteia* is whether Orestes had the right to kill his mother to avenge his father Agamemnon, whom she had killed in revenge for Agamemnon's sacrifice of their daughter Iphigenia, and whether killing a blood relative is graver than killing a spouse. The jury's verdict is undecided and Orestes is acquitted since he is *not sentenced* (Aeschylus, *Eumenides* 752–753). Athena's sleight of hand is the introduction of a jury to render the undecidability of the legitimacy of revenge into a decision that suspends the logic of revenge.

only one where "the object-choice has been effected on a narcissistic basis" (SE14:249). In other words, a resemblance to the "I" is what had made the loved one attractive in the first place, hence the stubborn refusal to stop loving it, and hence the ease with which accusations against the loved one can be disguised as self-accusations. In principle, however, identification is not a contrast to "object-choice"; Freud assumes:

> Identification is a preliminary stage of object-choice, that it is the first way—and one that is expressed in an ambivalent fashion—in which the ego picks out the object. The ego wants to incorporate this object into itself, and, in accordance with the oral or cannibalistic phase of libidinal development in which it is, it wants to do so by devouring it. (SE14:249–250)

The early conception of object-choice by way of "devouring" reappears in melancholia, its ambivalence as both appropriation and annihilation reappears in the contrast between intention and result of melancholic identification: Aimed at taking revenge on the loved object by exterminating it while, at the same time, perpetuating it, and preventing its loss. The melancholic incorporation of the lost love object turns out to cause an annihilation of the ego, exterminating the "I" that did not want to suffer a loss. Canetti summarizes the logic of such accidental self-consumption in a different context: "The thing which is eaten eats back."[68] Melancholia's ostentatious self-accusations, which are suspiciously correct and yet not fully true, expose the origin of "the function of judgement," described by Freud in the 1925 "Negation": "It affirms or disaffirms the possession by a thing of a particular attribute; and it asserts or disputes that a presentation has an existence in reality" (SE19:235). Yet the supposed rationality of propositional truth claims says nothing else than the "the oldest—the oral—instinctual impulses ... : 'I should like to eat this', or 'I should like to spit it out' ... 'It shall be inside me' or 'it shall be outside me'" (236). Melancholic self-accusations are thus not only pathological due to their painful accuracy but also dysfunctional in that they take the primordial oral relation to the world, and the essentially cannibalistic relation to others, literally. This is, however, one of the systematic points where the inquiry into the structure of mourning questions the strong distinction often assumed between healthy and pathological, normal and aberration.

First, however, there is need to clarify how the metabolism of melancholic (self-)accusations relates to the "Wolf Man's" lack of signs of sorrow at the death of his sister that Freud does not want to do without. The case history of the "Wolf Man" and "Mourning and Melancholia" do not

---

[68] Elias Canetti, *Crowds and Power*, 357.

interlock perfectly; the tensions between them seem to foreshadow Freud's revision of the theory of mourning in 1923, in which he attributes to regular mourning what he conceptualized as pathological melancholia in 1915. From the point of view of the *History of an Infantile Neurosis* it seems that the tears the "Wolf Man" sheds at Lermontov's grave are a surrogate for the "signs of sorrow" he could not produce for his late sister years before,[69] yet from the point of view of "Mourning and Melancholia," it seems that the tears for Lermontov are signs for abstaining from mourning the sister altogether and indeed feeling for the poet only. The theory of mourning and melancholia suggests that the "Wolf Man" complains about himself in order *not* to lament, and thus acknowledge, the death of his sister whom he has, rather, devoured in order to both continue loving her and eliminate her as a concurrent for his father's "preference."[70] This exchange is possible at the price of "consuming his ego" as well as the structures of his language: For the complaint that shall not name the cause for pain but still make that pain heard cannot but destroy those structures of language that allow comprehension. The "Wolf Man's" self-accusations and complaints about his symptoms voice the plaintive speech acquired from his mother not in order to speak of himself, but for speaking of himself as a stopgap, in order *not* to talk about his sister (and father).

What links the "Wolf Man's" particular disorder to the structure of mourning and plaintive language in general is that his discourse has already achieved the withdrawal of attachment to objects that Freud identifies as the aim of "the work of mourning." The "laments which always sound the same and are wearisome in their monotony" but "nevertheless take their rise each time in some different unconscious source" (SE14:256) ignore the reference of words and do not seek to portray any of the "single impressions" which make up the "presentation" of a loved object (256) through which the process of mourning works in a "slow and gradual" process (255). This means that with regard to the consumption of reference in plaintive language, there is no clear dividing line between the laments of mourning and the melancholic discourse of laments, complaints, and (self-)accusations. The metabolism of plaintive language consumes the stability of those linguistic structures that would allow to differentiate who laments over whom, or which loss, and whether signs are of sorrow, a painful lack of sorrow, or something else. What marks the relevance of the peculiar "Wolf Man" analysis is that

---

[69] A "mistake in his story" suggests that Lermontov is a surrogate: "He had repeatedly specified before that his sister had shot herself; but ... she had taken poison. The poet, however, had been shot in a duel" (SE17:23).

[70] "His father had an unmistakable preference for his sister, and he felt very much slighted by this" (SE14:17). It is hard to tell whether Freud censored the character of the "preference," which Abraham and Torok characterize as abuse, for his consciousness or that of his readers.

the metabolic cycle to which it testifies structures all plaintive language, undermining any distinction between healthy lamenting and pathological complaining, between mourning and melancholia. These distinctions indeed collapse in Freud's 1923 revision of the concept of mourning.

## Metabolism of Plaintive Language

In the course of revising the topology of the psyche in the 1923 *The Ego and the Id* (which adopts these concepts and sidelines *Cs.*, *Ucs.*, *Pcs.*), Freud touches upon his earlier work on mourning:

> We succeeded in explaining the painful disorder of melancholia by supposing that [in those suffering from it] an object which was lost has been set up again inside the ego—that is, that an object-cathexis has been replaced by an identification. ... Since then we have come to understand that this kind of substitution has a great share in determining the form taken by the ego and that it makes an essential contribution towards building up what is called its "character."
>
> ... *It may be* that by this introjection, which is a kind of regression to the mechanism of the oral phase, the ego makes it easier for the object to be given up or renders that process possible. *It may be that this identification is the sole condition under which the id can give up its objects*. At any rate the process ... is a very frequent one, and it makes it possible to suppose that the character of the ego is a precipitate of abandoned object-cathexes and that it contains the history of those object-choices.[71]

Although appearing more or less in passing, these remarks entail profound consequences for the theory of mourning: Everybody incorporates losses to the extent that the "character of the ego" is formed as the trace of lost love objects. Grief would thus always comprise, as Freud puts it in 1915, a regression to "the oral or cannibalistic phase of libidinal development" (SE14:249–250). The "normal affect of mourning" (243) would differ from a pathological structure in that the ego is not emptied "until it is totally impoverished" (253) but—analogous to the biological concept of metabolism—formed by the "precipitate" of the incorporated. Freud, however, does not spell out the consequences of his 1923 speculation for the 1915 theory of mourning, but glides from referencing the explanation

---

[71]SE19:28–29; my italics. "Introjection" is Ferenczi's term, conceived already in 1912 to correlate the externalizing projection.

of the "painful disorder" melancholia to the formation of the ego in general. The line between healthy and pathological has become irrelevant by 1923, after the First World War had made traumatic neurosis a common pathology.[72] What is remarkable with regard to the earlier concepts of mourning and melancholia is that in these later speculations, identification is no longer a simple replacement of the ego—and a pathological surrogate for the "normal" detachment of object-relations that leaves the "I" virtually untouched—but a process that alters and, in fact, creates the "I." The "character of the ego," one may conclude from Freud's speculations, results from the consumption of the clear difference between the ego and the incorporated other in the process of mourning—a process that is not only portrayed but essentially carried out in plaintive language which does not clarify to what "signs of sorrow" testify: who laments over whom, complains about what, or accuses whom of what, in whose words. Paying heed to the collapse of the distinction between "normal" and "pathologic," with reference not to individual patients but to psychical phylogenesis, Freud illustrates his 1923 understanding of incorporation as the source of the individual's "history." In a footnote he writes, again varying the archaeological demeanor of psychoanalysis:[73]

> An interesting parallel to the replacement of object-choice by identification is ... the belief of primitive peoples, and in the prohibitions based upon it, that the attributes of animals which are incorporated as nourishment persist as part of the character of those who eat them. As is well known, this belief is one of the roots of cannibalism and its effects have continued through the series of usages of the totem meal down to Holy Communion. (SE19:29)

The anthropological dimension of the ambivalence of perpetuation and annihilation in devouring had already been the subject of Freud's 1913 *Totem and Taboo*, his first rendering of psychoanalysis as a method for studying cultures. "By incorporating parts of a person's body through the act of eating," he writes in 1913, "one at the same time acquires the qualities possessed by him" (SE13:81). Just like the melancholic devouring of the lost object, cannibalism, in Freud's understanding, aims primarily at maintaining the incorporated by identification,[74] whereas the aspect of annihilation and

---

[72]Freud, "Introduction to Psycho-Analysis and the War-Neuroses." SE17:205–210, 208: "the precondition of the war neuroses, the soil that nourishes them, would seem to be a national [conscript] army; there would be no possibility of their arising in an army of professional soldiers or mercenaries." Cf. Conclusion, 247.
[73]For a criticism see Chapter 2.
[74]"The violent primal father had doubtless been the feared and envied model of each one of the company of brothers: and in the act of devouring him they accomplished their identification with him, and each one of them acquired a portion of his strength" (SE13:141).

excretion seems insignificant to him. The "totem meal" serves the same purpose of acquiring qualities and is, furthermore, parallel to grief in that it comprises mourning and lamenting. Yet Freud cites religious studies scholar Robertson Smith to qualify those plaints: "The mourning ... is not a spontaneous expression of sympathy ... but obligatory and enforced by fear."[75] Freud sees the plaint as an apotropaic epilogue to the incorporation: "When the deed is done, the slaughtered animal is lamented and bewailed. The mourning is obligatory, imposed by dread of a threatened retribution. ... its chief purpose is to disclaim responsibility for the killing" (SE13:139). Robertson Smith and Freud voice a profound conflict between ritual and modernity, where conventionality is taken to vouch against sincerity that is, in the modern notion, authenticity proven by unpredictability—whereas in ritual contexts, sincerity is understood as appropriateness marked by predictability. The incommensurability of the norms of ritual and modernity is a key reason why the discourse on trauma appears as a replacement of ritual mourning and lamenting in the *Studies on Hysteria*.

In spite of the estranged notion of what a ritual lament is, *Totem and Taboo* bears relevance for understanding plaintive language: The disorganization of linguistic structures in plaintive speech such as shifts between reference and addressee permits to pass on the responsibility for the killing onto the victim.[76] Just like melancholic self-accusations this lamenting and wailing is concerned with attributing the deed only insofar as it serves the purpose of being heard and, furthermore, of averting retaliation. In *Totem and Taboo*, plaintive language appears not merely as a "surrogate" for acts of revenge, as the *Studies on Hysteria* suggests, but equals it enough to answer and even forestall the urge to take revenge. There is, in other words, no doubt anymore that plaintive language is concerned with hearing and response. Written even before "Mourning and Melancholia," however, *Totem and Taboo* does not assume that the lamenting and wailing that is part of the "totem meal" leaves a trace within the lamenters and re-formulates their egos—analogous to how the incorporation of the meal alters them, and analogous to how the 1923 *Ego and the Id* states that incorporation forms "the character of the ego" as a "precipitate" of incorporated objects. Viewing ritual laments as "obligatory" rather than "spontaneous" and heartfelt is certainly not beneficial for conceptualizing plaintive language as medium for incorporating the lost object in mourning and for re-forming the self through consumption of established linguistic and psychical structures. And yet, in generalizing that melancholic devouring is the structure of all mourning, Freud's 1923 remarks call for this assumption insofar as they

---

[75] SE13:151, quoted from Smith, *Religion of the Semites*, 412–413.
[76] "A part of the ceremony consists of a dance accompanied by a song, in which the death of the slain man is lamented and his forgiveness is entreated. 'Be not angry ... Why were you our enemy?'" (SE13:36).

drop the cathartic paradigm under which plaintive language appears as a means only for expressing affects and cutting attachments—all as if to make sure the "I" remains untouched by others and by losses—in favor of a generative notion of mourning that alters the "I" by consuming its distinction from others. The assumption that the ego and its "history" are formed by incorporating abandoned object-relations similar to how communities are formed by incorporating the dead or a totem suggests that the language of lamenting and complaining works as a medium for the consumption of structures in language and the psyche—a consumption that is otherwise, in food and physis, brought about by meals and metabolism. This assumption is developed not in Freud but in theorists succeeding him: in the anthropologist Lagache, and in Abraham's and Torok's renewed inquiry into Freud's "Wolf Man" analysis.

In 1938, Lagache studies the work of mourning as addressing both "physical and mental pain."[77] Adopting Freud's 1915 thesis that if the work of mourning succeeds, "then it has consumed itself" (SE14:307), Lagache proposes that the structure of the process is best discernable in dysfunctional forms and in the institutions of foreign social orders. "The aim of mourning," he assumes, "is the accomplishment of a split between the dead and the living ... transposing the biological fact onto the human level, i.e. 'killing the dead.'"[78] The task of mourning is to remove the one who is no longer alive from the community in such a way that it persists in spite of being deprived by one of its elements. This social equivalent to Freud's 1915 theorem of a withdrawal of "all libido ... from its attachment to" a lost loved object (SE4:244) cannot be performed by merely affirming the inevitable, but—in order to enable this—requires participating in it:

> Human art, various practices, including endocannibalism, hasten or impede the efficacy of the forces of nature. The phenomenon of second funerals *consummates death on the human level*; it is correlated with a second death, not natural any more, but social, being accomplished by the society.[79]

Cultural practices like "secondary treatments"[80] of corpses do not consider themselves secondary in importance but crucial as they perform the social death and, thereby, conclude the otherwise solely biological process of death. They "consummat[e]" death as a social phenomenon for instance in disinterring the body, accelerating its decomposition by removing the flesh from the bones, thus forestalling uncontrolled decay.[81] In endocannibalism,

---

[77]Lagache, "The Work of Mourning: Ethnology and Psychoanalysis," 15.
[78]Ibid., 17.
[79]Ibid., 26; my italics.
[80]Metcalf and Huntington, *Celebrations of Death*, 11.
[81]Ibid., 34–35; 73–74. See Chapter 2, 110.

the bereaved perform the social death by consuming part of the dead so that the remains vanish in them, and survive. Lagache's French wording *consommé[r] la mort*[82] implies both that death is "completed" by consuming the dead and that death itself is "devoured" as the remains reenter the basic realm of the living: metabolism.[83] Freud's 1915 description of the melancholic incorporation of lost love suggests the ambivalence of "devouring" (SE14:249–250) that causes an identification as well as an annihilation. Lagache finds this ambivalence in endocannibalism, too: "It is tempting to see in it a maneuver that is both destructive (aggressive) and identificatory, which could be compared with introjection, the pivot of the psychoanalytic theory of mourning."[84] Although factual endocannibalism is a rare cultural praxis, it is an idea implied in many symbolic practices, not least in Christian Communion. What is relevant about "consummating death" by consuming the dead for the structure of mourning in general is that plaintive language, also, performs the role Lagache ascribes to endocannibalism in the "work of mourning": Lamenting and complaining perform the social death, make loss sharable: Lamenting and complaining do not record the lost but consummate the loss by way of disorganizing those structures of language that conventionally grant comprehension such as word reference and identification of author, object, and addressee. The disorganization of these structures foregrounds those phonetic and other material elements of language that demand hearing and response.

As Lagache emphasizes, mourning is a work done not only *in* but primarily *on* social communities. The language of lamenting and complaining assumes a seminal role in this process: Undermining the representational dimension of language, plaints focus on the address as basis of hearing, response, and maintaining social exchange in a bereaved community. Lamenting and complaining seek a hearing for the consumption of structure it carries out in order not to remain—owing to shock and loss—as still, isolated, and unheard as the deceased.[85] The consumption of structures brought about in the language of lamenting and complaining transforms the deceased, who is no counterpart anymore, into a part of the history of the "I" and, in turn, seeks to find someone to listen to the story of this transformation—since

---

[82]Lagache, "La travail du deuil," 254.
[83]*OED* 3:802, s.v. "consummate, v. 2b."
[84]Lagache, "The work of mourning," 27. While "the relationship of endocannibalism with aggression is not clear," since incorporating members of the own community serves different purposes than consuming the enemy in exocannibalism, it is clear that there is "aggression inherent in every inter-human relationship," aggression "provoked by the departure of the dead person," and "aggression inherent in the work of mourning, which is to destroy the love object" (ibid.).
[85]Ibid., 27: "If the deceased is treated like a living person, conversely, those remaining are treated like the dead: these are the 'people of death' whose interdictions turn the living body into a corpse. Immobility and silence are frequent dictates of mourning."

without hearing, response, and interaction, life is hard to tell apart from death. This is why the modern abandonment of mourning rites like dirges and lamentations is not merely one of many changes that occur in cultural practices over time but has a pathogenic effect, bringing forth neuroses.

Lagache's reading of Freud's theory of mourning via incorporation as a social practice suggests, literally, that in order to stomach a death (to tolerate it), it has to be swallowed (accepted). This might seem obvious or even an inane pun, however, Abraham's and Torok's re-readings of Freud's "Wolf Man" analysis and theory of mourning outline that these metaphors are unlike others in that they indicate an oral process at the very basis of symbolization—language—and mourning. A concluding look at these readings will provide a fuller understanding of the consumption of linguistic structures in lamenting and complaining.

In 1976, Abraham and Torok publish an analysis of the "Wolf Man's" treatment protocols. Instead of "signs of sorrow" (SE17:23) at his sister's death that Freud was looking for, they find a whole lexicon that serves both to hide and to articulate the incorporated sister. The "Wolf Man's" dream, which he describes as featuring a group of six wolves (while drawing only five) hides and, at the same time, articulates the sister in the Russian rhyme of шестёрка (shiestorka; the six, the group of six) with сестёрка (siestorka; the intimate diminutive of sister, sissy).[86] Abraham and Torok return to the differentiation between mourning and melancholia upon which Freud casts doubt in 1923 with a double "It may be" (SE19:28–29), transferring the explanation of the latter for the structure of all mourning. While they adopt Freud's assumption that the "Wolf Man" does not display any "signs of sorrow" (because he avoids mourning by way of incorporation in order to maintain the love relationship), Abraham and Torok detect no signs indicating that the incorporated sister had become part the history of the "Wolf Man's" ego, as Freud's 1923 concept of mourning would suggest. The sister, rather, persists like a trauma. In order to elucidate this structure, Abraham and Torok differentiate between "introjection" (Freud's 1923 term for the common incorporation in mourning that forms the character of the ego) and "incorporation," a fantasy and pathology.[87] Phantasies of ingestion are no metaphors, Abraham and Torok hold, yet fundamentally concerned with the possibility of forming metaphors and other images—such as describing plaintive language as rumination and thus bridging the difference that lamenting and complaining are concerned with expression while chewing, in contrast, is concerned with swallowing. Divergences in direction and intention, however, are irrelevant to the phantasy of "introducing all or

---

[86] Abraham and Torok, *Magic Word*, 17.
[87] Ibid., 4 and Abraham and Torok, "Mourning *or* Melancholia: Introjection *versus* Incorporation" [MM], 126.

part of a love object or a thing into one's own body."[88] Abraham and Torok explain this pathology in contrast to regular introjection, the structure of which they illustrate with the same scenario as Freud uses to explain wishing in *The Interpretation of Dreams*: a hungry infant.

> The initial stages of introjection emerge in infancy when the mouth's emptiness is experienced alongside the mother's simultaneous presence. The emptiness is first experiences in the form of cries and sobs, delayed fullness, then as calling, ways of requesting presence, as language. Further experiences include filling the oral void by producing sound ... The transition from a mouth filled with the breast to a mouth filled with words occurs by virtue of the intervening experiences of the empty mouth. (MM:127)

Abraham and Torok elaborate Freud's primal scene of wish-fulfillment as being based on the reappearance of the perception of food and being full (SE4:564) by underlining that the symbolic dimension of these infant experiences structures the psyche: The screams and other noises of appealing to be fed have an effect not only on others who understand them as indexes of hunger, the utterances also provide the infant with a remedy for the missing: with a substitute. The point is not, of course, that words substitute for food; they do not. The point is that the sounds initiate an abstraction: Instead of being captured by the lack of food, the sounds produced by the infant itself enable it to signify the lack, later on to name the lacking. "The absence of objects and the empty mouth are transformed into words" (MM:128) that allow to accept a lack of something, or loss of someone, while maintaining the wish for them—instead of being wholly dominated by the lack or loss. As something that is symbolized, that can be named and portrayed, the experience of lack or loss forms a precipitate within the ego. And it forms a community, as Abraham and Torok elaborate, thus transcending Freud's theories of individual mourning: "Introjecting a desire, a pain, a situation means channeling them through language into a communion of empty mouths. This is how the literal ingestion of food becomes introjection when viewed figuratively" (MM:128). The fantasy of corporation, on the other hand, does not transfer the lack or loss into a symbol to pass around, but destroys symbolization. When words cannot fill the void because it is impossible to say what is lacking or lost, then it is not solely words that are swallowed but the love object itself, so that its lack or loss can be denied:

---

[88]Ibid.: "possessing, expelling or alternatively acquiring, keeping, losing it—here are varieties of a fantasy indicating ... a basic intrapsychic situation ... created by the reality of a loss sustained by the psyche."

In order not to have to "swallow" a loss, we fantasize swallowing (or having swallowed) that which has been lost, as if it were some kind of thing. Two interrelated procedures constitute the magic of incorporation: *demetaphorization* (taking literally what is meant figuratively) and *objectivation* (pretending that the suffering is not an injury to the subject but instead a loss sustained by the love object). (MM:126–127)

The phantasy of incorporation abstains from using words associated with the loss in order not to intro-ject but re-ject it, reverting things in such a way that the ego did not sustain any loss and does not feel any pain. Rejecting the work of mourning by way of a fantasy of incorporation avoids symbolization and strives for a substitution of a different kind, "one mouth-work in place of another" (MM:128). What comes to pass by way of swallowing the lost is "an intrapsychic secret" that Abraham and Torok call a "crypt" (130): a hidden tomb to conceal all pain from consciousness, to contain all thoughts and feelings linked to the loss as well as the very lost love object itself. Such a crypt, they assume, regulates the "Wolf Man's" discourse. One complication, however, cannot go unnoticed: The differentiation between literal and figurative, physical and symbolic that supports Abraham's and Torok's distinction between functional and dysfunctional ingestion crumbles easily upon closer inspection: In spite of its thoroughly physical character, ritual necrophagia such as endocannibalism is not linked to the fantasy of incorporation, which takes the putting-into-the-mouth all too literal; instead, Abraham and Torok contrast it with this pathological structure—with good cause: Carried out in a group, the ritual consumption of the deceased is a symbolic practice, a form of a community of empty mouths filling the void with the lost in order to accept and swallow the loss together.[89] This approach is crucial to understanding many forms of ritual mourning and lamenting such as wakes, a "communion of survivors through the partaking of food. ... instead of the deceased we are absorbing our mutual presence in the form of digestible food" (MM:129). The theoretical distinction of such rites from a pathology such as the "Wolf Man's," however, can be attained only in view of the intention of the ingestion, hardly with regard to its literal or figurative character.

The refusal to mourn acted out in the fantasy of incorporation aims, paradoxically, not at stomaching and accepting loss but at preserving the lost. It is driven, Abraham and Torok assume, not by mere disappointment about being left by the deceased but by a conflict that predates the loss and escalates when the necessity of mourning arises: The bereaved shared a "shameful secret" with the loved one that also functioned as an ego ideal (MM:131)—like

---

[89]"Necrophagia is therefore not at all a variety of incorporation but a preventive measure of *antiincoporation*" (MM:130).

the "Wolf Man's" father, who was an ideal his son aspired to, as Freud notes.[90] Yet the son also witnessed the father abusing his daughter, as Abraham and Torok add.[91] What needs to be swallowed and buried in the crypt is the secret and the shame that would be brought upon the object if it was revealed, for that would entail a retroactive loss, proving that the object had never been the ideal as which it has been loved. Signs of sorrow such as laments that seek a hearing and response with others threaten to reveal their probably contrasting emotions, therefore, they must be swallowed, entombed within the self.

Yet the "Wolf Man" certainly speaks a lot. This is due to complications caused by the crypt. The insurmountable obstacle to mourning for the "Wolf Man," Abraham and Torok assume, is that his desire focuses onto a triangulation of himself with his father and sister, a constellation he cannot share with anyone. Instead of mourning, the "Wolf Man" incorporates both the sister and the father, who committed suicide shortly after her,[92] thus creating a community that neither gives away the shameful secret nor leaves him all alone, bereaved even of the organization of his desire. (And the mother? Her insistent complaining noted by Freud appears as that of the one who is left out: Abraham and Torok skip it.) The fantasy of incorporation does not settle the conflict but hides it from the "Wolf Man's" consciousness, wherefore he cannot comprehend his dreams, fears, complaints, or laments. The incorporation preserves the lost ones without assimilating them to the history of his ego, therefore, it is unclear *as whom* the "Wolf Man" speaks,[93] in whose words, when (considering the theorem of afterwardsness), and in which language. One important technique for silencing suspicious words are phonetic shifts into different languages, suggesting to Abraham and Torok that the wolf dream narrative may not be the report of a nightmare. They, rather, read it as complaint about the agony of having seen and having to silence himself: Retracing the wording Freud notes, "I dreamt" (SE17:29), to the corresponding Russian verb видеть сон (*vidiet son*), literally to "see a dream," Abraham and Torok identify echoes of the English words "son" and "witness"—key words of a hypothetical complaint lodged by the (soon dismissed) English nanny against the mother about a scene the boy saw.[94] Thus the fantasy of incorporation becomes apparent in a destruction of language—a destruction that serves the purpose of safeguarding secrecy but brings about the opposite insofar as it discernible as a symptom. Abraham and Torok call this destruction of language in the course of incorporation

---

[90]"From an early age he was proud of his father, ... declaring that he would like to be a gentleman like him" (SE17:17).
[91]Abraham and Torok, *Magic Word*, 4.
[92]In 1908; Gardiner, *The Wolf-Man*, 64–65.
[93]Abraham and Torok, *Magic Word*, 23: "But who, in fact, was he? Before and now? Freud in truth could never establish it. ... His official identity only served to cover up the other characters he clandestinely sheltered within himself: his father, his sister."
[94]Ibid., 33–34.

"antimetaphorical": "Incorporation entails the fantasmic destruction of the act by means of which metaphors become possible: the act of putting the original oral void into words, ... the act of introjection" (MM:132). The logic is simple, who puts things into their mouth cannot fill it with words and tell secrets. Still, the fantasy of introjection does not succeed in shutting up the subject because it is not only the secret that has to be hidden, but also the fact that there *is* a secret. The "Wolf Man" cannot but keep on speaking to disguise that he has silenced himself and swallows the crucial words.

In Abraham and Torok's view, the "Wolf Man's" main complaint about indigestion is no sexual wish-fulfillment but element of the "annulment of figurative language" that is a "crucial aspect of these fantasies of incorporation" (MM:132). It testifies to the flip side of the ambivalent gesture of incorporation by which the lost love object is preserved and, at the same time, "'fecalized', ... rendered excremental" (131). This much pertains to the metabolism of plaintive language. Dysfunctional and indeed unhealthy is that the "Wolf Man" puts feces (back) into his mouth and presents them—"under the innocent disguise of ... a complaint" (SE4:617)—as something he longs for. What he attains by presenting feces as the aim of his wish-fulfillment in monotonous complaints is ruining the figurative meaning of fecal invectives that could otherwise serve to malign his father, sister, mother, or to swear about the insoluble conflict of shame and desire. Yet if the "Wolf Man" speaks only in order *not* to tell a secret, if his laments and complaints seek a hearing and response only to withdraw attention from the shameful beloved secret in the crypt, then one question arises: "Should one believe that Sergei Wolf Man keeps speaking endlessly to analysts in order not to be heard?"[95] In French, Abraham's and Torok's question—*pour n'être point entendu?*[96]—leads the way to an answer via the double meaning of *entendre*: Inasmuch as the "antimetaphorical" consumption of linguistic structures serves the purpose of hiding the secret and masking the crypt, the "Wolf Man" speaks in order to not be *understood*. Yet inasmuch as the distraction succeeds only if the distorted wording of his complaint is given attention, the "Wolf Man" speaks in order to be *heard*. The psychic conflict that prevents mourning causes a destruction of language to the extent that listening to him, and taking him by his word, is tantamount to ignoring the trauma and conflict to which his words testify. Since the "Wolf Man's" complaint shall not name the cause for pain but still make that pain heard, he cannot but destroy those structures of language that allow comprehension. He must speak of everything but the important things, so that whoever answers its plea for hearing, and listens, in fact misses the point. Falling silent, however, is no option for the "Wolf Man" as being heard and receiving a response is the one thing that differentiates

---

[95]Ibid., 30.
[96]Abraham and Torok, *Cryptonymie. Le Verbier de l'homme aux loupes*, 137.

the living from the dead—the dead to whom he adapts himself as he does not acknowledge their passing but maintains their presence within himself.

While the "Wolf Man" certainly suffers from a grave psychical wound, the consumption and ruin of linguistic structures of his speech is no interesting exception from a norm but of fundamental relevance to understanding the dynamics of plaintive language in general. The disorganization of his speech—into a disguise for an unspeakable secret, a means for attaining satisfaction, and an inexhaustible plaint—by what Abraham and Torok call the fantasy of incorporation is crucial for understanding plaintive language in general because there is no other, cleanly distinguishable, healthy or at least regular form or lamenting and complaining that would testify to the desirable mourning-as-introjection, in which the loss is swallowed, stomached, and becomes part of the history of the self. Just as Freud's distinction between mourning and melancholia is certainly justified insofar as it serves to describe deeply dysfunctional cases of non-mourning against the background of the possibility to accept loss, Abraham's and Torok's differentiation between introjection and incorporation is certainly useful for its diagnostic and therapeutic purpose. These distinctions are, however, not supported by the language of lamenting and complaining. It is impossible to tell whether ruminating plaints testify to mourners who pass their loss around in a community of empty mouths, with the monotony and repetition of plaints insisting on the pain, the experienced of being overwhelmed, and the outrage that symbols claim to substitute for the lost—or whether ruminations testify to a refusal to mourn and the attempt to swallow the indigestible that turns the body into a tomb, and life into death. In both cases, lamenting and complaining testify to pain. In retrospect it is, of course, possible to tell whether or not the loss has been accepted and assimilated into one's own history; lamenting and complaining, however, mark a crisis in which this distinction is impossible to draw. Plaintive language is not merely a symptom of a dis-order but a disorganization caused by a loss or pain that erodes distinctions such as between pathological and healthy, functional or dysfunctional. Large parts of the *Iliad* are devoted to this complication, as the next chapter will outline. All signs of sorrow are marked by those features of the consumption of linguistic structures that characterize the "Wolf Man's" ruined speech, irrespective of whether the plaint is spontaneous, individual, ritual, a quotation, or other.

In its oftentimes repetitive, monotonous form, plaintive language insists on finding a hearing and response in exactly such situations that make reciprocity urgently necessary and, at the same time, highly unlikely. By way of fragmenting conventional structures of language, lamenting and complaining voice desertedness from attention and answer as well as experiences of being overwhelmed that leave neither breath nor room for a distinct portrayal. In rituals, devotional formulas, quotations from literary texts, and in individual neurotic complaints, repetition consumes the reference of words as plaints insist on something that cannot be communicated by naming and describing it. Repetition also consumes the possibility of a clear attribution of an utterance to an author since the originator of the plaint might be different from the one voicing (or penning) it: a latent subject in quotes, an anonymous subject in rituals, or an incorporated subject in neuroses. Moreover, not solely the "Wolf Man's" interlingual complaints raise doubts about the affiliation with a certain linguistic community—dirges and ritual wailing consume articulation and operate at the brink of noises and sobs. The rupture between hearing and understanding, audibility and attention is at the core of those existential situations that give rise to plaintive language, therefore, it communicates by way of consuming linguistic structures. The language of lamenting and complaining wonders whether there can be someone to hear and understand a speech that communicates by consuming and ruining linguistic structures.

Freund's inquiry into lamenting and complaining finds a metabolic structure in plaintive language that becomes apparent in individual pathologies but is relevant far beyond this scope, as the next chapter will outline by expounding parallel structures of ritual plaints. Focusing on the contempt for this form of speech that informs Freud's initial approach to therapy based on the assumption that complaints shall be silenced, a comparative reading of negotiations of tragic, liturgical, and other ritual plaints outlines that its profound doubt about symbolic substitution makes plaintive language a complication in sociopolitical discourses.

# 2

# Ritual and Modernity: On Silencing Plaints (with Aeschylus, Rilke, Veteranyi)

*"[Oughtn't we, still], have found wailing-women?*
*Women who [cry] for pay, whom one can hire*
*to wail the whole night long, when all is quiet.*
*Bring me customs! How bereft we are*
*of customs. They pass on, we [talk them down].*
*And so you must come back, and here with me*
*make up for the [lamenting] that you missed.*
*[Do] you hear that I am wailing now?"*[1]

The language of lamenting and complaining is a fundamental form of human speech concerned with attaining a hearing and establishing reciprocity. Plaintive language communicates by way of disorganizing and fragmenting conventional structures of articulate language, undermining not least the distinction between speech, voice, and noise. Many discourses respond to the apparent ruin of language in lamenting and complaining by way of historicizing plaints. Historical narratives are to oppose the disorganization of linguistic structures (which psychoanalysis allows to describe as consumption and ruin) by casting them in terms of the disappearance of a historic form of plaints. Lamenting and complaining feature prominently in discourses of modernization.

This chapter parallels criticism with anthropology, religious and classical studies to look into recurrent patterns of interpretations of ritual plaints in antiquity, modernity, and postmodernity, and outlines them in exemplary readings of Aeschylus's *Oresteia* and *The Persians*, Rilke's 1908 *Requiem for*

---

[1]Rainer Maria Rilke, *Requiem for a Friend*, 265; my brackets.

*a Friend* devoted to the late painter Modersohn-Becker, and Veteranyi's 2002 *Das Regal der Letzten Atemzüge* (The Shelf of Last Breaths). The chapter is organized thematically rather than historically to expound how structural aspects of plaintive language and historical instances of interpreting plaints mesh: The first section focuses on the temporal model that often informs current discourses on ritual plaints, which are positioned against ritual, liturgical, and other practices defined as belonging to a past, unrecoverable tradition. The second section highlights a series of dichotomies regulation discourses on ritual plaints since antiquity; the third contrasts the portrayal of ritual plaints in literary and anthropological texts to outline that ritual discourses cast doubt on the sovereignty of interpretation claimed by theory. The fourth section looks into antiphony as a ritual form of reestablishing reciprocity by way of consuming linguistic structures, and the last section revisits the structural issue of the closure of mourning, evoked in Chapter 1, as a political difficulty. This comprehensive survey of discourses on ritual plaints aims at underpinning that the common notion of rites as outdated impedes comprehending current ritual forms as much as analyzing the void left by the actual decay of rites in modernity. Some principal difficulties of any such comprehension require immediate attention: What precisely is a ritual plaint, and is it not indeed obsolete?

The latter question operates within a historicizing paradigm fundamental to many discourses that aim at enlightenment, comprehension, healing, etc. Freud refers to a historicizing hermeneutics when he understands the consumption of linguistic structures in plaintive language as symptom of trauma, that is to say of a prehistory that still wants representation, and when he parallels his inquiry with archaeology. The peculiarity of this approach stands out in his 1913 *Totem and Taboo*. In this cannibalistic prehistory to community and memory, the lament "is obligatory, imposed by dread of a threatened retribution" (SE3:139). Fear of revenge dictates the utterance—not sorrow, community, or habit, since these are only formed in this very scenario. One key factor, however, is missing from Freud's genetic analysis of "rituals of apologies and ceremonies of expiation" (SE13:103): repetition, which is essential to the invariance of a ritual order of words and gestures that establish social or cosmological order. In *Totem and Taboo*, ritual lament appears not as a reiterating realization of traditional forms but as timeless recurrence that collapses the difference between now and then. Durkheim's 1912 anthropological analysis of the death rites of the Australian Warramunga as "primitive mourning"[2] shares the chronotope of the timelessness of ritual. This presupposition predefines the subject under scrutiny, as Fabian points out: "'Primitive' being essentially a temporal concept, is a category, not an

---

[2] Émile Durkheim, *The Elementary Forms of Religious Life*, 398.

object of Western thought."³ The qualification as "primitive" relegates that to which it is attached into a realm outside of history and a-synchronous with modernity, whose inhabitants are incapable of a response (for instance to being called "primitive"), so that there can be no reciprocity with them, no exchange—such as is at the core of revenge practices. Durkheim refutes the Warramungas' own explanation of their mourning rites as averting revenge of the deceased⁴—as if the conventionality of ritual utterances disqualifies from answering the question about the sense of the rite.⁵ Concluding a lack of sincerity from ritual conventionality is still a common practice in discourses on ritual plaints.

Conventionality, however, may just as well be considered a pivotal element of ritual plaints that enables (rather than prevents) the relation to personal sentiments, as Urban emphasizes in his analysis of ritual wailing in Brazil. For it is not the obvious feeling of loss and desertedness that needs to be communicated in the face of death, but the wish for sharing a community as a remedy: "Loss occasions the wish to overcome loss through sociability, and it is sociability that is signaled through adherence to a culturally specific form of expression of grief." A strong "regularity" is, according to Urban, necessary for others to understand the communicated emotion and demonstrates the capability to interact.⁶ "Irregularity," the license to vary ritual forms, allows to demonstrate the sincerity of the individual emotion.⁷ Sincerity, individuality, intentionality, and historicity are not foreign to rituals, although it is not without reason that these traits are often denied ritual plaints: Lamenting and complaining doubt sincerity, individuality, intentionality, and historicity as they voice experiences that undermine or even prohibit them—like death, which terminates individuality and undermines the continuity of experience. What anthropologists call ritual wailing is the very utterance Rilke has in mind when he describes "wailing-women" as those "who [cry] for pay, whom one can hire/to wail the whole night long, when all is quiet" (*Klagefrauen ..., welche weinen/für Geld, und die man so bezahlen kann,/daß sie die Nacht durch heulen, wenn es still wird*⁸). The triangulation of crying, wailing, and quiet marks the ambivalent

---

³Johannes Fabian, *Time and the Other: How Anthropology Makes Its Object*, 18.
⁴Durkheim, *Elementary Forms*, 397: "mourning is not the spontaneous expression of individual emotions. ... it may be ... But it is more generally the case that there is no connection between the sentiments felt and the gestures made by the actors in the rite. ... They say that the dead wish to be lamented, that by refusing them the tribute of sorrow which is their right, men offend them, and that the only way of preventing their anger is to conform to their will. But this mythological interpretation merely modifies the terms of the problem, without resolving it."
⁵Ibid., 399: "Mythical explanations express the idea which the native has of the rite, and not the rite itself."
⁶Greg Urban, "Ritual Wailing in the Amerindian Brazil," 393.
⁷Ibid., 387.
⁸Rilke, *Requiem. Für eine Freundin*. RSW1:653.

status of wailing in many discourses: Wailing appears both as a pejorative of crying, which relates to the common reservation about the sincerity of ritual plaints, and as a contrast to silence, which indicates the purpose of plaintive language to attain hearing. "[Do] you hear that I am wailing now?" (*Hörst Du, dass ich klage?*[9]), Rilke's requiem thus asks. Urban highlights that with regard to the need for company and social exchange, "the question of the genuineness or falseness of the underlying expression of affect becomes irrelevant." Relevant is, rather, "the desire to do or show the socially correct thing"[10] to demonstrate both the lack of, and the capability to engage in, social reciprocity.

Thus far ritual plaints may be defined with reference to their communicative function. Delimiting a corpus of plaints, however, seems impossible due to the multifold contexts that occasion plaints. Anthropology pays attention mostly to laments for the dead, yet also to marriage laments,[11] laments from exile,[12] and city laments,[13] archaeology also to laments for deities,[14] theology and religious studies, moreover, to calendrical rites of mourning and lament such as Tisha B'av, which marks the anniversaries of the announcement of having to wander the desert for forty years after the exile from Egypt, of the destruction of both temples of Jerusalem, and of the crushing of the Bar Kokhba revolt. "Laments are windows on culture," Wilce writes, "insofar as they represent the ways people confront crises challenging the order of life." Apart from death, exile, and weddings, Wilce also counts proselytization, modernization, and globalization among the drastic changes in the structure of communities.[15] Ritual plaints performed on the occasion of such crises do not reinstall the challenged order but voice the crisis by disorganizing conventional structures of language. Entailing a crisis of articulate speech in words, the language of lamenting and complaining may itself be subject of plaints, as instances of the disparagement of plaintive language prove. Due to the characteristic instability of plaintive language, ritual laments can be defined only in approximation, as in Wilce: "Lament is a discursive and musical genre linked with crying and with funerary observances, but also used in other contexts."[16] What draws attention are mostly these

---

[9]Ibid.
[10]Urban, "Ritual Wailing," 399.
[11]For a proximity of dirges to marriage laments cf. Fred Blake, "Chinese Daughters"; Fei-wen Liu, "Expressive Depths" (China); Elizabeth Tolbert, *Women Cry with Words* (Karelia), Gail Kligman, *The Wedding of the Dead*, 90–96 (Transylvania); Wickett, *For the Living*, 110 (Upper Egypt); Susan Rasmussen, "Grief at Seeing a Daughter Leave Home" (Niger).
[12]Eckehard Pistrick, "Singing of Pain and Memory" (Epirus); Seremetakis, *Last Word*, 175–176 (Mani); Margaret Orbell, *Waiata*, 71–76 (Maori).
[13]F.W. Dobbs-Allsopp, *Weep, O Daughter of Zion*; Alexiou, *Ritual Lament*, 83–101.
[14]Bachvarova, "Sumerian 'Gala' Priests."
[15]Wilce, *Crying Shame*, 10.
[16]Ibid., 25.

contexts, in particular burials and mourning; the vocal or gestural language of lamenting and complaining is hardly in the focus of anthropological inquiry, as Feld and Fox note: "Despite the theoretical and ethnographic sophistication of this line of social and cultural inquiry, the actual discursive means (i.e. the laments) constituting these symbolic discourses on life have not been fully described or analyzed in the mortuary ritual literature."[17] The historicity of the lament ritual—its persistence, change, or fading—is mostly considered accidental rather than an integral part of the plaint as in literary genres. Still, a similar disregard for the historicity of ritual laments is to be found in literary studies where they feature mostly as source and starting point of tragedy. Purpose of the following inquiry is not to represent the whole range of the fields concerned with ritual plaints but to highlight a crucial moment that connects them: As a form of speech that consumes and ruins conventional structures of language because it communicates a profound doubt in the possibility of attaining hearing and establishing reciprocity, the language of lamenting and complaining appears—even in the conventionalized shape of ritual—as a disquieting source of concern that needs silencing. The disorganization of language in lamenting and complaining is retorted in recurrent interpretations of the disorganization as fading of a historical form of plaints. The next section shall, first of all, outline the temporal model employed in such responses to the structural complications of plaintive language.

## Tale of Lament's Life and Death

"The face of the earth has been changed by the religions of lament," writes Canetti in 1960, referencing Christianity, Shia Islam, and the cults of Aphrodite/Adonis, Innana/Tamuz, Cybele/Attis, Isis/Osiris.[18] Still, at the outset of the twenty-first century, ritual laments are "vanishingly rare," as Wilce puts it.[19] This is the result of policies of modernization. In 1963, the Second Vatican Council decides: "The rite for the burial of the dead should express more clearly the paschal character of Christian death,"[20] which is

---

[17] Stephen Feld and Aaron Fox, "Music and Language," 40.
[18] Canetti, *Crowds and Power*, 143. "Why is it that so many join the lament? What is its attraction? ... To all those who join it the same thing happens: the hunting or baiting pack expiates its guilt by becoming a lamenting pack. ... All they have done to others, another one now takes on himself; by attaching themselves to him, faithfully and without reserve, they hope to escape vengeance." Moments "of genuine lament," nevertheless, have "become rare" (145) in Christianity, Canetti holds: In fear of heretic masses, Catholic cult had become "an infinite dilution of lament ... It is the temporal lament mummified" (155).
[19] Wilce, *Crying Shame*, xi.
[20] Paul IV, *Constitution on the Sacred Liturgy*, III:81.

to say it should be less concerned with mourning and lamenting than the thus far mandatory 1614 Rituale Romanum. Anthropologists describe a worldwide fading of ritual forms, notably ritual laments, as a consequence of the formation of nation states, modern imperialism, and globalization. Crucial to these dynamics is the notion of bringing about an abolishment of older organizations of social life such as rituals, which are marked as archaic since they focus neither on individuals nor on authenticity. The concept of speech as expression of an individual thought or testimony of an authentic feeling entails the disparagement of ritual speech as imitative, insincere, and thus dubious. Complaints such as Freud's about "laments which always sound the same and are wearisome in their monotony" (SE14:256) and criticism of ritual plaints belong as essentially to modernity as laments over the vanishing of ritual. Whether approving or condemning, the concept of modernity is based on a narrative of the abolishment of ritual forms that is largely fixed in its wording and conventionalized in its performative context—which makes this narrative, in turn, ritual, as Wilce notes:

> "The loss of myth and ritual," ritually retold, *is* how we transmit our founding myth, the mythic loss underlying modernity. The representation of loss (of tradition, lament, or even culture) *constitutes* (post)modernity just as lament ritually held together or reconstituted "premodern" worlds.[21]

Noting that laments over the loss of traditional forms are part of the condition of modernity does not aim at denying the de facto disappearance of ritual forms and customs. It aims, rather, at correlating these two phenomena and paying heed to the fact that ritual forms provide alternative means for comprehending the changes to which they are subject—differing, above all, in that they do not presuppose a continuous authentic tradition to which modernity opposes itself in order to abolish it or, in postmodernity, to revive it. Anthropology analyzes many instances of modern modifications of rites: Ries describes a fusion of three traditional "formal genres of Russian speech, the traditional lament (a strictly female genre), Orthodox church litanies, and the declamatory style of Russian poetry reading" to form the new genre of "conversational litanies" during perestroika.[22] Ninoshvili describes a ritual transfer rendering the Georgian lamentation of the dead, *khmit nat'irali*, a genre or political accusations and public dispute in electronic media.[23] Pistick describes a shift of topic in Albanian and Green lament

---

[21] Wilce, *Crying Shame*, 11.
[22] Nancy Ries, *Russian Talk*, 86.
[23] Lauren Ninoshvili, "Wailing in the Cities," 2; cf. 1: "Women's traditional funerary laments and the contemporary, mediated performances broadcast to national audiences draw on a shared set of stylistic, gestural, and discursive-interpretive conventions to precipitate social and/or political change."

songs from dirges to laments of exile in the course of the depopulation of rural areas.[24] Seremetakis describes ritual dirges of the Peloponnesian Mani as metaphysical frame even for reflecting on the disappearance of ritual: "The continuum of historical destruction is thus comprehended through a metaphor of ingestion, eating, and forceful interiorization. Historicization as an oral practice replicates this process of cosmic injection."[25] Saunders describes the discontinuous and polyphonic techniques of modern literature as return of ritual forms repressed in modernity.[26] Central structures of the language of ritual plaints thus inform modernity's discourses, too, yet that is only part of the point. What is more, laments over the disappearance of ritual forms such as dirges and wailing play a substantial role in modern discourses. These laments inform popular culture as much as modern elegies and anthropology, one of the most important discourses into which ritual plaints are transferred, as Wilce shows. Analyzing ritual laments of diverse traditions, notably Bangla *bilāp* and Finnish-Karelian wailing, he conceptualizes anthropological accounts of the disappearance of laments as instances of "metaculture":

> Metacultural judgments are second-order cultural facts, and they slow or speed the circulation of the cultural forms they judge. Latifa's laments and her kinsmen's angry reactions to them are a pair of first- and second-order cultural facts. But so are *statements about "the death of lament"*—that "death" being a lower-order cultural "fact"—vis-à-vis my higher-order reflection that *these rumors of lament's death are not only exaggerated but constitute a new form of lament*, which turns the first "fact" (death) on its head, just as the second-order Javanese index turns the first on its head.[27]

Wilce's differentiation between "first" and "second-order cultural facts" is to describe that naming and evaluating rituals such as dirges regulates and modifies these practices. The processes Wilce seeks to describe, however, undermine the clear-cut differentiation between practice and commentary in a reflection: If the audience criticizes or rejects a ritual plaint, this is not necessarily part of the ritual order[28] but may as well result in the

---

[24]Pistrick, "Singing," 68: "The concept of migration in the musical sphere was positioned in reference to established genres, especially the ritual repertoire of death laments from which musical and textual formulas were used deliberately and in stylized form."
[25]Seremetakis, *Last Word*, 237.
[26]Saunders, *Lamentation and Modernity*, xiv.
[27]Wilce, *Crying Shame*, 119.
[28]Anthropology would usually insist on such unity; Victor Turner, "Betwixt and Between," 238: "A normal man acts abnormally because he is obedient to tribal tradition, not out of disobedience."

disappearance of the ritual. A collapse of the distinction between ritual and commentary marks numerous studies which describe the disappearance of the ritual and, at the same time, join in the lament. A striking instance is Liu's description of Hunan funerary and wedding laments (*kuge, kujia ge*) in the past tense which marks the aim "to reconstruct endangered kuge heritage, specifically its dialogic aspect, before it disappears under pressure from a rapidly changing modern China."[29] Remarkable about the disorganization of the differentiation between a ritual practice and its examination is that theoretical inquiry tends to constitute the object under scrutiny as obsolete and fading, while various modernizations borrow techniques central to the language of ritual plaints. Ritual plaints are a field crucial to forging historical narratives because lamenting and complaining negotiate the pastness of phenomena and the temporality of experience.

Many sociopolitical and religious modernizations criticize ritual plaints as symbolically, physically, or otherwise excessive. Luke the Evangelist recounts that when Jesus was on his way to Golgatha: "A great number of the people followed him, and among them were women who were beating their breasts and wailing for him" (Lk. 23:27; NRSV). Jesus's exorbitant role as the one who overcomes death is expounded when—while antiphonic dirges usually address the deceased in vain—he turns around to the wailing-women to answer and re-direct their plaint: "Do not weep for me, but weep for yourselves and for your children" (Lk. 23:28; NRSV). Theology explains this passage to the effect that believing in Christ's resurrection is tantamount to silencing dirges since the pain they voice has already been eased. Augustine thus writes that when his mother expired, his son broke into a *planctus*, a ritual plaint, and was silenced although he did what was conventionally expected. Augustine himself suppressed his *puerile* urge to cry—because dirges and tears are for those only who do not believe in overcoming death. Augustine says that he started to sing a psalm instead, and the others responded,[30] thus "modernizing" the form of antiphonic dirges into comfort.

Many other modernizations take action against ritual plaints, too, for instance early Christian church fathers against the concept of fate,[31] the Spanish inquisition against ritual laments considered Jewish relicts,[32] catholic and protestant clergy as well as English officials against Gealic *keening* in Ireland,[33] Lutheran clergy against marriage laments in the Finnish-Russian border zone,[34] social reformers in colonial India against

---

[29]Liu, "Expressive Depths," 207.
[30]Augustine, *Confessiones* IX.12.29–31.
[31]Hughes, *Lament*, 69–78, 83–97; Alexiou, *Ritual Lament*, 24–35; Wickett, *For the Living*, 236.
[32]James Amelang, "Mourning Becomes Eclectic," 21–27.
[33]Butler, "Symbolic and Social Roles," 110.
[34]Aili Nenola-Kallio, *Studies in Ingrian Laments*, 245–251.

wailing-women assumed to spur vendettas,[35] Russian Orthodoxy against ritual laments of preindustrial Russia and Ukrainian peasants,[36] "Russian-educated intellectuals" in Georgia at the outset of the twentieth century against the "social backwardness" of wailing,[37] currently "politically motivated and ultra-orthodox religious movements" in Egypt against female laments considered "non-Islamic,"[38] and the leader of Iran, Ayatollah Khamenei, against ritual self-mutilations as part of the Shia Ashura holiday, bewailing the death of Ali, grandson of prophet Muhammad, at the Battle of Karbala that may disconcert onlookers.[39] It is with equal reservation that Ries remarks on the litany of complaints as a common communicative genre during perestroika: "It seems clear that … citizens (and citizen activists) of democratizing societies need to move away from the kind of language … that in subtle ways symbolically reaffirms the distance between rulers and ruled."[40] The irreconcilability of ritual plaints is politically suspect—in Ries as well as in ancient Athens. For one modernization is in focus of the interest of classical, and literary studies in general, in ritual laments: the disappearance of dirges (*threnos* and *goos*) from the public of the Greek *polis* in favor of the praising funeral oration (ἐπιτάφιος λόγος, *epitaphios logos*) on the one hand, and on the other hand the transfer of ritual into tragedy (notably the *kommos*). This re-definition of the form of public discourse on death, mourning, and loss is accompanied by a segregation of the sexes: The presumably obsolete ritual plaint is defined as female, the newly established genres are defined as male to rearrange mourning rites presented very differently in, for instance, the *Iliad* into a modern political discourse. The last section of the chapter will discuss tragedy. Two seminal elements and arguments, however, that transform ritual plaints into tragedy inform the look onto ritual plaints persistently:

First, laments appear, Suter writes, "as a particularly gendered genre"[41] wherein gender codifications and genre conventions often interrelate—in ritual laments for the dead as well as in modern complaints of love. Berlant describes "the female complaint" as a gender-forming genre of US popular

---

[35]Parita Mukta, "The 'Civilizing Mission,'" 36.
[36]Christine Worobec, "Death Ritual among Russian and Ukrainian Peasants."
[37]Ninoshvili, "Wailing," 6.
[38]Wickett, *For the Living*, 240–241; Lila Abu-Lughod, "Islam and the Gendered Discourse of Death," 193.
[39]David Pinault, "*Shia Lamentation Rituals*," 299: "In his pronouncement of 7 Muharram 1415 (AD 1994), Ayatollah Khamenei declared 'unlawful and forbidden' acts of *matam* performed in public involving the use of weapons to shed one's blood. Khamenei's primary concern was the harm that might befall the image of Shia Islam if outsiders saw Muharram mourners scourging themselves." Lara Deeb, *Living Aschura in Lebanon*, 130pp.; Ali Hussain, "The Mourning of History and the History of Mourning."
[40]Ries, *Russian Talk*, 117.
[41]Suter, "Male Lament," 156.

culture,[42] Craik analyzes the literary "genre of male-authored, female-voiced lament," as negotiating the consequences of abolishing repentance and forgiveness in reformation England.[43] Second, ritual plaints are transposed into a far removed past, not last in order to explain the incomprehensibility of customs and words as ruins. Cicero thus describes not only female lamentations during funerals but even their legislative abolition as an instance of Rome's archaic heritage, recorded in a passage of the Law of the Twelve Tables which were once considered "a necessary chant" although the crucial word of the passage in question—*lessus*—had been incomprehensible already for the "old interpreters."[44] Cicero underlines the fading of the rite even though funerary laments (*nenia*) were common in his time.[45] Yet it is quite possible that *lessus*—a hapax legomenon—came from Cicero's pen, employing a historical fiction of the authority of ancient laws to convince his audience of the necessity of modernizing Roman legislation.[46] Constructions of a continuous tradition of ritual plaints often makes use of the same narrative motives as descriptions of their disappearance (and these two are often intertwined, as in Cicero): the seemingly prehistoric origin, and the genre-gender link. Just as Cicero's imagination of the authority of the Roman past may be read as a political complaint about his present, and just as the relegation of dirges from the public of the Greek *polis* pertains to warfare and the handling of casualties, it is sometimes easy to see that the purpose of a respective modern interest in ritual plaints undermining the theoretical distance between observer and observed: Three German studies on Greek lamentations of the dead, dating from 1938, 1941, and 1943 mention no present grounds for complaint yet speak in catachresis for dirges insofar as they seek to prove—in line with Nazi gender stereotyping and militarization of language—that ritual plaints such as portrayed in the *Iliad* do not aim at "expressing personal feeling in an 'unmanly' manner" but as doing a "holy duty."[47] The construction of proximity or distance to presumably ancient ritual plaints is a function of a historical "now."

---

[42]Lauren Berlant, *The Female Complaint*, 13: "The female complaint *is* a discourse of disappointment. But where loss is concerned, disappointment is a partner of fulfillment, not an opposite."
[43]Katherine Craik, "Shakespeare's *A Lover's Complaint* and Early Modern Criminal Confession," 438.
[44]Cicero, *De legibus* II.59.
[45]Dutsch, "Nenia," 262–263.
[46]Marie Theres Fögen, *Das Lied vom Gesetz*, 62–66.
[47]Eugen Reiner, *Die Rituelle Totenklage der Griechen*, 53 (a gender-bias strongly criticized in, Lüddeckens, *Untersuchungen*, 15–16 and images 21–21b displaying Albanian wailing-men); Ludwig Deubner, *Ololyge und Verwandtes*, 4–5 differentiates a "typically male" lament with a "distinctly active character" from a female, "involuntary, passive" lament. Fritz Boehm, *Die Neugriechische Totenklage*, 10–11 (authored 1943, published posthumously), focuses on denying any fear of a return of the dead, underlining the "hope for meeting again." All my translations.

Especially when the anthropological analysis of ritual plaints is linked to literary criticism, two temporalities collide: on the one hand "modern survivals" of old folk traditions, as Alexiou puts it[48] (Holst-Warhaft says "last remnants"[49]), on the other hand artistic forms like tragedy (or opera[50]) in which the assonant ritual is sublimated. Artistic genres are usually considered as forms of individual expression subject to historical change, folk traditions as anonymous realizations of "the unchanging ritual," as Shapiro says.[51] The contrast between a presumably original ritual and the art form that emerges from it (but is supposedly never reflected in the ritual) has shaped inquiries into ritual laments in the past[52] and persists, although unsupported by textual or archeological evidence:[53] There is no full account of a Greek or Roman funerary ritual;[54] elements are reconstructed from ancient literature and in analogy to current anthropological studies. It is largely uncontested, however, that while Greek tragedy portrays funerary rites, what it performs is a dramatic reproduction referring to the rite as an element of the religious and political life of the city state at least as much as to the poetics of tragedy. Greek vase-paintings are often read as proofs of a continuous tradition of the gestures of ritual laments,[55] yet these vases give a standstill impression of a ritual which literary sources portray as full of movement and sound. It is, therefore, fair to assume that images of lament rites employ a codified inventory of postures in order to be discernable, but their relation to the rites is not evident.[56] Folk traditions of rituals are, moreover, subject to change as Alexiou shows, even if her outline of Greek tradition aims at demonstrating the opposite: subject to Christianization, Ottoman conquest, wars with changing alliances that are never unanimous,[57]

---

[48] Alexiou, *Ritual Lament*, 36. Cf. Naomi Weiss, "The Representation of Lament in Greek Tragedy," 249.
[49] Holst-Warhaft, *Dangerous Voices*, 6.
[50] Weigel, "Lamento: Die Stimme von Klage und Oper" (lecture, Denkerei, Berlin, June 9, 2015).
[51] H.A. Shapiro, "Iconography of Mourning in Athenian Art," 655.
[52] Reiner, *Die Rituelle Totenklage*, 1–2.
[53] Neither is it supported by research on orality; Jeff Goody, *Myth, Ritual, and the Oral*, 41: "Oral 'literature' was the standard form (or genre) found in societies without writing. The term is also used to describe the quite different tradition in written civilizations where certain genres are transmitted by word of mouth or are confined to the unlettered (the 'folk'). ... While certain forms such as the folktale continue to exist especially among the unlettered component of complex societies, what might also be called the 'oral tradition' (to indicate that it is part of a wider constellation) is inevitably influenced by the elite, by written culture."
[54] Karen Stears, "Death Becomes Her," 139; Dutsch, "Nenia," 258.
[55] Alexiou, *Ritual Lament*, 6; Robert Garland, *The Greek Way of Death*, 25–33; Rush Rehm, *Marriage to Death*, 24–38; Silvia Schroer, "Biblische Klagetraditionen," 88–89; Christine Havelock, *Mourners on Greek Vases*, 51; Shapiro, "Iconography of Mourning," 635–636.
[56] Ingeborg Huber, *Ikonographie der Trauer*, 203–211.
[57] Alexiou, *Ritual Lament*, 24–130.

so that there is, at no point in time, one singular Greek folk tradition of laments.[58] Besides vase paintings, Greek funerary rites are reconstructed from literary texts and from accounts of their legal ban. Both sources are problematic insofar as they emphasize the dysfunctional character of ritual laments and complaints, and reconstructions tend to adapt this notion. Texts focusing on rites of lament like Aeschylus' *Persians* or Sophocles' *Ajax*, however, remain thus largely inaccessible to this approach. Still, the modern adaption of ancient reservations about ritual plaints is no coincidence: The language of lamenting and complaining disorganizes conventional structures of language, and these shifts or cracks is where fundamental distinctions crystallize that persist in historical discourses.

## Patterns of Looking at Ritual Plaints

In anthropology, Christian theology, as well as literary studies, ritual plaints are often portrayed as a prehistoric phenomenon vanishing just now, in the moment of examination. The tension between these two temporalities—one remote, one acute—is articulated in recurrent oppositions that are supposed to facilitate historic understanding by providing unequivocal distinctions such as male versus female, with lament being located on the female side. Conventionality versus authenticity is as seminal a contrast in descriptions of ritual plaints; it features prominently in discourses on wailing-women "who [cry] for pay," as Rilke says, thus raising the doubt that any conventionalized (that is to say symbolic) utterance of sensations vouches for the feeling it displays. Further oppositions for describing ritual plaints include:

—communality versus individuality, a contrast dominating readings of Greek tragedy since Hegel and Schelling, wherein ritual plaints are relegated to the side of the feminine and kinship, opposing male state rationality, the telos of history;[59]

---

[58]Dirges of the region Mani are discussed with regard to Athenian funerary laws (Holst-Warhaft, *Dangerous Voices*, 53pp.), but Mani was under the rule of Sparta (Seremetakis, *Last Word*, 11 & 18), a kingdom without the republican issues with war and its casualties, where lament was unrestricted (Alexiou, *Ritual Lament*, 17).
[59]G.W.F. Hegel, *Phenomenology of Spirit* C. (BB).VI.A.b, 279–289. Cf. Friedrich Wilhelm Joseph Schelling, *The Philosophy of Art*, 255: "The Greeks sought in their tragedies *this* kind of equilibrium between justice and humanity, necessity and freedom, a balance without which they could not satisfy their moral sensibility, just as the highest morality itself is expressed in this balance. Precisely this equilibrium is the ultimate concern of tragedy. ... that this guiltlessly guilty person accepts punishment voluntarily—this is the *sublimity* of tragedy; thereby alone does freedom transfigure itself into the highest identity with necessity." For criticism Simon Goldhill, "The Ends of Tragedy."

—rural versus urban, wherein ritual plaints are both "a source of embarrassment, indicative of rural backwardness and superstition"[60] and a token of nostalgia maintained in remote spaces.[61] The point of view is urban either way, situating ritual plaints "*on the Margins of Europe and Beyond*" or in "isolated pockets—remote areas of Greece and Romania, rural Ireland, Scotland, the Ingrian villages of Finland and Russia"[62]—in marginalizing topographies that incorrectly identify the contrast of tradition and modernity with the "rural/urban split";[63]

—foreign versus familiar, with ritual plaints appearing either exotic (for instance when the unaccompanied lament song "elegy" is called "Asian" in Euripides[64]) or strange in, and estranging from, the supposedly familiar tradition (when Plutarch quotes Solon's funerary laws as delimiting "harsh, artless, and barbaric"[65] dirges and when Plato, drawing up a more ideal state than Athens, ponders on the "music by hired mourners" escorting funerals[66]);

—madness versus sanity, with inarticulate wailing featuring as the excessive, irrational pole in current discourses[67] and already in Aeschylus' *Agamemnon*;[68]

—orality versus written word, concerning both the fact that ritual plaints comprise standardized yet non-verbal elements like wailing, "stylized sobbing,"[69] or "tuneful, texted weeping,"[70] and the question of authorship that rules most modern discourses but is problematic ritual agency.

Ritual plaints are, moreover, subject to genre distinctions such as *goos*, *thrēnos*, *nenia*, *planctus*, or "dirge" that serve to differentiate the lamenting and complaining from other forms and purposes of utterances which testify to a particular understanding of plaintive language. This notion might contrast with modern (western) conceptions. Finding praise in Sumerian city laments, for instance, Bachvarova writes: "The typical response of modern scholars is to note the unharmonious juxtaposition of paean and lament,"[71] because praising and complaining to (and about) someone

---

[60]Danforth, *Death Rituals*, 72; cf. Liu, "Expressive Depths," 208; Ninoshvili, "Wailing," 6–7; Seremetakis, *Last Word*, 162–165.
[61]Ernesto de Martino, *Morte e pianto rituale nel mondo antico*; Alexiou, *Ritual Lament*, 50.
[62]Evy Johanne Håland, *Women, Pain, and Death*, subtitle; Holst-Warhaft, *Dangerous Voices*, 6.
[63]Seremetakis, *Last Word*, 6: "Any rigid rural/urban split … ignores the history of the Mediterranean."
[64]Euripides, *Iphigenia in Tauris*, 146–147; 180.
[65]Plutarch, *Vitae Parallelae: Solon* 12.5.
[66]Platon, *Laws* 800e.1–3.
[67]Wilce, *Crying Shame*, 53–54.
[68]Aeschylus, *Agamemnon*, 1064.
[69]Ninoshvili, "Wailing," 3.
[70]Wilce, *Crying Shame*, xii.
[71]Bachvarova, "Sumerian 'Gala' Priests," 28. Praise and lament in Roman *nenia* cf. Dutsch, "Nenia," 261.

are conceptualized as different, even opposing utterances in modernity. In the Sumerian plaint genre, both belong to the concern for being heard and answered. In the *Oresteia*, Electra's *euchē* (prayer, vow, curse) also demands the chorus to both wail and praise the dead.[72] The name of the Roman dirge evokes a different semantic field, as Dutsch outlines: "The word *nenia* itself, in addition to meaning 'funeral chant', could denote a nursery rhyme, a load of rubbish, or magical incantation and it even ... had some obscure connection with the extremity of the intestine." Not only with reference to death, that is, "*nenia* belonged to a discourse associated with the crossing of boundaries."[73] In a *nenia*, the concern about being heard and answered, particular to plaintive language, focuses on reaching others across boundaries (like death) and moving them.

These dichotomies inform historical policies of silencing ritual plaints and are often adapted in current research, as a brief discussion of three major paradigms will outline: tradition, trauma, and orality in ritual plaints. Studies on ritual plaints often highlight the historical continuity of forms— not only in the case of Greek and Romanian rituals, on which the chapter will focus. Similarities of current ritual forms with descriptions in ancient texts are read as testimonies of a "continuity of tradition"[74] in Greek laments, or a "continuity of ... ancient performance conventions" in Egyptian dirges.[75] Yet modern Greek ritual laments are called neither *goos*, *threnos* nor *kommos* but μοιρολόι (*moiroloi*), a combination of *moira* (fate) and *logos* (speech)[76] denoting a genre of lamenting or "crying one's fate."[77] Such terminological change is supposed to be comprised in Alexiou's concession: "these laments are not unhistorical, because they are a poetic expression of a long chain of events throughout Greek history which have called for lamentation."[78] "Not unhistorical" means as much as not unchanging here. In the concept of a continuous tradition of ritual plaints, however, change is depicted as a continuous fading that threatens to end just now, in the moment of analysis. This notion is voiced in Caraveli-Chaves's 1980 study on Cretan ritual laments: "the present generation of lament poets is undoubtedly the last link in an uninterrupted chain of transmission ... in spite of past opposition against them by the church and, before the advent of Christianity, by the

---

[72] Aeschylus, *Libation Bearers*, 150–151.
[73] Dutsch, "Nenia," 258 & 272.
[74] Alexiou, *Ritual Lament*, 14; cf. Casey Dué, *The Captive Women's Lament*, 7; Håland, *Women, Pain, and Death*, 36–37; Holst-Warhaft, *Dangerous Voices*, 40.
[75] Wickett, *For the Living*, 166; criticism in Wilce, *Crying Shame*, 68. Lüddeckens, *Untersuchungen* outlines the change of lament rites in ancient Egypt.
[76] Alexiou, *Ritual Lament*, 110. In some regions the name is *nekratika traghoudhia* (Danforth, *Death Rituals*, 71); the Greek-American avant-garde musician Diamanda Galas adopts it in her Τραγούδια από το Αίμα Εχούν Φονός ("Songs from the Blood of Those Murdered," 1984).
[77] Seremetakis, *Last Word*, 3.
[78] Alexiou, *Ritual Lament*, 101.

state."[79] Presupposing a continuous invariant tradition of ritual plaints does not contribute to understanding the reasons for the disappearance of ritual in modernity and for the opposition to ritual dirges and wailing in earlier modernizations. Loraux states that "as far as historical reflection goes, we should not be content with the deus ex machina of continuity if we want to avoid the dreaded objection of 'evidence' ... The 'ancient Mediterranean stock' is no help."[80] Amelang shows that the narrative of ritual plaints as a just now vanishing archaism presupposes not one but three continuities: one temporal, one geographical ("the 'Euromediterranean' heartland of ritual lament"[81]), one formal ("of provenance or genre, through the interchange of literary and ethnographic texts and documents of actual historical experience").[82] With regard to correspondences between ancient lament texts and contemporary rites, research carefully avoids the question "survivals or similarities?," as Amelang puts it[83]—as if it was a source of concern that temporally and geographically remote rituals of lamenting and complaining communicate by way of similar modes of disorganizing conventional structures of language. It is this concern that there should be a systematic communicative role not only for the regular organization of linguistic structures, but even for their disorganization and the ruin of what is usually called comprehension that is kept at bay by presupposing a continuous tradition of ritual plaints. Parallels between rituals that transcend the presupposed link, such as between self-mutilations that are part of the Hebrew Bible and of Australian Warramunga funerary rites,[84] are disregarded in the insistence on historical continuity.

The narrative of a continuous tradition of ritual plaints was established largely by de Martino's 1958 study on South Italian dirges—a key piece of research that "exoticized, and mourned the passing of, the 'authentic' laments of other people in other times and places," as Wilce notes.[85] De Martino reads them as relics of ancient forms[86] maintained parallel to Christian customs in a remote region, although with a decline "from ancient plentitude through medieval challenge to modern irrelevance" and the "absence of a 'post mortem,'" as Amelang sums up.[87] The parallel worlds communicate, de Martino holds, in "the medieval figure of Mater Dolorosa, in which Mary assumed in silence the posture of pagan lament while articulating an

---

[79]Anna Caraveli-Chaves, "Bridge between Worlds," 129.
[80]Nicole Loraux, *Mothers in Mourning*, 29.
[81]Amelang, "Mourning," 10; cit. Martino, *Morte e pianto rituale*, 111.
[82]Ibid., 6.
[83]Ibid., 17.
[84]Kutsch, "Trauerbräuche" und "Selbstminderungsriten"; Durkheim, *Elementary Forms*, 394–396.
[85]Wilce, *Crying Shame*, 155.
[86]Martino, *Morte e pianto rituale*, 56–57, 225, 308.
[87]Amelang, "Mourning," 19.

exemplary Christian message."[88] Few current scholars reference de Martino yet most adapt his historiographic narrative of ritual lament, including its "ethnographic melancholy,"[89] as summed up by Amelang:

> The centuries-long decline and fall of lament involved few if any alterations in its repertory of gestures and speech. Its ill-fated entry into history meant instead its effective displacement from cultural and geographical centres to their equivalent peripheries—a fate that ended up by embracing virtually all categories of "paganism" in a Europe increasingly subject to the disciplines of reform.[90]

Amelang further notes that the common narrative of a "ruralization of public lament," pervasive in studies on Greek dirges, is inappropriately based on research on the disappearance of death from public life in Northern Europe.[91] The ruralization narrative also cannot do without the implication that the socially and politically marginalized rural realm was without a history[92] (while marginalization is, of course, a historical process) so that rural populations may practice customs that belong to different historical horizons. The narrative of ritual laments as ancient relict employs the Christian temporality of super-stition, of "jutting out" of pagan prehistory into historical time Anno Domini. Such relicts standing out of their context appear not only old, or anachronistic, but indeed "refer to a *spectral reality*," as Didi-Huberman puts it, a ghostly or uncanny[93] non-presence.[94] The term "survival" is, according to Didi-Huberman, the modern equivalence to superstition, both share "the *phantasmic time of survivals*."[95] "Survival" has, not only in anthropology, long been the name for everything that had become foreign and incompatible with the assumption of the continuity of tradition—remnants of old customs and habits in literature and the arts as much as the customs and beliefs of formerly other, then colonialized

---

[88]Ibid., 10; cf. Martino, *Morte e pianto rituale*, 334–344.
[89]Ibid., 19.
[90]Ibid., 7.
[91]Ibid., 20.
[92]Wilce sees this assumption in Martino's insistence of presence: "According to lamenters, culturally coded wailing can help maintain balance in the face of destabilizing events. Ernesto de Martino called that balance 'presence'—*a presence that is guaranteed in its relationship to and within the world* ... For de Martino, 'the crisis of presence', the crisis that death presents to the living, looms very large in 'traditional societies'" (Wilce, *Crying Shame*, 52; cit. Martino, *The World of Magic*, 223).
[93]Freud, "The 'Uncanny.'" SE17:240: "This uncanny is in reality nothing new or alien, but something which is familiar and old-established in the mind and which has become alienated from it only through the process of repression."
[94]Georges Didi-Huberman, *The Surviving Image*, 32.
[95]Ibid., 28; cf. 46–50. Georges Didi-Huberman, *Survival of the Fireflies*, 29: "de Martino, the great Italian anthropologist of survivals—who worked on the long tradition of ritual lament."

cultures corresponding with these relicts.[96] Survivals are like traumatic reminiscences, repeatedly interrupting the presence and providing no information about their origin. Rituals may appear like traumatic survivals insofar as repetition is essential to them, and ignorance about their origin does not reduce their effectiveness. Wickett thus entertains no doubt that in Upper Egypt dirges (ʿidid), spectral ancient customs survive, circulating even though obsolete: "Ancient ritual practices described in the laments and once performed for the benefit of the soul in the afterlife are now archaic but, as symbolic acts, they survive in the metaphoric domain of lament."[97] Cast in the narrative of survival-as-remnant, archaic rites remain active as dead metaphors in dirges. Problematic about this narrative is that it regards the relevance and comprehensibility of the current custom solely in terms of its genesis by decay—as something that belongs to the past and has no genuine place in the present world. The notion of survival-as-relict makes the disappearance of the ritual plaint, which it laments, the condition for studying it—as if it applied as much to criticism as to ritual that there shall be no lament without death.[98]

The fragmentary character of plaintive speech is, if not altogether ignored in the narrative of a continuous ritual tradition, often described in terms of trauma. Saunders thus analyses "the conception of the modern as a moment of traumatic loss" in which structures of presumably obsolete ritual plaints reappear, notably the undermining of comprehensibility: "Th[e] crisis of understanding and representation is one that is often thematized by the language of lamentation."[99] This thematization, Saunders rightly notes, does not have propositional structure since plaintive language voices the destruction and ruin of structures:

> The traumatic event and a language, like lamentation, that responds to it are ... not easily distinguished, for the language of lamentation cannot simply record catastrophe, but must also speculatively construct it. The traumatic moment is thus simultaneously phenomenal and rhetorical, recorded and produced by the language of lamentation; and the language

---

[96] Erhard Schüttpelz, Die Moderne im Spiegel des Primitiven, 399.
[97] Wickett, For the Living, xvii; cf. ibid.: "It is because of their sense of obligation and the continual performance of funerary lamentation by women after millennia that these laments survive today." This narrative casts even the ancient history of dirges in the pattern of survival-as-remnant, 179–180: "James P. Allen has noted that the grammar of the Pyramid Texts resembles a stage of language that disappeared from secular inscriptions fifty years earlier, and that some texts reflect burial practices older than the IVth Dynasty ... The 'survival' of these archaic references in the later texts reveals the ancient Egyptian penchant for preservation of ancient conceptions and rituals despite the adoption of new ideas and new funerary practices."
[98] On problematic requests for staged dirges Wickett, For the Living, 11.
[99] Saunders, Lamentation and Modernity, xi & 19.

of lamentation is simultaneously representational and performative, both a record, and the creation, of the traumatic moment.[100]

Saunders's reference to representation and production skips the difficulty that portrayals of trauma—a recurrent interruption of experience—require a disorganization of the means of portrayal. This undermines any clear notion of a response to trauma, as Freud's changing conceptions show, because Saunders fails to clarify whether responding means retorting trauma in language, or speaking in correspondence to trauma's disruptive character. Still, trauma could serve as tertium comparationis between modern, literary and older, ritual texts insofar as traumata do not belong to but interrupt historical horizons. Saunders's analysis of the discursive effects of trauma, however, wrongly transfers modern phenomena onto ritual contexts; anthropology contradict her thesis: "Lamentation disrupts social discipline."[101] Yet the ritual disorganization of social norms regularly serves the purpose of re-stabilizing the suspended order in times of crises, as Seremetakis outlines: "The construction of self and sentiment in the lament performance is an ongoing social process."[102] Saunders takes characterizations of ritual plaints that have historically served to silence plaints as timeless structures of plaintive language itself, thus demonstrating the necessity to carefully distinguish its structure from its discursive effect in different contexts: "Lamentation resists logical resolution ... Embedded in rituals that are historically prior to philosophy, it mingles with the primitive, the illogical, the feminine."[103] Localizing ritual plaints in a time "before philosophy" aims at claiming logic exclusively for theoretical thought articulated in terminological language, that is in delimitations. A fundamental one of these is a chain of characterizations suggesting a logical coherence of the illogical, the old, the primitive, and the female, marking a realm irrelevant to philosophy. These attributes feature prominently in descriptions of plaintive language and grant insight into the concern it raises, yet they cannot be paralleled with assumptions about the structure of lamenting and complaining as in Saunders who notes in the same list of characteristics: "Lamentation disorders the symbolic."[104] It does, and there is indeed ample reason to mistrust a grammatical and logical order that utters an ontological assumption by means of the same propositional structure as a defamation.

---

[100] Ibid., 47.
[101] Ibid., xvii.
[102] Seremetakis, *Last Word*, 3; cf. Wilce, *Crying Shame*, 44: "Lament and other forms of 'expression' help *constitute* social understandings and internal processes." Caraveli-Chaves, "Bridge between Worlds," 130: "The main effects of lamentation on the women of the 'patriarchal' Greek village society are the establishment of a strong sense of bonding among them, and the reinforcement of social roles and modes of interaction."
[103] Saunders, *Lamentation and Modernity*, xi.
[104] Ibid., x–xi.

Austin's reference to trauma in the analysis of plaintive language highlights the therapeutic aspect:

> Lamentation fulfills an important therapeutic role despite its apparent meaninglessness.
> In general, the *góos* occurs early in the pastoral, academic, or funeral elegy. It is traumatic language, as we say now: it sounds spontaneous and involuntary; it is meant to exhibit a mind and body temporarily out of control. Traumatic language signals internal dissociation, a state in which events are registered but not understood. The condition, as well as its symptomatic language, is unsustainable; it does not seem able to subsist apart from belated accounts of it, from a point of cognitive recovery.[105]

Anthropology conceptualizes the transitory character of plaintive language as ritual liminality, Scholem's theological approach regards lament as language bordering on of silence.[106] Austin's analysis "from a point of cognitive recovery," however, suggests that the normalization of speech to articulation, proposition, and terminological language is the ultimate aim of lamenting and complaining.[107] This might not only be an incorrect notion of the regularity of everyday speech and literary language, it reduces plaintive language to a self-regulating exception that passes without claiming a position in discourse. Austin thus notes: "Lamentation veers away from the cognitive and the pictorial toward sound ... the noise of trauma."[108]

Ritual plaints often appear as eminently oral, as Danforth writes: "Greek funeral laments are part of a longstanding oral tradition in which the literary concept of one authentic or correct version of a song does not exist."[109] This qualification emphasizes that ritual plaints appear, more precisely, as eminently oral within a culture of the written word, where they are restricted by the law and portrayed in literature. Delimitations of oral versus literal subjects relegating sound—which is indeed foregrounded in plaintive language as it prioritizes the search for hearing—out of phonetic script into the realm of (obsolete) orality are part of the theoretical approach to the world. And it is in accordance with theory that plaintive language is understood as although not rational but rationalizing remedy for suffering. Holst-Warhaft describes such a process:

> The structuring of pain into a song is itself an externalization of suffering. It may be that the shared activity of singing about another's pain shifts

---

[105] Austin, "Rhetoric of the Sublime," 285.
[106] Gershom Scholem, "On Lament and Lamentation," 6.
[107] For non-normalized trauma see Conclusion, 248–260.
[108] Austin, "Rhetoric of the Sublime," 279.
[109] Danforth, *Death Rituals*, 71–72.

the locus of pain from the individual to the group in the same way as the assignment of blame for the death shifts pain to anger, and anger frequently to a prescription for action. In both cases there is a movement from the inner world of private suffering to the outer, from one's own body ... to the object of one's hatred, from private tears to shrill cries that affect the landscape all around. ... Naming, blaming, fixing in a landscape: these are all gestures of order and control. For those who sing them, laments may be the reordering of one's inner emotional reactions to death into a tangible outward expression.[110]

Describing plaintive language as externalization is simpler than approaching it in terms of trauma. It implies that there is a pain predating, and consumed by, the utterance just as Breuer's and Freud's 1898 "cathartic method" (SE2:107) assumes. Freud dismisses the approach as it fails to establish a stable link between the utterance and the disappearance of affects. What is decisive is that lamenting and complaining communicate pain. It is, therefore, reasonable to assume that lamenting and complaining produce (rather than express) emotions, that is to say they voice and, at the same time, form them. The inside-outside split notorious in debates on affect and emotion shall be the last of the patterns of looking at plaints discussed in this section—not in the futile attempt of covering the field of affect and emotion studies but to outline the notion that will inform the subsequent readings.

The private interior in which Holst-Warhaft locates sensation matches modern Western psycho-topography but is inappropriate to texts from older or other contexts. Still, it is reasonable to assume an interval between plaintive language and suffering for if there was none, there would be no space for negotiating psychic topographies, and no shifts possible between the referent of a complaint, its cause, its author, and its audience. The interval is, however, not separating sensation from plaints, as Holst-Warhaft assumes, but constitutes both, as Pahl explains: "If we think that the authenticity of emotion lies in its immediacy, we will have a hard time experiencing emotion."[111] Experiencing anything requires some separation from the mere affected-ness, from being fully captured and consumed, so that the sensation may be compared to others, may be called sorrow, rage, or joy, that is to experienced *as* something.[112] The mourner who cries "Woe is me" has not, as Austin suggests, "disappeared into his or her grief"[113] but

---

[110]Holst-Warhaft, *Dangerous Voices*, 73.
[111]Katrin Pahl, *Tropes of Transport*, 91.
[112]Cf. Alain Ehrenberg, *The Weariness of the Self*, 30: "So that suffering may matter in and of itself, we must impose a language that allows the self not only to be expressed but also to be understood. The public function of the self, the common exchange, is the condition of the private experience."
[113]Austin, "Lament," 285.

managed to capture himself or herself *as* afflicted, and has thus reflected. Pahl outlines that "we need something in addition to the real in order to be able to lament. Affects ... have an immediate quality to them that gives us no means to lament."[114] What we need is indeed a gap:

> A slight gap or lag—precisely that which pain eliminates in its absolute rule. Without this interval, no lament, no language of pain is possible. ... we need fiction, metaphor, or theatre to create the interval that makes emotion resonate and allows us to experience it in the first place. *The sheer "reality" of pain is not an emotion; the lament is the true emotional experience.* Emotion is, thus, a manner of speaking. ... I need to find that distance to myself—to my own loss—that allows me to lament it. "Making a scene" thus involves reflecting and refracting the loss across various figurations of loss, self, and presence.[115]

This interval is neither the "order and control" Holst-Warhaft mentions, nor the "cognitive recovery" that is marked, according to Austin, when lamenting and complaining cease. The interval is, rather, prerequisite to any plaint. Audiences enjoy works of art that inspire sadness (rather than joy) because, Pahl says, they provide forms that may be borrowed in order to communicate their respective emotions.[116] Ritual plaints provide forms such as wailing, crying, tearing one's hair, and self-mutilations. It is only because emotions are formed while being communicated—rather than being pieces of cognitive content that find verbal or gestural expression—that Alexiou can ascribe opposing psychic functions to ritual plaints: "The function of the ritual lamentation of the women is the same as in antiquity. It soothed wrath in cases of cruel or untimely death; or, alternatively ... it roused the spirit of revenge ... grief, finding expression, is relieved and lightened."[117] Borrowing ritual or fictional forms in order to communicate emotions does not thwart the sincerity of the emotion but allows to produce it. Alienation, rather, marks those sensations that affect and capture the subject but cannot be compared to, or contextualized with, anything so that it cannot be felt *as* something but becomes a recurrent trauma interrupting all self-perception. The insistence on the authenticity of an "inner world of private suffering" (Holst-Warhaft) voiced in "spontaneous and involuntary" (Austin) utterances seeks to retort a disconcerting structure pointed out in Pahl: That emotions are formed by way of varying preestablished—ritual, artistic, or other—forms does not only imply a transfer of the productions of

---

[114]Pahl, *Tropes of Transport*, 90.
[115]Ibid., 91–92; my italics.
[116]Ibid., 90.
[117]Alexiou, *Ritual Lament*, 124–125.

others onto the respective "own" experience: It only becomes an experience because the transfer introduces a distance—not to the preestablished form, but to the self. "We lament only when we relate to ourselves as something else. ... emotion is an indirect way of speaking."[118] Emotions are relational, produced in exchange with and comparison to the productions of others in irreducible shift of reference, address, and attribution. Emotions are, writes Marcia Cavell, "orientations in the world that show how things matter to us, revealing the world in its relation to us, and ourselves in relation to the world."[119] Wickett objects to this relational notion of emotions with reference to translation:

> Despite the wealth of anthropological literature that asserts that emotions are socially and culturally constructed, from the wealth of emotions enumerated and repeated in the laments, it would appear that the apprehension of grief expressed here is rooted in the universal human experience of grief at loss.[120]

This is a standard objection aptly countered in Huntington's and Metcalf's remark: "Uniformity of human emotion does not explain the rituals of societies,"[121] which evidently differ. Regarding emotions as communicative faults that are produced in forms of speech such as, notably, the language of lamenting and complaining allows for the insight that observing the world, reflecting on it, and verbally segmenting it is no prerogative of theory, terminological language, and propositional formulas. Yet there is a fundamental difference in the ways theory and plaintive language segment, and grasp, the world: While concepts aim at the clearest possible differentiation, lamenting and complaining see the possibility of drawing and maintaining clear distinction undermined, for instance by the sudden death of someone who had been alive just seconds ago. Ritual plaints are concerned not so much with drawing distinctions but with negotiating their possibility and purpose. Therefore, they rarely presuppose a differentiation between occurrence and sensation but work toward the possibility of (re-) establishing a subject's and community's position in the face of crisis. Subject of the next section is how such ritual transfer of terms can be grasped in philology, in reading, without granting privilege to terminological language. Therefore, the section will proceed by comparing an anthropological analysis of liminality in dirges with their literary portray.

---

[118]Pahl, *Tropes of Transport*, 93.
[119]Marcia Cavell, *Becoming a Subject*, 126.
[120]Wickett, *For the Living*, 142.
[121]Huntington and Metcalf, *Celebrations of Death*, 61.

## "The Dead Are Hungry": Metaphor and Liminality

In her unfinished novel *Das Regal der letzten Atemzüge* (The Shelf of Last Breaths), published posthumously in 2002, the Romanian-Swiss author Aglaja Veteranyi follows the trajectory of her biography. In exile from Communist Romania since the age of five, raised in a circus touring the world, speaking Romanian and Spanish, temporarily schooled in Switzerland yet illiterate until her teen years, Veteranyi gives German a unique brevity and clarity unconsumed with stereotypes of modern progressiveness. Veteranyi confronts the (presumably female) first-person-narrator in Switzerland with the death of her aunt and mourning rites of her Romanian relatives such as preparing *Totenkuchen* (death cakes) made of boiled wheat. They have to be prepared for the burial because, her uncle explains to the geographically as culturally distanced relative: *Die Toten haben Hunger* (The dead are hungry). Commenting on this and other explanations of her family's unfamiliar customs, the narrator outlines a sensual instead of a strictly intellectual approach, as when she notes: *Ich verstand die Muttersprache mit dem Geruch* (I understood the mother tongue by sense of smell).[122] The Romanian her mother's relatives speak is not quoted and hardly even named in Veteranyi's writing. The Romanian language remains a hidden, unattainable source in the German text from which the narrator is as irreversibly estranged as from the funeral rites. Both the language and the rituals, however, still work insofar as they capture the narrator and grant some comprehension, first of all by way of an analogy between comprehension and eating. This culinary, often oral leitmotif, however, is not strictly a metaphor, a transference of the idea of internalization form the physical to the intellectual realm, as the "death cakes" make clear.

They are prepared for the dead, even if the dead are (most likely) not hungry—not because they are full, but because they cannot starve as they lack what keeps them alive—a condition called "hunger" with the living. It is thus in catachresis that "the dead are hungry." A more accurate description of their condition of general lack would have to be given by the dead themselves, which is, of course, impossible, as death is the end of all abilities. What is called "death" signifies the end of experience that, consequently, can be grasped merely in analogy to other experiences. The "death cakes" are such an analogy allowing to grasp the process of psychological disintegration and physical decomposition—not as something *else* than what it actually is, as the notion of a "metaphor" implies, but *as* something at all. For the hard task of mourning seems to be accepting—swallowing—what appears

---

[122]Aglaja Veteranyi, *Das Regal der letzten Atemzüge*, 9. Translations from this text are my own.

as nothing at all: a loss and lack. This section will return to the question of metaphoricity in order to discuss how ritual plaints work; before, a comparative reading of a literary and an anthropological portray of the ritual "death cakes" outlines how the supposedly obsolete form of ritual can be approached from a point of view in (or after) modernity.

The narrator in Veteranyi's text encounters rituals of mourning the lack of which is lamented in Rilke's *Requiem*. Veteranyi's narrator observes her Romanian relatives' preparation of ritual food, gestures of pain, and language of despair, commenting on it with reserve. Instead of citing dirges, Veteranyi's text adapts the structure of antiphony as stichomythic verse for portraying contradictions between modern, psychological, and presumably outdated, ritual approaches to emotion—emotions that arise over the losses of exile, individuals, and ubiquitous cruelty. Veteranyi's inquiry into a language to speak of loss started in her acclaimed 1999 novel *Warum das Kind in der Polenta Kocht* (Why the Child Is Cooking in the Polenta) that ponders the consumption of food as instance of identity. Polenta, which features prominently in the text, is a dish called *mămăligă* in Romanian. This term resembles the words *mamă* (mother) and *limbă maternă* (mother tongue). The dish would thus appear as a more-than-symbolic reunification with the mother, as a mater-ial compensation for her cruelty and the losses of exile—if *mămăligă* was named in the text. Yet it is not, polenta is evoked by its Italian name in the German text and appears as a secret emblem of loss that is, consequently, lost in symbolic substitution—which, however, enables the narrator to deal with loss. *Das Regal der Letzten Atemzüge* continues the inquiry for a language of loss and lament, examining "death cakes":

> Der Totenkuchen wartete in einem der drei Kühlschränke auf die Beerdigung der Tante.
> Bevor wir zum Friedhof fuhren, stürzte ihn Costel auf einen großen Teller.
> Puderzucker.
> Kreuz aus Nüssen.
> Smarties-Dekoration.
> 1 Kerze.[123]

> "The death cake was waiting for the aunt's burial in one of the three refrigerators.
> Before we drove to the graveyard, Costel turned it out onto a large plate.
> Icing sugar.
> Cross of nuts.

---

[123]Ibid., 12.

Smarties decoration.
1 candle."

*Sie aßen für sich und die Toten, sie sangen, sie weinten, sie schlugen
   sich zusammen.*
*Tagelang wurde der Totenkuchen gekocht.*
*In der orthodoxen Kirche reihte sich Tisch an Tisch für die
   Spenden der Tante. Geflochtenes Brot mit Kerzen, aufgetürmte
   Plastiksäckchen, darin 3 Trauben, 1 Stück Ziegenkäse, ½ Tomate.*
*Jeder Biß eine Erleichterung für die Seele der Toten.*[124]

"They were eating for themselves and for the dead, they sang, they
   cried, they beat one other up.
The death cake was cooking for days.
In the Orthodox church, one table followed the next with the aunt's
   donations. Plait bread with candles, mounted plastic bags, in them
   3 grapes, 1 piece of goat cheese, ½ tomato.
Every bite a relief for the soul of the dead."

What exactly "for" means is the seminal question in Veteranyi's observations of the rites surrounding "semolina cakes for the dead with smarties-decoration."[125] The custom of serving κόλλυβα (*kollyva* or *koliva*), *colivă* in Romanian—that is "boiled wheat mixed with sugar and cinnamon and decorated with nuts and raisins"[126]—has been described in anthropological literature about Greek funerals, too. A standard is Danforth:

> After coffee and biscuits are served, the priest lights a candle and places it in a tray of *koliva*, beside which are a glass of wine and a slice of bread. The *koliva*, wine, and bread are together known as the *makario* (that which is blessed). After the priest recites a prayer over the *makario*, he distributes it to the close relatives of the deceased to eat. Everyone then repeats the wish that God forgive the deceased. Finally a simple meal is served, usually consisting of rice, potatoes, or beans; olives, cheese, and wine.[127]

Danforth's portrayal does not hint at any instance of modern consumer culture permeating into the burial rite, marked by Veteranyi's mentioning of "smarties" (sweets akin to M&M's) and "plastic bags." In the anthropological text, the mode of portrayal is the index of modernity: While Veteranyi's text states without ascribing statements to a voice or perspective, Danforth's statements lead to an exegesis of the ritual. Citing van Gennep's concept

---

[124]Ibid., 84.
[125]Ibid., 14: *Grießkuchen mit Smartiesdekoration.*
[126]Danforth, *Death Rituals*, 21.
[127]Ibid., 43–44.

of "rites of passage"—"ceremonies whose essential purpose it is to enable the individual to pass from one defined position to another which is equally well defined"[128]—Danforth emphasizes that the consumption of *koliva* is as concerned with separation as with incorporation:[129] "In addition to marking the separation of the body from the soul and the dead from the living, these rites express concern with the incorporation of the soul into paradise, the body into the earth, and the close relatives of the deceased back into the world of the living."[130] Seremetakis argues against Danforth's emphasis on reintegration that the bereaved are not "momentarily detached from collective structures"[131] by death so that a funeral feast would primarily serve the reestablishment of family and community ties. As Lagache suggests, deceased, rather, first have to be detached from their respective community context, "transposing the biological fact onto the human level, i.e. 'killing the dead.'"[132] With regard to Freud's theory of mourning, the multi-stage consumption of *koliva* seems concerned with the common introjection of the ties to the deceased in order to reorganize the structure of each mourner's ego and their community. Abraham and Torok's elaboration of Freud points out that introjecting pain and loss does not mean swallowing and hiding them (this is the "Wolf Man's" pathology) but putting words and sounds into one's mouth which substitute the lost, and passing those around, in "a communion of empty mouths."[133] With the common meal, the absence of the deceased is made visible, approved, and accepted just as the dishes: Food is incorporated to enable communication about loss, the notorious nothing that seems to withstand symbolic substitution. The consumption of the "death cake" *koliva* is more complicated, however, it is as much a sign as a dish[134] containing a profound doubt in symbolic substitution.

Danforth says eating *koliva* goes along with wishing the dead absolution as if it was swap: the dish into the mouth for the living, the wish out of the mouth for the dead. The ritual assumes two analogies: one "between the consumption of food by the living at the memorial services and the consumption of the body of the deceased by the earth,"[135] and a "symbolic parallel between the 'dissolution' of the body and the 'absolution' of the soul."[136] The consumption of food promotes that of the body, which in turn supports the absolution of the soul. In this chain of analogy, however,

---

[128] Arnold van Gennep, *The Rites of Passage*, 3.
[129] Ibid., 11.
[130] Danforth, *Death Rituals*, 42–43.
[131] Seremetakis, *Last Word*, 13.
[132] Lagache, "The Work of Mourning," 17.
[133] MM:128.
[134] While *colivă* is a Romanian dish, Greek *koliva* are prepared only for funerals.
[135] Danforth, *Death Rituals*, 105.
[136] Ibid., 52.

the cake does not simply substitute for the human body[137] but functions as a ritual medium of transfer. The "death cake" does exactly not claim to bring somebody absent to presence; rather, it is an index pointing at the deceased as much as pointing out the insufficiency of symbolic substitution. *Koliva* is a plural corresponding to the ancient Greek singular κόλλυβος (*kollybos*, small coin),[138] which might refer to a similar form or a similar function as a placeholder in exchange, as Cicero calls *kollybos* the charge deducted by foreign exchange agents.[139] The "death cake" *koliva* promotes a shift in the ritual transfer: In Danforth, *koliva* are accompanied first by bread (just as Veteranyi's "death cakes"), later by wine and bread which, in Byzantine Rite, do not stand in for but become the body and blood of Christ.[140] The common consumption of the blessed *koliva* alongside wine and bread resembles an extended communion, but what would be the function of the additional element? Accompanying the sacrificial bread of the host, *koliva* corresponds to the *antidōron*: In case several loaves of bread had been prepared to choose the host(s)[141] among them, those left over are blessed and handed out to the parish after Eucharist[142] as a "return-gift,"[143] or "instead of a gift,"[144] in any case not as the body of Christ but to feed the bodies of the parishioners. Just as the handed-out bread suggests both a proximity to, and difference from, Christ since it could have been chosen for a host but was not, and thus further suggests both the proximity of, and difference between, Christ and Christians, the "death cakes" *koliva* adapt the idea of a proximity of crops to the corporeal without identifying them. On the contrary, *koliva* "constituted the diet of the 5th-C[entury] monks who refused to touch bread" because it could become a host."[145] What *koliva* have in common with the Orthodox host is thus not the Eucharist principle of realization-by-representation but a hermeneutic paradigm linking death and life in incorporation as a transition. Jesus voices this paradigm when he links the death of the crops (as brought about by cooking) to their reproduction,[146]

---

[137]Ibid., 105: "the koliva ... and bread consumed at death rites are identified symbolically with the body of the deceased." Alexandar Každan, *The Oxford Dictionary of Byzantium*, 1137, s.v. "Kollyba": "special cakes ... symbolized the human body."
[138]*LSJ*, s.v. "*kollybos*," http://www.perseus.tufts.edu/hopper/morph?l=kollubos&la=greek# lexicon, accessed December 4, 2019.
[139]Klose, *EA*, s.v. "*Kollybos*," 6:641. This hints at the long-standing use of corn as currency.
[140]Ken Parry, *The Blackwell Dictionary of Eastern Christianity*, s.v. "Prothesis," 391.
[141]Ibid., depending on date and region, Byzantine Rite requires one, two, or five host(s).
[142]Ibid., s.v. "antidoron," 33.
[143]*LSJ*, s.v. "*antidōron*," http://www.perseus.tufts.edu/hopper/morph?l=antidwron&la=greek# lexicon, accessed December 4, 2019.
[144]Parry, *Eastern Christianity*, s.v. "antidoron," 33.
[145]Každan, *Byzantium*, s.v. "Kollyba," 1137.
[146]Jn 12:24 (NRSV): "Very truly, I tell you, unless a grain of wheat falls into the earth and dies, it remains just a single grain; but if it dies, it bears much fruit." Cf. Danforth, *Death Rituals*, 97.

Paul says: resurrection.[147] Therefore, *koliva* features prominently in the repetition of funerary rites three, nine, and forty days, six months, and one year after the burial analogous to the after-life of Christ.[148] Consuming *koliva* does not imply symbolically eating the dead, still, the proximity to the host points out that eating "for" the dead—on the occasion of their funeral and in order to promote their absolution—is concern with the consumption *of* the dead.

The ritual consumption of "death cakes" is the ambivalent act of both portraying and negating the dissolution of the corps in the earth: By consuming "the aunt's donations," as Veteranyi writes, that is the cakes given by (not to) the dead, the mourners accept her death, and on the one hand their metabolism dissolves the cakes just as the aunt is consumed by the earth. On the other hand, the consumption accentuates and preserves the life that distinguishes the mourners from the dead—currently at least, as menacing lament songs point out, which accompany the "death cakes" in Greece, and as the dying aunt herself explains in Veteranyi:

*Die Erde wird nie satt, sie will immer essen.*
*Die Tante spricht von der Erde wie von einem Kind.*[149]

"The earth is never full, it always wants to eat.
The aunt speaks of the earth as of a child."

This warning hints at a further dimension in this rite of passage: The "death cakes" are eaten in order to promote the aunt's transition into a different state of being, yet with the cakes the bereaved also seem to swallow the obligation to follow the dead. The enjambment in the warning passage marks the distance between the dying aunt and her relatives as well as the hiatus between ritual insider and observer. This hermeneutic hiatus comes to the fore when Danforth explains Greek lament songs that accompany the funerary rites, such as:

"The earth eats tender bodies and muscular shoulders.
It eats children who have mothers, and brothers who have sisters."
"The earth is insatiable. It will never be satisfied.
Insatiable earth, how many people have you eaten! You will never let
    me go."[150]

---

[147]1 Cor. 15:42 (NRSV): "So it is with the resurrection of the dead. What is sown is perishable; what is raised is imperishable."
[148]Danforth, *Death Rituals*, 44–45.
[149]Veteranyi, *Regal*, 13.
[150]Danforth, *Death Rituals*, 100.

The songs from which these lines are taken explain what links the funeral to the feast: the notion of decomposition as consumption by the earth that is checked, displayed, and lamented in the exhumation and second funeral of the (ideally) blank bones five years after the first burial.[151] Danforth reads this link in terms of a cycle:

> If plants are food, and if human beings are like plants, then human beings must also, at least in some context, be food. *It is proof of the internal coherence of the symbolic system under consideration* that the metaphor of human beings as food is well developed in the laments.
> A person's body, which is transformed into a corpse with the departure of his soul at death, becomes food and is consumed by the earth during the rite of burial and the gradual process of decomposition that follows. *The image of a human body being eaten by the earth is one of the most graphic and frightening in the entire corpus of Greek funeral laments.*[152]

Danforth's reading is remarkably condescending when he grants the ritual "coherence" as if semantic incoherence was the rule. His reading of the ritual notion of consumption in terms of a cycle of life seems to serve as much to comprehend the rite as to avert the observer's fear. For the idea of a cycle is introduced to the Orthodox funeral not by the dirges, which scandalize decomposition and scold death, but by the priest, whose words Alexiou renders in English: "'Earth thou art, and to earth thou shalt depart.'"[153] Seremetakis criticizes Danforth for situating the rites not merely in the local context of, but also in semantic coherence with the Orthodox Church, since the relation between ritual and liturgy (Christian ritual) is one of hermeneutic concurrence rather than of mutual completion.[154] Seremetakis finds no vegetable cycle in the notion of decomposition as being "consumed by the earth"[155] but a concept of carnivore violation: "Death is frequently equated with theft, illicit consumption, and flesh eating."[156] With regard to this alternative description, a remarkable parallel in Danforth's text comes to the fore: Both the ritual consumption of *koliva* and its anthropological description by Danforth assume the ambivalent attitude of portraying the decomposition of the deceased as consumption while, at the same time, disavowing it:

---

[151] Ibid. 16–20.
[152] Ibid., 99–100; my italics. The address of the deceased as plant 98–99; cf. 102: "While people are alive, then, culture consumes nature, but when they die, nature consumes culture."
[153] Alexiou, *Ritual Lament*, 44.
[154] Seremetakis, *Last Word*, 13 and 170–174. Cf. Alexiou, *Ritual Lament*, 47: "This feast, pagan in origin and at one time forbidden by the Church, is now presided over by the priest."
[155] Ibid., 185; cf. 186: "Below the roofed enclosure of the gravestone is the *lákos* ... the 'eater of the dead.'"
[156] Ibid., 153.

there is a clear parallel between the consumption of food by the living at the memorial services and the consumption of the body of the deceased by the earth. Both kinds of food, the *koliva* ... and bread, on one hand, and the body of the deceased, on the other, must be eaten in order for the soul to enter paradise.[157]

In this explanation, there is no trace left of "the most graphic and frightening" idea of being physically eaten. The ritual consumption of *koliva* portrays this idea but also introduces a significant turn: It is not the dead who are consumed, but the living consume food just as they do in order to stay alive. The *koliva* does not stand in for the deceased, its consumption does not imply a participation in death and resurrection as with Eucharist bread, even if both share some ideas. Consuming "death cakes" means accepting—actually swallowing—the loss by performing the decomposition that happens to the deceased, but the incorporation also emphasizes that the mourners are still alive.—So far, as the accompanying lament songs point out while explaining the ritual meaning of the other mouth-work, the consumption of the dish. Both cast doubt on the principle of symbolic substitution they are based on: no utterance can compensate for the loss, no symbol can incarnate the deceased. In Danforth, this doubt is sidelined by the implicit hierarchy of the text that describes ritual practices, and cites ritual laments, to comment on them. Veteranyi's text introduces no such hierarchy but presents a polyphony and plurality of perspectives without identifying them with binary oppositions such as moderns/traditional, Western/Eastern, rational/irrational. Veteranyi's text, rather, contradicts the homogeneity of experience implied in such oppositions. This becomes apparent when the dying aunt mistrusts the transition the "death cakes" are supposed to promote, expressing her doubts *in* the ritual in the hermeneutic frame *of* the ritual:

> *Der Onkel ... drehte die Tante von einer Seite auf die andere und*
>   *wusch ihr Arme, Beine, Brust und Rücken.*
> *Die Tante kratzte sich Löcher in die Haut.*
> ...
> *Gleich geht's Dir besser, sagte er.*
> *Besser, besser! rief sie. Bevor du bei Gott ankommst, fressen dich die*
>   *Heiligen!*[158]

> "The uncle ... turned the aunt from one side to the other and washed
>   her arms, legs, chest and back.
> The aunt was scratching holes into her skin.
> ...

---

[157]Danforth, *Death Rituals*, 105.
[158]Veteranyi, *Regal*, 20.

Soon you will be better, he said.
Better, better! she cried. Before you get to God you are eaten by the Saints!"

In Veteranyi, ritual appears not as a closed interpretative cosmos that eliminates doubt but as shared practice that provides a frame and a vocabulary to articulate doubt in interpretations of life and death, and thus as a distant relative of poetic language. While Danforth's anthropological text aims at establishing the coherence of the rituals under scrutiny, Veteranyi's literary approach highlights that these practices and their interpretation are constantly subject to negotiation. Contradictions are essential to any language of lament as it speaks of disintegration. Adequately, laments formulate distress and being inconsolable by casting doubt on the—ritual, Eucharistic, secular, or other—terms they voice and on the very principle of symbolic substitution they rely on. Veteranyi's texts grants no position priority: Familiarity with the rituals is not tantamount to trust in their effectiveness, as the aunt proves, just as ignorance of the customs, and distance from their practice, does not hinder participation in them. Looking back at traditional customs—such as preparing "death cakes"—appears as one of many ways of continuing them:

> *Die Toten haben Hunger, sagte Costel.*
> *Der Stoffkalender mit den orthodoxen Feiertagen war seit Jahren abgelaufen, seit Onkel Petrus Tod. Die Feiertage waren ein Küchentuch geworden, sie warteten auf ihre Verwendung. Für mich hatte Costel keine Verwendung, ich stand neben ihm und vergaß über das Beobachten der Totenvorbereitung das Weinen.*[159]

> "The dead are hungry, Costel said.
> The fabric calendar indicating Orthodox holidays had run out years ago, since uncle Petru's death. The holidays had turned into a tea towel, they were waiting for their use. For me Costel had no use, I stood next to him and, whilst watching the burial preparations, forgot to cry."

The relative's custom gives mourning a form other than crying: uncle Costel prepares "death cakes" instead, the narrator observes him instead. The practice appears as a profanation because it customizes the Orthodox calendar, a prescription indicating when rituals have to be practiced, into a tea towel used to carry out a ritual. The theme of profanation is evoked by uncle Petru's name: Latin *Petrus*, English Peter, is the apostle opposing Paul in the issue of whether gentile Christians have to obey Jewish dietary

---

[159] Ibid., 9.

and circumcision laws (Gal. 2:11-14). Paul reports that Peter lost, therefore, since "Petru's death," what will be called Christianity turns away from the rules he had observed. Yet Veteranyi's text continues: *Das Vergessen hebt die Dinge nur deutlicher hervor.*[160] (Forgetting only accentuates things.) Illogical at first glance, this dictum nevertheless voices the psychoanalytical insight that an experience which is not realized remains ever-present as trauma. In Rilke's *Requiem*, mourning customs are foregrounded because they have been forgotten and are now missed: "Bring me customs! How bereft we are/of customs. They pass on, we [talk them down]."[161] Repeating the word *Verwendung* that denotes usage but comprises the idea of a turn (*Wendung*), Veteranyi's text suggests a conclusion of a different kind: The Orthodox-calendar-turned-tea-towel indicates that the movements of turning away from customs and re-turning to them do not contradict each other but depend on one another. Turning away from a habitual usage, or profaning it, indeed appears as prerequisite to adapting it to current needs, to modifying customs so that they can remain present. Encountering estranged customs, Veteranyi's text underlines that customs do not consist of a regulated repetitions of the ever-same but persist as usage that is applied when needed. The effects of rites and other customs are not brought about by merely following guidelines—effects such as forgetting to cry for the dead in view of burial preparations which marks the observer's distance from the ritual and, at the same time, participation in it. Customs bring about effects by way of a *Verwendung* of traditional forms, that is both by their application and their adaptation, by using them and turning them into something else, so that the ritual meets the requirements of particular situations—just like words are standardized forms that receive a different particular meaning with every usage.

Rilke's *Requiem* harps on *Gebräuche*, a plural denoting customs or traditions, while the singular (*Gebrauch*) means usage like Veteranyi's term *Verwendung* but also comprises the idea of needing or requiring (*brauchen*): *Gebräuche her! wir haben nicht genug/Gebräuche. Alles geht und wird verredet.*[162] (Bring me customs! How bereft we are/of customs. They pass on, we [talk them down].) What marks Rilke's as a particularly modern outlook onto rituals is an ambivalence quite different from Veteranyi's postmodern link of forgetting and carrying on: Rilke's lines lament that customs are vanishing and being talked down (as obsolete, backward, irrational, etc.), at the same time, they participate in *verreden* customs insofar as this itself rather obsolete verb also denotes driving away by means of speech.[163] This is the effect of the *Requiem* that speaks of needing customs instead of using

---

[160]Ibid.
[161]Rilke, *Requiem for a Friend*, 265; my brackets.
[162]Rilke, *Requiem*, RSW1:653.
[163]*DW* 25:999, s.v. "verreden."

them, asking in irrealis mood: *Ob man nicht dennoch hätte Klagefrauen/ auftreiben müssen?* ([Oughtn't we, still], have found wailing-women?)[164] The norm this question refers back to has irreversibly been broken, no wailing-women have been sought, the custom of dirges is out of usage. Wilce explains, citing Urban, why the modern nostalgia that points out the need to lament in a proposition is no way to usher in dirges but drives them away:

> "In cultures with a developed ritual wailing or lamentation tradition, as in many central Brazilian Amerindian societies, grief is expressed by means of formalized crying. Your stylized weeping tells others of your grief. Contrast this expressive style with one in which an individual says referentially—as is often the case in American culture—'I'm feeling sad.'" Urban situates this difference in relation to broader contrasts. In all societies, language serves as a tool for reference—"talking *about*" something. Its referential function becomes paramount in Western ideologies of language. However, there is no cross-cultural agreement that emotional expression should primarily consist of rational reference to feelings—"I'm feeling sad."[165]

Propositions do not guarantee sincerity or authenticity—on the contrary, Urban notes: "Ritual wailing is precisely not talking about feeling. That is what makes it convincing."[166] Propositions privilege clarity in naming emotions, ritual wailing privileges the display of affectedness.[167] Ritual plaints, therefore, rarely articulate statements (for instance about what death is) but majorly communicate transformation. They do not only describe transformations of life brought about by death, funerals, weddings, or exile, but seek to have a transforming effect. Ritual plaints are involved in what they lament over, or complain about, therefore, they are neither primarily (distancing) statements nor majorly (spontaneous) expressions. Transmuting emotions and forms, such as sorrow into

---

[164]Rilke, *Requiem*, RSW1:653/*Requiem for a Friend*, 265.
[165]Wilce, *Crying Shame*, 130; cit. Greg Urban, *Metaphysical Community*, 175–176.
[166]Urban, "Ritual Wailing," 397.
[167]The relevance of this differentiation becomes apparent in Holst-Warhaft's analysis of Greek dirges, wherein it is ignored. She presupposes: "I will not attempt to deal with the non-verbal elements of this lament—with voice quality, melodic and rhythmic elements, gesture, etc., but simply with a text as it appears in transcription" (*Dangerous Voices*, 55). Later on, she states: "The most obvious feature of the language ... is its dry, impersonal tone, its apparent lack of emotion" (67). This is a consequence of ignoring most linguistic means of communicating emotion. Holst-Warhaft thus reaches a conclusion that contradicts her presupposition: "Like the cries that puncture the text, so sobs, sighs and sudden intakes of breath are integral to the performance of lament. Singers of dramatic or plaintive songs from opera to blues will use their breath for heightened emotional effect. Since soul and breath are synonymous in Greek culture ..., manipulations of breath in laments may carry additional emotional weight" (70).

hope and lament into praise, as many psalms do,[168] is thus essential to "ritual laments in the fullest sense," as Wilce notes, "i.e. those designed to *transform* and not only express."[169] Turner conceptualized the principle that "ritual is transformative,"[170] following up on van Genneps sequencing of rites of passage "into *rites of separation, transition rites*, and *rites of incorporation*."[171] If rites of passage transfer individuals or groups from one social "position" (Gennep) or "state" into a different one, Turner concludes, they are not stable and distinct, but equivocal: "during the intervening liminal period, the state of the ritual subject (the 'passenger') is ambiguous; he passes through a realm that has few or none of the past or coming state."[172] Removed from their previous state but not yet incorporated into their future one, liminal ritual subjects are "structurally ... invisible"[173] as they cannot be grasped in the cultural terms in between which they are moving.[174] The symbols of liminal stages are, therefore, often borrowed from other contexts, in initiation rites for instance from death, metabolism, or birth.[175] Danforth and Seremetakis describe Greek funerary rites, from dirges to second burials, as a liminal process that transposes the deceased and the living to different physical, social, and emotional states.[176] Turner's concept of liminality permits to sum up: "The symbolism attached to and surrounding the liminal persona"—such as the consumption of the "death cakes" *koliva*—"give[s] an outward and visible form to an inward and conceptual process."[177] The consumption and the accompanying dirges do not merely depict the decomposition of the body and the absolution of the soul but see themselves as promoting this transfer while also showing that they do not symbolically stand in for the deceased. The doubt in symbolic substitution is owing to ritual liminality since the transfer that can be named only in catachresis, still, happens de facto.

It is misleading when Holst-Warhaft characterizes laments as "reinforcing the concept of liminality ... through their metaphors of transition."[178] Rites of passage transfer subjects into a different state, they no not merely cast something in different terms as metaphors do. Rites of passage seek, as Turner says, "to effect an ontological transformation; ... not merely to

---

[168] Chapter 3, 171.
[169] Wilce, *Crying Shame*, 29–30; Cf. Seremetakis, *Last Word*, 2: "Mourning ceremonies are transformative and not merely expressive performances."
[170] Turner, "Betwixt and Between," 235; ibid.: "... ceremony confirmatory."
[171] Gennep, *Passage*, 10–11.
[172] Turner, "Betwixt and Between," 235.
[173] Ibid., 234–235.
[174] Ibid., 236.
[175] Ibid.
[176] Danforth, *Death Rituals*, 36–37; Seremetakis, *Last Word*, 55 & 70.
[177] Turner, "Betwixt and Between," 235.
[178] Holst-Warhaft, *Dangerous Voices*, 19.

convey an unchanging substance from one position to another by quasi-mechanical force."[179] The differentiation between metaphoricity and ritual liminality does not follow the path of devaluating figurative language as "just a metaphor," on the contrary: the distinction between literal and metaphorical usage presupposes statements as the standard form of speech, which is an approach utterly unsuited to comprehending literary language, the language of lamenting and complaining that communicates by undermining structures, and ritual speech that seeks to bring about an ontological shift. And yet, the assumption of a metaphoricity is pervasive in anthropological and critical studies of ritual plaints. Wickett thus speaks of the "the metaphoric domain of lament,"[180] and Danforth explains *koliva* in terms of "the metaphor of human beings as food."[181] The crux is that explaining ritual laments as metaphors implies the position of a privileged observer whose hermeneutic sovereignty enables them to name in plain terms what the rite casts in supposedly figurative language. Veteranyi's text does not assume that there can be such a position, therefore, it parallels the observer's with the ritualist's outlook onto customs. This parallelism, however, has to do without an explanation of the kind Holst-Warhaft gives, citing a dirge noted in Danforth that speaks from the point of view of the deceased:

"Just tell them that I have married and taken a good wife.
I have taken the tombstone as mother-in-law, the black earth as wife ..."
... By the use of such metaphor, the finality of death is denied; it becomes a transition rather than a permanent state.[182]

Customs such as second burials, which display decomposition, indeed suggest that death is a transition, as does the concept of resurrection. Weddings are rites of passage[183] paralleled with death not only in Greek dirges[184] since both imply a separation from the present community. Yet while a wedding is a transition, marriage is indeed "a permanent state," no

---

[179]Turner, "Betwixt and Between," 238.
[180]Wickett, *For the Living*, xvii.
[181]Danforth, *Death Rituals*, 99.
[182]Holst-Warhaft, *Dangerous Voices*, 19; cit. Danforth, *Death Rituals*, 81.
[183]Gennep, *Rites of Passage*, 116–145.
[184]Alexiou, *Ritual Lament*, 120pp.; Stears, "Death Becomes Her," 144pp.; in tragedy Rehm, *Marriage to Death*. The parallel is drawn particularly for unmarried deceased; Holst-Warhaft, *Dangerous Voices*, 19: "Among Iraqi Jews, as recently as the 1950s, ... lamenters would chant antiphonally at such funerals, alternating wedding songs with laments." They are buried in their wedding apparel (Alexiou ibid.), the dowry is taken to the graveyard (Seremetakis, *Last Word*, 148); cf. Veteranyi, *Regal*, 37: "The shroud had been a wedding gown." Cf. parallel Kligman, *The Wedding of the Dead*; Wickett, *For the Living*, 86–91.

mere passage, as Holst-Warhaft erroneously suggests. Her assumption that paralleling death with a wedding aims at negating the "finality of death" is adopted from Danforth, too:

> The metaphor of death as marriage is ultimately an attempt to mediate the opposition between life and death. It attempts to do this by establishing marriage as a mediating term and then asserting that death is marriage, *that death is not what it really is*, a polar term in the opposition between life and death, but that it is the mediating term.[185]

This explanation of dirges suffers from a structural misunderstanding: Neither analogies nor metaphors identify a tertium comparationis in order to claim that something is that in-between, rather, analogies and metaphors identify two obviously different phenomena because they have a particular trait in common (the tertium comparationis). Highlighting this trait permits of a particular insight into one, or ideally both, of the identified phenomena. Lamenting death as a marriage does not establish marriage as a third between life and death but emphasizes the irreversible separation from the family that both have in common in a patrilineal world without divorce.[186] Yet Danforth's explanation also suffers from a misconception of its own hermeneutic capacities: Lamenting death as marriage does not imply the claim that the deceased is not really dead but casts the departure in terms of a passage whose other side (married life) is known and discernible: Just as the deceased played a role in their social context in life, they are obliged to the grave in death. The analogy of death and marriage is rhetorically a metaphor, yet its ontological status is more complex: While metaphors casts something as something *else* than what it intrinsically *is*, in and of itself (for instance Achilles as a lion[187]), it is neither known nor knowable what death is in and of itself because death is the end of the possibility to know and experience. What death *is* is exactly the question that paralleling it with marriage seeks to answer. This is the fundamental hermeneutic difficulty Danforth ignores when he explains the dirge as asserting "that death is not what it really is" while he is certain to know that it is "a polar term in the opposition between life and death," which is a mere ex negativo: death is the opposite of everything that can be experienced. Phenomenology as well as anthropology suggests that what is particular about death is that there seems to be no *as such*.[188] "Death does not just exist," Barley thus notes: "In order to have coherence and to find its place, it has to be integrated into a

---

[185] Danforth, *Death Rituals*, 83; my italics.
[186] Ibid.: "Like death marriage involves departure and separation."
[187] Aristotle, *Rhetoric*, 1406b/3.4.1.
[188] Jacques Derrida, *Apories*, 35–37.

wider scheme of things." One of the strategies for grasping death in spite of it's a-phenomenal character "is to imagine death as being *like* something else that is more readily accessible,"[189] that is to say portraying death in heuristic metaphors.

The issue of explaining ritual plaints as metaphoric is not limited to dirges and portrayals of death but merely culminates with its heuristic inaccessibility. Approaching ritual language requires reflecting the observer's position and relinquishing the theoretical prerogative of statements. Danforth and Holst-Warhaft read dirges as statements about death instead of communications of emotion that promote ontological transfers by transposing conventionalized forms into individual speech. The customizing of ritual plaints—the use and alteration of metric, music, and figurative conventions of ritual laments songs, wailing, and gestures—formulates structures such as statements and metaphors.[190] Yet they serve neither to name nor to conceal emotions but to communicate how the world appears to those who have reason to lament or complain, and how the world should appear to others who shall be moved upon hearing the plaints. Ritual or other plaints are not metaphorical just because they differ from the point of view, or vocabulary, of observers who see themselves as hermeneutic corrective such as Danforth: "By asserting similarity where there exists difference, by demonstrating identity where there exists opposition, metaphors force us to see things in a different light ... The power of metaphors lies in their ability to change the way we view our world."[191] Metaphors do have a heuristic function; however, it lies not in distorting a plain, non-metaphorical view but in forming a hermeneutic context that can be called "world." The corrective presupposed by calling ritual plaints "metaphors" may be part of the cultural context under scrutiny, as Seremetakis notes:

> Danforth interprets the alternation between ritual cognition and ideology of common sense as women's rational and "realistic acceptance" of the biological separation of death. He ignores that this polarity between ritual cognition and common sense is gender-based and that the local male ideology coincides with that of western scientism.[192]

---

[189]Nigel Barley, *Dancing on the Grave*, 151.
[190]Cf. Margaret Jaques, "Metaphern als Kommunikationsstrategie" (Mesopotamia); Tolbert, "Women Cry with Words" (Karelia).
[191]Danforth, *Death Rituals*, 82.
[192]Seremetakis, *Last Word*, 246; cf. Danforth, *Death Rituals*, 50: "The corpse may have failed to decompose fully because the deceased himself or one of his ancestors committed a sin that was not forgiven. ... Some villagers, particularly men and younger people, offer a more naturalistic explanation for the fact that some corpses fail to decompose fully. They argue that the condition of the remains when they are exhumed is influenced by drugs taken prior to death, by the quality of the soil, and by other natural factors."

Caraveli-Chaves also describes "men's ambivalent attitude toward women's lamentation ranging from outright hostility to uneasy mocking of the tradition," and relates them to the contrast of ritual and modernity.[193] Calling for reservation with regard to installing a corrective to the observed rituals and their explanation by ritualists is not to rule out critical distance or terminology, rather, it calls for an added attentiveness so as to reflect on the role of the observer in order to grasp the whole discourse of the respective ritual plaint. The crux in Danforth's observation of second burials and accompanying dirges, which lacks sufficient reflection of this kind, is that he grants only his view "reality," for instance in noting: "the mediation attempted by the exhumation fails because the contradiction between life and death is real. The exhumation can never bring the dead back to life." It is him who assumes that exhuming bodies follows the logic that digging out initiates the passage from death to life just as the burial initiated the passage from life to death.[194] An analysis of the "death cakes" *koliva* rather suggests that the exhumation seeks to find full decay—and in ambivalent addition to that, probably also the return to life. Liminality is not only the status of ritual subjects experiencing a passage between states of life, liminal is also the language of lamenting and complaining: ritual plaints undermine the difference between speech and sound in techniques such as wailing, thus evoking distinctions such as between social or gender roles in order to delimit the disorganization.

A prominent form of ritual plaints for negotiating doubts in reciprocity and giving voice to liminality is antiphony, a polyphone chant that, as Seremetakis sums up, "emerges as an articulation between these linguistic and extralinguistic media, between poetry and prose, music and screaming."[195] Antiphony is a ritual form of the consumption of referential and phonetic structures of language that constitutes and, at the same time, undermines reciprocity. Antiphony is, therefore, a prominent target for criticism in ritual plaints aiming at silencing them.

## Antiphony: Response and Dissent

The function of antiphony is best illustrated by an example: As far as we know, Roman burial rites started when the dying did not respond any

---

[193] Caraveli-Chaves, "Bridge between Worlds," 130; Wickett, *For the Living*, 107. Cf. Rasmussen, "Grief at Seeing," 392 on the *techawait* ritual of Niger Tuareg: "Men told me matter-of-factly that the women's cries were 'not real grief, only ritual cries', whereas women told me that the women were crying from 'very real grief, in seeing their daughter leave.'"
[194] Danforth, *Death Rituals*, 66–67.
[195] Seremetakis, *Last Word*, 106.

more, as Dutsch explains: "when the relatives summoned the deceased by name (*conclamatio*); no reply was taken as a proof of death."[196] The rite ends with *illicet* (you may go) as soon as the liminality brought about by a corpse who had just been alive moments ago is delimited, that is when the ashes of the cremated have been gathered and the differentiation between life and death, bodies and bones has been reestablished. "Only then were the people standing around and responding to the lamentations (*fletibus*) of the *praefica* [professional mourner and leading voice] free to go."[197] Antiphony is centered on the difficulty of receiving a response and establishing reciprocity—on the lacking answer that marks death, and the reestablished exchange among mourners. The dirge is addressed to the deceased, who cannot respond anymore,[198] so that others respond to the lament in the deceased's name. "Antiphony," Seremetakis explains, "is an extension of the ethic of helping"[199] wherein the voices of some stand in for the pain of others in order to reformulate the community that has been disorganized with the death of one of its members. The roles in antiphonic dirges are distributed in accordance with the responsibilities, ascribed to different degrees of relationship, for someone who cannot speak for themselves such as a deceased. Exercising the responsibility means responding to other relatives, or community members, in antiphonic laments.[200] Ritual plaints are, more often than not, set in kinship contexts and antiphony is, as Seremetakis explains, a form of "weaving conflict" between family members that have divergent interpretations of the life, death, and heirs of deceased relatives.[201] Just as the line separating life from death is porous during the rite of passage of burial, and family relations are negotiated and redefined, the differentiation between language, voice, and sound is undermined in polyphonic antiphonic lament. Death becomes apparent in language when the name does not evoke the named any longer, thus eliciting doubt in the referential and representational claims of articulate language that lie at the basis of talking to someone and speaking in someone's name. Rilke's *Requiem* thus addresses the friend whose death it laments, voicing doubt in the communicative functions of language: "[Do] you hear that I am wailing now?" (*Hörst Du, dass ich klage?*)[202] An adequate communication of pain, the poem proceeds to point out, would require the destruction of the aesthetic and hermeneutic texture of the text that enables communication:

---

[196]Dutsch, "Nenia," 259.
[197]Ibid., 262.
[198]Ibid., 265. Cf. Alexiou, *Ritual Lament*, 136–137; Danforth, *Death Rituals*, 117; Caraveli-Chaves, "Bridge between Worlds," 141.
[199]Seremetakis, *Last Word*, 100.
[200]For Greek contexts Alexiou, *Ritual Lament*, 12–13.
[201]Seremetakis, *Last Word*, 126–158.
[202]Rilke, *Requiem for a Friend*, 265/*Requiem*, RSW1:653.

*Ich möchte meine Stimme wie ein Tuch*
*hinwerfen über deines Todes Scherben*
*und zerrn an ihr, bis sie in Fetzen geht,*
*und alles, was ich sage, müßte so*
*zerlumpt in dieser Stimme gehn und frieren;*[203]

I'd throw my voice as if it was a cloth
over all the fragments of your death,
tear at [it] until it [goes] to tatters,
and everything I say would have to go
in [the] rags [of this voice] and freeze;[204]

The destruction of the phonetic, syntactic, and semantic coherence of speech—summed up in the idea of a "voice"—suggests itself as the poem's metric and semantic organization seems to negate more than to portray the lamented loss: the structures of speech proceed as if nothing was missing. Rilke's lines do not in fact carry out any disorganization of speech; rather, it appears to be averted by spelling out the wish. This adherence to propositional discourse is due to the problem that if the verse did realize the wish to voice loss and pain by way of ruptures in voice and text, it would become hard or impossible to comprehend what they are communicating, to whom, or in response to what. The broken voice would, in turn, require regularly organized speech to explain the disorganization—which would primarily point out that the disorganization of the voice communicates nothing. Ritual antiphony confronts this difficulty by way of voicing pain, loss, and sorrow in *conventionalized* forms so that the disorganization is comprehensible *as* lament. Seremetakis explains: "the voice of the mourner supplements the silence of the corpse,"[205] yet rather than imitating the living voice of the deceased, the laments disrupt articulate speech and the harmony of gestures and chants (just as the "death cakes" disrupt the representational claims of Eucharist bread-as-corps): "Women represent the violence of death though their own bodies. Their postures, gestures and general facial expressions function as corporeal texts which reaudit the experience of death as passage and disorder on behalf of the now silent and immobile dead."[206]

Social and the linguistic disorganization correlate in antiphony: Antiphonic lament rites are a liminal means for achieving a social re-organization by way of a dis-organization of language. A large part of the *Iliad* is devoted to pondering the ritual organization of the consumption of social and linguistic

---

[203]Rilke, *Requiem*, RSW1:653.
[204]Rilke, *Requiem for a Friend*, 265.
[205]Seremetakis, *Last Word*, 97.
[206]Ibid., 74.

structures. In Hector's funeral, the dissolution of articulate speech into moaning is given a conventionalized place and function: The lament song (*goos*) of Andromache, Hecuba, and Helena is each answered by moaning:

> "so she spoke, weeping: the women added their own lament [*stenachonto*, groaned]" (*Iliad* 24.746)
> "So she spoke, weeping, and stirred up unending lamentation [*goon*]." (760)
> "So she spoke, weeping, and the countless throng lamented [*estene*, groaned]." (776)

*Goos* is Homer's usual term for laments, cries, and other forms of moaning or groaning (*stenō*) and maintains this function in Aeschylus. Since the disorganization of articulate speech into moaning and wailing is given the conventionalized place of a response in antiphonic lament, even the reduction of speech to mere noise remains comprehensible as a linguistic sign and part of an exchange—instead of decomposing reciprocity and comprehensibility, as in Achilles' lament for Patroclus: Starting in book 18, Achilles is characterized mostly by the epithet "groaning" (18.323) which is the same verb as the women's wailing in response, and in book 23 "the lamentation for Hektor at Troy merges with the laments for Patroklos in the Achaean camp."[207] Achilles, however, disrupts the ritual order he commands.[208]

> "... let us now drive close
> to Patroklos, and mourn him: this is the dead man's privilege.
> Then, when we've had our fill of painful lamentation [*olooio ... gooio*],
> We'll unyoke our horses and all take our evening meal together.
> So he spoke: they all cried out as one [*ōmōxan aollees*], and Achilles led them:" (*Iliad* 23.8–12)

Rather than naming the "moaning," these lines convey a phonetic impression of it when the emphasized O of *goos* spreads out into the vocabulary, just as Achilles' lamenting transcends the ritual frame. While he orders the myrmidons to stop (*Iliad* 23.48) and they comply and return to work (53–54), he does not respond to their actions but goes on: "Pēleus's son lay on the shoreline of the thunderous sea, heavily sighing [*stenachōn*], with all his Myrmidons around him" (59–60) and demands more lamenting: "he spoke, and stirred in them all the urge for lamentation [*gooio*]" (108). The organization of lamenting in ritual antiphony aims at nothing less

---

[207] Nicholas Richardson, *The Iliad: A Commentary*, 6.167.
[208] Not least as he times the feast before the funeral; ibid., 166–167.

than reestablishing temporal continuity[209] which has come to a halt as, on the one hand, Hector's corps is consumed neither by decomposition nor by Achilles' mutilations,[210] but Achilles, on the other hand, is as consumed with grief as Patroclus' corpse by the flames.[211] The extraordinary role of the antiphonic lament for Hector that re-institutes the progression of time (and war) is emphasized in the singular vocabulary of the passage: "singer," "dirge," and "leader of the chorus," that is to say "ἀοιδός, θρῆνος, θρῆνεῖν, and ἔξαρχος occur only here in the poem."[212] Lamenting outside any ritual order, as Achilles does, is excessive in the *Iliad* because the disorganization of articulation and reciprocity does not lead into a reorganization. In ritual antiphony, the decomposition of structures allows for their negotiation and alteration. Modernizations, however, regard ritual plaints as an excess of convention that prohibits spontaneity and individuality. Veteranyi confronts both views in a portray of antiphonic lament. Unlike Rilke's *Requiem*, Veteranyi's text does not comment on the destruction of speech as utterance of pain but undermines the syntactical texture of articulate speech in favor of ambiguity, the logical equivalent of polyphony:

> *Meine Mutter schluchzte ins Telefon: Ich bin böse mit Gott! Er hält nicht zu uns!*
> *Dann hielt sie ihrer toten Schwester den Hörer hin. Aus dem Apparat drang ein rumänisches Klagelied. Neben der Tür schluchzte Costel. Mama Reta ist gegangen!*
> *Er schlug sich auf den Kopf, ins Gesicht, auf die Lippen, schlug sich die Wörter in den Mund zurück.*[213]
>
> *Ich setzte mich zur Tante, die sich immer noch das Klagelied aus dem Telefon anhören mußte: Sehnsucht und Trauer haben mich gepackt, sie drücken mich wie ein enger Gürtel.*[214]
>
> *Meine Mutter saß am Tisch mit den Verwandten im Telefon und weinte. Sie schüttelte sich. Sie schlug mit der Stirn gegen ihre Faust. Die Blumen auf ihrer Bluse hüpften rauf und runter. Sie ist gegangen! Unsere Mutter ist gegangen!*

---

[209]Priamos' outline of the ritual emphasizes this purpose in counting days: "*Nine days* we would mourn him in our halls, and then/on the *tenth* we'd inter him, and there'd be public feasting;/on the *eleventh* we'd raise the funeral mound over him—/and on the *twelfth*, if we have to, we'll join battle once again" (*Iliad* 24.664–667; my italics).
[210]*Iliad* 24.414–418.
[211]*Iliad* 23.182. The disintegration of articulate discourse and figure is underlined by a further parallel: Just as Achilles is standing at Patroklos' stake "ceaselessly sobbing" or groaning [*stenachizōn*] (23.225), the sea groans [*estenen*] when he finally falls silent and asleep.
[212]Richardson, *The Iliad* 6.351.
[213]Veteranyi, *Regal*, 15.
[214]Ibid., 17.

*Meine Mutter weinte auch meine Tränen. Ihre Stimme drang wie Glassplitter in meinen Kopf ein.*[215]

"My mother was sobbing into the telephone: I am angry with God! He is not on our side!
Then she presented the receiver to her dead sister. A Romanian dirge was sounding from the telephone. Uncle Costel was sobbing next to the door. Mama Reta has gone!
He was beating his head, his face, his lips, he was beating the words back into his mouth.
...
I sat next to the aunt, who still had to listen to the dirge from the telephone:
Longing and sorrow have taken hold of me, they press me like a tight belt.
...
My mother was sitting at the table with the relatives in the telephone and cried. She was shaking. She was beating her forehead against her fist. The flowers on her blouse were bouncing up and down.
She is gone! Our Mother has gone!
My mother cried my tears, too. Her voice penetrated my head like a glass splinter."

Adapting ritual antiphony to a world shaped by technology, the dirge transmitted by telephone translates kinship relations into geographical terms: distant relatives sing, close relatives sob in response.[216] Veteranyi's scene of technology-based antiphony portrays liminality by contrasting ontological with grammatical structures: It is still possible to address the aunt as she is physically present,[217] yet the deceased is no longer capable of the self-relation implied in the reflexive German verb *sich anhören* (to listen for oneself). Gestures of lament—beating the head and face—display the self-relation that is lost with death, the end of the self. The gestures reassure the mourners of their remaining self-relation, an assurance that is necessary since the aunt's death has disorganized her relatives' integrity, too. They are seized by the correlation of the dead aunt, who has fallen mute, with the "relatives in the telephone," whose voices replace hers: Located not on but "in the telephone," their voices seem to have lost their bodies just as, vice versa, her body has lost its voice. Corresponding to what Seremetakis calls an "ethic of helping" underlying ritual antiphony,[218] "the relatives in the

---

[215]Ibid., 21.
[216]This is the order of Greek ritual antiphony; Alexiou, *Ritual Lament*, 12–13.
[217]Ibid., 21: *Das ist die Stirn der Tante, dachte ich./Das ist noch ihre Stirn.* (This is the aunt's forehead, I thought./This is still her forehead.)
[218]Seremetakis, *Last Word*, 100.

telephone" stand in for the crying uncle, the narrator, and her mother, just as the mother steps in to cry the narrator's tears in her place. This exchange, however, consumes clear distinctions between positions: "Mama Reta," the aunt, is not the same as "our mother." The polyphony of voices makes it unclear who is the "me" pressed by a "tight belt," whether this is a line of the dirge, or an interior monologue of the narrator listening to the dirge. Antiphony undermines the distinction of positions, not least that between ritual practitioner and observer. Blurring the line between insider and outsider is constitutive for ritual antiphony, as a brief glance at Seremetakis' anthropological analysis of rituals in the Greek Mani allows to point out. Just like in Veteranyi's tele/anti/phony, sobbing is part of the discourse:

"The acoustic signification in the lament can be presented as a single, tripartite structure: sob/discourse/sob. The movement from the nonlinguistic (sob) to linguistic media is antiphonic."[219] It is worth noting that the discourse Seremetakis describes undermines the schematic distinction between "nonlanguage" and "language"[220] just as it decomposes articulation and syntax. For Seremetakis continues: "Stylized sobbing establishes the aesthetic-acoustic structure of *moirolói* as a signifying system autonomous and independent of any specific verbal content."[221] The sobbing is significant exactly because it differs from articulate speech; it confirms emotionally what has been articulated in propositional discourse:

> This antiphony seals the juridical value of speech through nonlinguistic expression of pain in a manner analogous to the acoustic and bodily techniques by which the chorus confirms, resonates, and memorializes the juridical authenticity of the entire performance of the *koriféa* (soloist).[222]

The alteration between sobbing and articulate propositions constructs pain and mourning as shared. In this ritual context, pain is valid not as a private sensation best expressed by silence as the modern paradigm of the inwardness of emotion would dictate, rather, sorrow and pain are valid as a phenomenon that is "socially constructed in antiphonic relations."[223] Only if somebody feels with it is pain valid as a basis for claiming a different social role. Therefore, "the histrionic display is an essential element of lament performance," as Wickett points out.[224] It is from the point of view of the modern paradigm in particular that ritual performance seems histrionic. These two notions collide in Veteranyi's text, casting the historical antithesis

---

[219] Ibid., 116; cf. Wickett, *For the Living*, 106.
[220] Seremetakis, *Last Word*, 117.
[221] Ibid., 117.
[222] Ibid., 116–117.
[223] Ibid., 120.
[224] Wickett, *For the Living*, 71.

of modernity and tradition in an antiphonic structure. However, Veteranyi's text also outlines that the position of modern distance to ritual becomes an element of antiphonic performance. The silence of listeners is as relevant to ritual antiphony as the pause to music, Seremetakis explains: "The men are *not* ignored by the women mourners during the ceremony, nor are they oblivious to what is happening within the circle of mourners; they function as a silent chorus."[225] This same logic can be found in Veteranyi's text, counteracting the narrator's distance from the rituals: From the point of view of the ritual, the at-times skeptical audience functions as witnesses of the plaints and the distress they voice. Ritual antiphony expounds that what is essential is not agreement but being listened to because it marks the difference between life and death: "*Hearing is the doubling of the other's discourse.* ... The absence of hearing is equivalent to the 'silent' death. The 'silent' death is also the social death of the mourner without witness."[226] Relying solely on the voice to establish interpersonal relations, the technological medium of telephony that might appear as a disruptive element in Veteranyi's text indeed foregrounds the ritual's social purpose.

Telephony, however, casts doubt on the attribution of voices to speakers just as ritual antiphony casts doubt on the link between (felt) emotion and (expected) utterance while undermining articulation in wailing, and audibility in polyphony. Wickett's anthropological study of contemporary Upper Egypt dirges explains the phonetics of ritual antiphony as medium of social and psychological negotiation: "Through the device of antithesis the lamenter accentuates the ambiguities surrounding death, and the psychological dilemma created by loss."[227] The ambiguity is voiced in dissonance, dissecting the inarticulate tone of crying in the articulate lexicon:

> Orchestrated by the interaction between the *badaya* [lead singer] and her respondent and the creation of a heterophonous convergence of voices, the experience of shared sorrow is created. ... the *badaya* and her respondent may sing different lines simultaneously ... but their voices still merge at the cadences in a single, sustained sound, "aaa."[228]

Veteranyi's literary text points out that the fragmented speech of antiphony causes further ruptures when the voice "penetrated" the narrator's "head like a glass splinter." Since ritual antiphony fosters liminality to bring about reorganization by way of a disorganization, it may have a traumatizing effect, adding to the shock, or sorrow, caused by the lamented loss or pain; the next section will elaborate on this issue. The violence caused

---

[225] Seremetakis, *Last Word*, 100.
[226] Ibid., 104.
[227] Wickett, *For the Living*, 94.
[228] Ibid., 106.

by disorganizing language is displayed particularly when the uncle is, in Veteranyi, "beating the words back into his mouth": No word seems appropriate for communicating the pain of grief, however, tearing apart the texture of his speech, and replacing it by a violent gesture of speechlessness, is comprehensible *as* communicating grief since it follows the gestural code of a mourning ritual. Comparable to the institution of literature, the conventionality of lament rituals permits undermining and disorganizing conventional structures of language in order to communicate a unique affectedness and emotion that is comprehensible as such. Literature as well as ritual requires the recognition of the disorganization of those structures of language that usually permit comprehension as variation of a form, therefore, genre and ritual conventions are a constitutive, even if constantly re-negotiated, element of both.

The form, and deformation, of discourse in ritual antiphony relates to its social purpose. Veteranyi evokes the kinship context of many ritual laments in the tribal logic in of the lamenter's cry: "I am angry with God! He is not on our side!" Ritual antiphony is a form of a controversial reformulation of self and community, including criticism in social stereotypes.[229] Antiphonic ritual plaints are, as Solzhenitsyn says with a contemptuous ring, "politics" (политика).[230] Ritual lament and antiphony in particular inspired criticism as it does not aim at settling cases. Wickett explains: "The phenomenon of antiphonic performance ... emulates the turn-taking of dialogue," yet: "The aim is not unison but divergence."[231] Just as neurotic complaints, ritual antiphony voices conflict in a shift between key elements of speech: While in ritual lament, unlike in neurotic complaint, occasion and expression correlate according to social convention, expression and emotion might differ widely. One does not need to feel what one, still, has to say. This shift, considered pathological in neurosis, is element of the liminality of rite in ritual laments. Yet it is cause for concern in both contexts. Antiphony causes strife since setting a limit to liminality proves to be difficult, as Achilles' endless mourning and wrath demonstrates. Transforming pain and sorrow into concrete accusations and demands can, nevertheless, be conceptualized as part of the passage ritual plaints perform.[232] Yet while ritual antiphony foregrounds the role of hearing in communication, the reciprocity it establishes is no harmony but dissent. Solzhenitsyn's 1959 story "Matryona's Home," thus portrays ritual antiphony performed by wailing-women (плакальщицы) as "a coldly calculated age-old ritual" (искони заведенный порядок) every bit as double-tongued and mendacious as Soviet

---

[229]Wickett, *For the Living*, 11; Caraveli-Chaves, "Bridge between Worlds," 138pp.; Holst-Warhaft, *Dangerous Voices*, 41pp.; Seremetakis, *Last Word*, 126pp.; Liu, "Expressive Depths."
[230]Aleksandr Solschenizyn, "Matryona's Home," 51/"Матрёнин Двор," 143.
[231]Wickett, *For the Living*, 179.
[232]Ninoshvili, "Wailing"; Worobec, "Death Ritual," 24–25.

rule.²³³ Criticism in ritual plaints often targets wailing-women and forms a gender bias against ritual plaints that informs Freud's discourse as well as current debates on "the female complaint." Therefore, it appears worth the while to look into this strain of the debasement of plaintive language linked to gender.

In antiquity, the institution of wailing-women is present in the Greek context and, as Alexiou somewhat carelessly puts it, "prevalent among the more civilized Chinese, Egyptians and Romans as among more primitive peoples, and it survives today among the Greeks and other Balkan peoples, in Asia Minor and in Spain."²³⁴ The Tanakh frequently mentions wailing-women, and they have been common in many Jewish diaspora communities until modernity.²³⁵ In such heterogeneous realms as Upper Egypt,²³⁶ Rajasthan,²³⁷ and Styria,²³⁸ wailing-women are still a part of some funerals. Three points are cited as reasons for reservations against ritual plaints. A first point that easily appears disconcerting under the modern paradigm of the inwardness of authentic emotion is a lack of spontaneity. Holst-Warhaft's statement is true for all of these institutions: "There was nothing spontaneous about the ancient Greek lament."²³⁹ A second point of criticism is that wailing-women mourn not only the losses in their own circle of family and friends but intone dirges at other funerals, too—voicing, it may seem, a pain they do not feel, which suggests that ritual antiphony is, as Amelang puts it, "less the expression of emotional crisis than a form of dissimulation."²⁴⁰ This practice is based on a shift of reference, as Wickett explains: "As well as lamenting the dead, at each funeral the performers 'lament their own.'"²⁴¹ After reassuring us that "these women are not professional mourners in any sense," which would apparently make their performance invalid in Danforth's eyes, he explains along the same lines: "They are usually women who have become good singers and have learned many laments because they have had much experience with death. Often the women who lead the singing are themselves in mourning and through their singing express their own grief for their own dead."²⁴² Skepticism about the sincerity of antiphonic wailing is neither new nor indicating its disappearance, as a passage from the New Testament demonstrates, in

---

²³³Solschenizyn, "Matryona's Home," 51/"Матрёнин Двор," 142–143.
²³⁴Alexiou, *Ritual Lament*, 10.
²³⁵Schroer, "Biblische Klagetraditionen," 86pp.; Paloma Díaz-Mas, "Sephardic Songs of Mourning and Dirges"; Tova Gamliel, "She Who Mourns Will Cry."
²³⁶Wickett, *For the Living*.
²³⁷Ajay Sekher, "Gender, Caste, and Fiction."
²³⁸As witnessed by the author.
²³⁹Holst-Warhaft, *Dangerous Voices*, 103.
²⁴⁰Amelang, "Mourning," 25.
²⁴¹Wickett, *For the Living*, 71. Cf. Homer, *Iliad* 19.301–302: "So she spoke, weeping: the women lamented with her, for Patroklos professedly, but each one for her own sorrows."
²⁴²Danforth, *Death Rituals*, 73.

which Jesus mocks his adversaries: "They are like children sitting in the marketplace and calling to one another, 'We played the flute for you, and you did not dance; we wailed [*ethrēnēsamen*: sang a dirge], and you did not weep.'"²⁴³ In this passage, ritual antiphony appears as shorthand for obstinate social conformity, expecting that the Messiah can be given orders he will follow such as, in ritual antiphony, wailing is followed by sobbing or beating.²⁴⁴

Crucial is that modern criticism in the lacking authenticity of ritual practices like antiphony often duplicates traditional discourses as it ignores that the lacking possibility of self-determination, and the mocking of a supposed insincerity, may be part of what is bewailed in the ritual. In Aeschylus' *Libation Bearers* the unnamed chorus-leader, a female slave, praises—or marvels at—Orestes' wet nurse for her "unpaid pain" over a child she had been paid to raise.²⁴⁵ The astonishment points out that dirges and wailing belonged to the duties social inferiors took for payment. This payment is the third, and probably most important, point raised as vouching against the sincerity, and social productivity, of wailing-women "because they pre[y] on the grieving."²⁴⁶ This notion ignores that professional mourners are mostly socially and economically marginalized, often widows,²⁴⁷ who have experienced loss and whose life in poverty and abjection is hardly lacking is lamentable subjects.²⁴⁸ An often male-voiced charge Wickett quotes—that "they weep not for the deceased but for themselves"—is thus conveniently true and yet cynical, all the more as wailing-women are linked to prostitution not only with regard to their low social status, as both Wickett's anthropological analysis of Upper Egypt *naddabat* and Devi's literary portray of Rajasthan *rudali* rituals point out.²⁴⁹ Discussing Devi's portrayal of "rudali work,"²⁵⁰ Sekher points out that hierarchy is seminal to the ritual: "The upper castes lament not for the dead. ... making the low caste women weep over the body of the dead upper caste male," she explains, is "humiliating and symbolically mutilating assault"²⁵¹ as they are paid to lament those who scorn and exploit them as wailing-women and prostitutes. In the course of her field work in Egypt,

---

[243] Lk. 7:32, NRSV; parenthesis LXX.
[244] Cf. Mt. 11:17.
[245] Aeschylus, *Libation Bearers*, 733; my translation.
[246] William Hoy, *Do Funerals Matter?*, 64.
[247] Not necessarily female: Isabella Clark-Decès, *No One Cries for the Dead*, 96pp. describes Tamil Dalit men, so-called "untouchables," as professional mourners.
[248] Wickett, *For the Living*, 99: "The public forum of the funeral is also acknowledged to be a legitimate setting for the expiation of personal grief, centering around the suffering and tribulations of the mourners in general: widowhood, poverty and loneliness."
[249] Ibid., 33; Mahasweta Devi, *Rudali*, 91.
[250] Devi, *Rudali*, S. 116.
[251] Sekher, "Gender, Caste, and Fiction," 4423.

Wickett finds that the anthropological observation that is emotionally distanced and, at the same time, requests the performance of lament songs duplicates the disparagement and exploitation wailing-women otherwise encounter.[252] Criticism pointing at the supposed inauthenticity of payed wailing duplicates the hierarchy inherent to the social context of the ritual in the lacking differentiation of what payment means: Just as Danforth describes that the mourners are invited to a funeral feast, professional wailing-women are often paid in food[253] (not least because in ancient Egypt, grain has long been currency). What may seem as payment to someone who starves may appear as hospitality to those who do not—it is not hard to see this difference as a source of sorrow. In the English term "to sing placebo" it is a source of contempt for a "flatterer, a sycophant, a parasite," who sings *placebo*—"the first word in the first antiphon of vespers in the Office for the Dead"—to profit from the feast afterward.[254] As wailing-women were silenced in modern England, hired mourners became "mutes," men clothed in black bearing a solemn face.[255]

The persistent criticism in the inauthenticity of ritual laments, wailing, and antiphony elucidates that authenticity of emotion is a norm inappropriate for understanding ritual performance. Gamliel emphasizes that "the modern distinction between expert performance and personal emotion turns out to be yet another false dichotomy in the context of wailing."[256] What is false is identifying payment with commodity-character and, consequently, insincerity—an association that accompanies, according to Wilce, the redefinition of social relations, dismissing (visible) worth in favor of (invisible) inwardness: "in South Asia ... [p]ayment represented material recognition of the value of social relationships. Professional wailers first gave way to unpaid wailers, who still sang improvised songs of grief and protest. Now both yield to silent weepers."[257] Authenticity is a capitalist norm that silences ritual plaints by deeming only those things, utterances, and acts sincere that cannot be bought and which, given that they evade the equalizing means of

---

[252] Wickett, *For the Living*, 32. The same can be found in literature: Sekher sees "fiction's affiliations with the dominant and hegemonic ideologies" in Devi's narrative of a self-transformation of wailing-women into the paradox of a "gendered caste, specifically a low caste of 'whores'" ("Gender, Caste, and Fiction," 4425) that fixates abjection and analphabetism while the fiction participates in "the texts of culture and history" (4424). Mukta, "Civilizing Mission," 36pp. similarly points out that the abolishment of dirges in colonial India reproduced gender- and caste-hierarchies.
[253] Devi, *Rudali*, 91–93.
[254] *OED* 11:942, s.v. "placebo."
[255] *OED* 10:148, s.v. "mutes."
[256] Gamliel, "She Who Mourns," 497.
[257] Wilce, *Crying Shame*, 100; cf. Barley, *Dancing on the Grave*, 21: "Other people are unspeakably shocked that we hand over the bodies of our dead to complete strangers to strip, eviscerate and do with as they will. We in turn are scandalized by the employment of paid mourners who simulate pain."

money, do not follow any convention—short of the rule of unpredictable newness. With regard to this rule, ritual plaints are twice compromised as traditional (old) and conventional (unoriginal).[258] Innovation is a paradigm springing from consumer capitalism as much as from the culture of the printed word. Danforth considers the issue of the medium: "Greek funeral laments are part of a longstanding oral tradition in which the literary concept of one authentic correct version of a song does not exist."[259] Under the conditions of orality, originality and sincerity are constructed in ways that differ profoundly from the expectation of innovation in cultures of the written word,[260] as the Egyptian author Khakheperre-sonb bemoans already in 1800 BCE:

> Had I unknown phrases
> Sayings that are strange
> Novel, untried words,
> free of repetition ...[261]

In functional orality, repetition is crucial, yet not necessarily the repetition of an exact wording, as required in the antiphons of Christian liturgy but, rather, as compliance with rules regarding metric, vocabulary, phonetics, and interaction. The purpose of following these rules is a social one: It is the social role, the position in relations to others, that is claimed publicly in the common yet dissenting ritual antiphony. "Affective display is *conventionally* expected,"[262] as Wilce explains, not to prove the veracity of the feeling of loss but to display the capability for engaging in interaction. Modernity's turn from sociality toward the inwardness of emotion means that "one must 'perform oneself' rather than a more distanced role. Performance itself, in this sense, becomes more salient, as does the scope for performance-shame."[263] Ritual display of emotion becomes shameful if it is not taken as pattern for making social claims (for instance as a widow against the deceased's family) but as an exposure of intimate relations (informing others about the quality of the marriage). This transformed comprehension of emotional display is the reason why, in analyses of ritual plaints, the distance imperative to any theoretical investigation is often diminished or consumed, to the effect that studies reproduce traditional discourses on ritual plaints instead of

---

[258] Wilce, *Crying Shame*, 102: "under a metacultural embrace of newness ..., all cultural products, including the self, must constantly take on *new* forms."
[259] Danforth, *Death Rituals*, 71–72.
[260] For ritual versus textual coherence Jan Assmann, *Cultural Memory and Early Civilization*, 123–124.
[261] Ibid., 84.
[262] Wilce, *Crying Shame*, 201.
[263] Ibid., 124.

scrutinizing them: It is the same modernization that has established the distanced observation—of phenomena, prizes, and the self—as a norm and that has dismissed ritual plaints. Reckwitz sums it up:

> The rise of rationalism that took place within bourgeois modernity against the affective cultures of aristocratic society, popular rural and craftwork cultures and religion, particularly Catholicism, showed up in the trade economy, self-employment and the professions, as well as the neutrality of bourgeois law, modern science's claim to objectivity, and the discipline and self-reflection of the bourgeois self.[264]

Rilke's *Requiem* articulates the break with ritual forms such as dirges and wailing inherent to this transformation in a line split up by a full stop: *Gebräuche. Alles geht und wird verredet* (customs. They pass on, we [talk them down]).[265] In this line, customs appear as fixed forms incompatible with their discursive negotiation which causes their disappearance. Yet the differentiation between, on the one hand, monolithic "customs" about which nothing further can be said because they consist in identical repetition and, on the other hand, dissecting reflection is itself a nostalgic re-flection: a glimpse backward at past ritual forms and societies. Necessarily so, for in the conflict of paradigms between conventionality and authenticity, there is no third point of view. No look at ritual can be unbiased, which calls for a careful reflection of the position of the analyst. The comparative discussion Danforth's anthropological and Veteranyi's literary approach to ritual plaints points out that faced with the historiographic difficulty of an inevitably biased stance, literary language is capable of providing a more differentiated outlook since, unlike theoretical language, it does not prerequisite the claim to distance and noninvolvement.

One seminal question remains to be addressed in the closing section of this chapter: Ritual plaints are a liminal means of social re-organization by way of a disorganization of linguistic structures, however, setting a limit to liminality proves to be difficult, as Achilles' consumption by mourning demonstrates as much as Freud's difficulties in conceptualizing the closure of mourning.

## Ta(l)king Revenge: No End to Lamentation

Van Gennep calls the last phase of rites of passage concerned with the "incorporation" into a new organization "postliminal,"[266] suggesting that

---

[264] Andreas Reckwitz, *The Invention of Creativity*, 203.
[265] Rilke, *Requiem*, RSW1:653/*Requiem for a Friend*, 265.
[266] Gennep, *Passage*, 11.

liminality—the suspension of clear distinctions that enables the passage—has been overcome at this point. The limitation and prohibition of ritual plaints that occur in diverse historical and cultural contexts, however, is incurred by a difficulty inherent to the logic of liminality that undermines van Gennep's sequencing: Liminality tends to suspend even those conventions that are supposed to delaminate the rite. This complication of ritual plaints points at a general structure: Ending the consumption of structures inherent to the language of lamenting and complaining presents a difficulty inside and outside of ritual contexts. This difficulty is at the center of Freud's revised theory of mourning, and it is no coincidence that his revision does not reach a definite conclusion: While the 1915 notion assumes that "when the work of mourning is completed the ego becomes free and uninhibited again" (SE4:245), the revised 1923 theory assumes that accepting loss does not mean relinquishing emotional ties but internalizing them so that "the character of the ego is a precipitate of abandoned object-cathexes" (SE19:29). Mourning thus forms the ego as a growing ruin, and it becomes hard to tell when—or whether ever—mourning is over, and what distinguishes mourning from melancholia. Achilles' mourning for Patroklos is liminal to the extent of decomposing the order of the ritual lament that enables liminality; consequently, "for Achilles, a complete return to normality seems excluded."[267] Veteranyi's text does not tell of an end of the dirge for the aunt and a reestablished difference of the narrator's, her mother's, and her relatives voices, but of how ritual plaints cause lasting ruptures: "My mother cried my tears, too. Her voice penetrated my head like a glass splinter."[268]

That the proliferated consumption of linguistic structures in ritual plaints undermines comprehension and audibility is why it serves as a poetic principle of formulating distress in Greek tragedy. Portraying ritual antiphony in stichomythic verse, Aeschylus' 472 BC *Persians* (the oldest known full text of an Attic tragedy) closes with fragmenting articulate speech to vowels:

Ξέρξης βόα νυν ἀντίδουπά μοι.
Χορός οἰοῖ οἰοῖ.
Ξέρξης αἰακτὸς ἐς δόμους κίε.
Χορός ἰὼ ἰώ. [Περσὶς αἶα δύσβατος.]
Ξέρξης ἰωὰ δὴ κατ' ἄστυ.
Χορός ἰωὰ δῆτα, ναὶ ναί.

---

[267]Richard Seaford, *Reciprocity and Ritual*, 167: "By the combination of abnormal ritual expressions of death-in-life with the knowledge that his own death has been made inevitable by that of Patroklos."
[268]Veteranyi, *Regal*, 21.

Ξέρξης γοᾶσθ᾽ ἁβροβάται.
Χορός ἰὼ ἰώ· Περσὶς αἶα δύσβατος.
Ξέρξης
ἠὴ ἠή, τρισκάλμοισιν,
ἠὴ ἠή, βάρισιν ὀλόμενοι.
Χορός πέμψω τοί σε δυσθρόοις γόοις.

**Xerxes** Cry aloud now in response to me.
**Chorus** [oioi oioi!]
**Xerxes** With sounds of wailing go to your homes.
**Chorus** [iō iō]! [Persian land, grievous now to walk upon!]
**Xerxes** [Cry iō] through the city.
**Chorus** [iō, of course! yes, yes]!
**Xerxes** Pour forth your wails as you move along with soft steps.
**Chorus** [iō iō]! O Persian land, grievous now to walk upon!
**Xerxes** [iē iē]! Those that perished
[iē iē]! in three-tiered galleys [...]!
**Chorus** I will escort you with dismal sounds of woe. *Exeunt omnes*[269]

Sounds (*ai, iō*) are dissected from words and join the formulas of wailing (*oioi, iē*). Translating these vowels as "alas" or "woe me" is more standard than the outline of the Greek text's soundscape given above, yet such translations hide what is crucial to this final scene. It is "repetition," as Gurd writes on the language of *Persians*, that "empties even signifying language of its semantic reference and raises the level of sound in the mix."[270] Still, this disorganization of articulation has a communicative purpose: Xerxes addresses the chorus (of Persian men) twice before in the exact same wording, asking them to respond to his lament[271] and demanding wailing, self-mutilation, and hair-pulling as gestures of lament[272]—as if to reassure himself of the effect of his words, and the power of his rule, after the defeat at Salamis due to which he had returned to Persia "stripped of [his] escort."[273] The antiphonic lament serves Xerxes to re-supply himself with the chorus as an escort that duplicates his vowels, answers his request, and restores his rule. Or so it seems, for insofar as he requests the same thrice, he does not easily get an appropriate response, and the response he evokes is nothing else than a lament. Xerxes's reestablished rule is one over, and in, lament. It does not compensate for the destructions caused by the defeat the Persians suffered (by giving loss a metaphysical sense, or planning retaliation) but proliferates loss in an ongoing destruction of linguistic structures. The play's

---

[269] Aeschylus, *The Persians*, 1066–1076; my italics, underlining, and brackets.
[270] Sean Alexander Gurd, *Dissonance*, 70.
[271] Aeschylus, *The Persians*, 1040, 1048.
[272] Ibid., 1046, 1054, 1056, 1062.
[273] Ibid., 1036.

last word, *goois* (wailing, lamentations), promises further reiterations of the ruin of linguistic structures. The liminal status of the king returning to his homeland defeated and without an escort is not overcome—of course not, since the tragedy serves to display a *lasting* Greek triumph. Still, the almost-melancholic repetition of plaints and proliferated destruction of structures are general complications in the language of lamenting and complaining that elicits prohibitions of (ritual) plaints. This juridical response to the consumption of structures in plaintive language has shaped tragedy, too: Herodotus reports that Athens imposed a fine on Phrynichos after his presumably 492 BCE[274] play portraying the sack of Miletus (an Athenian colony) by the Persians two years prior moved the whole audience to tears as it was reminded of their "own calamities" *(oikēia kaka)*.[275] Ever since, Attic tragedy portrays calamities of distant times or realms, or Athens's adversaries,[276] however, not the 480–79 sack of Attica by the Persians. An exemplary discussion of a related prohibition of ritual plaints that features prominently in criticism shall elucidate the logic of responses that seek to silence the language of lamenting and complaining.

Studies on the history and (gender) policy of Attic tragedy often refer to the legislative delimitation of dirges in numerous Greek *poleis* (city states) between the sixth and the fourth centuries BCE.[277] Plutarch and Cicero report that Solon had achieved a reform of burial rites.[278] Its interpretation is difficult since the wording of the laws themselves has been preserved as little as the details of the targeted funerary rites; merely comments on both have been handed down. One of them is Plato's imagination of the funerary regulations in an ideal state that sums up all others: The size of graves as well as the expenditure on burials shall be limited to "moderation,"[279] just as the public display of mourning:

> The laying-out of the corpse ... shall be carried out in accordance with the custom concerning such matters, but it is right that custom should give way to the following regulations of State law:—Either to ordain or to prohibit weeping for the dead is unseemly, but we shall forbid loud [lamenting] [*thrēnein*] and [screaming] [*phōnēn*] outside the house, and we shall prohibit the carrying out of the dead on to the open roads and making lamentation while he is borne through the streets, and the funeral party must be outside the city-bounds before day-break.[280]

---

[274] *EA*, s.v. "Phrynichos," 9:970.
[275] Herodotus, *Histories* 6.21.2.
[276] Loraux, *Mothers in Mourning*, 86.
[277] Josine Blok, "Solon's Funerary Laws."
[278] Plutarch, *Vitae Parallelae:* Solon, 12; 21; Cicero, *De legibus* 2.59.
[279] Plato, *Laws*, 958e–959d.
[280] Ibid., 959e–960a; my brackets.

This passage rules that crying for the dead is a private matter out of place at public funeral processions which, in turn, seem to be altogether out of place in the ideal polis and are thus relegated to the night. And it articulates the fundamental principle of any modernization to justify such politics, and policing, of emotion by downgrading customs from social norms to mere habits incomparable to state law. Funerary customs are a primal scene of sociopolitical modernizations because they perform the ruling interpretation of life and death. It is not missing in Plato either: "one ought never to spend extravagantly on the dead, through supposing that the carcass of flesh that is being buried is in the truest sense one's own relative; but one ought rather to suppose that the real son or brother … has departed in furtherance and fulfillment of his own destiny."[281] Plutarch reports along the same lines that Solon, a founding father of Athens's democracy, reformed inheritance and funerary regulations to the effect that the clan is not the inevitable heir and disorderly behavior is prevented, which pertains particularly to travel expenses of women, burial gifts, and laments: "Laceration of the flesh by mourners, and the use of set lamentations (*to thrēnein pepoiēmena*), and the bewailing of any one at the funeral ceremonies of another, he forbade."[282] Solon thus prohibits what Xerxes orders the male chorus to do. Yet by lamenting in such a way, Plutarch voices Solon's concern, "they indulge in unmanly and effeminate extravagances of sorrow when they mourn."[283] Athens's mourners are thus forbidden to do what the tragic chorus does in singing a *kommos* (dirge): to perform sorrow in public in singing prepared/poetic laments.[284] Solon's laws seem to target wailing-women in particular, who would be wailing "at the funeral ceremonies of another." Pericles' paradigmatic funerary oration for the victims of the first year of the Peloponnesian War (or Thucydides' paradigmatic portray thereof) consequently closes with the order: "And now that you have brought to a close your lamentations for your relatives, you may depart."[285]

While archaeological research often views this legislation as testifying to a changed notion of death, philological approaches explain them as part of a political dispute, targeting specific groups: either women, who do not count as *politai* (citizens) and shall be excluded from the public life of the polis, or clans, whose "vertical rivalry" threatens to plunge the polis into

---

[281]Ibid., 959c.
[282]Plutarch, *Vitae Parallelae: Solon*, 21.4.
[283]Ibid., 21.5.
[284]Edith Hall, *Inventing the Barbarian*, 83–84 suggests that Aeschylus portrays the lamenting Persians as effeminate; other scholars find nothing female about their lament (Holst-Warhaft, *Dangerous Voices*, 131; Dué, *Captive Women's Lament*, 57–90; Suter, "Male Lament," 161ff.) Disparaging the enemy as effeminate would diminish the Greek triumph, therefore, it appears as an unlikely poetic strategy.
[285]Thucydides, *The Peloponnesian War*, 2.46.2.

civil war.[286] Both interpretations have shortcomings, therefore, the following is not to take a decision; what matters here is that both have a crucial point in common: the issue of delimiting the liminality of ritual plaints. Both women and clans, it is assumed, use dirges to elicit revenge, transferring the disorganization of language into political unrest. The fear of this transferal is fundamental to understanding the political consequence of the structural disorganization caused by plaintive language.

In spite of foregrounding the female role in ancient Greece, readings that connect the funerary laws to a restrictive gender politics are, still, indebted to Hegel's notion of the polis. Based on a reading of Sophocles's *Antigone* he concludes that "womankind in general" is the political community's "internal enemy" who rebels against the suppression of the family in the state.[287] Notably Holst-Warhaft argues that the prohibition of public dirges is a means for isolating women in the polis as ritual plaints were traditionally female-voiced[288] (which disagrees with Homer, wherein men and women lament[289]). Ritual dirges, Holst-Warhaft continues, were silenced in the militarized polis, and contained in tragedy, to substitute it with a male commemoration of the soldiers killed in action in the *epitaphios logos*, the funeral oration such as Pericles'.[290] Purpose of "the taming of lament"[291] was to substitute the insistence on pain voiced by ritual laments with the insistence on the "furtherance and fulfillment of his own destiny," as Plato puts it, that gives death a political meaning. The effect is that in Solon/Plutarch as well as Pericles/Thucydides, lament is gendered and relegated out of the public realm, such that women are "handicapped to the level of silence."[292] The reason for this policy, Holst-Warhaft assumes, is "the connection between the women's laments and incitement to revenge": ritual dirges served female relatives to incite male relatives to vendetta.[293] Alexiou hints at the association of Greek dirges with blood feuds, too, yet

---

[286] Lorna Hardwick, *Philomel and Pericles*, 156. Cf. Alexiou, *Ritual Lament*, 17–18; Blok, "Solon's Funerary Laws," 133–235; Garland, *Greek Way of Death*, 21pp.; Seaford, *Reciprocity and Ritual*, 74–86; Stears, "Death Becomes Her," 143pp.

[287] Hegel, *Phenomenology of Spirit* C.(BB).VI.A.b, 288. Readings of Sophocles's *Antigone* and Hegel's Antigone are countless; for a recent reading in terms of political theory cf. Bonnie Honig, *Antigone, Interrupted*.

[288] Holst-Warhaft, *Dangerous Voices*, 114pp.; Helene Foley, *Female Acts*, 23pp.

[289] Inappropriate gendering leads Foley to the inappropriate conclusion: "The *Iliad*, then, does not repress the marginal discourse of lament, but appropriates it in the service of its own plot structure" (*Female Acts*, 44). Lament is neither exclusively female nor per se, let alone in the *Iliad*, a "marginal" discourse. The same misunderstanding in Weiss, "Representation of Lament," 250.

[290] Holst-Warhaft, *Dangerous Voices*, 119–169.

[291] Ibid., 127.

[292] Stears, "Death Becomes Her," 148.

[293] Holst-Warhaft, *Dangerous Voices*, 118–119.

neither refers to Durkheim's systematic interlinking between the two. On the occasion of bloody lament rites he writes:

> One cannot fail to be struck by the resemblances which these practices present to those of the vendetta. Both proceed from the same principle that death [calls for] [*la mort appelle*] the shedding of blood. The only difference is that in one case the victims are the relatives, while in the other they are strangers. ... vendetta ... is connected with the rites of mourning, whose end [*la fin*] it announces.[294]

Destructive rites of lament such as (self-)laceration and planctus as well as vendetta suggest that death requires a response. Death literally "calls for" an answer—by more blood, which effects a proliferation of destruction that claims to be a compensation. This ambivalence of claiming to strive for compensation but causing the proliferation of destruction is what links revenge to lament, according to Freud a response to traumatic affection which aims at compensating for the injury but effectively perpetuates it as trauma. Acts of revenge promise to hurt the originator of an injury yet they are subject to the same shifts and dispersions due to which neither curses nor condemnations can guarantee to meet the ear and heed of those who matter. Dirges and vendetta strive for response and reciprocity where it appears to be hopeless and thus all the more urgent. Durkheim's ambivalent reference to "the end" of mourning illustrates the interrelation: The call to revenge may be taken as *conclusion* of lamenting insofar as it moves to action, or as the *purpose* lamenting is after. It is the latter sense that the chorus of Aeschylus' *Libation Bearers* sees in lamenting, suggesting that dirges function not as announcements of vendetta or their surrogate, as Freud assumes, but as the very agent of revenge:

> The murdered man has his dirge [*thrēskōn*];
> the guilty man is revealed.
> Justified lament [*goos endikos*] for fathers and for parents,
> when raised loud and strong,
> makes its search everywhere.[295]

The dirge is associated to justice as it finds out the culprit for the lamentable cause and accuses them—whether or not it is just, as the Erinyes later suggest,[296] is the crucial issue the *Oresteia* settles by avoiding a decision. The chorus of the *Libation Bearers* is female, yet Durkheim's interlinking of dirge and vendetta does not require a gendered reading, it is

---

[294]Durkheim, *Elementary Forms*, 394/*Les formes élémentaires de la vie religieuse*, 658.
[295]Aeschylus, *Libation Bearers*, 327–332.
[296]Aeschylus, *Eumenides*, 511–512: "'Justice!' 'Thrones of the Furies!'"

equally suited to read the funerary legislation as targeting clan structures. According to Durkheim, the relatives who injure themselves in ritual lament correlate to foreigners who are killed in revenge. Following kinship logic, the Erinyes count Clytemnestra's husband, whom she murders in revenge, among the foreigners unrelated by blood.[297] Viewed from this perspective, what is crucial to interdicting public dirges is the question of who is related to whom, and who is an "other" whom to bewail Solon/Plutarch forbids. In 508/07 BCE, about fifty years before the *Oresteia* premiered, this distinction was subject of the reforms of Cleisthenes that abolished clans, stripping noble families of their escort.[298] This entails a fundamental modification of the reciprocity seminal to kinship societies: Members of a clan are no longer obliged to one another (for instance by avenging each other), but every citizen is obliged to the state (to appeal to its courts). Blood relations are delimited to the household and thus excluded from the polis—such that women belong solely to a family while men are members of two profoundly different organizations, state and household. The "others" targeted *at* the end of—or *as* an end to—lamenting are thus found not inside but outside the polis, as Athena orders in the *Oresteia*: "Let their war be [outside the gates],"[299] and the Erinyes-turned-Eumenides consent: "discord, greedy for evil, may never clamor in this city ... and ... cause ruinous murder for vengeance to the destruction of the state."[300]

Silencing ritual plaints seeks to ban civil war from the polis. Against this background, the fear of liminal impurity that is sometimes given as a reason for the funerary legislation (testifying to an altered notion of death that requires a clear separation from life[301]) may be interpreted as fear of violent confrontation erupting at funerals.[302] Vendetta and kinship systems are not per se instances of a chaotic lack of organization first sorted out by codified state law, as legal history's largely Roman terms suggest, but sociopolitical organizations in their own right.[303] Vendetta and kinship systems are despotic, as Veteranyi points out, since they permit of is no neutral position: "My mother was sobbing into the telephone: I am angry with God! He is not on our side!" Kindship structures tend not to distinguish between life and death but between pro and contra the "enduring reality"[304] of the family substance, as Hegel puts it. It is this approach to community the

---

[297] Ibid., 211.
[298] Jochen Martin, "Von Kleistenes zu Ephialtes," 178.
[299] Aeschylus, *Eumenides*, 864.
[300] Ibid. 976–980.
[301] Blok, "Solon's Funerary Laws," 199.
[302] Seaford, *Reciprocity and Ritual*, 188.
[303] This is profoundly mistaken in Simon Stow, *American Mourning*, 6, where vendetta is characterized as "Eroding all considerations of reciprocity, justice, and even self-interest in favor of its own singular perspective."
[304] Hegel, *Phenomenology of Spirit* C.(BB).VI.A.a, 277.

funerary legislation targets, Blok holds: Laments are delimited to restrict the living's duty for the dead, which is imperative in order to lay fallen soldiers, wars, and the question of blame to rest.[305] It is no contradiction when Arendt writes: "The organization of the polis ... is a kind of organized remembrance. It assures the mortal actor that its passing existence and fleeting greatness will never lack the reality that comes from being seen, being heard, and, generally, appearing before an audience."[306] The genre of funerary oration serves to install unchanging presence, adopting the clan structure's co-presence of the living and the dead, division of the cosmos into parties, and incitement to revenge, and turns them against enemies outside the polis.

With regard to the difficulty of delimiting liminality, it appears that calling for revenge—although inciting unrest—still effects a re-stabilization insofar as it reintroduces the propositional form of attribution and judgment. Rilke's *Requiem* returns to propositions as it finds that while the destruction of the texture of speech seems an appropriate expression of pain, it fails to communicate anything:

*und alles, was ich sage, müßte so*
*zerlumpt in dieser Stimme gehn und frieren;*
*blieb es beim Klagen. Doch jetzt klag ich an:*
*den Einen nicht, der dich aus dir zurückzog,*
*(ich find ihn nicht heraus, er ist wie alle)*
*doch alle klag ich in ihm an: den Mann.*[307]

and everything I say would have to go
in [the] rags [of this voice] and freeze;
[would I stick to lamenting.] But now [I accuse:]
Not the [one] man who pulled you from yourself
(I can't find him [out], he [is] like all the others),
but in him I accuse them all: [the] man.[308]

Rilke's *Requiem* does not stick to lamenting the fact that neither a nostalgic reference to rituals nor current poetry appropriately communicates mourning. Just as it seems to fall silent with a full stop after *Klagen* (lamenting), the *Requiem* finds a way to speak on by turning to propositions. In German, it is a slight shift from *klagen* to *anklagen*, from lamenting to accusing. Attributing responsibility to someone re-stabilizes the poems' discourse even though it is actually impossible to single out a culprit. The

---

[305]Blok, "Solon's Funerary Laws," 237.
[306]Arendt, *The Human Condition*, 176–177.
[307]Rilke, *Requiem*, RSW1:653.
[308]Rilke, *Requiem for a Friend*, 265.

*Requiem* leaves no doubt that reintroducing proposition serves not to form just judgments but to communicate immeasurable pain that threatens to overcome conventional structures of language and disorganize speech to the point of incomprehensibility. Generalizations such as "all men, man as such" are a form of excess, too, yet appear as shapely terms. Modersohn-Becker, to whom the *Requiem* is devoted, died after giving birth. The indeterminate *Ein[e]* (one) might be the father of the child, a doctor, or death (a grammatical male in German). Yet the point of attributing responsibility is not to identify one but to direct the lament (*Klage*) to (*an*) someone who is called to listen and respond. Attributing responsibility is a way of reassuring hearing and reciprocity, onto which things that give reason to lament or complaint cast doubt. Nietzsche thus sees attribution, accusation, and revenge as the purpose of all plaintive language:

> No one accuses without an underlying notion of punishment and revenge, even when he accuses fate of himself. All complaint is accusation [*Alles Klagen ist Anklagen*] ... we always make some one responsible.[309]

Zarathustra includes even inarticulate utterances in this equation: "'Is not all weeping a lament? And is not all lament an accusation [*Und alles Klagen nicht ein Anklagen*]?'"[310] Nietzsche, the classicist, certainly satirizes Western philosophy's commitment to propositional forms, however, Greek tragedy agrees with him: incessantly lamenting and complaining, tragedies never fail to attribute causality—not only due to a historical proximity of tragic plaints to revenge: Accusations are part of plaintive speech insofar as it cannot do without propositions if it seeks to articulate what it laments over or complains about. Chapter 5 will return to the prepositional normalization of plaintive speech in juridical discourse. What is relevant here is that the proximity of ritual lament to vendetta might be a projection in the psychoanalytical sense rather than a historical analysis; and that the accusations inherent to many laments and complaints as a means for finding hearing and response are a receptive object of projection.

Sourvinou-Inwood objects to Holst-Warhaft from an archaeological point of view: "The notion that women's laments in sixth-century Athens or classical Delphi incited to revenge is based on no ancient evidence."[311] Following a psychoanalytic approach, Loraux thus reads the link between ritual dirge and blood feud drawn in the *Oresteia* as a projection of fears aroused by warfare. Greek funerary legislation, Loraux holds, is concerned

---

[309]Friedrich Nietzsche, *Human, All-Too-Human*. Vol. 2, 43 (*Miscellaneous Maxims and Opinions* no. 78)/*Vermische Meinungen und Sprüche* 78, KSA2:409.
[310]Friedrich Nietzsche, *Thus Spake Zarathustra*, 250/*Also Sprach Zarathustra*. KSA4:280.
[311]Christiane Sourvinou-Inwood, "Review of *Dangerous Voices*, by Gail Holst-Warhaft," 68.

with protecting the polis from emotions that are detrimental to military order, notably mourning.[312] The sense of guilt that, according to Freud, accompanies all mourning[313] is dangerous for the polis since the blame for the death of soldiers cannot be attributed solely to the enemy: It is the polis which sends out soldiers. Rather than internalizing the blame as a bad conscience and hesitating in further campaigns, the male *politai* (citizens) of the polis project the feeling that they might be to blame onto the fallen soldiers' mothers, and fear their revenge.[314] In order to relieve citizens from the feeling of guilt, Loraux argues, ritual dirges are relegated to the women's charge and interpreted not merely as calls for revenge but as signs of remorse for a bloody deed already committed—following the model of Clytemnestra, who had killed her husband to avenge their daughter, whom he had killed. Loraux writes:

> As if there were only one model for all mourning women: at the same time maternal and desperately deadly.
> We can guess the consequences of such a configuration: it suggests that all feminine mourning may be less wound or anger but remorse. Is a woman in tears originally guilty of whatever makes her cry?[315]

This projection of blame abolishes both nagging mourning and the uncomfortable disorganizations stirred up by ritual plaints. For if all those who engage in dirges must be regarded as potential murderers of their citizen husbands, it is nothing short of imperative not to lend them an ear. The legislative gender segregation of mourning thus appears to result from the attempt to politically sort out the ambivalence of mourning. In the *Oresteia*, motherless Athena ascribes herself exclusively to the male principle with the establishment of a "perpetual" (*aeí*) citizen court[316] to replace vendetta.[317] With the gender segregation of mourning, the citizens' love for the polis undergoes a catharsis of all ambivalence, now contained in the feminine realm of the household—which is not a part of the polis, as Aristotle's *Politics* will later fixate.[318] Tragedy displays the segregation, expounding the ambivalent sentiments of mourning detrimental to community. Tragedy, according to Loraux, produces the conflict averted by the polis as "practice of consensus."[319] It points out that what is detrimental to politics about

---

[312]Loraux, *Mothers in Mourning*.
[313]Freud, *Thoughts for the Times on War and Death*. SE14:293.
[314]Loraux, *Mothers in Mourning*, 43–56.
[315]Ibid., 55.
[316]Aeschylus, *Eumenides*, 684.
[317]Ibid., 736–737.
[318]Aristotle, *Politics*, 1252a.
[319]Loraux, *The Mourning Voice*, 24.

mourning is not only the concoction of specific acts of revenge but already the insistence on pain and its perpetuation as rage: "wrath in mourning, the principle of which is eternal repetition, willingly expresses itself with an *aeí*,[...] and the fascination of this tireless 'always' threatens to set it up as a powerful rival to the political *aeí* that establishes the memory of institutions."[320] Irreconcilable and, therefore, dangerous for a political community are, as Freud puts it, "the laments which always sound the same and are wearisome in their monotony" (SE14: 256). Because repetition, be it melancholic or ritual, does not let the dead rest but recalls them to presence just as Dareius' and Agamemnon's shadows shall be raised from their graves in Aeschylus.[321] Funerary legislation delimiting the length, occasion, and publicity of ritual laments testifies to a political mistrust toward, as Loraux writes, "the paralyzing seduction of mourning and the pleasure taken in immortalizing the voluptuousness of tears."[322] Both Achilles and Priamos take their fill of "dire lamenting" (*olooio ... gooio*) that consumes them, all other life, and articulation into a mere o-sound.[323] They follow the "desire of wailing" and in turn "rouse" this yearning in others,[324] so that lament does not cease. Along the same lines of a gluttony of plaints the chorus of Trojan women comments in Euripides: "[O how pleasant] to sufferers it is to weep, to mourn, lament, and chant the dirge that tells of grief!"[325]

The exemplary discussion of Greek funerary laws expounds a paradox that feeds the political relevance of lamenting and complaining: the lament that does end in a call for action as well as the endless lament are politically destructive—the former because the return to propositional discourse may call to revenge, war, or other forms of dissent that proliferate the destruction of structures brought about by plaintive language, the latter because it perpetuates the liminal dissolution of terms and the consumption of linguistic structures. In short, the disorganization caused by plaintive language cannot be put aside easily. This structural insight calls for some reservation with regard to the discussion above:

Greek funerary legislation does not seek to capture the form and purpose of ritual lament but to serve the polis. These laws portray a chaotic prehistory and lasting threat permanently kept away by the order of the polis: civil war. This is why ritual plaints appear archaic, feminine, and barbaric in this discourse—as that which is foreign to the political order of Attic tragedy. Tragedy takes part in this political shaping of the past but expounds that

---

[320]Loraux, *Mothers in Mourning*, 98.
[321]Aeschylus, *Persians*, 683pp.; *Libation Bearers*, 124pp.
[322]Loraux, *The Mourning Voice*, 202.
[323]Homer, *Iliad*, 23:10; 98.
[324]Ibid., 23:14; cf. 23:108.
[325]Euripides, *Trojan Women*, 608; my brackets.

it aims at ruling out ambivalences for the sake of societal consensus. In speaking of a fundamental femininity of (ritual) lamenting and complaining, or an eastern origin of plaints,[326] research duplicates rather than analyses the legislative discourse. Tragedy produces ritual plaints and their political delimitation, for instance when in the *Oresteia* Cassandra's prophetic lament is mocked, and later proven right.[327] The publicity of ritual plaints provided by Attic tragedy is delimited on the one hand by the fixed wording of the tragic text that dictates wailing, moaning, and the end of dirges, on the other hand by the distance of the produced plots from Athens's own calamities.

The exemplary discussion of the danger that both ending and endless lamenting and mourning represents for the polis expounds a structural excess in plaintive language due to which it is often denigrated and silenced: doubt in the principle of symbolic substitution makes the language of lamenting and complaining irreconcilable, disconsolate, and thus violent. The silencing of ritual laments and complaints in the Greek polis, Christian churches, and other forms of communities that presents itself as an instance of modernization abolishing the archaic call for revenge appears, in turn, as a form of revenge—revenge on the language of lamenting and complaining as a form speech that keeps claiming attention while refusing symbolic substitution in order to insist that they cannot be answered, satisfied, or appeased by political, metaphysical, or therapeutic concepts. Some studies classify the language of lamenting as progressive: Foley, for instance, describes lament as "a form of political or social resistance" best illustrated by Sophocles's *Antigone*, who supposedly points out "the potentially revolutionary force of women's role in rituals performed for the dead."[328] Baggini characterizes complaining in general as "emancipatory"[329] because: "Complaint is a secular, humanist act. It is resistance against the idea, promulgated by religion, that suffering is our divinely ordained lot."[330] The language of lamenting and complaining may certainly be an instance of resistance, its profound doubt in symbolic substitution, however, makes it unsuited as an element of any sociopolitical agenda. Irreconcilability is a resistance to any claim of a symbolic compensation for pain or sorrow and cannot be classified under the progressive social forms alone. It has been, rather, in the name of sociopolitical progress that communal forms of displaying pain and sorrow in lamenting and complaining have been debased

---

[326]Hall, *Barbarian*, 83; Alexiou, *Ritual Lament*, 13; both refer to the 1911 Martin Nilsson, "Ursprung der Tragödie," 78, who only mentions that antiphony appears in cuneiform texts, too.
[327]Aeschylus, *Agamemnon*, 1050–1166.
[328]Foley, *Female Acts*, 33.
[329]Ibid., 18.
[330]Baggini, *Complaint*, 12.

and violently silenced. Resisting all narratives of historical progress for better or worse, the language of lamenting and complaining may appear—depending on context and perspective—subversive as well as reactionary.

The following chapter compares two theoretical approaches to the excess of plaintive language which insists on the hearing of others but refutes all answers aiming at consensus and settlement.

# 3

# Voicing Pain and Destruction: Wittgenstein and Scholem

*"So in the end when one is doing philosophy one gets to the point where one would like just to emit an inarticulate sound."*[1]

*"lamentation is language at the point of disappearance."*[2]

Lamenting and complaining undermine the stability of linguistic structures indispensable for forming concepts and theses. Freud's analyses of his patients' complaints expound the consumption of word reference and shifts in the relations between author and speaker, cause and occasion of a complaint; ritual plaints entail a similar decomposition of linguistic structures that extends to the level of articulation. Studies on ritual lamenting and complaining, moreover, often consume the distance between observer and observed prerequisite to theory. As the previous chapters demonstrate, neurotic and ritual plaints effect a psychical or social reorganization by way of a disorganization of fundamental structures language, thus questioning the concept of language as a coherent system that can be grasped by a distinct number of grammatical or other rules. Wittgenstein's *Philosophical Investigations* and Scholem's epilogue to his translation of the *Eicha*, the biblical book of Lamentations, are theoretical approaches to plaintive language that heed to this consumption of structures: Wittgenstein in his notes on pain, Scholem in remarks on the tension between semiotics and semantics. Both focus on the role of the response and thus elaborate systematically what appeared, so far, as a difficulty in neurotic, ritual, poetic, and quotidian plaints: How to respond to laments and complaints without silencing them? How to answer a speech that refutes symbolic substitution?

---

[1]Wittgenstein, *Philosophical Investigations* [PI] §261.
[2]Gershom Scholem, *Lamentations of Youth: The Diaries 1913–1919*, 216.

While Wittgenstein and Scholem are prominent authors, their texts on the language of lamenting and complaining have not yet gained the critical attention their arguments deserve. Wittgenstein's discussion of knowing about pain has been widely read with regard to the private language argument and the problem of other minds, however, his notes on complaining and lamenting which communicate pain from the second, non-numbered part of the *Philosophical Investigations* are rarely discussed.[3] This avoidance might not be accidental, as Wittgenstein's remarks on laments and complaints form an extremum in his criticism of traditional philosophical thinking, fathoming the limitations of speculative thought.

Wittgenstein and Scholem provide no manual for dealing with plaints but examine how the structure of plaintive language that highlights the crucial role of hearing and response can be conceptualized. Wittgenstein's notes grant the insight that in order to comprehend the language of lamenting and complaining systematically, the response has to be added to the structure of the utterance. Scholem's essay allows to elaborate more precisely that in order to comprehend the seminal role of hearing and response in plaintive language, even silence and muteness have to be taken into account as possible utterances instead of disregarding them as mere absence, or failure, of communication. Since the two texts correspond systematically as groundwork and precision, they will be discussed in this order, although Scholem's is older than Wittgenstein's. This chapter outlines that the prominence of hearing and response as well as the move to silence plaints can be discussed not only in historical terms. The history of the attempts to silence ritual plaints and their return in neurosis is, rather, based on the structure of plaintive language that—in orality and writing—centers upon reciprocity.

Pain and destruction are a possible content of speech in Wittgenstein and Scholem as well as a particular structure of speech. The heterogeneous texts—Wittgenstein's a set of notes by a well-known philosopher; Scholem's an apodictic essay by a youngster returned from deployment in the German army in the First World War[4]—are concerned with one difficulty: How is it possible to speak adequately of sensations and events that do not allow to keep one's distance? In both texts, the inquiry into lamenting and complaining is accompanied by the decomposition of the self-conception as theory, as a distanced examination conducted in terminological language: Wittgenstein

---

[3] Discussions are referenced below; texts not mentioning Wittgenstein are not listed here for reasons of redundancy.
[4] Lina Barouch, "Lamenting Language Itself," 5. The war is of course not the only context, cf. Lina Barouch, *Between German and Hebrew*, 27: "Itta Shedletzky, the editor of Scholem's published letters, has described his intensive work on the lamentations as a reflection of his mourning for a Judaism lost to emancipation and assimilation."

sees philosophizing—owing, no least, to reading Frazer's ethnology[5] and Freud's psychoanalysis[6]—as a contrast to theoretical discourses and terminology; Scholem's theological diction focuses on the connection between sign and sound as a fundamental yet rather unapproachable aspect of language. Wittgenstein's approach starts with a (presumably) more approachable structure: the sentence.

Written between 1936 and 1948, Wittgenstein's *Philosophical Investigations* are published posthumously in 1953.[7] They comprise reflections on a broad scope of topics, articulated in notes, questions, and objections rather than one continuous argument.[8] Unlike the 1918 *Tractatus Logico-Philosophicus*, the *Philosophical Investigations* does not presuppose that there is a single basic form of language such as the proposition or statement,[9] or a distinct number of grammatical or other forms, but

> countless different kinds of use of what we call "symbols", "words", "sentences". And this multiplicity is not something fixed, given once for all; but new types of language, new language-games ... come into existence, and other become obsolete and get forgotten. (PI:§23)

A "language-game" is a historically and culturally variable convention that resembles the concept of genre. Establishing the notion of "language-games," Wittgenstein in his turn leaves the language-game of theoretical speech. For contrary to the conventions that apply to the use of philosophical terms, the term "language-game" is introduced neither by means of a syllogism nor by way of an argument. Wittgenstein, rather, appeals to the recipient: "Review the multiplicity of language-games in the following examples, and in others" (PI:§23). Unlike in Platonic dialogues, this request remains unanswered within the text, hence it seems to actually address the reader in front of the text whom the genre of theory usually passes over. The imperative is followed by a list of fifteen items, including "Giving orders" (as in the imperative "Review"), "Forming and testing a hypothesis" (the concern of theoretical language), "Singing catches—/Guessing riddles—,"

---

[5]Ludwig Wittgenstein, "Remarks on Frazer's *Golden Bough*."
[6]For both Frank Cioffi, *Wittgenstein on Freud and Frazer*.
[7]William Child, *Wittgenstein*, 13–15.
[8]This is not necessarily the volume's intended form; PI:§122: "A perspicuous presentation produces just that understanding which consists in 'seeing connexions' ... The concept of a perspicuous presentation is of fundamental significance for us. It earmarks ... the way we look at things." In the course of writing, however, Wittgenstein explains in the foreword, he finds that he "should never succeed" in bringing the notes into "a natural order ... without breaks" (PI:vii).
[9]Wittgenstein, *Tractatus Logico-Philosophicus*, translated by David Pears [TLP], "1.1: The world is the totality of facts, not of things. ... 2. What is the case—the fact—is the existence of states of affairs. 2.01 A state of affairs (a state of things) is a combination of objects (things)."

and, as the very last: "Asking, thanking, cursing, greeting, praying." (PI:§23) This list comprises the range of the *euchē*, the "plea, prayer, vow, wish" and "curse," Aristotle's instance of a speech other than the either true or false statement that alone is relevant to theory.[10] Wittgenstein even exceeds Aristotle's concession. What "Asking, thanking, cursing, greeting, praying" have in common is the direction at others who are expected to respond. Wittgenstein does not name lamenting or complaining in this note, still, what matters is that he breaks away from the primacy of the *logos apophantikos*, the statement forming judgments, in favor of non-apophantic (neither true nor false) modes of speech which are not at all beyond the concern of his consideration of language.[11]

One language use illustrating the limitations of Aristotle's binary distinction between the proposition as the basic form of speech and the *euchē* as a catch-all example of other kinds is a funeral oration, an example Wittgenstein notes in the second non-numbered part of the *Philosophical Investigations*:

When it is said in a funeral oration "We mourn our ...." this is surely supposed to be an expression of mourning; not to tell anything to those who are present. But is a prayer at the grave these words would in a way be used to tell someone something. (PI:189)

In both cases, the truth or falsity of "We mourn our ...." is not crucial for understanding the utterance, even if it is grammatically a statement. Yet whether the sentence is an expression of, or an information about, affects (be it even for God) depends not on the grammatical structure of the utterance but on its context. And this pertains not only to ritual speech: Context is always crucial for understanding language-games. A "funeral oration" and a "prayer at the grave," however, are no strictly separated genres. The initially baroque genre of funeral orations (heir to both the classical *epitaphios logos* and the liturgical funeral sermon) as well as its variation in eighteenth- and nineteenth-century German poetry combines oration and prayer to a guidance of affects: The praise of the deceased is followed by the lamentation of the bereaved, and eventually leads to consolation. The aim of the genre of funeral orations is to consume its occasion, to overcome mourning and grief.[12] As in other funerary rites, lamentation is concerned not only with expressing grief but, first of all, with stirring affects of loss in

---

[10]Aristotle, *On Interpretation* 16b.26–17a.3; Introduction, 7.
[11]Wittgenstein is fully aware of breaking away from the paradigm, as the end of §23 indicates: "It is interesting to compare the multiplicity of the tools in language and the ways they are used, the multiplicity of kinds of word and sentence, with what logicians have said about the structure of language. (Including the author of the *Tractatus Logico-Philosophicus*.)"
[12]Eva Horn, *Trauer schreiben*, 38–39.

order to channel them, thus reorganizing a community disorganized by the death of one of its members.[13] Keeping this purpose of the genre and ritual context in mind, Wittgenstein's note on the funeral oration shows more than that one sentence can be read differently in different language-games, or that diverse language-games complement one another. The note, moreover, points out that the rules of the respective language-game determine what exactly "telling" (*Mitteilung*)[14] means: information in an apophantic sense, ritual evocation, spontaneous expression, etc. Wittgenstein's thesis of an indefinite multiplicity of language-games undermines the clear-cut distinction between a stable theoretical terminology on the one hand and, on the other hand, ritual, poetical, ordinary, and all further language uses as object under scrutiny.

Relinquishing the idea that there is one fundamental form of speech, the *Philosophical Investigations* formulates a maxim of formal plurality:

> Instead of producing something common to all that we call language, I am saying that these phenomena have no one thing in common which makes us use the same word for all,—but that they are *related* to one another in many different ways. And it is because of this relationship, or these relationships, that we call them all "language." (PI:§65)

The assumption of a plurality of language-games allows to state what might have appeared as a complication so far: The language-game of plaints is related to other games (to pleading due to emphasis on address, to praise in the funeral oration, to descriptions due to the use of propositions) but not fully identical with them. Breaking away from the theoretical dominance of the statement and the idea of a basic form of speech in general is not without consequences for Wittgenstein's discourse: The *Philosophical Investigations* proceeds as an argument in the dialogical sense not unlike antiphony, as a dispute between contrasting notes that highlights contradictions and details difficulties rather than eliminating them, as a traditional theoretical discourse would attempt to. The assumption of an irreducible plurality of linguistic forms thus follows from an affirmed objection:

> Someone might object against me: "You take the easy way out! You talk about all sorts of language-games, but have nowhere said what the essence of a language-game, and hence of language, is ... you let yourself off the very part of the investigation that once gave you yourself most headache, the part about the general form of propositions and of language."
> And this is true. (PI:§65)

---

[13]Chapter 2, 102–121.
[14]Ludwig Wittgenstein, PI:189/*Philosophische Untersuchungen* [PU], 512.

A later speculation is answered, and stopped, with the comment: "A strange question" (PI:§263). Against this background, lamenting and complaining do not appear foreign to an inquiry into language but as one of many obvious forms of speech. Talking about pain is a language-game for which Wittgenstein holds particular interest because it marks a sore point in the Aristotelian paradigm that foregrounds truth claims and word reference.

## Naming and Claiming Pain

Pain, as Wittgenstein sees it, calls the structure and purpose of the "language-game of telling" (PI:§363) in question since while I[15] cannot tell of my pain so as to make somebody else actually feel it, I myself do not need to tell of and reflect on my pain in order to realize it. Yet not only is the syntactical structure of talking about pain unclear, the issue already starts at the lexical level: "How do words *refer* to sensations?" (PI:§244) The conventionality of a word seems to contradict rather than indicate the individuality of the sensation,[16] first, as not all of the sensations that are called "pain" feel the same (a basic problem of words), second and more importantly,[17] as it is impossible to know, or sense, what exactly it is that others call "pain."[18] Concerning the first issue, Wittgenstein points out that the problem is posed not by the conventionality of the word but by the fact that the rules of the language-game apply to any other, more individual designation just as well:

> It would not help either to say ... that when he writes "S", he has something—and that is all that can be said. "Has" and "something" also belong to our common language.—So in the end when one is doing philosophy one gets to the point where one would like just to emit an inarticulate sound.—But such a sound is an expression only as it occurs in a particular language-game, which should now be described. (PI:§261)

In this note, part of the much-discussed private language argument (§243), the unavoidable logical inversion in talking about language commonly called hermeneutic circle appears, rather, as a trap. In Wittgenstein, there is no way out of the conventionality of language-games, so much so that even

---

[15] I adopt Wittgenstein's habit of speaking in the first person singular for the sake of brevity.
[16] Ludwig Wittgenstein, PI:§384: "You learned the *concept* 'pain' when you learned language."
[17] Given that I can at least compare my sensations, Wittgenstein considers the former a minor difficulty: "What I do is not, of course, identify my sensation by criteria: but to repeat an expression. But this is not the *end* of the language-game: it is the beginning" (PI:§290).
[18] The latter is a problem which talking about pain has in common with talking about color, discussed throughout PI, starting in §1.

a cry or sigh of distress at this insight ("an inarticulate sound"[19]) can be placed within the net of language-games—which alone makes the utterance comprehensible *as* cry or sigh of despair. The conventionality not solely of words but just as much of grammatical structures that might appear as a hindrance to communicating the particularity of the sensation is, at the same time, the condition for being comprehended by others. The relation between word and sensation is no key to the language-game of telling of pain. Wittgenstein's remark concerning the second above point underpins this suspicion.

There is no way to know, or sense, what exactly is called "pain" by others. Yet if only my own pain can be called "pain" with certainty, then communication becomes impossible: Everybody else would be equally unable to comprehend what I tell about my pain.[20] And, what is more, this solipsistic point of view—or speech—also begs the question: "Which are *my* pains? What counts as a criterion of identity here?" (PI:§253) In the earlier *Philosophical Remarks*, Wittgenstein indeed ponders on the possibility that "only our bodies are the principle of individuation" (PR:§60). The *Philosophical Investigations* asks more profoundly: "Is it the *body* that feels pain?" Rather not, Wittgenstein decides, because "if somebody has a pain in his hand, then the hand does not say so (unless it writes it) and one does not comfort the hand, but the sufferer: one looks into his face" (PI:§286). The language-game of telling of pain requires reciprocity as much as word reference (denoting "hand" and "pain") and propositions (ascribing the pain to the hand).

Wittgenstein's approach is remarkable since in terms of modern subject theory, for instance in Hegel, pain is regarded as an alienation from the self that can be relieved by expression, for instance in crying, while stating one's pain appears as a self-reflection both facilitated and necessitated by the split within the self.[21] This relation mirrors the binary distinction implied in the notion that words refer to things. According to Scarry, pain brings about a split between the self and the world and is thus characterized by "unsharability" and a "resistance to language"; in reducing articulation

---

[19] I do not follow Hacker here, who see the "inarticulate sound" as a reference to the "'S'": "We, as philosophers, are reduced to trying to characterize what role 'S' has in the private language by an inarticulate noise. We now want a sound *unconnected with grammar*" (P.M.S. Hacker, *Wittgenstein*, 127).
[20] Ludwig Wittgenstein, PI:§293: "If I say of myself that it is only from my own case that I know what the word 'pain' means—must I not say the same of other people too?"
[21] Hegel, *Encyclopaedia of the Philosophical Sciences* III: *Philosophy of Mind*, §382: "the essential, but formally essential, feature of mind is Liberty: i.e. it is the notion's absolute negativity or self-identity. ... it can thus submit to infinite *pain*, the negation of its individual immediacy: in other words, it can keep itself affirmative in this negativity and possess its own identity. All this is possible so long as it is considered in its abstract self-contained universality." Cf. §401.

to mere cries, pain even brings about "the destruction of language."[22] Schmidt combines canonical and modern notions in assuming that suffering disconnects from any community or common sense of self, and results in a general "speechlessness," compared to which the expression of pain appears as an act of overcoming suffering since it grants a "salutary distance" so that it might be at least "alleviated."[23] Against such rigorous distinction of the suffering body from the mind, or self, Adorno's 1966 *Negative Dialects* insists that "all pain and all negativity" are "the moving forces of dialectical thinking" because "the physical moment tells our knowledge that suffering ought not to be, that things should be different."[24] Wittgenstein's earlier reflections approach suffering on a lower level of abstraction, subverting the body–mind distinction even more radically. Wittgenstein considers talking about pain not as a matter of distancing oneself from the sensation but as an integral part of *being* in pain. He calls an utterance of pain a "pain-behaviour" not unlike the cries of children or certain gestures (§244). An utterance is not identical with the sensation of pain, still, it makes no sense "to try to use language to get between pain and its expression" (§245) in order to draw a terminological distinction between the concept of pain and the concept of its expression. Articulate speech, on the other hand, is no decisive criterion, as Hacker emphasizes: "Utterances of pain, e.g. the exclamation 'it hurts' or the groan 'I am in pain', ... are acculturated extensions of natural pain-behaviour."[25] The way they refer to pain is no other than in an infant's cry: "The verbal expression of pain replaces crying and does not describe it" (PI:§244).

Yet what is the structure of the reference in talking about pain? And what is it that I claim to have when I say "I have an ache"—a sentence that, in terms of grammar, appears as a proposition ascribing an object to a subject (me)?[26] One might find it unsatisfying to point out that the proposition "I have an ache" is a pain-behavior as conventional as any other, even inarticulate cries, and comprehensible due to its context, not verbatim. For what is peculiar about pain is that it grants no distance, neither to regard it from afar nor to refer to it as an object. With regard to the lacking distance that would allow for a contemplation one might just as well say that "an ache has me." Yet if

---

[22]Elaine Scarry, *The Body in Pain*, 5–6. Unlike Hegel and Schmidt, Scarry supposes this to be true only for physical pain: "*Psychological* suffering, though often difficult for any person to express, *does* have referential content" (11). This ignores a basic consensus of trauma studies that psychological pain is a fracture in the psychic structure rather than a "thing" with a content.
[23]Schmidt, *Klage*, 16 and 153; my translation.
[24]Theodor W. Adorno, *Negative Dialectics*, 202–203.
[25]Hacker, "Knowledge," 246.
[26]"Having an ache" is preferred over the more usual "being in pain" here as it is closer to Wittgenstein's German *Schmerzen haben* (PU:§286).

the words "I have an ache" do not actually denote something I *have*, might speaking of pain be in fact completely independent from feeling pain?

Wittgenstein ponders on this notion because it seems plausible that even if the sensation is seminal to the motivation and context, it is irrelevant to the structure of the communication about it. "The thing in the box has no place in the language-game at all; not even as a *something*: for the box might even be empty" (PI:§293). Otherwise it would be impossible to speak of pain without actually feeling it, for instance in a recollection, a lie, or an article. But where, then, is the experience of pain in the language-game? Certainly not within the sufferer as if in a box, the outside of which is formed by (verbal) pain-behavior. In other words, the model is insufficient if the pain has no place in it. Wittgenstein explains: "If we construe the grammar of the expression of sensation on the 'model of object and designation' the object drops out of the consideration as irrelevant" (PI:§293).

The conventional model of word reference, canonically illustrated by means of a tree in Saussure,[27] does not hold for sensations because, unlike trees, they are hardly objects to regard. Hallett explains that "the tree may exist without my seeing it, whereas grief, anger, and fear cease to exist if not 'felt.'"[28] What is crucial, however, is that neither these emotions nor pain permit *not* to feel them, so that I cannot (without medication) make pain vanish by deciding not to feel it. The canonical model of word reference appears to be modeled after the optical perception—*theōria*—of objects distanced from the observer, such as trees that are (relatively) stable in their independence from their perception. Pain is unfit to serve as such a theoretical object. What can be observed are expressions of pain. And if it is impossible to access the sensation in any other way than by means of its expression, Wittgenstein suggests, it is not helpful to speak of expressions at all but, rather, necessary to view utterances and gestures of pain as part of the sensation. With the conventional model of reference that implies a distance between the naming and the named—a distance prerequisite to theory—there is no systematical place for pain in the structure of speaking about pain. "The paradox disappears only," Wittgenstein concludes, "if we make a radical break with the idea that language always functions in one way, always serves the same purpose: to convey thoughts—which may be about houses, pains, good and evil, or anything else" (PI:§304).

Pain may be subject of quite different language-games. In medical papers, it appears as object of theoretical inquiry, however, in telling somebody that I am in pain, it is neither a thought (even if one may have thoughts about it) nor an object of observation but a state of the one who is speaking. The most seminal feature of this state is that unlike objects and thoughts, it can neither be disregarded nor regarded in the strict sense as it grants no

---

[27]Ferdinand de Saussure, *Course in General Linguistics*, 65–67.
[28]Garth Hallett, *A Companion to Wittgenstein's Philosophical Investigations*, 649.

distance. Speaking of pain poses a challenge not solely for the canonical notion of word reference but just as much for its conventional alternative, the notion of language as an outward expression of a previously felt, or formed, interior. Wittgenstein does view pain as internal insofar as it is peculiarly inaccessible to others. The term "expression," however, conveys no precise concept of the interior it implies:

> Misleading parallel: the expression of pain is a cry—the expression of thought, a proposition!
> As if the purpose of the proposition were to convey to one person how it is with another: only, so to speak, in his thinking part and not in his stomach. (PI:§317)

The criticism of the notion of language as expression leads to the same conclusion as the one of language as mere designation: Unlike cognitive processes, pain sensations have no object but belong to the one who senses them. The language-game of telling of pain remains incomprehensible if analyzed in terms of referring to a sensation and ascribing it to a sensor, therefore Wittgenstein's notes turn to the other with whom the game can be played.

## Knowing and Doubting Pain

The question appropriate to "the grammar of the word 'pain'" is not: "How has he done this naming of pain?!" but "what was its purpose?" (PI:§257) Asking for help, a remedy, or sympathy may come to mind as possible aims. Yet Wittgenstein's concern is not the felicity of the speech act[29] but the structure of the language-game that seeks to establish a relation.

> One would like to say: "Telling brings about that he knows that I am in pain; it produces this mental phenomenon; everything else in inessential to the telling." As for what this queer phenomenon of knowledge is—there is time enough for that. ... (It is as if one said: "The clock tells us the time. *What* time is, is not yet settled. And as for what one tells the time *for*—that doesn't come in here.") (PI:§363)

The particular challenge of the language-game of telling of pain seems to be that knowing, a propositional organization, is not at all the point. For what would the subject-matter of that knowledge? Hardly my sensation

---

[29] John L. Austin, *How to Do Things with Words*, 14.

as it depends on me to feel it. And even this is not quite right, since the propositional structure in common utterances of pain is misleading. One says "I am in pain," or "I have an ache," still, as Wittgenstein puts it: "I do not point to a person who [has an ache], since in a certain sense I [do not know] *who* [has it]."[30] Pain leaves no room for regarding and comprehending, neither the pain itself nor, consequently, myself as being in possession of, or affected by, anything. Hence the point of telling someone of my pain is not, as Wittgenstein notes, "to draw the attention of others to a particular person," but "to draw their attention to *myself*" (PI:§405) in a condition of being disabled to reflect on myself as one person among others. In sentences like "I am in pain" or "I have an ache," the "I" functions as grammatical subject, however, the pain or ache that is the topic of the utterance (as well as, maybe, intonation) point out that the one uttering it is has no authority over the experience communicated. Wittgenstein suggests that the "I," rather, appears as the center of an overwhelming sensation, as the site where a sensation occurs, and it is this site to which the attention of others shall be drawn. Yet telling of pain indicates an aim of the utterance, or a clue as to the expected form of reply, as little as groaning does. Telling of pain does not predetermine the form of the attention it strives for, it is concerned with being heard at all. That, however, leads back to Wittgenstein's question of what it is that telling of pain seeks attention "*for*": What can be told about pain?

Essential to the German *Mitteilung*, usually translated as "telling" in Wittgenstein, is the idea of sharing (*teilen*) with (*mit*) others. What can be shared about pain is neither the sensation nor any knowledge of this sensation, as Wittgenstein states in a much-discussed note:

> It can't be said of me at all (except perhaps in a joke) that I *know* I am in pain. What is it supposed to mean—except perhaps that I *am* in pain? …
> The truth is: it makes sense to say about other people that they doubt whether I am in pain; but not to say it about myself. (PI:§246)

This difficulty is not identical with the abovementioned one that pain leaves no room to regard and reflect. Stating that one can neither know nor be in doubt about one's pain, Wittgenstein casts doubt on the Cartesian ego, sovereign of its sensations and sentences. The issue of pain shakes the modern concept of the subject to the very foundations, namely, Descartes's method of securing certainty by way of doubt: Everything can and shall be doubted in order to find safe ground for thinking, even one's own body and the world surrounding it. Descartes finds that the only thing impossible to doubt is that he *is*, because when I doubt—which he assumes tantamount to thinking—I am. For Descartes, this conclusion: *cogito ergo sum*—"I think,

---

[30] Wittgenstein, PI:§404.

therefore I am" is, therefore, the fundamental principle of philosophy.[31] Not the only one to disagree with Descartes's concept of being as incorporeal thinking, Wittgenstein counters not, for instance, with a different concept of being but with the multifold discussion of the experience of pain, pointing out that, first, neither thinking nor speaking are incorporeal and that, second, it is not the business of philosophy to secure certainties and to eliminate doubts. Wittgenstein imitates Descartes's gesture of a fresh start beyond all conceptual conventions in order to stick to his observations and to develop their complications.[32] Part of this project is the provocative statement, "It can't be said of me at all ... that I *know* I am in pain," when nothing seems to be more evident than pain. Yet exactly this evidence is the issue at stake. Scarry explains what she calls the "unsharability" of pain (without reference to Wittgenstein):

> For the person in pain, so incontestably and unnegotiably present is it that "having pain" may come be thought of as the most vibrant example of what it is to "have certainty," while for the other person it is so elusive that "hearing about pain" may exist as the primary model of what it is "to have doubt."[33]

Certainty and knowledge, however, can only be where there could just as well be uncertainty and ignorance. This is not the case with pain: If I have it, there is no way for me not to know it, even if I might not necessarily know why. Temkin explains the problem of saying "I know I have an ache":

> In order for this to be a statement of significant fact, rather than a grammatical proposition, its denial ... must also be significant. That is, it must make sense to say 'It seems to me that I am in pain, but I may not really be in pain', and this is the kind of doubt that Wittgenstein says is excluded from the language-game.[34]

Robjant objects that it is possible to be ignorant of one's own pain, for instance by mistaking emotional for physical pain.[35] This mistake is a common hermeneutic difficulty in psychoanalysis, for instance in Freud's analyses of the "Wolf Man," whose physical symptoms appear to be expressions as much as suppressions of emotional pain, most notably of the grief for his late sister—in which the patient does not believe (SE17:23). Wittgenstein was well aware of Freud's description of defense mechanisms

---

[31] René Descartes, *Discourse on Method*, 25.
[32] Ibid., 7–11.
[33] Scarry, *Pain*, 4.
[34] Jack Temkin, "Wittgenstein on Epistemic Privacy," 108.
[35] David Robjant, "Learning of Pains."

of the unconscious such as repression and displacement. Yet ignorance of the causes of emotional pain or physical aches does not contradict Wittgenstein's note on the impossible uncertainty or doubt about the ach*ing*. That he feels a pain so strong it undermines his ability to live is evident to the "Wolf Man," too, hence he consults Freud. His complaints and symptoms testify to this pain. It is just that, according to Freud, the patient assigns them to the wrong parts of the body, and to the wrong causes. From the point of view of Wittgenstein's notes on pain, these displacements testify to a basic complication in telling others of pain rather than (merely) to a pathological psychic disorganization.[36] The difficulty is caused by the propositional structure even of simple utterances such as "I am in pain."

According to Temkin, Wittgenstein's provocative note aims at the Aristotelian identification of a grammatical statement with a judgment as if it was "a quasi-empirical proposition ..., as stating a peculiar (because necessary) sort of fact."[37] Without this identification, Descartes's groundbreaking conclusion *cogito ergo sum* is unthinkable. Wittgenstein formulates no general objection against this, or any other, philosophical principle but sticks to particular problems such as the tension between the experience of pain and the Cartesian concept of the *ego*. General principles as well as principal objections all suffer from the same limitation: they apply often, yet always at the price of ignoring individual experience. This is why there is nothing like "Wittgenstein's concept of pain" but scattered notes portraying facets and parts of a particular language-game: The shortcoming of general principles cannot be overcome by yet another principle. Given that understanding language-games requires looking at different parts and points of view (or speech), the question of what can be told—and thus shared—about pain becomes all the more pressing.

While it might be possible to describe the quality and intensity of my sensation, it is impossible to share them with others *as* sensation since it depends on me to feel it. The sensation is not assigned to an interchangeable subject as if it was an object or attribute, even though the propositional structure of sentences such as "I am in pain" or "I have an ache" suggests just that. The sensation captures the one who feels it and remains impenetrable to everyone else, hence the ubiquity of doubt in the pain of others that troubles Wittgenstein. The apparent impossibility of sharing pain casts doubt on the possibility of sympathy, compassion, or pity, ideas that figure prominently in traditional notions of ethics, and that one might suspect to be an answer to Wittgenstein's still pending question as to what *for* one tells of pain anyway. Sym-pathy and com-passion promise what seems impossible in the language-game of telling of pain: suffering with others.

---

[36] Freud's revised theory of mourning comes to a similar conclusion: *The Ego and the Id.* SE19:29–30.
[37] Temkin, "Privacy," 109.

"If one has to imagine someone else's pain on the model of one's own," Wittgenstein writes, and a different approach is indeed not in sight, "this is none too easy a thing to do: for I have to imagine pain which *I do not feel* on the model of pain which *I do feel*" (PI:§302). The difficulty is not just that I might not have experience with pain in the same part of the body:[38] If I have to imagine someone else's pain on the model of my own sensations, I have to replace the uniqueness of the pain, the individuality of the sensation that the other's groaning or articulate report testifies to. In the *Philosophical Remarks*, Wittgenstein thus writes: "When I feel sorry for someone with toothache, I put myself in his place. But I put *myself* in his place" (PR:§63). In terms of grammar, this substitution is unproblematic: Just like in the sentence "I have an ache," "I" is a shifter everyone may insert himself or herself for in order to appropriate the pain symbolically. In terms of logic, however, it seems odd to replace the pain *with* which I seek to have sympathy or com-passion. And in terms of ethics, one might find it problematic that sympathy with the pain of others is structurally nothing but self-pity, as Wittgenstein further notes in the *Remarks*: "When I am sorry for someone else because he's in pain, I do of course imagine the pain, but I imagine that *I* have it" (PR:§65). Sympathy thus appears as an imagination of my own suffering that does not side but disregard the other.

One might, of course, dismiss the question of how sympathy is constructed in favor of the ethically more decisive question of whether sympathy is actually displayed. And hardly anything is a point so much against expressing sympathy as the impression that somebody is simulating pain, an issue Wittgenstein touches upon a couple of times.[39] Yet even if such an impression is not gained, displaying sympathy is not completely independent from its construction by substitution insofar is it leads to a logical complication sketched in a note from the *Philosophical Investigations*:

> How am I filled with pity *for this [hu]man?* (...) (Pity, one may say, is a form of conviction that someone else is in pain.) (PI:§287; my square brackets)

The (round) brackets in Wittgenstein's sentence contain a severe complication for the language-game of telling of pain: In order to arouse sympathy, the one in pain has to raise in others a certainty about the pain that whoever is in pain cannot have—because pain captures and leaves no room, neither to be convinced of it nor to be unsure about it. No matter whether sympathy or help is at stake, others must be convinced of the reality

---

[38] Wittgenstein, PI:§302: "what I have to do is not simply to make a transition in imagination from one place of pain to another."
[39] Ibid., §250, §310.

of my pain even though its sensational reality for me is that it does not permit me to make logical judgments about it because the propositional structure is inappropriate to the sensation. The language-game of telling of pain is fundamentally asymmetrical: For someone in pain a sentence such as "I have a headache" is no statement attributing the object "headache" to the subject "I" because pain leaves no distance from which to behold it. For those who hear the sentence, however, it assigns their experience of pain to their perception of the one who is speaking in a way that can be true or false, credible or not. What can be shared about pain, it seems, is not the sensation that is inseparably linked to the one who feels it but the experience of disorganization: The logical inappropriateness of the grammatical structure of the proposition, and of the "conviction" thus raised in others, to pain sensations relates to the experience of being captured and overwhelmed by pain. The uniqueness of pain, it seems, can be communicated only in the paradox manner of finding that no linguistic structure does justice to the particular sensation. This inappropriateness, however, is again perceptible only for the one who is in pain.

The question of how the character of a sensation can be comprehended from what others tell of their pain is still pending. And this is where Wittgenstein's notes on the language of lamenting and complaining come into focus.

## Complaint by Response

The second part of the *Philosophical Investigations* comes back to pain, discussing the "problem" that "a cry, which cannot be called a description, ... [nevertheless] serves as a description of the inner life" (PI:189). Phonetically, a *Schrei* (cry) is to be found in a *Be-schrei-bung* (description), yet in terms of the language-game the reverse is true: Even an inarticulate, non-propositional cry can be understood as a description of "the inner life" of the one who utters it. Contrary to what Lascaratou notes on this passage, Wittgenstein does not hierarchize a "primary, basic role of avowals of pain which he describes as ... 'expressions', 'natural cries' etc., on the one hand, and derived, more sophisticated uses of verbal utterances, on the other."[40] Wittgenstein's point is that an utterance of whichever sort can be perceived in both ways. Hacker and Gebauer/Stuhldreher discuss this issue in terms of an expressive or descriptive function of the utterance, all voting for the expressive, and all disregarding a possible appellative one.[41] The function of

---

[40] Chryssoula Lascaratou, *The Language of Pain*, 25.
[41] P. M. S. Hacker, "Knowledge," 245; Gunter Gebauer/Anna Stuhldreher, "Wittgenstein," 630.

an utterance is determined by the position from which it is heard. Telling of a sensation as private as pain is possible because the utterance can have an expressive and appellative function for the one uttering it while serving a descriptive function for the one hearing it, no matter whether it is articulate or inarticulate.[42] This is to say that while sympathy rests on a propositional structure, it can be evoked by quite different, non-propositional utterances. And it appears that the fundamental asymmetry in the language-game of telling of pain is what enables the reciprocity indispensable to it.

If even an inarticulate pain-behavior such as crying serves as a multidimensional "description of the inner life," this is all the more true with articulate utterances. Wittgenstein notes: "if 'I am afraid' is not always something like a cry of complaint [*etwas der Klage Ähnliches*] and yet sometimes is, then why should it *always* be a description of a state of mind?" (PI:189/PU:512) Grammatically a proposition, the syntagma may serve as a description, call for help, or cry of complaint. This multidimensionality of utterances puzzles Wittgenstein because rather than being a comfortable solution for the question of how language-games are set up, it creates difficulties for differentiating language-games the way genres are differentiated—in order to determine what is a cry of complaint and what merely "something like a cry of complaint." A further note suggests a solution for this difficulty:

> We surely do not always say someone is *complaining* [*klagt*], because he says he is in pain. So the words "I am in pain" may be a cry of complaint [*eine Klage*], and may be something else. (PI:189/PU:512)

The words "I am in pain" may be a piece of information for a doctor, as Kenny exemplifies: "But this would not make them, in the full sense, a description; for the doctor may acquire the same information from a wordless cry."[43] A description "in the full sense" would thus be only a syntagma that could not be replaced by a cry or some other pain-behavior. Discussing the difference between complaints and descriptions in terms of the proposition, however, leads nowhere as Wittgenstein's consideration sets out with breaking away from regarding this the standard structure of language. The issue requires a profound change in perspective toward reciprocity: What the words "I am in pain" are depends neither on the structure nor solely on the context of their utterance but, first and foremost, indeed on whether or not "we ... say" that someone is complaining or lamenting (the German Verb covers

---

[42] There is a broad variety of utterances between these polar terms: "A cry is not a description. But there are transition. And the words 'I am afraid' may approximate more, or less, to being a cry" (Wittgenstein, PI:189).
[43] Anthony Kenny, "Verification Principle and Private Language Argument," 150.

both). Calling an utterance a cry of complaint does, of course, require a proposition, yet the structure of this sentence of recognition is not the point. Crucial for understanding the language-game of complaining is that it requires reciprocity on a fundamental level: It requires some pain-behavior and a response acknowledging that someone is complaining—our response. The question is whether "we ... say someone is *complaining*." Wittgenstein does not leave the response with just any hypothetical someone, but ascribes it to himself and his readers. The complaint, or lament, is one dimension of an utterance concerned about "the attention of others" (PI:§405). It seems, therefore, that every utterance can be a complaint or lament insofar as it is called thus, when this proposition in turn may be called true or false.

This may sound simplistic or arbitrary but it entails an enormous complication for a theoretical approach: Theory considers itself as looking at objects without interacting with them, as Wittgenstein notes: "'Observing' does not produce what is observed (That is a conceptual statement.)" (PI:187). If, however, what matters in the language-game of lamenting and complaining is to realize its direction at my attention, my hearing—a constitutive interaction—then it is impossible to observe and theoretically grasp complaints and laments. What remains, then, is comprehending the parts and possible facts of the language-game. Turning to individual experience and specific cases is an argument in Wittgenstein's discourse as well as the form of his argument, as Goppelsröder notes: "He *practices* the sublation of theory by evoking its condition, a language use aiming at universality and completeness, though in order to let it fail."[44] A theoretical approach that cannot but disregard interactions with its object necessarily finds that a sentence such as "I am in pain" is a proposition and hence a description indicating, for instance, the necessity of medical treatment. This is why Cavell, rather, considers Wittgenstein's hints at the role of interaction:

> I said that the reason "I know I am in pain" is not an expression of certainty is that it is an expression of pain—it is an exhibiting of the object about which someone (else) may be certain. I might say here that the reason "I know you are in pain" is not an expression of certainty is that it is a response to this exhibiting; it is an expression of *sympathy*. ("I know what you're going through"; "I've done all I can"; ...)
>
> But why is sympathy expressed in this way? Because your suffering makes a *claim* upon me. It is not enough that I *know* (am certain) that you suffer—I must do or reveal something (whatever can be done). In a word, I must *acknowledge* it.[45]

---

[44] Fabian Goppelsröder, *Zwischen Sagen und Zeigen*, 86; my translation.
[45] Stanley Cavell, "Knowing and Acknowledging," 68.

For Cavell, Wittgenstein's view of sympathy as "conviction that someone else is in pain" (PI:§287) does not suffice, the conviction must also be expressed in words or deeds. This is not necessarily the case, as Cavell underlines: "I do not mean that we always in fact have sympathy, nor that we always ought to have it. The claim of suffering may go unanswered."[46] The necessity of expressing the conviction of the other's pain is not at all ruled out in the *Philosophical Investigations*; it, rather, seems to go without saying, for instance when Wittgenstein notes: "if somebody has a pain in his hand, ... one does not comfort the hand, but the sufferer: one looks into his face" (PI:§286). Such an acknowledging response appears to be what one tells of pain *for*. Even a gaze can be a response to pain-behavior because what it aims at is drawing the other's attention. And this acknowledgment does not require a verbal form. Yet that does not exactly simplify the issue of communicating pain to others because it means that the language-game comprises the quite diverse aspects of establishing conviction that someone else is in pain (which requires a propositional organization) as well as verbal or active attention to the pain-behavior (that can even do without speech).

Outside poetical or juridical contexts, complaints and laments hardly call themselves "complaints" or "laments." This is not only because many utterances do not realize they are complaints and laments, as a psychoanalytic inquiry may point out. Even if this is understood, hardly anyone complains about pain by saying: "I complain about pain." Doing so seems odd because the language-game of telling of pain fundamentally requires reciprocity. Somebody else must not only be convinced of my pain but just as much realize the need for attention in my utterance. The realization can be demonstrated in responding words, gestures, or other acts of "acknowledging," and these comprise not least calling an utterance a complaint or lament. One more note in the *Philosophical Investigations* points out the fundamental role of hearing and interaction in the language-game of telling of pain, and it may also serve to make clear why comprehending this particular language-game matters for thinking about language in general:

> Think of the expression "I heard a plaintive melody" [*eine klagende Melodie*]. And now the question: "Does he *hear* the plaint?" [*das Klagen*]
> And if I reply: "No, he doesn't hear it, he merely has a sense of it"— where does that get us? One cannot [name] a sense-organ for this 'sense'.
> Some would like to reply here: "Of course I hear it!"—Others: "I don't really *hear* it." (PI:209/PU:545)

The answer depends, of course, on the scope of the respective concept of hearing. Elsewhere Wittgenstein notes: "The truth of the matter is: 'Wailing'

---

[46]Ibid., 69.

[*Klagen*] is not a purely acoustical concept."[47] From a philosophical perspective, the complex of complaining and lamenting might not appear as an acoustical concept at all, but as this complex comprises wailing and cries of complaints, a phonetic aspect is undeniable. With regard to Wittgenstein's question, "'Does he *hear* the plaint?,'" one might find it easy to counter that what is perceived are sound waves the character of which is sensed and named a certain way, depending on cultural, historical, social, and individual parameter such as the familiarity with requiems, dirges, or ritual wailing. Yet the question draws attention to the fact that complaining and lamenting are acoustical phenomena not merely in music. The language-game of complaining and lamenting always depends on being heard (or read).

Wittgenstein's notes on complaints and laments outline what the much-discussed notes on pain alone cannot make clear: Every "language-game of telling" (PI:§363) relies on an utterance and its context as much as, furthermore, on hearing and a response. A language-game is mostly played by, at least, two instances. The language-game of complaining and lamenting makes this particularly clear because it is not based on a single utterance that would call itself "complaint" or "lament," and grants reflexive distance from pain or sorrow, so that the utterance would overcome the problem it voices and does not need to be listened to. Rather, the language-game of complaining or lamenting requires interaction as it is concerned not solely with pain, sorrow, or any deplorable matter, but just as well with the consequent doubts in the possibility of gaining someone's attention, establishing mutuality, and sharing the matter by means of language. Calling something "plaintive" or a lament is one way of interacting, and while this acknowledgment itself has a propositional structure, what matters about it in terms of the language-game is its direction.

Hanfling's discussion of Wittgenstein's notes on the "plaintive melody" demonstrates that more conventional concepts do not suffice to comprehend its structure:

> Why should anyone want to listen to a complaint? Again, a complaint has to be *about* something, and what the complaint is about is normally stated in the very act of making it. ("I complain," just by itself, does not make sense.) But a piece of music, plaintive or otherwise, is not a suitable medium for such communication. Again, who would be making the complaint? ... These difficulties vanish, however, if we accept that "plaintive" and "complaint" are being used here in a secondary sense and resist the assumption that their logic here must be the same as with the primary sense.[48]

---

[47] Ludwig Wittgenstein, *Last Writings on the Philosophy of Psychology* [LW] §748/*Letzte Schriften über die Philosophie der Psychologie* [LSPP].
[48] Oswald Hanfling, *Wittgenstein and the Human Form of Life*, 156.

That nobody is willing to listen to a complaint, which Hanfling seems to regard as a rule, is often part of what laments or complains are "about." The reading is based on a misconception: In spite of the etymological link between plaint and complaint, "a plaintive melody" is closer to the terms lament, dirge, or wailing and resembles instructions in scores such as *dolendo* or *doloroso*. Apart from testifying to a terminological misjudgment, Hanfling's insistence on the propositional structure he finds to be inappropriate testifies to a lack of that which is necessary for comprehending an utterance, a melody, or a text as a lament or complaint: the willingness to listen, transcend propositions, and do something else than scrutinizing objects, or issues, without conceding that they, in turn, might affect the onlooker. Therefore, Wittgenstein ponders on the question of whether "we ... say someone is *complaining*" as a personal one, concerning "us."

A melody may be a lament or complaint as much as a cry, groan, or syntagma because what matters for the language-game is the proposition not in the utterance but in the response of the hearer, or reader, who acknowledges it. To the extent that it is established in reciprocity, the language-game of complaining and lamenting is unlike a literary genre. Literary texts do, of course, respond to the expectations and traditions associated with a genre; Rilke's *Requiem for a Friend*, for instance, does this extensively. Yet Wittgenstein's notes point out that in order to see such interaction, there need to be not only intertextual references but, moreover, readings outlining the link between numerous texts that is called genre, which is to say: interaction with the texts. If, however, the concept of a genre rests on the interaction with texts, and such interaction is constitutive to the use of language for complaining and lamenting, then concepts of genres cannot vice versa be the guideline for looking into laments and complaints.

In the language-game of complaining and lamenting, room for playing is neither between pain and utterances of pain (there are merely conventions), nor between sorrow and expressions of feeling sorrow (Wittgenstein dismisses such conceptual distinctions), but in between these utterances and the one who hears, listens, and responds to them—if there is someone, and if they do. For the response can only be an acknowledgment if it may as well not happen, so that no one hears the plaint, or wants to hear it, or someone hears a plaint in an utterance that was not meant as one—which brings us back to Wittgenstein's question what it can mean to "mean pain," when pain leaves no room to regard it from afar. The language-game of pain is not based on a judgment about the truth or falsity of the pain. Yet if the language of lament and complaint is eminently non-theoretical, and the language-game of telling of pain is not based on an apophantic structure but only evokes a proposition, then every utterance of pain can be accused of simulation. And as it cannot be verified or falsified, such accusation is suited not as a heuristic means but as a means for silencing laments and complaints—an issue as prominent in Greek tragedy and Christian church history as in politics and psychotherapy.

## A Nasty Move: Silencing Plaints

The decisive role of reciprocity in the language-game of pain does, of course, not rule out that something misplaced and inappropriate might be said in response. On the contrary, reciprocity is called into question in laments and complaints as it is often quite unclear what could be an appropriate acknowledgment or answer. Cavell passes over this complication of the language-game of telling of pain that is one of the essential issues in the book of Job. One denying rather than appeasing phrase in particular bothers Wittgenstein:

> I tell someone that I am in pain. His attitude to me will then be that of belief; disbelief; suspicion; and so on.
> Let us assume he says: "It's not so bad."—Doesn't that prove he believes in something behind the outward expression of pain?—His attitude is proof of his attitude. (PI:§310)

Playing the language-game of complaining and lamenting is governed by a profound asymmetry: by the necessity to raise certainty about pain or sorrow in order for it to be acknowledged by others, when this acknowledgment alone is appropriate to the telling of pain and sorrow, not the apophantic structure of being sure or unsure. The dismissive reply in Wittgenstein's note points out a structural trait of complaints and laments that complicates the establishment of reciprocity. Complaints and laments insist that it is "bad," indeed very "bad"; they insist on being inconsolable. Wittgenstein voices the indignation of the sufferer not listened to and not taken seriously, yet the unconciliatory mood of the scenario points to a greater complication: Be it in psychotherapeutic, ritual, romantic, societal, or other contexts, lamenting and complaining speech appears as a scandal because, while claiming attention, it refutes to be answered, and thus silenced, by metaphysical or political concepts. Yet to the extent that is does not remain or fall silent, lamenting and complaining speech keeps pointing out that your presence, our hearing, does not suffice to end suffering. It is quite possible than no acknowledgment will ever suffice to satisfy a complaint or lament. A response does not end but open the language-game of complaining and lamenting.

In preliminary notes to a second part of the *Philosophical Investigations*, Wittgenstein elaborates his approach of thinking in scenes and ponders on to the cultural conditions of responding to complaints:

> A tribe unfamiliar with the concept of simulated pain. They pity anyone who indicates that he is feeling pain. They are unfamiliar with the suspicious attitude toward expressions of pain. A traveller coming from our culture to theirs frequently thinks that a complaint [*ein Klagen*] is exaggerated, indeed, that its only purpose is to generate pity; ... A missionary teaches the people our language; in the process he also educates them and under his tutelage they learn to distinguish between a genuine and a pretended expression of pain. For he mistrusts many an expression of pain and suppresses it, and teaches the people to be suspicious.—They learn our expression: "to feel pain", and also: "to simulate pain", and the question is: were they taught a new concept of pain? (LW/LSPP:§203)

> And how could they remain unaware of the difference of sometimes they would complain [*klagten*] when they were in pain, and sometimes when they were not? Am I to say that they always thought it was the same?— Certainly not. Or am I to say that they didn't notice any difference?—But why not say: the difference wasn't important to them? (LW/LSPP:§205)

This fictional scene imitates anthropological accounts in order to gain distance from those parameter of thinking about language that vary historically and culturally. Wittgenstein's scenario is drawn up against the backdrop of the modern Western paradigm of authenticity, the assumption that utterances must be external manifestations of a prior, unattainable interior in order to be valid. In the wake of imperial colonization and capitalist globalization, authenticity replaces the older paradigm of conventionality that insists on the regularity of any utterance thus evoking, for instance, emotions appropriate to a ritual. Wittgenstein's scenario is fictitious, still, it describes a historical process and points out a gap in conventional approaches to language based on propositions that form either true or false judgments, a basis mirroring the authenticity paradigm. This conventional approach cannot take into account that what matters in complaints and laments is the aim: attention, hearing, acknowledgment, comprehension *as* complaint or lament. In view of this aim, the truth or falsity of the supposed pain is irrelevant, yet this distinction says nothing about the truthfulness of the need for attention and interaction. Wittgenstein's scenario expounds that the language-game of complaining and lamenting is not based on an apophantic structure, that is, it cannot be understood by deciding whether it expresses genuine or simulated pain, however, it evokes such a structure: It starts as soon as an utterance is taken for and called, or answered as, complaint or lament. Otherwise the opening of the language-game is repudiated, as by the fictitious missionary. Honig is right to point out that "this is no crazy counterfactual. We are that tribe. This is how we, in our own culture, often respond to pain."[49] This structure has severe consequences: As no complaint or lament is based on a judgment about the truth or falsity of the pain or sorrow it voices, every complaint and lament may be suspect of simulation. And since the accusation can be neither verified nor falsified, a demand of the truthfulness of the voiced pain is useless as a heuristic means yet extremely suitable as a (personal, political, etc.) means for silencing complaining and lamenting speech. This move hits efficiently because the language-game only arises from reciprocity.

The language-game of complaining and lamenting is not at all a stable exchange, therefore, Wittgenstein does not describe it as one coherent theorem. One important aspect generally omitted in Wittgenstein is indicated in a note quoted above:

> So in the end when one is doing philosophy one gets to the point where one would like just to emit an inarticulate sound—But such a sound is an expression only as it occurs in a particular language-game, which should now be described. (PI:§261)

In this passage, Wittgenstein's discourse localizes pain not in some hypothetical body part, as usually, but in the very act of thinking about the complex organization of communicating pain. Wittgenstein's notes, however, do not allow themselves to heave a sigh, or to make an appeal to someone that would be misplaced in the genre of theory. Wittgenstein challenges the foundations of theory and appeals to the readers of his notes several times, yet he remains grounded in theory enough to rule out that the difficulties of playing the language-game, or of comprehending it, may be a genuine source of pain and cause to complain. The experience of disorganization that appears to be so crucial for sharing pain shall, still, not affect its analysis. Concluding that Wittgenstein does not take the regard to reciprocity serious enough would be too easy; Freud struggled with the notorious difficulty of mutual transference just as much.[50] And yet the fact remains, Wittgenstein's note stops short of looking further into how his consideration is affected by its subject matter. The wish "just to emit an inarticulate sound" that seems to become a complaint about the object under consideration is put to silence by a contradiction that focuses back onto the object and dismisses the complaint.

This is just a single sentence among Wittgenstein's many remarks on pain and plaints, yet it points out that these others leave a gap: Emphasizing

---

[49] Honig, *Antigone, Interrupted*, 134.
[50] Freud, *The Dynamics of Transference*. SE12:97–108.

the constitutive role of reciprocity in the language-games of telling of pain, complaining, and lamenting, Wittgenstein's notes always assume that there is someone to hear the utterance so that the language-game can be played. This presupposition appears to be a conclusion from, or side effect of, the speculative discourse that evokes scenes of pain and complaints or laments in order to look into them, so that there is indeed always someone who listens. In everyday speech, however, it is everything but understood, or certain, that there is someone to listen and respond. This is a main concern of many complaints and laments as well as a consequence from the asymmetrical structure of the language-game of complaining and lamenting (for instance about pain).

While the *Philosophical Investigations* casts doubt on the axioms of Aristotelian notions of language and, moreover, on theoretical approaches to speech in general, it, still, proceeds as monologic examinations of reciprocity, which hinders them from considering the pains caused by language. Wittgenstein's *Philosophical Investigations* demonstrates why the language of lamenting and complaining is inaccessible to a strictly theoretical approach—not by overcoming this difficulty in all aspects, but by bringing it out clearly.

## Relationality and Symbol

On December 2, 1917, at the age of twenty, Scholem translates the *Eicha*, the biblical book of Lamentations, from Hebrew into German[51] and writes an afterword entitled "On Lament and Lamentation."[52] Both are published only posthumously. Scholem's essay hardly mentions characteristics of the *Eicha* or biblical lament genres but discusses lament as "a completely autonomous order" (LL:10) of speech.[53] In diary entries of the time, Scholem rigorously distinguishes biblical lamentations from elegies or Rilke's modern poetry.[54] "On Lament and Lamentation," however, draws no such distinctions but emphasizes the privileged access of poetry to lament, its proximity to tragedy (LL:7), and concludes: "lament, as long as it is lament, remains always self-same" (LL:8).

It is not inappropriate to call Scholem's apodictic style the "tendentious, judgmental, megalomaniacal, pretentiously self-dramatizing meanderings of

---

[51]Gershom Scholem, *Tagebücher 1917–1923*, 112–127.
[52]Gershom Scholem, "On Lament and Lamentation" [LL]; dated in Scholem, *Diaries*, 201.
[53]Scholem's view is thus far from Gunkel's paradigmatic notion, first published in 1913, that a genre or form is defined by its performative context and function (*Sitz im Leben*); cf. Fuchs, *Klage als Gebet*, 278–302.
[54]Scholem, *Tagebücher*, 147 and 324. On elegy in Scholem Daniel Weidner, "Movement of Language" and Transience, 246–250.

an adolescent," as Braiterman does.⁵⁵ Still, this same adolescence might have been what enabled Scholem to radically undermine the canonical distinction between speech and silence that is inadequate to comprehending plaintive language. Scholem's essay is often read in view of his claim to continue Walter Benjamin's 1916 "On Language as Such and on the Language of Man,"⁵⁶ although Benjamin refutes this claim.⁵⁷ Rather than pursuing this historical context, the following reading expounds Scholem's unique view of the role of the response in plaintive language in comparison to Wittgenstein's notes, and comes back to Benjamin in the next chapter.

In Scholem, as in Wittgenstein, the approach to lamenting and complaining entails a departure from theory as enterprise of a distanced, uninvolved observer. Yet Scholem does not relinquish the claim to terminological language, as a 1918 diary entry shows:

> The essay in the songs of lamentation must be seen as a description of my inner state. *With this in mind*, God will have nothing to do with anyone who doesn't understand this. And the essay is *also* just such a description. This is what gives it meaning—namely, that I have managed to use the quiet language of theory to express that which is most glowing. For this reason, the essay is eternal truth.⁵⁸

In Scholem, theory appears as god-forsaken theology: without an instance to reveal insight and yet with the same claim to formulate "eternal truth" in stable terms. Weidner describes the essay as one of Scholem's "esoteric texts"⁵⁹ which examines its object—the Jewish tradition and poetry of lament—and contributes to it at the same time, thus forming a "theoretical practice."⁶⁰ Theory operates in terms, that is, in distinctions; Scholem's fundamental one reads:

> Lament is certainly not the opposite of any type of language such as jubilation, happiness, or the like ... For happiness has an inner core (*Kern*), but lament is nothing other than a language on the border, language of the border itself. (LL:6)

---

⁵⁵Zachary Braiterman, Review of *Lamentations of Youth*, by Gershom Scholem, 196.
⁵⁶Scholem, *Diaries*, 201. For such readings, see Ilit Ferber, "A Language of the Border"; "'Incline thine ear unto me'"; Barouch, "Lamenting Language Itself," 11–12; for a critical view see Paula Schwebel, "Tradition in Ruins."
⁵⁷Walter Benjamin, *The Correspondence 1910–1940*, 121: "I openly admit that the theory of the lament in this form still seems to be burdened by some basic lacunae and vagueness. Your (and my) terminology has not as yet been sufficiently worked out to be able to resolve this question. ... I continue to doubt the clear relationship between lament and mourning."
⁵⁸Scholem, *Diaries*, 212.
⁵⁹Daniel Weidner, *Scholem*, 192.
⁶⁰Ibid., 21.

Scholem's dissociation between lament and emotional terminology seems to contradict a phrase in Lamentations 2:19a discussed in the introduction: *Steh auf!/Schreie in der Nacht*[61] is Scholem's rendering of the call to daughter Zion—"Arise, cry out in the night" (AV, NRSV)—to become a wailing-woman instead of remaining silent in the face of destruction. Besides crying and lamenting, the Hebrew verb also denotes cheering and rejoicing, that is crying out loud for a joyful reason.[62] Yet this opposition is not the "border" Scholem refers to because (just as in Wittgenstein) the crucial structure of lamenting and complaining is not to be found on the level of word reference. "Happiness has an inner core," Scholem writes, a reason rejoicing talks about. Lamenting has a reason, too—the destruction of the temple and the city of Jerusalem in the case of the *Eicha*—however, the organization of plaintive language is such that it destroys the structure of "about-ness" because it undermines symbolization. Undermining the structure of the symbol is what makes, according to Scholem, lament the expression of mourning, which has a complex relation to symbolic substitution, as Freud expounds at about the same time as Scholem. Explaining this relation in Scholem's terms requires a set of definitions that open his essay:

> All language is infinite. But there is one language whose infinity is deeper and different from all others (besides the language of God). For whereas every language is always a positive expression of a being, and its infinity resides in the two bordering lands of the revealed and the silenced (*Verschwiegenen*) ... this language is different from any other language in that it remains ... on the border between these two realms. This language reveals nothing, because the being that reveals itself in it has no content (...) and conceals (*verschweigt*) nothing, because its entire existence is based on a revolution of silence. It is not symbolic, but only points toward the symbol; it is not concrete (*gegenständlich*), but annihilates the object [*Gegenstand*]. This language is lament. (LL:6; my square brackets)

This opening refers to a differentiation in Benjamin's essay which follows Genesis 1:19: In the paradisiac state of language, the name reveals the named.[63] That so-called natural languages are means not only of naming and insight but just as well of judging in statements (and, by extension, of insult, demagogy, and deceit) is what Benjamin calls the "fall of the spirit of language."[64] Fallen language speaks in words instead of Adamitic names:

---

[61]Scholem, *Tagebücher*, 118.
[62]Cf. Introduction, 22–23.
[63]Walter Benjamin, "On Language as Such, and on the Language of Man." *Selected Writings* [SW] 1:65–70; cf. Chapter 4, 188.
[64]SW1:71.

in forms that claim the same reference principle as proper names but are used for very different things, *and* ignore this difference. Scholem simplifies Benjamin's multi-stage primal scene of language into a geographical distinction, wherein the "realm" of "the silenced" or, literally, unsaid is not one of muteness but "that of the symbolized, silenced" (LL:7). Symbols silence insofar as they voice (or show in phonetic script) something else than the entity they refer to—which Scholem, therefore, sees as being silenced or hidden. This fold is to be found in metaphors as much as in words that often do not sound the same as the entity they name. Human speech, according to Scholem, comprises both "realms," using symbolic means to get involved with the world. Solely laments speak otherwise, they use and consume symbols, and thus all objects:

> For if revelation means the stage at which each language is absolutely positive and expresses nothing more than the positivity of the linguistic world ... then lament is precisely the stage at which each language suffers death in a truly tragic sense, in that this language expresses nothing, absolutely nothing positive, but only the pure border. (LL:7)

The opposition of revelation and lament does not collide with that "of the revealed and the silenced," at the border of which Scholem locates lament. The first distinction is concerned with effect of speech, the latter with the relation between beings and speech: While revelation does without symbolic substitution, lament is about nothing else. Lamenting is no "positive expression of a being" (LL:6) but an expression of lack: "the mental being whose language is lament is mourning, ... which is of an exclusively symbolic nature" (LL:8). Unlike Freud, Scholem discusses mourning not as psychical state but as position in the structure of symbolization. "Mourning is a condition of each thing, a state into which everything can fall" (LL:8)—when it becomes a placeholder that does not fill the position of the absent other but merely marks its place, and thus turns into an appearance of lack. This, however, is the common notion of the written symbol since Plato: It is not only a substitute of the absent voice but signals its own muteness, too, as it cannot answer questions about its meaning.[65] Mourning after Scholem is the state of a being that has become a symbol, therefore, mourning marks the border between the insight into beings gained by means of speech on the one hand, and the structure of the word on the other. Lament articulates this border. I has no "positive" content, as Scholem puts it, since the mourning it voices is concerned with lack. What the principle of symbolic substitution reveals in lamenting is, therefore, nothing but the structure of symbolic substitution. Insofar Old Testament scholar Plöger is not completely wrong

---

[65]Platon, *Phaidros* 275d-e, cf. Exod. 3:1–4:17.

when he writes (although with the intention to say some else than Scholem) that "in a lament song the lament is without an independent meaning":[66] lamenting exposes the structure of the symbol, and calls it in question. "It is not symbolic, but only points toward the symbol" (LL:6), Scholem writes, because it does not present any idea but only that it substitutes something else which is missing. Scholem refers to the profound doubt in symbolic substitution that has been expounded, in the previous chapter, in dirges and ritual mourning when he opens his essay stating that lament "is not concrete (*gegenständlich*), but annihilates the object" (*Gegenstand*).

Just as Wittgenstein, Scholem does not approach lament on the basis of word reference or addressed topics but in view of the structure of the utterance. Its characteristic according to Scholem—the turn of symbolic substitution toward itself—is a reflection that presents the fundamental linguistic form of symbolic substitution[67] and, at the same time, destroys it. Yet this means that the structural logic of mourning according to Scholem— the symbolic state of a being in which it marks the absence of an other and its own insufficiency—inclines toward silence because it appears absurd to expound the voidness of symbols by means of symbols. The structure of plaintive language Scholem describes is, therefore, dynamic; Scholem calls it "the most powerful revolution of mourning's innermost centre (*Mittelpunktes*)":

> In order to induce mourning's self-overturning, which, as a result of its own reversal, allows for the course toward language to emerge as *ex*pression. ... What appears here is the truest anarchy, which emerges most clearly in the *im*pression made by lament, in the utter inability of other things to answer lament in their language. There is no answer to lament, which is to say, there is only one: falling mute (*das Verstummen*). (LL:9)

This might seem to contradict Wittgenstein's notion that reciprocity is fundamental to lamenting and complaining but Scholem's concept of a "revolution" inherent to lament does, in fact, correspond to Wittgenstein's dynamic approach. "Revolution" is no marginal term in 1917, still, in Scholem's essay on lamenting, it corresponds to the older notion of a cosmological circulation more than to the political notion of overthrowing empires. Lamenting "is based on a revolution of silence" (LL:6), as Scholem initially states, insofar as mourning is expressed in language, the very system of symbolic substitution that is exposed as void in mourning, in order to

---

[66]Plöger, *Klagelieder*, 162. My translation; Introduction, 14.
[67]Ferber, "Incline," 112: "the self-reflexive movement of lament does not express a 'self' in a subjective sense (it is not an 'I' of any kind who is lamenting); it is, rather, the self-presentation of pure linguistic form."

then fall silent. Scholem cites the destruction of the temple in Jerusalem as "the most eminent example" of those "unheard of (*unerhörte*) revolutions" (LL:10) that can only be expressed by repeatedly falling silent insofar as the lament over the destroyed temple was the impetus for establishing the tradition of Jewish scripture in diaspora. In Scholem, the forceful, even violent "*ex*pression" is the beginning of lament yet—like "pain behavior" in Wittgenstein—only the beginning. Mourning is *ex*pressed to create a devastating "*im*pression" that renders speechless, so that silence returns. Every liturgical recitation of the *Eicha*, the book of Lamentations, completes this cycle: As in other ritual plaints, the songs lend their words to lamenters who might be mourning something else than the destruction of the Jerusalem temple, still, singing the songs is a vehicle for expressing their desolation and a medium that allows to *fall* silent together instead of just remaining mute and isolated in the face of destruction.

Scholem's notion of the Hebrew lament song *kina* (LL:12), Bielik-Robson proposes, provides an outlook onto a concept of language that differs profoundly from the Aristotelian paradigm of language as transporting information: "*logos* protects itself against its traumatic origins by producing a plethora of meaning that immediately repairs the broken world—while *kinah* ... delays the moment of sense-bestowing"[68] and "reenacts the trauma of the destruction."[69] Language-as-*logos* seeks to compensate for lacks and losses, language-as-lament communicates the damage. Scholem's concept of plaintive language thus centers on the very proliferation of destruction that is the reason why, in Athens, ritual mourning is contained in tragedy and wholly silenced in other contexts.

But where, again, is reciprocity in Scholem's notion of lamenting? There seems to be none when he writes: "There is no answer to lament, which is to say, there is only one: falling mute" (LL:9). This does certainly not mean that there might not be inappropriate responses to lament such as the one that bothers Wittgenstein: "It's not so bad." What Scholem is concerned with is that there is no consolation for the destruction of the temple. Even the fact that it was the impetus for centuries of Jewish learning does not redress any loss or death, just as little as there is a word to compensate for the pain someone complains about. "There is no answer to lament" means that there is no response that can do justice to plaints the way an explanation does justice to a question, or a particular act satisfies an imperative. This is impossible as lamenting undermines the symbolic substitution active in such exchange. The "utter inability of other things to answer lament in their language," Scholem insists, results from the fact that unlike questions, instructions, or theories, laments do not refer to any

---

[68] Agata Bielik-Robson, "Unfallen Silence," 135.
[69] Ibid., 143.

"thing" but speak of lack, and expound the absence of the "thing" that serves as symbol (of something else).

Falling mute—according to Scholem to only appropriate response to lament—is no capitulation but may indeed do justice to lamenting. Taking into account the two characteristics of lamenting and complaining expounded in Wittgenstein and Scholem—first the direction at the others' attention, second the doubt in symbolic substitution—it turns out, paradoxically, that while it is necessary to respond something to a plaint this cannot be done in words. Words would merely confront lamenting with the symbolic structure the insufficiency of which it mourns. Therefore, even an affirmative response would structurally resemble the dismissive "It's not so bad." Still, falling mute hardly appears as a response in Wittgenstein's sense. Some further elaboration is necessary by way of revisiting Wittgenstein note: "We surely do not always say someone is *complaining* [klagt], because he says he is in pain" (PI:189/PU:512): Scholem's essay allows to add to the previous discussion: On the one hand, calling the utterance a plaint means taking it seriously, on the other hand this response does not suffice. Cavell comments on Wittgenstein's discussion of pain that "your suffering makes a *claim* upon me"[70] to be acknowledged in words, gestures, and deeds. Scholem's essay introduces the reservation that the mourning or suffering voiced in lamenting and complaining appears as *claim* upon me because while they cannot be sufficiently answered by way of following conventions (since no word, no comprehensible gesture, and hardly any action is sufficient to alleviate suffering) lamenting and complaining, still, leave no doubt that it would be unacceptable to remain unmoved by them. Just as ritual plaints, especially ritual antiphony, are no harmonious monolithic customs but forms of a controversial reformulation of self and community, the "language-game" of lamenting and complaining in general is no stable, routine exchange of conventions but a dynamics of language that explores the limits of conventionality and reciprocity.[71]

This is why Scholem calls lament "the only possible ... volatile (*labile*) language" (LL:7). Concerned with the state of things, all other forms of speech "can leave its sphere, can go into other spheres and return" (LL:7); a dialogue, an essay, or a narrative may return to previous subjects, digress, add something, or contradict. "But once lament has left its line (*Linie*), it can never win itself back" (LL:7) because as soon as it speaks of things other than the insufficiency of symbolic substitution, it does lament no longer. Deviating from this "line," however, is no mistake but inherent to the "revolution of silence." "There is no stability of lament" (LL:7) because it aims at a response while expounding the insufficiency of symbolic

---

[70]Cavell, "Knowing and Acknowledging," 68.
[71]Scholem on ritual wailing *Tagebücher*, 387–388.

substitution, thus undermining all speech. Where it does not return to silence, plaintive language in the Hebrew Bible and elsewhere moves on to other modes of speech: to curses and calls for revenge (as in the first and third song of the *Eicha*, and the *Oresteia*), to praise (as in many psalms[72]), or to a different voice that starts over lamenting (as in the passage from a female to a male voice between the second and the third songs of the *Eicha*).

Scholem sums up this shift of genre inherent to lament in a harsh term: "Language in the state of lament destroys itself, and the language of lament is itself, for that very reason, the language of destruction (*Vernichtung*)" (LL:7). After the Shoa, it is impossible not to read Scholem's German term *Vernichtung* as "annihilation" and "extinction," and the catastrophe commemorated in the *Eicha* certainly justifies such reading. However, in the 1917 context of Scholem's essay, lament is the "language of destruction" not because death, genocide, and war were inevitably the subject of lamenting; Scholem's concern is not for propositions or word reference. "Language in the state of lament" is associated with the destruction, or annihilation, of speech because it is articulated for the sole purpose of expounding the insufficiency of symbolic substitution and, thereby, collapsing into either silence or a different mode of speech. Scholem, therefore, summarizes in a March 1918 diary entry: "In a word, lamentation is language at the point of disappearance."[73] Scholem speaks of lament instead of lamenters,[74] still, it is worth the while to evoke Abraham and Torok's notion of an oral consumption of symbols in mourning to comprehend Scholem's theses. For the second and the forth songs of the *Eicha* articulate the destruction of humans, temple, and city in terms of consumption:

Lam. 2:5 The Lord has become like an enemy;
he has destroyed [swallowed up] Israel.
He has destroyed [swallowed up] all her palaces,
laid in ruins its strongholds,
and multiplied in the daughter Judah
mourning and lamentation. (NRSV, parenthesis AV)

Lam. 4:10-11 The hands of compassionate women
have boiled their own children;

---

[72]Cf. Ps. 6:7-10. In 1934, Begrich paradigmatically links the sudden change in mood to a "certainty of hearing" (*Gewißheit der Erhörung*) in the liturgical context that has since been disputed (discussed in Federico Villanueva, *The "UNcertainty of a Hearing,"* 2–27). Villanueva emphasizes that hearing seems uncertain as psalms do not always switch from lament to praise but may alternate between them (Ps. 31:28-29; 163–185) or move on to cursing (Ps. 31:187-212).
[73]Scholem, *Diaries*, 216.
[74]Scholem, *Tagebücher*, 388: *Es gibt keinen individuellen Klagenden, der die Klagen klagte.* (There is no individual lamenter who laments the lamentations.)

they became their food
in the destruction of my people.
The Lord gave full vent to his wrath;
he poured out his hot anger,
and kindled a fire in Zion,
that consumed its foundations. (NRSV)

Abraham and Torok analyze the disorganization of language on the basis of the psychic structure of mourning; Scholem approaches lamenting, vice versa, as a dynamics inherent to the structures of language that permits to articulate experiences of devastation and destruction. It is primarily in poetry, Scholem writes, that the "language of destruction" is articulated (LL:10). Yet while "Hebrew has only one word both for lament (*Klage*) and lamentation (*Klagelied*): *kina*" (LL:11), both are not identical to Scholem: Lamentations differ in form with time, language, and culture whereas "lament, as long as it is lament, remains always self-same" (LL:8)—the same dynamics of expounding the insufficiency of symbolic substitution and falling silent, the same consumption of linguistic structures to the extreme of muteness.

Scholem reads the Hebrew title of the book of Lamentations, *Eicha*, as an emblem of muteness in articulated speech: "there is hardly any other word in human languages that cries and falls silent more than the Hebrew word איכה (*eicha*, how), with which the dirges begin" (LL:11). *Eicha* is both the exclamation "oh!" and the word "how," and serves as genre marker of Hebrew dirges. As the first word in four out of five total songs (except Lam. 3), the first letter of the word *eicha* also opens the alphabetic acrostic that structures the first four songs of the *Eicha*, wherein the first letter of every verse (Lam. 1 and 2) or strophe (Lam. 3 and 4) follows the order of the letters in the alphabet. In this function, *eicha* marks a rupture between spoken voice and written letter. First because the acrostic is a dimension of the lament that can only be seen, not heard, as it crosses the linear order of speech, and second since the phonetic realization of letter and word differ: The first letter of *eicha* (and of Lam. 3) is aleph (א), which represents the onset of a vowel at the glottis. While holding the first position in the Hebrew alphabet or, rather, alephbet, in the context of the word *eicha* aleph is realized as "e" rather than "a."[75] Scholem's essay mentions the alphabetic acrostic in passing, speculating that it "has a symbolic meaning that is at least connected with the fact that lament encompasses *all* language and destroys all language" (LL:11). Picturing the devastation of Jerusalem and the temple, the order of the alphabetic acrostic might seem to contradict the portrayed chaos. Yet the acrostic spells out the completeness of the destruction, articulating the devastation in the erosion of the referential

---

[75]Ulrich Berges, *HThKAT: Klgl.*, 75.

structure of words by expounding the individual letter. No stone is left standing, neither in the city nor in language. The alphabetic acrostic gestures toward the countless possible combinations of letters to words that would *all* be required to appropriately portray the immense destruction. Between 1918 and 1919, Scholem notes in his diary: *Das ist der tiefste Grund des Akrostichons: es ermöglicht den empirischen Schluss der Klage, indem es symbolisch ihr unendliches Fortklingen anzeigt.* (This is the deepest of the grounds for the acrostic: it enables the lament to come to an empirical end by symbolically indicating its infinite continuation of sound.)[76] Yet how can a form of language that focuses on falling silent by way of consuming articulation and word reference establish a tradition or learning?

## Lamenting Tradition

In Scholem, *lamenting tradition* does not mean mourning its disappearance (as discussed in Chapter 2) but continuing it. What seems puzzling is that Scholem's notion of tradition comprises not only the task of commemorating losses but silence, too:

> The teaching encompasses not only language, but it also encompasses, in a unique way, that which lacks language (*das Sprachlose*), the silenced, to which mourning belongs. The teaching that is not expressed, nor alluded to in lament, but that is kept silent, is silence itself. (LL:9)

The link between tradition, teaching, and silence can easily seem obscure in Scholem's apodictic idiom; however, it corresponds to the claimed role of silence that he does not elaborate on it. Linafelt explains that the link is established in the *Eicha*; without reference to Cavell he writes: "The lament requires that the experience of the one lamenting be looked at and acknowledged."[77] This is demanded, for instance, in these passages:

> O Lord, look at my affliction, for the enemy has triumphed! (Lam. 1:9, NRSV)
> Look and see if there is any sorrow like my sorrow ... (Lam. 1:12, NRSV)[78]

It is unclear whether or not God beholds; the *Eicha* report on no response. The addressed instance of God does not participate in the language-game

---

[76]Scholem, *Tagebücher*, 365; my translation.
[77]Linafelt, *Surviving Lamentations*, 44.
[78]Ibid.

of plaints the way Wittgenstein describes it for "us." This, in turn, is bemoaned in the last song of the *Eicha* that opens with "Remember, O Lord" (Lam. 5:1):

> Lam. 5:20 Why have you forgotten us completely?
> Why have you forsaken us these many days?
> 21 Restore us to yourself, O Lord, that we may be restored;
> renew our days as of old—
> 22 unless you have utterly rejected us, and are angry with us beyond measure. (NRSV)
> [22 But thou hast utterly rejected us; thou art very wroth against us. {AV}]
> [22 Or do you despise us so much that you don't want us? {CEV}]
> [22 For if truly you have rejected us, bitterly raged against us ...[79]]

The four versions of Lamentations 5:22 illustrate the profound difficulty in translating the concluding sentence of the *Eicha*, which does not give a definitive conclusion on the previous articulation of pain and suffering. Linafelt writes:

> The final phrase of verse 22 is a poignantly appropriate way to end the book, inscribing in its near decidability the very lack of closure represented by God's nonresponse and the poetry's refusal to move beyond lament. As virtually all commentators note, it is difficult to know how to render the opening Hebrew phrase of 5:22, ... (*kî'im*), which may be literally translated as "for if." ... one might expect the phrase *kî'im* to introduce a conditional statement, but ... the second colon of 5:22 does not seem to state the consequence of the first ..., leaving a protasis without an apodasis, or an "if" without a "then." The book is left opening out into the emptiness of God's nonresponse. By leaving a conditional statement dangling, the final verse leaves open the future of the ones lamenting.[80]

The silence of the unfinished conditional clause forms the realm wherein tradition, translation, and commentary of the *Eicha* can speak, in catachresis for an answer. What Scholem calls "teaching" is not a particular one of these translations and commentaries but their plurality. Teaching is linked to silence and speechlessness because they establish the possibility for reciting the *Eicha*, and for speaking about them. Linafelt thus concludes:

> So reader after reader has attempted to complete the incompletion by filling the void that exists in the place of YHWH's response and by

---

[79]Ibid., 60.
[80]Ibid.

addressing Zion's anguished concern over the fate of her children. Within the borders of Lamentations Zion's children do not survive, but in moving beyond those borders, to the afterlife of this biblical text in other tests, survival becomes possible.[81]

Scholem's translation of the *Eicha* and his commentary on the "revolution of silence" participates in the articulation of the survival that seems at risk in the songs by revoking the destruction of temple and people. "Language in the state of lament" formulates both destruction and tradition. This must seem incompatible to an Aristotelian notion of language based on propositions; however, Scholem's essay participates in the tradition of lament not by describing the destruction of the temple but by speaking the way lament communicates according to him: by losing its object. In his diary he notes in March 1918: "All lamentation grieves that it loses its object ... It is precisely the countenance of this process that makes up the expression of lament."[82]

Barouch points out the ambivalent consequences of Scholem's notion of lament as a "state" rather than a historical genre or corpus: "Scholem elevates lament to a non-referential language, thereby ejecting the concrete object of lament: the historical Temple and its destruction."[83] This entails, on the one hand, "that destruction is not considered a finite event. Rather, ... destruction is elevated from the empirical object of lament to a linguistic precondition and practice of transmission."[84] Lamenting transcends the particular event that gave rise to it and, rather than marking its conclusion, lament vouches for the survival of the event in tradition. Scholem thus marks in his diary, in a note dating between 1918 and 1919, that the *Eicha* contain *eine Warnung an die historische Exegese der Bibel. Es kann niemals Aufgabe werden, den Sinn ausfindig zu machen, den der {...} [›mekonen‹, der Klagende] mit ihm verbunden hat* (... a warning to the historical exegesis of the Bible. The task can never be to identify the meaning that the ... [*mekonen*, {the lamenter; the one who sings the *kinah*}] saw in it).[85] This, however, means on the other hand, as Barouch writes: "Scholem absurdly weakens the link of lamentation to the historical event that gave rise to a whole tradition of Hebrew

---

[81]Ibid., 61.
[82]Scholem, *Diaries*, 211.
[83]Barouch, *Erasure and Endurance of Lament*, 20–21. Barouch describes Scholem's essay as *apophasis*, "a discourse of 'un-saying' or 'speaking away'" (21) that describes and, at the same time, imitates the unstable language of lament. The Aristotelian term, however, seems an unfortunate choice: Scholem's approach to language departs from the hegemony of propositional language while *apophasis* is a "negation" and thus one of two possible forms of statements (Aristotle, *On Interpretation* 17a.23–26).
[84]Barouch, "Lament," 16.
[85]Scholem, *Tagebücher*, 330; my translation.

lamentations."[86] It is, therefore, reasonable to read Scholem's essay in the context of his translation of the *Eicha* which speak of the historically concrete destruction from which his afterword abstracts. Reading them together expounds that the tradition of lament (*genitivus subjectivus* and *objectivus*) happens, according to Scholem, by way of a ceaseless consumption of both the lamented event and the structures of language that permits portraying objects and events. The link of destruction and tradition is based not on a particular interpretation of the historical event but is, vice versa, what allows for such interpretation the same way as silence is what makes it possible that speech is heard.

Wittgenstein demonstrates that plaintive language is not merely a particular type of utterance but a structure of interaction that requires a response but can, therefore, as Scholem permits to add, be appeased by no single answer since lamenting and complaining reserve a fundamental openness for, or insistence on, further answers. This structural openness of plaintive language is the beginning, not the end, of historical discourses. The fourth chapter features Benjamin's famous theses on the concept of history, along with their precursors in Herder, on the ancient motif of the lament of nature, which assumes that apart from communicating particular, individual or communal, experiences of suffering, complaints and laments are fundamental to all language, world-relation, and the notion of history. The point of view of theory and terminological language, which appear problematic in Wittgenstein's and Scholem's approach to lamenting and complaining, come clearer into critical focus with Benjamin.

---

[86]Barouch, "Lament," 25.

# 4

# Lament of Nature: Benjamin, with Herder

*"It is a metaphysical truth that all nature would begin to lament if it were endowed with language ... even when there is only a rustling of plants, there is always a lament."*[1]

Scholem calls lamenting "language at the point of disappearance."[2] Wittgenstein's notes on pain outline that the fundamental role of reciprocity in the language-game of lamenting and complaining consumes the distance between observer and observed indispensable for theory. In Benjamin and Herder, however, the reverse seems to be true: In their inquiry into the origins of language, lamenting and complaining appear not as instance of fading language but as a natural substratum underlying, and inhabiting, the genuinely human articulate speech in words, even the conceptual language of theory. These two figures—vanishing rest and enabling foundation—form no opposition but two sides of one model for conceptualizing the peculiarity of plaintive language that makes a structural, rather than a historical, claim: Laments and complaints manifest a fault line and contact zone between the specifically human language on the one hand and linguistic phenomena of other living beings and even the inanimate world on the other hand. Unlike Wittgenstein and Scholem, Benjamin and Herder do not discuss laments to precisely define a mode of speech, or text, but for the sake of a comprehensive concept language and world in which plaints mark an important—instable as well as fundamental—

---

[1] Walter Benjamin, "On Language as Such and on the Language of Man." *Selected Writings* [SW] 1:72–73.
[2] Scholem, *Diaries*, 216.

moment. In Herder, lament links human language to the organic and even inorganic world, from which articulate speech stands out although the nonhuman remains present—a connectedness which, in turn, could not be pointed out without articulate language. The fault line marked by lament structures all language and testifies to the complex relation between human and nonhuman animals. Herder's inquiry into lament, however, will be commented in the following only insofar as it is suited to access Benjamin's short, erratic, and highly reflexive notes on lament. In Benjamin, lament indicates the necessity of criticism in the conceptual context within which it appears. It is particularly within a theological context—philosophy's conceptual incubator—that lament points out what remains unheard and unrecognized in a system of terms.

Benjamin's 1916 essay "On Language as Such and on the Language of Man" and Herder's 1772 "Treatise on the Origin of Language" question the conventional notion of language as distinctively human feature by varying the ancient motif of a lament of nature. In Hittite literature, a personification of nature voices the sorrow of drought; in the Epic of Gilgamesh and in the myth of Orpheus, nature's lament participates in mourning the hero,[3] pointing out the economic and phonetic connectedness[4] of humans to the animate and inanimate world. The medieval *De planctu naturae* is an allegoric discourse of gender norms[5] wherein nature is no superior but fellow creation, mediating between humans and God.[6] Benjamin and Herder adapt the motif of a lamenting nature in the inquiry into the origin of (human) language, wherein "origin" is no reconstruction of a historical point of departure but a hypothetic scenario of the systematic question for the conditions of the possibility of human language.[7] In both authors, this question evokes the ethical necessity of thinking language and communication other than as a distinctive feature, separating humans from other beings in such a way that they are at the disposal of humans without mattering as fellow creation. Current approaches such as (human) animal studies and ecocriticism are dedicated to the same necessity, and it is in view of such theorization that expounding the doubt cast on theory's gaze

---

[3]Volker Haas, *Hethitische Literatur*, 317–319.
[4]Ovid, *Metamorphoses* XI.44–53.
[5]Alain de Lille, *De planctu naturae*. In a 1924 letter to Scholem, Benjamin notes that he "had taken up the Alanus de Insulis ... and noted that he has nothing to do with my subject" (*Correspondence*, 256).
[6]Ernst Robert Curtius, *European Literature and the Latin Middle Ages*, 92–93.
[7]Johann Gottfried Herder, *The Spirit of Hebrew Poetry* 2:6: "The best conception of a thing is obtained from a knowledge of its origin." Benjamin, *The Origin of Tragic German Drama* [O], "Origin (*Ursprung*), although an entirely historical category, has, nothing to do with genesis (*Entstehung*). The term origin is not intended to describe the process by which the existent came into being, but rather to describe that which emerges from the process of becoming and disappearance."

and gestures in Benjamin's (and Herder's) readings of lament is particularly relevant. While Wittgenstein's and Scholem's approaches to complaining and lamenting leave key conventions of theoretical discourse behind, Benjamin and Herder explicitly link their speculative discourse to poetry and theology rather than setting them apart. Their discourses are speculative inasmuch as they draw up primal scenes of language in order to analyze them by means of terminological language—because the origin of language cannot be examined from a theoretical distance, that is to say from a point of view outside of language, such that Wittgenstein's line would apply: "'Observing' does not produce what is observed" (PI:187). The origin of language has to be produced by the discourse analyzing it which is, therefore, as much poetical as theoretical.

Rather than discussing the many aspects tied together in Benjamin's 1916 language essay, which has been extensively done elsewhere, this chapter will follow his modifications of a sentence that repeatedly—in the 1916 essay and elsewhere—locates lament at the heart of different conceptualizations of mourning, language, and history: The first part reads Benjamin's early conceptualization of lament as linking feeling and speech, the second part briefly discusses the term "nature" in Benjamin, the third part returns to the lament of nature in the essay on language, the fourth part traces the vanishing of lament from Benjamin's notion of history, and the last part sums up the peculiar status of lament in theory as outlined by Benjamin.

## *Trauerspiel* and Tragedy: "The ear for lament"[8]

Between June and November 1916, Benjamin examines the link between feeling and speech in the essay "The Role of Language in *Trauerspiel* and Tragedy." This essay first features a phrase on a lament of nature that Benjamin will vary in the more prominent 1916 "On Language as Such and on the Language of Man" (written parallel or afterward),[9] pick up in his 1924–5 *Origin of German Tragic Drama*, ponder in notes written in the late 1920s, and rephrase in a sketch to the theses "On the Concept of History" in the early 1940s. In Benjamin, lament is no stable set of genre conventions, and not even, as in Scholem, the "volatile language" (LL:7) of a set of texts (*kinah*), but part of a theoretical process wherein lament is consumed: In 1916, the lament of nature indicates what communicates in inarticulate sounds (feelings and nonhuman beings), and which articulate speech claims to represent but actually silences; *The Origin of German Tragic Drama* picks up these notions yet deletes lament. From the 1930s on,

---

[8]Benjamin, "The Role of Language in *Trauerspiel* and Tragedy" SW1:60.
[9]Dating see Benjamin, *Gesammelte Schriften* [GS] 2:930.

Benjamin addresses the vanishing of lament as characteristic of Modernity's notion of history as progress. The terminological context wherein lament appears throughout Benjamin's work varies tremendously, however, its appearance always marks the position where what is at stake is, first, a notion of language that transcends the concept of distinctive *logos*, or *ratio*, and, second, a clarification of the link between nature and history, ontology and historicity. In 1916, Benjamin considers tragedy and its reception in baroque tragic drama or, literally, mourning play (*Trauerspiel*), as two forms negotiating these issues:

> The tragic is situated in the laws governing the spoken word between human beings. ... dialogue is neither sad nor comic, but tragic. ... For sadness, unlike tragedy, is not a ruling force. ... It is merely a feeling. What is the metaphysical relation of this feeling to language, to the spoken word? (SW1:59)

Unlike Aristotle and even Scholem,[10] Benjamin defines tragedy with reference not to lament songs (*threnos* and *kommos*) but to the exchange apparent in antiphony and stichomythia. Sadness is voiced in sounds fading away. This seems close to Scholem's notion of lament as volatile language of mourning that either falls silent or becomes a different form of speech, however, Benjamin talks about a fading of the inarticulate that is fundamentally incompatible with words. Rhetoric is conventionally seen as what links feelings to speech, yet Nägele points out that Benjamin has good reason to stick to scenic forms:

> Theater and theory are intimately linked not only through their common Greek root in *theorein* (to watch, to see) but also in the two German verbs *vorstellen* (put forward, present, imagine) and *darstellen* (present, represent, depict). ... The dominant *Vorstellung* of theater since the eighteenth century has been theater as drama: (re-)presentations of human subjects who affirm themselves in antagonistic dialogues and self-reflexive monologues.[11]

Benjamin's link of theory to tragedy is heir to a tradition of thought that does not so much put tragedy on the stage but expound the structure of subjectivity, community, and history on the basis of the tragic text.[12] Yet Benjamin names neither Lessing, Schelling, Hegel, Kierkegaard, nor

---

[10]Aristotle, *Poetics* 1452b.24–25; cf. Introduction, 8; Scholem, LL:7: "The language of tragedy is most intimately related to lament."
[11]Rainer Nägele, *Theater, Theory, Speculation*, 4.
[12]Benjamin, "*Trauerspiel* and Tragedy." SW1:55–57; written around the same time in 1916.

Nietzsche[13] in 1916 but short-circuits theory and tragedy as two prominent domains of speculation:

> When language has an impact by virtue of its pure meaning [*tragenden Bedeutung*], that impact is tragic [*tragisch*]. The word as the pure bearer [*Träger*] of its meaning is the pure word. But alongside this, we find a word of another sort that is subject to change ... Language in the process of change is the linguistic principle of the mourning play. Words have a pure emotional life circle in which they purify [*läutert*] themselves by developing from the natural sound [*Laute*] to the pure sound of feeling. For such words, language is merely a transitional phase within the entire life cycle, and in them the mourning play finds its voice. *It describes the path from natural sound via lament to music.* In the mourning play, sounds are laid out symphonically, and this constitutes the musical principle of its language and the dramatic principle of its breaking up and splitting into characters. The mourning play is nature that enters the purgatory of language only for the sake of the purity of its feelings; it was already defined in *the ancient wise saying that the whole of nature would begin to lament if it were but granted the gift of language.* For the mourning play does not describe the motion through the spheres that carries feeling from the pure world of speech out to music and then back to the liberated sorrow of blissful feeling. Instead, midway through its journey nature finds [*sieht*: sees] itself betrayed by language, and that powerful blocking of feeling turns to sorrow [*Trauer*: mourning]. (SW1:60/GS2:138; my italics)

Unlike in tragedy, language in the mourning play is no interaction of positions but transformation: Feelings are initially voiced in natural—neither articulate nor referential—sounds (*Laute*). Sounds become speech by being "laid out symphonically," that is, by being articulated in words and distributed onto dramatis personae. Yet this symphonic differentiation does not transfer natural sounds of feeling through speech into the sphere of music, rather, speech betrays feeling: The sentence "nature [sees] itself betrayed by language" hints at the character of the breach of promise as it speaks not of sound and accord but in an optical register. Natural sounds are alien to articulate speech in words because rather than merely differentiating phonemes and voices, symphonic differentiation transposes sounds into signifying words, into the semantic realm, where feeling is denoted rather than felt: The word "mourning" is not mournful. Even granted that no word is "pure bearer of its meaning" since a material signifier is indispensable, still, semantics—rather than sound—dominate discursive speech. Mourning

---

[13]Julian Young, *The Philosophy of Tragedy*, 68–187; Joshua Billings, *Genealogy of the Tragic*.

plays, according Benjamin's 1916 essay, describe the betrayal of feeling in language as sounds become a mere means for the non-sensory ends of reference and proposition.

Before Benjamin fully spells out this transformation, he formulates a phrase he will keep coming back to: "the ancient wise saying that the whole of nature would begin to lament if it were but granted the gift of language."[14] What it primarily says is *not* that nature laments but, rather, that her lament is legitimate but impossible. And it is exactly this: that nature lacks the means to lament, what gives her reason to lament. Benjamin's essay implies no claims about the communicative faculties of nonhuman beings, the irrealis mood of nature's lament, rather, refers to an structure within human language: It is impossible to transfer natural sounds into words without rendering them something utterly different, anthropomorphic to wit: "meaning" (signification, not significance). Benjamin's text states as well as demonstrates the break between sound and signification, and the breach of promise language commits by preferring the latter over the former: "When language has an impact by virtue of its pure meaning [*tragenden Bedeutung*], that impact is tragic [*tragisch*]"—not, however, due to the accord of *trag-end*, *trag-isch*, *Träg-er* (bearer), and trag-edy, on which the passage harps, but because dialogue hosts agreement, misunderstanding, as well as dispute. Likewise, the promise that words "purify [*läutert*] themselves by developing from the natural sound [*Laute*] to the pure sound of feeling" is suggested not by the seeming figura etymologica *Laut*—*läutern*, but by the traditionally cathartic poetics of tragedy. According to Grimms' Dictionary, *Läuterung* denotes both purification and terminological clarification (*Erläuterung*).[15] In Benjamin, the transition from sound to explanation appears not as purification but as betrayal of feeling detectable only in phonetics.

There is more at stake than an obscure baroque drama genre when Benjamin detects a betrayal of feeling underlying the motion from sound to explanation, because this transfer is at the heart of psychoanalytic theory, itself well known by 1916. In Benjamin's notion, naming and explaining a feeling might indeed lead to its comprehension, as Freud assumes, yet at the expense of transposing whatever feeling it had been into mourning: "sorrow [*Trauer*, mourning] fills the sensuous world in which nature and language

---

[14]Benjamin cites no source. Two contexts might have evoked the subject of nature's lament: First, the myth of Orpheus in Hölderlin's *Dichtermuth* (The Poet's Courage), discussed in the fall 1915 "Two Poems by Friedrich Hölderlin" (GS1:20–21), second, the transformation of antique to medieval notions of nature in the summer 1916 "Über das Mittelalter" (GS2:132–133, On the Middle Ages). The lament of nature allegorized appears to be an eminently medieval motif without imminent antique precursors (Mechthild Modersohn, *Natura als Göttin im Mittelalter*, 90).
[15]DW 12:389, s.v. "Läuterung."

meet"[16] (SW1:60/GS2:139). Because, as Benjamin's details, midway through the symphonic differentiation of sound, words leave the feeling behind, turn to signification, and "errant feeling gives voice to its sorrow" (SW1:61) or more precisely: "raises the lament of mourning" (*erhebt ... die Klage der Trauer* [GS2:139]).

Unlike the aforementioned impossible lament of "the whole of nature" (SW1:60), feeling's lament over being left behind by articulate language is not put in irrealis but can actually be raised because the natural sound has already been adapted to articulation—which is the very reason to lament. Benjamin notes that "this lament must dissolve itself" (SW1:61) and become music as it voices nothing else than the impossible presence of feeling in language. Just as ritual antiphony consumes the reference of words in dissecting plaintive sounds from their phonetics, lament in baroque tragic drama retreats into sound "laid out symphonically," to music. Benjamin concludes his 1916 essay on the "world of the mourning play":

> These plays represent a blocking of nature, as it were an overwhelming damming up of the feelings that suddenly discover a new world in language, the world of signification, of an impassive historical time ... the faculties of speech and hearing still stand equal in the scales, ultimately everything depends on the ear for lament, for only the most profoundly heard lament can become music. Whereas in tragedy the eternal inflexibility of the spoken word is exalted, the mourning play concentrates in itself the infinite resonance of its sound. (SW1:60–61)

One might, of course, object that texts like Aeschylus's *Persians* or Euripides's *Trojan Women* display no "inflexibility of the spoken word" at all, considering the prevalence of wailing in them, however, Benjamin is concerned with tragedy primarily as a contrasting term for contouring the less prominent mourning play (*Trauerspiel*).[17] What is important beyond the schematic complementary distribution of "meaning" to tragedy and feeling to mourning play is what this parallelism points out: While tragedy relies on reciprocity in dialogue, mourning play requires both voicing and "hearing." Assuming that "only the most profoundly heard lament can become music," Benjamin grants the addressee a seminal role in what Wittgenstein calls, seemingly along the same lines, the language-game of lamenting and

---

[16]Parallel in the *Trauerspiel* book, yet without any mentioning of lament; O:209: "For the baroque is and remains something purely sensuous; meaning has its home in written language. And the spoken word is only afflicted by meaning, so to speak, as if by an inescapable disease; it breaks off in the middle of resounding, and the damming up of the feeling, which was ready to pour forth, provokes mourning."

[17]Inflexibility is characteristic of tragedy in Benjamin as he takes it to be a "sequence of ceremonial images that form the nucleus of myth around which tragedy crystallizes" ("Calderón's *El Mayor Monstruo* ..." SW1:365).

complaining. Yet Benjamin's point is not that somebody needs to call the sound "music." The point of "lamentation and its resonance"—as Benjamin puts it in *Origin of German Tragic Drama*, commenting on Opitz's and Werfel's versions of *Trojan Women*[18]—is phonetics, not word reference. It is, more precisely, neither just naming nor merely expressing because while symphonic differentiation does require voice, Friedlander rightly emphasizes: "dispersion *cannot* be sung. ... It is a matter of sensing the attunement between different voices rather than the peaks of passion in the voice of the individual."[19] Just as antiphony is assembled in hearing, symphonic accord is generated in the ear rather than the throat. Benjamin, therefore, underlines that hearing is not accidentally added but intrinsically belongs to lament as "the ear for lament" (SW1:61), or, more literally, "the ear of lament" (*Ohr der Klage* [GS2:140]).

Still, (at least) three questions remain: First, what if nobody listens to the feeling's fading sounds—don't they, still, lament? And with all the more reason? Benjamin's 1916 language essay picks up this issue, addressing a second question raised but hardly answered in the *Trauerspiel* essay: "What is the metaphysical relation of ... feeling to language ...?" (SW1:59) In order to approach these questions, a third one requires clarification: What is "nature" in Benjamin?

## Benjamin's "Nature"

Benjamin's notion of nature differs throughout his oeuvre. The 1916 language essay is based on Genesis 2:19, evoking nature as creation. During the 1920s, Benjamin's concept of nature becomes differentiated, yet the notion of nature presented in Genesis remains fundamental even in the idea of an industrial and ideological mastery of nature. For the exploitation of nature is based on its conceptualization as passive surroundings waiting to be recognized and named by "mankind," even natural sciences and other fields of theory often imply this approach to nature. Reshaping the approach to nature is, therefore, one of the seminal interests in paralleling theory and tragedy.

Benjamin follows Kant, who has paradigmatically provided every approach to nature with the proviso that concepts correspond not at all to what nature is or is not, but to the observer: Humans cannot but form concepts under the assumption of a teleology of the observed, of a purpose that an author had in mind when arranging the object under scrutiny, even if nature might have neither a personal author nor, therefore, a finality or

---

[18]O:54.
[19]Eli Friedlander, "On the Musical Gathering of Echoes of the Voice," 641.

"*purposiveness*": "nature is represented by means of this concept, as if an Understanding contained the ground of the uniformity of the manifold of its empirical laws."[20] Kant's concession to the inevitability of the axiomatic assumption of a creating god crucially interlinks the concepts nature and art: Nature cannot but be perceived as though it was art, whereas art is interesting as it portrays the intricate relation between nature's necessarily assumed purpose and probable freedom from purpose.[21] Benjamin radically foregrounds the perspective inherent to all approaches to nature in scattered remarks, suggesting that the domain of nature is formed less on the basis of the assumption of a similarity among the inorganic, nonhuman beings, and human bodies, but due to a crucial feature of the human outlook onto the world: language. The 1916 language essay thus opens apodictically:

> There is no event or thing in either animate or inanimate nature that does not in some way partake of language, for it is in the nature of each one to communicate its mental contents. This use of the word "language" is in no way metaphorical. For to think that *we cannot imagine anything that does not communicate* its mental nature in its expression is entirely meaningful; consciousness is apparently (or really) bound to such communication to varying degrees, but this cannot alter the fact that *we cannot* imagine a total absence of language in anything. (SW1:62; my italics)

The recurrent "we" of this passage is not merely Benjamin's royal *we* but comprises humans in general, above all the author and readers of these lines who contemplate on the language of nonhuman beings. Openly accounting for the human perspective links Benjamin's text to Kant's that likewise notes: "The song of birds proclaims gladsomeness and contentment with existence. At least so we interpret, whether it have this design or not."[22] With reference to the interpretation of human interactions with nature, however, Benjamin's conclusions reach further. Unlike conventional notions of language as distinctively human feature, Benjamin sees language neither as a faculty nor as an instrument nonhuman beings lack but as medium for interaction with them: Without some participation of living and inorganic nature in language, "we" would be incapable of speaking about it. Assuming that whatever notion of something other than humans is based on them sharing "mental contents"—something that can be imagined or known—with humans, Benjamin contradicts Modernity's purpose-oriented rationality. By the early 1940s, he describes it as a "progress in mastering nature" (SE4:393) which supposes that nature is ready for usage and

---

[20] Immanuel Kant, *Critique of Judgement* §4:19.
[21] Ibid. §45:187–188.
[22] Ibid. §42:181–182.

consumption. Capitalism, social democracy, and fascism agree, Benjamin writes, the view that "nature ... 'exists gratis'" (394).

In different texts and contexts in between 1916 and the 1940s, Benjamin opposes the presupposition that nature is a homogenous realm, separate from "mankind," devoid of language and history. Not all of these require outlining in order to highlight the peculiar link between life, nature, and history in Benjamin. In 1921, he writes: "The range of life must be determined by the standpoint of history rather than that of nature, least of all by such tenuous factors as sensation and soul" (SW1:255). "That life was not limited to organic corporeality" (254), as a biologistic view would suggest, but comprises historicity to the same extent, is an important principle in *The Origin of German Tragic Drama*, which states: "The life of works and forms ... is a natural life" (O:47). Benjamin hardly uses the canonical German term *Gattung*[23] that assimilates a textual *genre* to a biological *genus*, mostly in view of a developmental hypothesis. Benjamin's concept of life, rather, suggests the reverse, an understanding of biological life in analogy to textual forms: as unities formed in human language.

Benjamin, moreover, does not only analyze the baroque notion of nature presented in mourning plays but also adapts this notion to other contexts without explicating the concept's historicity. This historical critique of Modernity gives rise to a provocative ambiguity because rather than filling an empty continuum of time, historical insight is, as Benjamin outlines in his theses "On the Concept of History", a construction informed "by now-time" (*Jetztzeit*) (SW4:395/GS1:701) in which the look back is based. Yet the world of the baroque mourning play is hardly Benjamin's now—except for a parallel to expressionism it suggests: both are "periods of so-called decadence" (O:55), as the *Trauerspiel* book puts it, times of heavy losses to lament. The notion of nature implicit in the baroque concept of history, Benjamin further outlines here, "is quite different from the nature of Rousseau": Rather than releasing history as its foundation, baroque "nature of creation ... absorbs history back into itself" (O:91).[24] Baroque nature is, to Benjamin, the suspension of historicity. Anachronistically adapting this link between nature and history for modern contexts to counter the instrumental notion of nature as present resource, and history as mere trace left behind, Benjamin, first and foremost, exposes that both terms are subject to formation in language. Benjamin's concept of natural history "refers," as

---

[23]He rather undermines it: "A major work will either establish the genre or abolish it; and the perfect work will do both" (O:44).
[24]"From the point of view of the baroque, nature serves the purpose of expressing its meaning, it is the emblematic representation of its sense, and as an allegorical representation it remains irremediably different from its historical realization. In moral examples and in catastrophes, history served only as an aspect of the subject matter of emblematics" (O:170–171).

Santner explains, "not to the fact that nature also has a history" but to the structure of the relation between life and symbol:

> Natural history is born out of the dual possibilities of that life can persist beyond the death of the symbolic forms that gave it meaning and that symbolic forms can persist beyond the death of the form of life that gave them human vitality. ... For Benjamin, natural history ultimately names the ceaseless repetition of such cycles of emergence and decay of human orders of meaning.[25]

What is "natural" about Benjamin's notion of history is no contrast to history as res gestae but that human history is shaped by decay and death, which underlie the symbolical sphere as absence and loss. In a review of Hofmannsthal's mourning play *The Tower*, Benjamin writes that "lamentation is the primal sound of nature's creatures" (SW2.1:104). Sounding is, however, not indispensable to lamentation, as Benjamin's 1916 language essay points out, where he locates the main feature of nature's lament in silence—in the complication of finding an "ear for lament" (SW1:61) which testifies to the genuinely human outlook that synthesizes the rest of creation into one coherent realm called nature. A 1918 note from Scholem's diaries is suited to illustrate the structure Benjamin outlines:

> *The statement "I exist" is always a lamentation.* The landscape also exists visually, and this is the reason for its lamentation. The landscape converges upon the genius, and its visage lets out a lament. Why? I don't know yet.[26]

One reason for landscape to lament is that it needs to "converg[e]" upon the viewer in order to become a landscape in the first place—upon a viewer who is concerned less with the nature he beholds but, rather, with his authoritative outlook as "genius." In his 1919 dissertation, Benjamin comments on this Romantic outlook that "one can also call this ... an *ironic* observation. ... No question put to nature lies at the basis of this experiment. Instead, observation fixes in its view only the self-knowledge nascent in the object" (SW1:148). Scholem quotes the Romantic topos of self-reflection via nature to hint at a logical—rather than phonetic—dissonance in creation marked by lamentation. Within the theological framework provided in Genesis, Benjamin's 1916 language essay expounds an ontological dissonance informing the structure of language.

---

[25]Santner, *On Creaturely Life*, 16–17.
[26]Scholem, *Diaries*, 252.

## Language as Such, and Terminology: Looking Away

"On Language as Such and on the Language of Man" examines language in terms of a primal scene of naming outlined in Genesis:

> Gen. 2:19 So out of the ground the Lord God formed every animal of the field and every bird of the air, and brought *them* to the man [Adam] to see what he would call them; and whatever the man called every living creature, that *was* its name.
>
> 20 The man [Adam] gave names to all cattle, and to the birds of the air, and to every animal of the field; (NRSV, brackets AV)

The scene is a topos in thinking about language, fundamental to Herder's 1772 "Treatise on the Origin of Language," too. Benjamin's mentioning of Herder tends to be dismissive, still, a glance at his treatise serves to clarify what is at stake in Benjamin's essay. In the 1935 *Problems of the Sociology of Language*, Benjamin calls Herder's the "most popular" thesis about the origin of language, "notwithstanding its primitive form ... 'Man himself invented language from the sounds of living nature,' says Herder. In this he is merely taking up some ideas from the seventeenth century" (SW3:69). Rather than eighteenth-century thinkers like Condillac and Rousseau, whom Herder discusses,[27] Benjamin references "Gryphius and the other Silesian poets"—authors of baroque mourning plays—to point out "what resonance the purely phonetic side of language attained at that time" (SW3:69). Benjamin's criticism sidelines that Herder's primal scene of language is twofold, with one "purely phonetic" side, and one founded on "understanding, reason, thinking-awareness (*Besinnung*)."[28] These faculties form, Herder notes, "the sounds of living nature" into articulated, signifying sounds.[29] The view and recognition of a sheep leads to an act of naming, and thus to the invention of human language, when the first speaker says: "Aha, you are the bleating one!"[30] What is invented in view of the Christological animal is, in Herder's terms, the "artificial language"[31] of words, based on abstraction, reflection, "thinking-awareness." Yet this strictly human language would have neither air for vocalizing nor any intention to be heard without the contributing "language of nature,"[32]

---

[27]Herder, "Treatise on the Origin of Language", 75–77.
[28]Ibid., 82.
[29]Ibid., 99: "The human being invented language for himself!—from the sounds of living nature!—to be characteristic marks of his governing understanding! And that is what I prove."
[30]Ibid., 88.
[31]Ibid., 66.
[32]Ibid.

operative in the sheep's as well as the naming man's utterance. This natural substratum of language is the cry uttering violent sensations of the body as well as passions of the soul—"as though," Herder says, "it [the creature] breathed more freely by giving vent to its burning, frightened breath; it is as though it moaned away a part of its pain."[33] Herder's example for this basic feature of creaturely life is neither an animal nor a human but Sophocles's Philoctetes, a tragic character. Herder thus infers the therapeutic purpose of natural cries from reading a work of art. Weissberg remarks: "If one can speak of any origin of language here, it has to be an artistic one already. Philoctetes' cries are created for, and appear on, stage."[34] Kant will describe this approach to nature, just a few years later, in 1790, as the inevitable "transcendental concept of a finality of nature" which "ascribes nothing to the Object (of nature), but only represents the peculiar way in which we must proceed in reflecting upon the objects of nature."[35] In order to see anything in nature, "we"—humans—have to regard it as if—"as though"—it was a product of human artistry, when it very obviously is not. The notion of a homogenous, sharply defined realm called "nature" is such a product of human artistry, a concept. In discourses that refer to nature as a creaturely fundament of an exclusively human faculty, the living beings and inanimate phenomena subsumed under the concept of nature are met with a particular disregard, a quite open (and indeed lamentable) ignorance. Herder's scenario of the origin of human language thus does not spend one word on the question of why the sheep is bleating, or whom its addresses. What is at stake for Herder, particularly on the basis of a common "language of nature," is the invention of an utterly human language. It is this fault line, dividing the notion of a language of all nature from human language, operative in concepts, that is examined in Benjamin's 1916 language essay. At its core is, yet again, nature's lament in an irrealis mood: "It is a metaphysical truth that all nature would begin to lament if it were endowed with language" (SW1:72).

This phrase is taken from a complex paragraph that demonstrates a problematic violence in critical approaches to nature. It starts with an asymmetry: "The life of man in the pure spirit of language *was* blissful. Nature, however, *is* mute. ... it can be clearly felt in the second chapter of Genesis how this muteness, named by man, itself became bliss, only of lower degree" (SW1:72; my italics). The temporal contrast emphasizes that nature has a share neither in the Fall, nor in (salvific) history. What Benjamin calls "the communicating muteness of things (animals) toward the word-language of man, which receives them in name" (70), remains unaltered. Human speech is about creation, addressed to humans, and perceived

---

[33]Ibid., 65.
[34]Liliane Weissberg, "Language's Wound," 559.
[35]Kant, *Critique of Judgement* §5:24.

in the image of God (65). It might seem easy to dismiss this theological frame of thinking about language in favor of, for instance, an evolutionist one, however, Benjamin's point is that every framework evokes the same difficulty: All axioms of insight are based on a human point of view, and of speech, from which a metaphysical instance is invoked. Benjamin's insistence on nature's muteness, still, seems paradoxical as nature is full of noise, and given that the essay also states that "the whole of nature, too, is imbued with a nameless, unspoken language, the residue of the creative word of God" (74). "We only know of no *naming* language other than that of man" (64). Viewed from the perspective of human "word-language," however, in which distinct phonemes are the smallest parts of the codification of sound for signification, nature appears mute, even if it can be denied neither intentionality nor expressivity. The complication Benjamin demonstrates is the impossibility to abandon this perspective, even if the view it permits appears violently ignorant. The paragraph continues:

> After the Fall, ... the appearance of nature is deeply changed. Now begins its other muteness, which is what we mean by the "deep sadness of nature." *It is a metaphysical truth that all nature would begin to lament if it were endowed with language* (though "to endow with language" is more than "to make able to speak"). This proposition has a double meaning. It means, first, that she would lament language itself. Speechlessness: that is the great sorrow of nature. ... This proposition means, secondly: she would lament. Lament, however, is the most undifferentiated, impotent expression of language. It contains scarcely more than the sensuous breath; and even when there is only a rustling of plants, there is always a lament. (SW1:72–73; my italics)

The Fall is seminal to Benjamin's essay since the corruption of divinely inspired language is the origin of human speech. Yet the tale of this origin-in-rupture (*Ur-sprung*) is disrupted at a decisive point: The issue of nature's lament disrupts the narrative of the development of human language with a shift to the subjunctive and back, and the consequent cloudiness[36] of its relation to human language. Benjamin does not say "that all nature would begin to lament if it" had been "endowed with language," but "if it were," as if that was still possible, as if creation was not complete. It is indeed not perfect, as nature's lament indicates. Identifying "speechlessness" (*Sprachlosigkeit*, lack of language [GS2:155]) as source of nature's sadness, however, is surprising after the essay's initial outline of the ubiquity of language. Yet that "we cannot imagine a total absence of language in anything" (SW1:62) means that even the assumption of a ubiquity of language is linked to the human

---

[36]The cloud as Benjamin's figure of undermining terminology cf. Werner Hamacher, "The Word *Wolke*—If It Is One."

point of view. And from the vantage point of the articulate human language of names and judgments, "the communicating muteness of things (animals)" (70) may just as well appear as an utter lack of language. In terms of phonology—of distinct, signifying sounds—nature seems mute. Hence the ambivalence Hanssen notes: "can mute nature ever speak or does nature's lament (*Klage*) already constitute a prosopopeia and thus a logocentric anthropomorphism?"[37] Both options are, of course, anthropocentric.

It is more than a circular argument when Benjamin regards creation in terms of the human language of names articulated in phonemes, and finds that it thus appears mute, speechless, even devoid of language. Benjamin adopts the axioms of Genesis in his essay, according to which language is the medium of creation. The privation is, therefore, no mere question of perspective—of humans regarding creation as "nature"—but turns into a quality of nature, of "things" and "animals." For the same reason, however, it is impossible for Benjamin to regard a scene of the origin of human language as if it was staged, as Herder does with Sophocles's Philoctetes. For Benjamin, it is impossible to abandon the human point of view formed by human language. This entails no lack of analytical distance, quite the opposite: In Benjamin, language appears first and foremost as a medium of distance, founded on the "combination of contemplation and naming" (SW1:70) of nature in order to communicate to God.

Yet Benjamin's parenthesis outlines that "speechlessness" does not even pertain primarily to phonology. To "endow with language" is more than "to make able to speak" exactly because, from a human point of view, language is a "combination of contemplation and naming" (SW1:70)—a matter of observation, insight, and recognition, whereas the utterance of sounds appears subordinate. Not being endowed with a *naming* language can, in this limited, but unavoidable human perspective, appear tantamount to a general absence of language. This lack of difference between the "nameless, unspoken language" (SW1:74) of nature on the one hand and mere "speechlessness" on the other—this human indifference toward nature—is the source of her sorrow.

Now it might seem that if nature was able to lament this sorrow, and articulate her complaint, that is to say that if she *was* bestowed with language, there would be noting to complain about. Wohlfarth thus asks: "If nature were no longer mute, what would she still have to complain

---

[37]Beatrice Hanssen, *Walter Benjamin's Other History*, 161. See Weber, *Theater, Theory, Speculation*, 196 for "the allegorical personification of a mourning nature" in Benjamin. In Herder, a reflexive prosopopeia marks that all notions of a natural substratum of language are inevitably logocentric projections: the hand of a prosopopeia of nature is what forms human language as intention to be heard: "This was, so to speak, the final, maternal imprint of nature's forming hand, that she sent all into the world accompanied by the law: 'Do not have sensation for yourself alone, but may your feeling resound!'" (Herder, "Treatise on the Origin of Language", 66).

about? Would she resemble the Jewish mother who, when her son calls, does not stop complaining that he never calls her?"[38] Comay puts this question in the indicative: "Once it is necessary to lament, there can be no possibility of doing so; by this very token it is always necessary, and thus impossible, and therefore all the more necessary, to lament, and so on ... Lament is either superfluous ... or impossible."[39] The reverse conclusion, however, proves this reading to be a violent one, suggesting that every audible lament or complaint is, in fact, no legitimate one—because it has the means to make itself heard. This implies nothing else than that nobody needs to listen to complaints, or grant laments any attention, as Schmidt concludes, since expression alone already grants the salutary distance from suffering necessary for overcoming it.[40] It is precisely such dismissal and indifference that Benjamin points out as fundamental to nature's lament.

This, however, is only one part of the story. The other part develops the issue of indifference: For even if nature were "endowed" with language the way language appears from a human point of view, she would not discuss but lament—which means, to Benjamin, she would remain at the verge of human language. Benjamin calls lament "impotent" because it is "expression" rather than contemplation, and "undifferentiated" (SW1:73) because moaning and groaning often remains inarticulate, forming neither words nor statements. The "sensuous breath" (73) is not considered the enlivening moment in language here, but an organic residue in a faculty for abstraction. At this point, where one might wonder why lament is counted as an "expression of language" at all, there is a further disruption: Switching from subjunctive back to indicative, Benjamin proceeds to concede that "there is always a lament" (73) audible in nature. Although pervasive in myth and poetry, such lament is not considered communication in Benjamin's essay, which steadfastly locates the language of nonhuman creation in "muteness" (70; 72). Insofar as language arises from the "contemplation and naming" of nature—and not also from the creaturely expression of sensations, as in Herder—audible laments of nature cannot be considered part of nature's language. Benjamin's radical reservation about the human perspective on language and nature (a unity formed in the human eye) does not prevent listening to nature, but averts embracing her noises in a theoretical, that is to say visually informed concept of language.

"That all nature would begin to lament if it were endowed with language" means that if Benjamin's consideration endowed nature with language, one could say that nature laments. Yet such endowment would take more than outlining a fairy tale of speaking nature: language would have to be considered from a nonhuman point of view. And whereas such

---

[38]Irving Wohlfarth, "On Some Jewish Motifs in Benjamin," 172.
[39]Rebecca Comay, "Paradoxes of Lament," 274.
[40]Schmidt, *Klage*, 153–158.

shift of perspective is thinkable insofar as Benjamin outlines the limitations of the human view, it is impossible to fully abandon this view. Therefore, nature's endowment with language, and the relevance of lament for theory, remain in the subjunctive, in irrealis mood. For a brief moment, Benjamin's essay observes nature's lament as unheard, and then looks away; the shifts between indicative and subjunctive indicate this movement of listening, and then looking away. Theory's deaf approach to nature is reinstituted when the essay concludes, in spite of all of the above:

> Because nature is mute, nature mourns. Yet the inversion of this proposition leads even further into the essence of nature; the sadness of nature makes her mute. In all mourning there is the deepest inclination to speechlessness, which is infinitely more than the inability or disinclination to communicate. (SW1:73)

Lamenting and complaining are an essential part of what is "more" to speechlessness in mourning than unwillingness: a plaintive language that communicates by refuting symbolic substitution and by destabilizing those structures of language that allow to form propositions. Benjamin's essay traces how a strictly conceptual approach to the world is incapable of comprehending these dimensions of language and must, rather, perceive the aberration from terminological language as mere lack of language. Benjamin's 1916 essay of language thus outlines the disturbance plaintive language causes in the conceptual grasp on the world, as lamenting and complaining emphasize that which is not fixated in concepts but abandoned by them. In provocative ambiguity, Benjamin highlights what Hamacher calls the "horizon-less-ness" of language:[41] No given mark provides orientation in language because it is, vice versa, language that permits orientation in the world by way of naming, describing, drawing distinctions—which means that orientation springs from indifference. Critical reading shares with plaintive language the querulous insistence that the attempt to come to terms with something is a violent reduction obsessed with seeking shelter from that which does not cease to touch, concern, bother.

Benjamin's 1916 language essay outlines that the theoretical and theological foundation of the modern, industrialized, and technology-centered concept of nature which "'exists gratis'" (SW4:394) entails a particular understanding of human language: As a "combination of contemplation and naming," language is, first and foremost, a medium of distance, of talking about things without considering any response on

---

[41]Hamacher, "Bemerkungen zur Klage," 96; my translation: "that all nature would raise their voice to lament if it were endowed with language, as Benjamin writes ..., is no metaphysical hyperbole of a melancholic, but an objective definition of the horizon-less-ness of what language, and speech acts, means beyond conventionalistic norms of acknowledgement."

their part, and of communicating insight—not for sharing sensations, as in Herder. The essay thus also points out what criticism means in Benjamin, the necessity of which is marked by the very appearance of lament. As North writes:

> Theory is not enacted, applied, put into practice in language or in ethical relations as if something fundamentally alien to it. ... Any theory of language has a theory-in-practice within it that it by and large denies. A true theory of language is not what we can say about language but what we do say in and as writing and talk when we write and talk.[42]

In Benjamin's 1916 essay as well as in later texts, lamenting or complaining marks the point where critique has to set in, criticism of the context in which it appears. But the lament is just an indicator for Benjamin—a liminal phenomenon, like in ritual contexts—that gets dropped as the critique unfolds: Revisiting the "ancient wise saying," or "metaphysical truth," about nature's lament in later writings, Benjamin substitutes mourning for lament, a symbolical structure that can do without voice or noise.

## Vanishing from History

In the *Origin of the German Tragic Drama*, Benjamin rephrases the passage on nature's lament from the 1916 language essay, drops lament, and replaces it by a conception of allegory that is close to Scholem's notion of symbolization: Allegory brings nature to naught by rendering it a placeholder for something else which exposes primarily its non-identity with that referent.

> Guilt is not confined to the allegorical observer, who betrays the world for the sake of knowledge, but it also attaches to the object of his contemplation. This view [is] rooted in the doctrine of the fall of the creature, which brought down nature with it ... *Because it is mute, fallen nature mourns. But the converse of this statement leads even deeper into the essence of nature: its mournfulness makes it become mute. In all mourning there is a tendency to silence, and this is infinitely more than the inability or reluctance to communicate.* (O:224; my italics)

The second half of the passage is almost identical with the 1916 language essay, the last sentence could alternatively be rendered: "In all mourning

---

[42]Paul North, "Apparent Critique," 90 based on, yet not limited to, Benjamin's *The Concept of Criticism in German Romanticism* (SW1:116–120).

there is the inclination to speechlessness, which is infinitely more than the inability or disinclination to communicate." What Benjamin comes back to is thus, notably, the reinstitution of theory in the 1916 essay, wherein the previously heard lament is disregarded. Even more so than the 1916 language essay, Benjamin's *Trauerspiel* book performs the symbolic structure it describes, betraying nature for the sake of an insight into a symbolic structure—which does, however, do justice to the problem that "nature" is a concept that pertains more to the conceptualizers than the referent. This background also informs the temporality of the rephrasing: The *Trauerspiel* book locates nature's silent mourning in earthly time after the "fall," while the 1916 essays see the fundamental ontological dissonance in creation per se.[43] Benjamin's concept of history, formed during the 1930s, corresponds better to the earlier version of the passage, wherein creation has always had reason to lament, even before becoming "the setting for history" (SW1:255) while remaining alien to it.

It is no singular event that the lament of nature Benjamin drafts vanishes from finished works; it is, rather, a paradoxical consequence from the theoretical implications of the drafted structure of the language of lamenting and complaining, as a brief look at two other such textual histories proves. The first instance is concerned with the juridical dimension of plaintive language. In the late 1920s, Benjamin writes on Karl Kraus: "If he ever turns his back on creation, if he breaks off in lamentation, it is only to file a complaint at the Last Judgment" (SW2.2:443). Nature's lament, as it (almost) appears in the 1916 language essay, is irreconcilable with propositional speech in attributions, accusations, and judgments. Turning to one is tantamount to rejecting the other. This irreconcilability is object of Benjamin's 1927 "Idea of a Mystery," noted while working on an essay on Kafka, in a letter to Scholem—and the irreconcilability may also be the reason why the *Idea* did not find its way into the essay's final version:

To represent history as a trial in which man, as an advocate of dumb nature, brings charges [*Klage*] against all Creation and cites the failure of the promised Messiah to appear. ... The court does not dare to declare that it cannot make up its mind. For this reason new grievances keep being introduced, as do new witnesses. There is torture and martyrdom. The jury benches are filled with the living, who listen to the human prosecutor and witnesses with equal distrust. ... At the end, the entire jury has fled; only the prosecutor and the witnesses remain. (SW2.1:68/GS2:1153)

---

[43]Wohlfarth, "On Some Jewish Motifs," 176: "Even before the Fall, the slight but palpable injustice of human language seems to have compounded the ontological inequity of the world."

"Charges against all Creation" are not actionable, hence the mistrial. The human prosecutor, "advocator of dumb nature," betrays nature in the same way as the 1916 language essay, which hears lament as a dissonance in the ontological order yet turns away, toward language as it appears from a human point of view. Articulating "charges" or complaints (*Klage*), the advocate faces the court, thus turning his back to "dumb nature," the plaintiff. Logically, this turn away from nature is an implication not only of propositional speech in words—speech judging creation instead of recognizing it in Adamic names (SW1:71)—but already of advocacy, of talking in the name of "dumb nature," which is thus exposed as being, or declared, incapable of doing so herself. In Benjamin's "Idea of a Mystery," the human mastery of language implies the dominion over creation, and no juridical ruling can compensate for the separation, at the origin of language, between those who communicate in articulate referential speech and those who communicate otherwise. Therefore, "new grievances keep being introduced." The next chapter will come back to the violence inherent to advocacy with Kafka's *Stoker*. Already Benjamin's draft points out that charges and complaints dispense no justice because they cannot succeed in containing the excess of lamenting and complaining that refutes symbolic substitution while insisting on hearing and response in unambiguous attributions. Legal charges, rather, replace those in the name of which they claim to be brought forward for the sake of procedure. Ignoring the difference between plaintive and propositional language exerts the same violence as Benjamin's 1916 language essay, which concedes that there *is* a lament of nature, but lends it no ear. Benjamin's criticism of Krauss thus concludes: "Lamenting, chastising, or rejoicing? No matter" (SW2.2:457)—the voice of the advocate, such as raised in Kraus's texts, is concerned solely with raising (above other things).

The final version of Benjamin's 1934 essay on Kafka comments on "legal authorities"—literally: jurisdiction, *Gerichtsbarkeit* (GS2:412)—"whose proceedings are directed against K" (SW2.2:797). In the *Idea of a Mystery*, jurisdiction appears, to quote Weber, as one of "Benjamin's abilities,"[44] one of the ambiguous terms ending in -*barkeit*, a suffix evoking an abstraction as much as a privation (*bar*): Just as the 1916 concept of "communicability" (*Mitteilbarkeit* [GS2:145; cf. SW1:66]) comprises the foundation of communication as well as its obstruction, the notes on jurisdiction (*Gerichtsbarkeit*) comprise the structure of juridical institutions as well as their failure. The Kafka essay's final version characterizes the jurisdiction over K. historically: "It takes us back, far beyond the time of the giving of the Law on twelve tablets, to a prehistoric world, written law being one of the first victories scored over this world" (SW2.2:797). The *Trauerspiel*

---

[44]Samuel Weber, *Benjamin's – abilities*.

book revisits the 1916 thesis that tragedy is essentially dialogue (rather than lament) when quoting a 1924 letter by Rang on "the relationship of dramatic dialogue ... to Attic legal procedure"[45] which points to the reciprocity of kinship and revenge logic as discussed in the previous chapter: "A trial in antiquity—especially a criminal trial—is a dialogue, because it is structured on the dual role of accuser and accused [*Kläger und Beklagtem*] (without an official procedure)."[46] Mourning play and nature's lament derive from the juridical sphere, too, yet of a different, Christian, manifestation:

> The language of pre-Shakespearian *Trauerspiel* has been aptly described as "bloody legal dialogue" (*blutiger Aktendialog*). The legal analogy may reasonably be taken further and, in the sense of the medieval literature of litigation, one may speak of the trial of the creature whose charge against death—or whatever else was indicated in it—is only partially dealt with and [filed away] at the end of the *Trauerspiel*. (O:137; my square brackets)

Just as in the *Idea of a Mystery* the charge is impossible to decide but left pending, mourning plays keep treating "the same subjects" in order not to settle them but to "necessitate ... repetition" (O:137). Nothing seems as repetitive to baroque *Trauerspiel* as death. Incessant dying, however, is nature's demeanor even beyond the *Trauerspiel*: Benjamin's "Idea of a Mystery" is "to represent history as a trial (*Prozess*)" (SW2.1:68/GS2:1153) which refers to historicity, the articulation of temporality as process, as much as to jurisdiction and procedure. While the law keeps nature pending without doing it justice, history—according to Benjamin the actual realm of "life"—consumes nature, staging it in order to make it die.

The disappearance of nature's lamenting and complaining from history and from the Kafka essay is as a paradoxical consequence from Benjamin's description of plaintive language as the very "volatile (*labile*) language" (LL:7) Scholem diagnoses: a fault line in between concepts accessible to poetic design but opaque to terminology. In notes on his translation of Job 3,[47] Scholem writes in 1918: "*All* lamentations according to their innermost essence accuse, and this one in particular, but they do so not by accusing any particular being—this is what is so particular in this kind of accusation—but rather language itself."[48] Benjamin seems to say something very similar in his 1916 language essay, noting on nature that "if it were endowed with language ... she would lament language

---

[45]Benjamin, *Correspondence*, 234–235.
[46]Ibid., 235; parenthesis from Benjamin, *Briefe* I:337; quoted in O:116.
[47]Scholem, *Tagebücher*, 544–545.
[48]Scholem, "Job's Lament," 321.

itself" (SW1:72–73). Yet Benjamin's claim is in the conditional, unlike Scholem's indicative: "Lament is an accusation that can never turn itself into a verdict."[49] Benjamin's "Idea of a Mystery," and his reading of the *Trauerspiel* as complaint filed away, suggest the same without proposing it as a thesis. Because any thesis straightforwardly claiming that laments and complaints—be they Job's or nature's—accuse language turns to propositional speech and thus necessarily away from those who have cause to complain as they remain unheard in this realm of language, and vanish. To the extent that Scholem's notion of lament as "volatile language" is taken seriously, it cannot be articulated as a concept: Those who would have cause to complain, or reason to lament, cannot—and even claiming this implies a language use that duplicates the reason to complain as much as comprehending it. This is why there is a concise "concept of plaintive language" in Benjamin as little as in Freud, although their respective discourses are incessantly concerned with lamenting and complaining.

Lamenting and complaining appear in irreducible afterwardsness (*Nachträglichkeit*)[50] in Benjamin—be it that natural sounds first have to fade away in order to find an "ear for lament" (SW1:61) in which it is symphonically differentiated and recognized *as* lamenting (in the 1916 *Trauerspiel* essay), be it that nature's lament (dis)appears at the brink of a theoretical outlook onto creation as an ontological disharmony prerequisite to this very outlook (in the 1916 language essay), or be it in the look back forming history: In "Commentaries on Poems by Brecht," Benjamin notes in the 1930s that "lament" is "one of the greatest forms of medieval literature." Brecht's Von den *Sündern in der Hölle* (On the Sinners Down in Hell) "harks back to old laments in order to lament something new: that even lamentation no longer exists" (SW4:227). The fading of lament is, literally, the "latest" (*dies Neueste* [GS2:550]) thing to lament. Benjamin thus joins Modernity's lament over the loss of ritual forms in modernizations—especially the eradication of ritual and liturgical lamentation in reformation, which Benjamin describes as baroque mourning plays' historical context,[51] and the transformation of experience and narration in the First World War[52]—a lament over the loss of lament that renews the lost form one last time, as does Rilke's *Requiem for a Friend*.

In a second instance of a sketch of lament's role in history fading from the final version of the text, Benjamin identifies a particular notion of history, or historiography, as reason for the fading of lament. In paralipomena to "On the Concept of History" Benjamin notes:

---

[49]Ibid., 322.
[50]Cf. Chapter 1, 37.
[51]O:78–80; Comay, "Paradoxes of Lament," 275–276.
[52]Conclusion, 245–247.

> The "scientific" character of history, as defined by positivism ... is secured at the cost of completely eradicating every vestige of history's original role of remembrance (*Eingedenken*). The false aliveness of the past-made-present, the elimination of every echo of "lament" ["*Klage*"] from history, marks history's final subjection to the modern concept of science. (SW4:401/GS1:1231; my square brackets)

The objectivity claimed by a positivist approach to history eradicates lament because it sympathizes, as the final version of the "Concept of History" notes, "with the victor. And all rulers are heirs of prior conquerors" (SW4:391). Sticking to documents and monuments as "dates" and "facts," positivist historiography passes over the victims of those who wrote, or erected, them, thus mimicking victory in "scientific" objectivism. In this notion, it is no longer (solely) the ontological dissonance due to which natural sounds of feelings are alien to articulate speech and "impassive historical time" (SW1:60), as the 1916 essays outline but, rather, a particular, itself historical concept of history that eradicates lament. This latter notion, however, comprises an eminent complication: If any echo of lament or complaint has indeed been eliminated from history, then there is no noticeable remnant of plaintive language that might serve as a basis for lamenting over, or arguing for, its elimination. Then there is only: Silence on the issue of plaints. The commentary on Brecht's text, which laments "[the latest]: that even lamentation no longer exists," hence hurries on to mark: "But the poem does not properly lament this lack of tears" (SW4:227). Of course not, because there is no "prope[r]" lament anymore, none unmarked by the notion of an anachronism of the genre. In the sketch for the "Concept of History," Benjamin's quotation marks embracing "*Klage*" seem to acknowledge this difficulty: To the extent that the claim of an echoless elimination of lament from history is true, it cannot be articulated. Benjamin thus takes into account that laments and complaints are up to those of whom there is no remainder in history and terminological language because they are lost to the violence of the formation of history and terminological language. It is, therefore—in tantalizing ambiguity—as consistent as alarming that the note on the elimination of lament is not included in the final version of the thesis "On the Concept of History." Lament vanishes not only from the historiography of the victors and from terminological language but even from the critical analysis of their constitutive shortcomings. Not linking plaintive language to any promise of compensation or restoration in propositional language, it seems that unlike Freud, Benjamin sees no way for theory to respond to plaintive language, to "work it out," and that this is not even at the ruin of theory—which is, of course, all the more ruinous. It is only in his notes on the widespread experience of trauma in the First World War, discussed in conclusion of this volume, that Benjamin hints at a discontinuity that remains after the echoless elimination of lament from history: a speechlessness.

The elimination of lament from history is not solely analyzed as aftermath of a positivist notion of history but just as well performed throughout Benjamin's oeuvre. A concluding look at the *Origin of the German Tragic Drama* shall outline the consequences of Benjamin's ambiguous approach to lament for the inquiry into the structure of lamenting and complaining in general.

## Lament and Theory, Once Again

While revisiting the idea of nature's mourning and muteness, the 1925 *Trauerspiel* book discusses lament neither with regard to nature nor in the context of a "theory of mourning" (O:139). In the *Trauerspiel* book, the "fragmentation of language" (O:ii) is an effect not of lamenting, as in Scholem, but of allegory, which takes the focal position lament holds in the 1916 *Trauerspiel* essay. One, even if certainly not the sole, reason for this substitution is that the gaze of theory, as articulated in Benjamin, itself makes lament vanish—"betrays" it, as the 1916 essay holds (SW1:60).[53] A rarely commented passage in the *Trauerspiel* book illustrates that it does not merely keep silent on lament but indeed silences it. In this passage, Benjamin refers to a dispute between Winckelmann, Lessing, and Herder, formative for enlightenment aesthetics, on how to read crying, wailing, and lamenting in Greek art: not at all, as in Winckelmann's praise for Laocoon's silent suffering,[54] as "natural expression of bodily pain,"[55] as Lessing counters with reference to Sophocles's *Philoctetes*, vouching for the proximity of Greek art to nature, or as artifice, as Herder in turn counters Lessing, pointing out the irreducibly poetic fabrication of everything "natural" in human language.[56] Benjamin writes:

> It was as ... laments that the *Sturm und Drang* read the choruses of tragedy, hereby retaining an element of the baroque interpretation of tragedy. In his criticism of (Lessing's) *Laocoon* in his first part the *Kritische W[ä]lder* Herder writes ... of the loudly lamenting Greeks with their "susceptibility ... to gentle tears". *Really the chorus of tragedy does*

---

[53] Allegory, it might be further assumed, appears not as one among many rhetorical devices in the *Trauerspiel* book but as the seminal figure of Christian hermeneutics—since Paulus' Gal. 4:24—which undergo a profound transformation in baroque mourning play in the wake of reformation.
[54] Simon Richter, *Laocoon's Body and the Aesthetics of Pain*, 90–106.
[55] Gotthold Ephraim Lessing, *Laocoon; or the Limits of Poetry and Painting*, 5.
[56] Herder, *Critical Forests* 1:2, 57 (quoting Lessing ibid.): "Where are 'the laments, the cries, the wild curses ...' Where are they? On the stage? Yes, but they are merely described ... the cries are not enacted."

*not lament*. It remains detached in the presence of profound suffering; this refutes the idea of surrender to lamentation. It is a superficial view of such detachment to seek to explain it in terms of indifference or even pity. Choric diction, rather, has the effect of restoring the ruins of the tragic dialogue to a linguistic edifice firmly established—in ethical society and religious community—both before and after the conflict. Far from dissolving the tragic action into lamentations, the constant presence of the members of the chorus, as Lessing already observed, actually sets a limit on the emotional outburst even in dialogue. The conception of the chorus as a *Trauerklage* (lamentation) in which 'the original pain of creation resounds', is a genuinely baroque reinterpretation of its essence. For the chorus of the German *Trauerspiel* does, at least partially, have this function. (O:121; my italics)[57]

This passage revisits the 1916 *Trauerspiel* essay's assumption: "The tragic is situated in the laws governing the spoken word between human beings" (SW1:59). In the 1925 book, Benjamin refers to Lessing in reading the function of the chorus as delimiting the affects evoked in dialogue. Benjamin's conclusion, however, that "really the chorus of tragedy does not lament," contradicts contemporary and current research on chorus and *kommos*, the "song of lament shared by the chorus and the actors on the stage."[58] Unlike Weigel suggests, Benjamin's claim is not "solidly grounded in the verbal enormity displayed by the Greek chorus."[59] That the chorus delimitates affects might be correct for Sophocles's *Philoctetes* yet in Aeschylus's *Persians* and *Oresteia*, or Euripides's *Trojan Women*, the

---

[57]Note 47: Herder, *Critical Forests* 1:3, 61: "The susceptibility of the Greeks to gentle tears is so familiar to us from any number of testimonies that unlike Mr. Lessing we need not take only a single example." Cf. Lessing, *Laocoon*, 9: "It is remarkable that, among the few tragedies which have been preserved to us from antiquity, there are two in which bodily pain is not the least of the misfortunes with which the suffering hero is assailed. Besides the Philoctetes, we have the Dying Hercules, who is likewise represented by Sophocles as moaning, weeping, and shrieking with pain."—note 48: Lessing, *Hamburg Dramaturgy* no. 59: "But we moderns who have abolished the chorus and, for the most part, keep our characters within their four walls, what grounds can we have then for such decorous, fastidious, pretentious speech? No one hears it other than those the characters allow to hear it, nobody speaks but people who are also involved in the action and who are therefore in the heat of passion themselves and have neither the inclination nor the leisure to control their expressions. That was the domain of the chorus, which, as tightly as it might have been woven into the play, nevertheless never took part in the action and always judged the active characters more than it really sympathized with their fates."—note 49: Hans Ehrenberg, *Tragödie und Kreuz*, 1:112-113: "The chorus says what humankind has suffered until Aeschylus' days. ... The sound of lament swoosh over us, who stand at the grave, burying the deceased. The original pain of creation resounds" (My translation).
[58]*Poetics* 1452b.24–25; Introduction, 8.
[59]Sigrid Weigel, "Brünnhilde's Lament," 6.

chorus laments extensively, dissolving articulation—the "linguistic edifice firmly established"—into sounds of pain, lament, and wailing. The notion of a "surrender to lamentation," or literally: lamenting devotion (*klagend[e] Hingebung* [GS1:300]) is solitary in this passage, Benjamin never mentions it again. What matters to him is, like in the 1916 *Trauerspiel* essay, emphasizing tragedy's stark contrast to baroque mourning play,[60] where lamenting devotion is to be found in the chorus (*Reyen* [GS1:300]) as "ornamental ... frames enclosing the act" (SW1:121) first as "dancing chorus," later in the genre history as "spoken, oratorical chorus" (211). An optical frame of the presented action is, for instance, the list of "mute choruses" of women, murdered ghosts, virtues, death, and love (*deß Frauen Zimmers. Der ermordeten Geister. Der Tugenden. Deß Todes vnd der Liebe*) in Gryphius's 1657 *Catharina von Georgien* (Catherine of Georgia), an acoustical frame is the paradoxically voiced "chorus of princes strangled by Chach Abas" (*Reye der von Chach Abas erwürgeten Fürsten*).[61] Benjamin's claim, that "really the chorus of tragedy does not lament," rests on no specific notion of lament but follows from the rather schematic complementary distribution of feeling to mourning play and dialogue to tragedy. The latter, in turn, rests not only on his 1916 essay, but just as well on his reading of Rosenzweig's 1921 *Star of Redemption*.

Bielik-Robson has shown that Benjamin's view of tragedy as dialogue draws strongly on Rosenzweig's notion of silence as the form of speech appropriate to the tragic hero.[62] Benjamin emphasizes particularly the "silence residing in lamentation."[63] With reference to the hero's silence, Rosenzweig attributes a particular function to the chorus: "In ancient tragedy, what else is the chorus but this breaking in of the outer world upon the hero, this call addressed to the figure that is as mute as marble?"[64]

---

[60] An emphasis of the distinction seems all the more pressing since Benjamin's material contradicts it: Opitz's definition of baroque *Trauerspiel* calls it *Tragödie* (O:62/GS1:242), Lessing, in the passage alluded to in Benjamin's O:121 note 47, refers to Greek tragedy as *Trauerspiel[e]* (*Laokoon, oder Über die Grenzen der Malerei und Poesie*, 20).
[61] Andreas Gryphius, *Catharina von Georgien*, 11 and 63; cf. the latter's final sequence (65:413–416): "*Ernster Richter! übe Rache!/Wache! grosser Gott erwache./Wache! Wache! Wache! Wache;/Rache! Rache! Rache! Rache!*"
[62] Agata Bielik-Robson, *Jewish Cryptotheologies of Late Modernity*, 96–99; cf. Franz Rosenzweig, *The Star of Redemption*, 85: "The tragic hero has only one language that is in perfect accordance with him: precisely, silence." Quoted in O:108.
[63] Bielik-Robson, *Jewish Cryptotheologies*, 97; cf. 89–90: "Benjamin very consciously conflates the tragic hero with Job ... The tragedy, thus messianized, turn into 'the trial before the higher court' ..., where the laws of natural life are being questioned and impeached, and the chorus only barely prevents 'from dissolving tragic action into lamentations' ... which, like Job's eloquent and vitriolic *kinah*, lurk constantly behind the stubborn silence on the tragic hero (this is why the baroque evolution of the chorus in the *Trauerklage* seems like an obvious development)."
[64] Rosenzweig, *Star of Redemption*, 222.

Choral odes are a social medium in Rosenzweig. The choral "We" forms no unison but "all the voices have become independent" and synthesize. In this "harmony" the "true mystery of language" appears: "the word speaks."[65] Benjamin adopts Rosenzweig's notion of chorus and dialogue to support his thesis: "The tragic devised itself the tragic form of the drama precisely so as to be able to present silence," to bring out "the experience of speechlessness" from dialogue (O:108). If the chorus is determined to form the background for silence, it cannot (also) be the medium for the disorganization and consumption of the structures of articulate dialogic speech but must, on the contrary, safeguard these—hence Benjamin's surprising thesis: "Really the chorus of tragedy does not lament" (O:121). Where a notion originates and what it entails, however, are two different things.

Localizing lament neither in natural sound that touches articulate language (as in the 1916 *Trauerspiel* essay) nor in tragedy but in the chorus (*Reyen*) of baroque mourning play, the *Trauerspiel* book renders lamenting an ornament in the image of the incessantly passing, of constant death. Benjamin writes:

> The chorus of the baroque drama is not something external. It is as internal to it as the carving of a Gothic altar behind the open wings on which stories from the lives of the saints are painted. ... In the chorus, or the interlude, allegory is no longer colourful, rich in historical associations, but pure and severe. (O:190)

The *Trauerspiel* book follows this up with an extensive theory of allegory while lament is not mentioned again, even if it has been declared "internal" to mourning plays as element, or "devotion" (GS1:300), of the chorus. One might sum up the contrasting poetics of tragedy and *Trauerspiel* as Weber:

> The Greek hero ... does not and cannot know the meaning of his silence—or his death. The German *Trauerspiel*, by contrast, thinks it knows the meaning of what is said and done, but knows it as pure negation. This is why its basic stance is that not of silent resistance, but of noisy complaint and accusation: not *Trotz* but *Klage*.[66]

What is missing from this comparison of poetics, however, is Benjamin's falling-silent on lament, compared to the pivotal role it plays in the 1916 essays. Benjamin's poetics of theory, as it were, is highly ambivalent with regard to lament. For against the backdrop of his 1916 assumptions, first, that "ultimately everything depends on the ear for lament" (SW1:60), second, that lament indicates a fault line in between the concepts of creation

---

[65]Ibid., 254–255.
[66]Samuel Weber, "Tragedy and *Trauerspiel*," 101.

and language within which those who would have to lament and complain must remain unheard, and the later claim that lament has been eliminated from history, the fading of lament from the *Trauerspiel* book permits of two contrary conclusions: Does Benjamin simply drop his 1916 notion of *Trauerspiel* as passage from natural sounds to lament and, therefore, does not mention it? Or is the silence of lament a consequence from his earlier notion of lament as something that is lost on propositional speech and terminological language? The latter poetics of silence-as-indicator—"a mute address"—is seminal, for instance, to Felman's reading of Benjamin's silence on the death of his friend Hessel.[67]

Benjamin's texts radically portray the eminent difficulty any inquiry into plaintive language faces: While texts and genres of lament and complaint may be read critically (as in this study), they evade abstraction into a poetic, aesthetic, or other theory because the language of lamenting and complaining neither fixates nor constitutes but decomposes structures, thus expounding fault lines and dissonances in the contexts wherein they appear. Should the fading of the issue of lament from Benjamin's later works indeed be an, although paradoxical, conclusion from the thesis on plaintive language formulated in early works and later drafts, this radically comments the question, raised in the 1916 language essay, what communicating means: Can something be communicated by, or communicate in, silence? In view of Benjamin's assumption that tragedy releases the "experience of speechlessness" and "dumb anguish" (O:107–108), the fading of nature's lament might even be viewed as a release of "the communicating muteness of things (animals)" (SW1:70) proposed in the 1916 language essay, which is otherwise named and thus in a certain sense eliminated.

These assumptions certainly push the concept of critical reading beyond defendable limits. Reading what is not being said is merely claiming, and the release of lament in silence is indistinguishable from remaining silent due to a disinterest in lament, or suppressed mourning. Yet it is nowhere else than at the brinks of theory where Benjamin's "Epistemo-Critical Prologue" to the *Trauerspiel* book locates what he calls an "idea." Explaining that his study neither writes the history of a genre nor formulates a concept comparable to that of "the tragic" in philosophy, Benjamin notes: "As ideas, however, such names perform a service they are not able to perform as concepts: they do not make the similar identical, but they effect a synthesis between extremes" (O:41). An idea is hence no means for ordering discourses, just as little as it is a theoretical object: "Ideas are not among the given elements of the world of phenomena. ... The being of ideas simply cannot be conceived of as the

---

[67]Shoshana Felman, "Benjamin's Silence," 218: "Benjamin's whole writing could be read as work of mourning, structured by a mute address to the dead face and the lost voice of the young friend who took his own life in desperate protest in the first days of the First World War."

object of vision, even intellectual vision" (35). Rather than a concept of a genre under which phenomena (texts) are subsumed, Benjamin's idea of the mourning play (*Trauerspiel*) informs the critical analysis of baroque tragic forms, as he somewhat cryptically formulates: "Truth is an intentionless state of being, made up of ideas. The proper approach to it is not therefore one of intention and knowledge, but rather a total immersion and absorption in [fading into] it" (O:36/GS1:216). Benjamin's outline of the idea of the *Trauerspiel* is no distanced examination of a dramatic form made for being viewed from a certain distance[68] but itself a *poiēsis*, a poetical creation expounding the structure and limits of *theōria*, the beholding; it is criticism. The *Trauerspiel* book's concern is not for concise concepts but for the analysis of structures of language such as mourning plays or lament, one of its constituents.

The *Trauerspiel* book and later texts point out the structural condition for terminological language that Wellbery (with reference to Lessing) calls "pathos of the limit," the "operation of delimitation" separating a concept from a non-theorized realm that, still, has to be evoked for the sake of distinction.[69] Beneath their terminology, Benjamin's texts let the transgression of delimitations show through that is prerequisite to forming a concept when, in analyzing the *Trauerspiel*, the motive of nature's lament falling silent in human language first appears seminal and later vanishes for the sake of a coherent argument.

With reference to the language of lamenting and complaining Benjamin's initial discussion and later silence points out a complication Wittgenstein ponders, too: Whether or not an utterance is called lament or complaint is not external but fundamental to it because the "language-game" of lamenting and complaining comprises someone's hearing, response, and acknowledgment. Benjamin's texts, however, underline that the discursive imbalance which marks the language game—the power of someone else to call an utterance lament (even if disparagingly) and the inability of lamenters to do so themselves—is often an essential element of the cause to complain, or reason to lament respectively. In Benjamin even more than in Wittgenstein it becomes apparent that the constitutive dependency on an acknowledging response does not conclude and appease but drive the language-game of plaints, not least by frustration. Benjamin's notes on the laments of nature, however, also add a more problematic insight to Wittgenstein's analysis:

---

[68]This is true for all scenic forms, of course, yet for baroque mourning plays in particular: "Their images are displayed in order to be seen, arranged in the way they want to be seen. ... The spectator of tragedy is summoned, and justified, by the tragedy itself; the *Trauerspiel*, in contrast, has to be understood from the point of view of the onlooker" (O:119).

[69]David Wellbery, "The Pathos of Theory," 49–50: "I want to insist here on the notion of pathos, which I take, following recent psychoanalytical research, to mean primarily affectability by the other, an openness to the other that precedes any stable self-identity."

A theoretical examination of the language-game of lamenting and complaining duplicates the imbalance of power essential to it even in pointing it out. Because an analysis cannot but proceed in articulate, propositional speech that silences the very different aspects of language relevant in lamenting and complaining at least as much as comprehending them: phonetic materiality, formed to attain hearing, response, and reciprocity. And in spite of claiming a superior stance, conceptual language suffers from the same complication as lamenting and complaining and, by extension, all speech: not being capable of guaranteeing the reception toward which it is oriented.

The mimetic participation of Benjamin's *Trauerspiel* book in its subject matter, the mourning play, has been repeatedly been pointed out, most notably with regard to the concept of melancholia. Reinhard Luton and Reinhard comment on Benjamin's as compared to Freud's notion: "The distinction between tragedy and *Trauerspiel* emerges in an historicism of melancholy that arises as such in defining, imagining, and deforming its categories in retrospect."[70] They infer that just as melancholia is mourning over a more proper form of mourning which is, however, only formed in retrospect and thus fundamentally improper,[71] *Trauerspiel* is a retrospective view of the ancient form, itself mirrored in Benjamin's look back at the baroque form: "Benjamin's text traces and enacts the passage of literature into theory, through narratives of expulsion, vengeance, guilt, and mourning, and through their failure."[72] Although Fenves contradicts the conclusion that tragedy is concerned with mourning, he notes: "Benjamin's theory of tragedy, like tragedy according to this theory, ends in a *non liquet*[...]: the decision—about the tragic hero, about the treatise in which his theory of tragic heroism is advanced—is final, to be sure, but the case itself is not."[73] All the more unsolved, and imperfect, is the *Trauerspiel* that is concerned with mourning and melancholia. Yet mourning plays are, Benjamin writes, "not so much plays which cause mourning, as plays through which mournfulness finds satisfaction: plays for the mournful" (O:119). Mourning is the form rather than the content of the plays, Fenves explains, as they are about the incessant return of that which does not stay: antiquity, its gods, nature—and exactly this is "the law of mourning: everything must come back again and again."[74]

---

[70] Julia Reinhard Lupton and Kenneth Reinhard, *After Oedipus*, 57.
[71] Ibid: "Melancholia mourns mourning—laments, that is the lack of a genuinely anterior, legitimate, 'normative' paradigm. Mourning is 'primary' only in the sense that melancholia needs to posit an origin from which to deviate."
[72] Ibid., 53.
[73] Peter Fenves, *Arresting Language*, 227; with reference to Benjamin, *Correspondence*, 231: "I would be inclined to deduce that the conclusion of a tragedy is still somehow removed from the sure triumph of the person-salvation-God principle, and that even there a kind of non liquet lingers an undertone. Of course, I want to deal only briefly with the theory of tragedy."
[74] Fenves, *Arresting Language*, 234.

A comparison of Benjamin's with Freud's notion of mourning and melancholia is suggested, first, by the *Trauerspiel* book's emphasis on "the relationship between mourning and ostentation" (O:140; cf. 119) which Freud notes, too (SE14:247), and, second, by the seminal role of afterwardsness (*Nachträglichkeit*) in constructions of collective and personal history. Beyond Benjamin's and Freud's notion of mourning and melancholia,[75] what suggests a link between both approaches to thought is the pivotal role of primal scenes (hypothetical scenic presentations of otherwise opaque origins) in the formation (rather than mere illustration) of concepts. Both Freud's and Benjamin's approach to theory leave hardly any fundament untouched, as Nägele points out: "The difference of this scene from the commonplaces of psychology and literary criticism affects above all the central figures of these commonplaces: subjectivity, interiority, experience, and history."[76] The role of lamenting and complaining in Benjamin and Freud, however, is not addressed in comparisons of their works. And this is hardly astonishing as plaintive language holds a problematic position in both: Psychoanalytic therapy sets out as the impetus to eliminate complaining but becomes theorized as a hermeneutics of complaining about pain and (not) lamenting losses confronted with the difficulty of having to comprehend something else than that which is being said. Benjamin, in contrast, gives detailed descriptions of the structure of lamenting and complaining as language at, or beyond, the brink of human speech in his early works while he later, to the extent of taking his early claims methodically seriously, falls silent on the topic. Still, in both Freud and Benjamin, the language of lamenting and complaining marks decisive fault lines in between nature and history, physical organization and psychic dynamics. An indicator of fragile links in conceptual textures, plaintive language is never stabilized as a concept in neither Freud nor Benjamin but appears as part of—or problem in—a particular scenario under scrutiny that drives, and is absorbed by, its theorization.

---

[75]Comparisons in Ferber, *Philosophy and Melancholy*, 16–66; Horn, *Trauer schreiben*, 28–33.
[76]Nägele, *Theater, Theory, Speculation*, 70–71.

# 5

# (No Way) From Complaining to Legal Action: Kafka

> *"You mustn't think—here his voice failed him and he gesticulated with his hands— that I am complaining for the sake of complaining."*[1]

Plaintive language evokes and transcends the law. A complaint is, according to the *Oxford English Dictionary*, an "outcry against or because of injury."[2] Grimms' German Dictionary similarly defines *Klage* as cry for legal action: *geschrei, mit dem man seinen schädiger beschuldigt, dasz es möglichst alle hören, und die hilfe des richters anruft* (shouting by which the wrongdoer is accused for everyone to hear, and a judge's help is appealed to).[3] Although lamenting and complaining often suppress accusations, as Freud analyzes, although lamentations threaten to move on to calls for revenge, as discourses on ritual plaints as well as Scholem suggest, and although a lament might comprise a fundamental charge against the ontological order, as Benjamin assumes, plaintive language neither necessarily leads to legal action, nor can it be appeased by juridical discourse. Lamenting and complaining give impetus to accusations, charges, and judgments but transcend these because pain, insults, death, and many losses cannot be undone. Therefore, the laments and complaints communicating loss and suffering refute symbolic substitution. Plaintive language transcends the juridical discourse it evokes just as testimony transcends a mere proof and requires something more: lamentation,[4] hearing.

That a form of speech as omnipresent as lamenting and complaining transcend the law, however, is a grave thing to say, given that the law is a

---

[1] Franz Kafka, *Amerika* [A], 7.
[2] *OED* 3:608, s.v. "complaint, n.3."
[3] *DW* 11:910, s.v. "klage."
[4] Weigel, "Zeugnis und Zeugenschaft, Klage und Anklage," 131.

central instance of conflict settlement in Western societies. The upcoming chapter will, therefore, examine the claim thoroughly in reading texts by Kafka. For Kafka, the insurance lawyer, often attends to the insufficiency of juridical terms and processes for comprehending phenomena and settling conflicts in general, and the insufficiency of the propositional means of statements and judgments for doing justice to plaints in particular. Scrutinizing the possibility of appeasing laments and complaints by resolving disputes, the reading will refer back to previous chapters.

Portraying divergent genres of plaints, Kafka's texts emphasize the violence with which lamenting and complaining claim attention, for instance the lament of exile in "The Stoker" which borders on nationalist populism, the complaint of love in the same text that comes close to harassment, or the neurotic complaint in "The Neighbor" that turns into slander. Juridical discourse counters the violence in plaints with the violence inherent to accusations, delimitations of a case, and judgments on guilt or liability. These responses, however, do not silence plaintive language, as Kafka's texts demonstrate, because its concern is not for decision and settlement but for hearing and reciprocity. The violence with which plaints demand exchange may characterize the exchange they attain, turning it into dispute, polemics, or reciprocal repudiation. This dynamics is analyzed in the chapter's first section on a complaint about language that voices the counterpart to Benjamin's ontological lament of those silenced in human speech: Kafka analyzes the uncanny estrangement from what is supposedly one's own language, as opposed to many foreign ones. The relation of plaintive language to modern institutions, Kafka expounds, pertains primarily not to law but to politics, the negotiation of how to live together. The second section explores what "understanding" plaints can mean, the third section analyzes the collision of a complaint of love with juridical action in "The Stoker," the fourth section examines how advocacy, be it juridical or political, feeds on the complaints it claims to voice while silencing them, and the concluding section analyzes the outcry for justice as a popular form of plaint in modern politics as partaking in these problematic structures.

## "With every complaint understanding [subsides]"[5]

In a 1912 "Introductory Talk on the Yiddish Language," or literally: *Jargon*,[6] given at the Jewish Town Hall in Prague to open a reading of Yiddish poems,

---

[5] Franz Kafka, "An Introductory Talk on the Yiddish Language" [IT], 263, my brackets.
[6] Kafka, "Einleitungsvortrag über Jargon." *Nachgelassene Schriften und Fragmente* [NSF] 1:188.

Kafka assures his audience of "how much more Yiddish you understand than you think" (IT:263). It is only in a second step that Kafka hints at the common history of German and Yiddish due to which "everyone who speaks the German language is also capable of understanding Yiddish" (IT:265). In a first step, Kafka addresses the "arrogant attitude to" and "dread of" Yiddish (263) common among German native speakers at the time,[7] particularly among Jews.[8] In view of "our Western European conditions dread mingled with a certain fundamental distaste" for this language from Eastern Europe "is, after all, understandable" (263), Kafka continues, sarcastically casting the tensions tearing up the multinational and multilingual Austro-Hungarian empire at the eve of the First World War as a harmony of discord:

> We live in positively cheerful concord, understanding each other whenever necessary, getting along without each other whenever it suits us and understanding each other even then. From within such an order of things who could possibly understand the tangle of Yiddish—indeed, who would even [have the desire] to do so? (IT:263–264)

An audience that came to listen to Yiddish poetry might feel this desire (*Lust* [NSF1:188]), one might assume. Yet Kafka's question is more than a captatio benevolentiae trying to elicit a responding "we" from the audience: Kafka's question turns the notion of understanding away from phonetic and lexical knowledge to will and desire. The primary obstacle to understanding Yiddish might not be the unknown designation of individual words but the connotation of the whole idiom. Yet rather than reproducing the condescension onto rural, non-assimilated Eastern Judaism, Kafka discusses the peculiar structure of its idiom, Yiddish, because unlike the "distaste" for its speakers, this structure is accessible for criteria that permit of comparison: Yiddish, "the youngest European language," has "no grammars," "consists solely of foreign words," elements of the language areas crossed and inhabited in diaspora, and comprises "fragments of recognized linguistic laws," but has formed no standard language: "Yiddish as a whole consists only of dialect, even the written language" (IT:264). Therefore, "obvious though the idea might seem," "no sensible person thinks of making Yiddish into an international language," solely "thieves' chant" borrows extensively.[9] In short, Yiddish fits ill into the Western European paradigm of homogenous

---

[7] Patrick Fortmann, "Kafka's Literary Communities," 1059.
[8] Vivian Liska, *When Kafka Says We*, 30: "Kafka expects there to be a deep unease among his listeners that evening and confronts them with their repression of their own status as parvenus. To them Yiddish embodies an earlier, more primitive stage of 'civilization' which they themselves have left behind, regard with contempt, and would like to make contact with only from a great distance."
[9] On the "thieves' chant" background David Suchoff, *Kafka's Jewish Languages*, 29–30.

national languages and states—indeed as little as "our Western Europeans conditions" in the multilingual and multinational Prague of 1912.

The first personal plural Kafka employs is an extremely unclear form in Prague 1912, mostly of either polemic or nationalistic use, and every bit as confusing as Yiddish. Kafka's sarcastic evocation of a "cheerful concord" of understanding in contrast to "the tangle of Yiddish" expounds that the distinction justifying the "distaste" (IT:263) for Yiddish is untenable. Kafka explains how the structure of Yiddish, which is grounded in diversity, pertains to those speaking (German) under the paradigm of national languages, in which the "concord" of a "we" is formed by condescension onto those who are separated as foreign—that is to say by discord. Kafka counters this strategy with a reference to the peculiarity of Yiddish to do without a differentiation between that which is one's own and what is foreign, and without formal standardization. That it should be possible to do without all this is what arouses fear.

Yiddish as a "linguistic medley of whim and law" (IT:264) inspires fear since its structure seems so far apart from that of other European languages and yet "everyone who speaks the German language is also capable of understanding Yiddish" (IT:265). Since both languages descend from Middle High German, as Kafka explains, "the superficial comprehensibility of Yiddish is"—from the point of view, or speech, of a German native speaker—[formed by] the German language" (IT265/NSF1:192). Therefore, "Yiddish cannot be translated into German" (265) because Yiddish is not foreign to German but participates in it as an alternative articulation. Dread is inspired by this parallel of in-translatable proximity and foreign distance which concerns not solely a Jewish "we" but indeed "everyone who speaks the German language": Because if it is possible to understand Yiddish as a German native speaker then German, too, must be a "linguistic medley of whim and law"—comprehensible not due to its standardization as national language but because it hosts an immeasurable diversity of phonetic, grammatical, lexical, and other varieties. Kafka thus traces the "dread of" and "distaste" for Yiddish not only to resentment against non-assimilated Jews but just as well to fear *for* a certain notion of the own language (two moments that are, of course, interlinked in the issue of assimilation). Understanding Yiddish entails the insight that the German language is not monolithic and opposed to other, presumably foreign languages but permeable to them (not just to Yiddish but, just like Yiddish, to many languages) and, furthermore, that neither German nor any other language is a monolithic block in the possession or mastery of a speaker but comprises unknown varieties.

What Kafka's "Introductory Talk on the Yiddish Language" introduces to the audience is no particular knowledge of Yiddish that would be necessary to understand the subsequent poems but an altered notion of understanding which implies that whoever is able to understand his talk can understand the poems, too. Kafka calls this the capacity "to understand Yiddish intuitively" (IT:266). Understanding by way of feeling (*fühlend zu verstehen* [NSF1:193]) calls for no a- or antirational reading[10] but for a will to consent, *con-sensus*: to feeling with others as a precondition for thought and comprehension[11] which is—unlike the will to "cheerful concord"—not based on the imperative of homogenous uniformity. The will to *consensus* makes it possible that even "dread of Yiddish, dread mingled with a certain fundamental distaste, is, after all, understandable, if one has the good will to understand it" (IT:263). What has to be willed in order to achieve such understanding is the suspension of exclusiveness that permits only of either my own or an other's view and feeling—an exclusiveness at the heart of "our Western Europeans conditions" of nation states and languages in 1912, yet alien to Yiddish. Kafka thus prefaces the Yiddish poems with a sociopolitical version of the hermeneutic circle: Understanding Yiddish requires the very insight that is granted by understanding Yiddish. The will to *consensus* is the entry into the circle:

> It is only here that the interpreter can help, reassuring you, so that you no longer feel shut out from something and also that you may realize that *you must cease to complain that you do not understand Yiddish. This is the most important point, for with every complaint understanding [subsides]*. But if you relax, you suddenly find yourself in the midst of Yiddish. (IT:266/NSF1:193; my italics)

Who talks cannot listen, but this is not the sole reason why Kafka urges the audience to remain silent. He interdicts complaining about not understanding Yiddish because it serves no other purpose than preventing *consensus* and making understanding subside—the understanding of Yiddish as well as of the proximity of "the tangle of Yiddish" to the structure of German and, by extension, any other so-called national language. As an instance of resistance, however, the complaint about not understanding Yiddish has perfect comprehension of what it refuses: that which happens when keeping silent: "once Yiddish has taken hold of you and moved you ... you will [not recognize] your former reserve. Then ... it will frighten you, yet it will no longer be fear of Yiddish but of yourself" (IT:266/NSF1:193). Complaining

---

[10]Fortmann proposes that understanding intuitively is about "the reception of poetry as a physiological process," psychical and logical ("Kafka's Literary Communities," 1059). He refers to Kafka's diary entry on the occasion of having finished "The Judgement": "Only *in this way* can writing be done, only with such coherence, with such a complete opening of the body and the soul." (Kafka, *Diaries 1910–1913*, 276).

[11]*Verständnis* (understanding, sympathy, comprehension) and *Verstand* (reason) are both translations of *intellectus* and *sensus*; DW 25:1596–1599, s.v. "verständnis." Cf. *OED* 18:985, s.v. "understand, v.2.c": "to understand each other, to be in agreement or collusion."

about not understanding Yiddish serves to avert being held and moved—not by a particular wording or scenery of the subsequent poems, which Kafka mentions rather in passing (IT:265), but by the Yiddish idiom as a wholly different understanding of language—which entails the insight that all languages grant comprehension without being totally mastered, even one's supposedly own (native) language. If the complaint about not understanding Yiddish is a resistance to the insight enabled by understanding Yiddish, then the complaint testifies that the insight has been gained in a certain way. According to Freud, an adequate reaction corresponds to the unwanted affect it repels, be that reaction crying, revenge, or complaining (SE2:7). Freud notes on insistent negations, as in the complaint about not understating Yiddish: "Negation is a way of taking cognizance of what is repressed; indeed it is already a lifting of the repression, though not, of course, an acceptance of what is repressed" (SE19:234–235). Complaining about *not* understanding Yiddish thus articulates the understanding but refuses to acknowledge it—and masks this repression by rendering it a complaint, which portrays the non-understanding as unwanted and unpleasant. Yet what exactly does Kafka mean by "understanding"? What can it mean, against the backdrop of all previous readings of this book, to understand plaintive language?

## Understanding, Comprehension, Sympathy, and Inconsolability

In a negation, Freud notes, "the intellectual function is separated from the affective process" (SE19:235). In the complaint about not understanding Yiddish, the intellectual process comprises the listening comprehension of the Yiddish texts as well as its implication for the concept of language in general, the contrasting affective process spans from the "distaste" for the idiom to the lacking desire to embrace the structural insight it communicates. Kafka, however, does not separate but link the rational and the emotional in his reference to "understand[ing] ... intuitively" (IT:266), that is by way of feeling (*fühlend* [NSF1:193]). And Kafka lays emphasis on the complaint, not on the negation: "This is the most important point, for with every complaint understanding [subsides]" (IT:266/NSF1:193). Understanding (*Verständnis* [NSF1:193]) has a double meaning here.

On the one hand, the "understanding" that subsides in complaining is comprehension, the intellectual as well as emotional grasp of something: If there is a will to "understand Yiddish intuitively," that is to *consensus*, then "the interpreter can help, reassuring you, so that you no longer feel shut out" (IT:266) from getting a grasp for what is being said and be, in turn, seized by the unfamiliar idiom. This notion of a (lacking) will to comprehend can be paralleled with insights from previous chapters: Neurotic complaints resemble ritual laments in voicing one persistent wording in diverse context and on different occasions.[12] This verbatim conventionality is a complication for understanding complaints as it undermines word reference and propositional meaning. Anthropological analysis, therefore, assumes just like Freud that complaining does not primarily communicate the cause to complain but the will for social interaction. Urban notes that it is not the obvious feeling of loss and desertedness that needs to be communicated in the face of death, but the wish for sharing a community as a remedy.[13] In the audience's complaint about not understanding Yiddish Kafka's talk anticipates, the communicated sense of isolation is multifold: it refers to the exclusion of German-speaking assimilated Jews such as Kafka from Hasidic Judaism and from Yiddish as the "not so long ago ... familiar colloquial language of German Jews" (IT:266) and, furthermore, to the parallel exclusion of the assimilated from recognition as part of Austro-Hungary's German bourgeoisie. Obtaining the latter is the hidden agenda in reproducing the commonplace complaint about not understanding Yiddish (anymore) (as assimilated Jew). The crux is that while the complaint is reproduced because the recognition as bourgeoisie remains denied, it renews the former exclusion. Understanding Yiddish the way Kafka envisages it, furthermore, entails the dreaded experience of feeling estranged from German as it points out that even one's native and supposedly own language is not completely familiar but permeable to unknown forms. "The most important point," according to Kafka, is that complaining about not understanding Yiddish communicates the need for social interaction to the same extent as refusing the presently possible community, the common listening to Yiddish poems. The complaint about not understanding Yiddish, rather, forms a complication due to which it must remain inconsolable: As a complaint, it says: I do not comprehend, hence I feel excluded; as a negation it says: I do not understand because I do not want to. The complaint remains inconsolable because it finds the incomprehension and isolation as lamentable as the possible comprehension and the community it would entail.

Yet Kafka does not only give a guideline for overcoming the "distaste" for Yiddish. On the other hand, "with every complaint understanding [subsides]" (IT:266) also means: The sympathy[14] for the complainer, the com-passion of the listener, ceases with every further complaint. Plaintive language indeed seems to prevent and destroy the community it seeks to attain. Freud speaks of neurotic "complaints" that keep reappearing "with a wearisome monotony" (SE7:45) and of an "insistent communicativeness which finds

---

[12]Freud, SE7:45, SE14:256.
[13]Urban, "Ritual Wailing," 393.
[14]*DW* 25:1600, s.v. "verständnis."

satisfaction in self-exposure" in melancholic (self-)accusations (SE14:247). Such complaints voice pain as well as a defense against the knowledge of their cause(s). Therefore, they communicate by ostentation rather than proposition, putting a strain even on the analyst's nerves. For the complaints insist on not finding the adequate, consoling community—least of all in the analyst who points out that they cannot find such community because pathological complaining is designed to remain inconsolable. Refuting all consolation while insisting on hearing and response, the irreconsilability of complaining raises adversarial affects and makes sympathetic understanding subside.

The complication of subsiding comprehension pertains to all lamenting and complaining: It arises due to lack of comprehension, in the face of the unfamiliar and strange, and develops no understanding because, rather than arousing compassion, it inspires disgust and refusal. For this reason, lamenting and complaining are often put in brackets so as to voice and, at the same time, prohibit the unnerving language. In his earliest story, "Description of a Struggle," Kafka thus writes:

> No, I [want] to go away—and this at once—to my relatives and friends who [are] waiting for me. But if I didn't have any relatives and friends then I must fend for myself (what [is] the good of complaining!), but I must leave here no less quickly.[15]

This complaint is voiced neither about the disagreeable whereabouts the speaker wants to leave urgently (*möchte nur weggehen* [NSF1:134]), the lack of friends and family, nor about his helplessness in leaving, but about the futility of complaining that is unable to help with any of these things. And even this complaint is reduced to a sigh of resignation, indicated by the exclamation mark, while the grammar of the subordinate class is that of a question. But there is no hope for a response to the, therefore, suppressed question that reads literally: Of what help is complaining (*Was hilft die Klage* [NSF1:134])? Complaining and lamenting are often bracketed in Kafka, and a 1929 reading concludes: "Kafka does not complain. Unlike in Job, there is no complaining in his works. The most unheard-of suffering, the most dreadful fates are told, but no complaint resounds."[16] Plaints indeed hardly resound in Kafka, they are, rather, voiced and silenced at once, expressed in the course of interdicting themselves, in phrases similar to those by means of which theoretical texts, too, insist on

---

[15]Kafka, *The Complete Stories* [CS], 16; my square brackets after NSF1:134.
[16]Margarete Susman, "Das Hiob-Problem bei Franz Kafka," 65; my translation. Scholem, on the other hand, tells Benjamin to start his inquiry into Kafka with Job; quoted in North, *The Yield*, 308n71.

being "not merely a lament."[17] Scrutinizing the notion of understanding, Kafka analyzes the intricate relation of plaintive language and negation in a number of texts. This link is remarkable since lamenting and complaining evade propositional logic, the basic structure of affirmation and negation. In "The Judgment," the only one to voice a verbatim complaint—the outcry because of injury indispensable for a juridical judgment—is the protagonist Georg Bendemann's absent friend. Before being sentenced to death by his father, Georg thinks of

> his friend, who had actually run away to Russia some years before, being dissatisfied with his prospects at home. Now he was carrying on a business in St. Petersburg, which had flourished to begin with but had long been going downhill, as he always complained on his increasingly rare visits. (CS:77)

In "Description of a Struggle" as in "The Judgement," the complaint is about not getting on. Unlike in the early text, the negation is not syntactically included but added by Bendemann's father. Before sentencing his son, he casts doubt on all propositions by means of which Georg gave an image of the friend: he questions whether he "really" has this friend (CS:82), denies the friend altogether (CS:83), later claiming the greater intimacy with this friend for himself, calling him "a son after my own heart" (CS:85) whom Georg allows to go "to pieces in Russia" (CS:87). There is no way of determining whether father and son compete for the Russian friend's sympathy, or negotiate their conflict in terms of the projection of a friend afar, Georg's doppelgänger, to whom they attribute all complaints, fears of failure, expectations of loyalty, and ideals of getting on in live.[18] In Aristotle, attributions are the logic form of statements which form judgments.[19] In Kafka's "The Judgment," however, attributions appear not as stable propositions but, rather, as neither true nor false volatile phantasmagorias which serve to picture what is otherwise unsayable but must be said nevertheless—for instance that one would prefer being son somewhere else, or having a different son. Plaintive speech complements the discourse of attribution-as-projection as the form of speech that searches a hearing and attention for that which has to be said, or shown. Yet since the proposition functions as a projection, complaints in Kafka are—if not voiced to be silenced, as in "Description of a Struggle"—often attributed to an indistinct

---

[17]Massumi, *Parables for the Virtual*, 88; Introduction, 6.
[18]A sentence in the draft, following the quoted passage above, emphasizes that Georg and the friend are complementary; Kafka, *DL:Apparatband*, 95: klagte. *[Georg dagegen war in der Heimat geblieben.]* (visits. [Georg, on the other hand, had stayed at home]).
[19]Aristotle, *On Interpretation* 17a.8–26 on affirmation (*kataphasis*) and negation (*apophasis*); Introduction, 7.

doppelgänger figure. "My Neighbor," written in 1917, develops a mirror figure about whom to complain is the text's sole, and yet carefully denied, purpose:

> My business rests entirely on my own shoulders. Two girl clerks with typewriters and ledgers in the anteroom, my own room with writing desk, safe, consulting table, easy chair, and telephone: such is my entire working apparatus. So simple to control, so easy to direct. I'm quite young, and lots of business comes my way. *I don't complain, I don't complain.* (CS:424; my italics)

In the neighboring apartment, "a young man" named Harras has taken up "a business similar to mine" (CS:424). While the narrator "never got a good look at him yet," he can hear him all the better through "the wretchedly thin walls," which "betray the honorable and capable man, but shield the dishonest" (425). A telephone is installed at the dividing wall. Outlining the complication that "everything" said in his office "could be heard in the next room" (425), the insistently *un*complaining narrator projects himself to the other side of the wall, from where he considers himself being listened to. "My Neighbor's" complaint is caught up in a feedback loop: The narrator's certainty that "everything" can be heard on the other side of the wall can rest on nothing but his listening to Harras's office. His lurking gives him reason to assume that his neighbor eavesdrops him, yet he himself is the lurking neighbor. This mirror logic finds approval even in silence, which is understood as sign of the fact that someone is listening next door. The silent neighboring room becomes a soundbox for the listener's paranoid discourse.[20] The very complaint about being listened to, however, which could clear up the situation, cannot be heard next door because it is not communicated by means of the voice but in a silent text. The accusation projects a counterpart on the other side of the wall, succeeding in silence, to complement the narrator who works audibly with unclear success:

> Because of all this my business decisions have naturally become unsure, my voice nervous. What is Harras doing while I am telephoning? If I wanted to exaggerate—and one must often do that so as to make things clear in one's mind—I might assert that Harras does not require a telephone, he uses mine, he pushes his sofa against the wall and listens; while I on the other side must fly to the telephone, listen to all the requests of my customers, come to difficult and grave decisions, carry out long calculations—but worst of all, during all this time, involuntarily give Harras valuable information through the wall.

---

[20]Carolin Duttlinger, "Kafkas Poetik der Aufmerksamkeit," 90–91.

Perhaps he doesn't even wait for the end of the conversation, but gets up at the point where the matter has become clear to him, flies through the town with the usual haste, and, before I have hung up the receiver, is already at his goal working against me. (CS:425)

Harras, the neighbor, is logically the mirror-image of the narrator yet modeled after the invisible partner at the other end of the telephone line. This, as it were, personified receiver, appears as contrary as complementary: "Perhaps ... working against me," he might also be working toward the speaker; *mir entgegenzuarbeiten* (NSF1:372) carries both notions. The narrator's complaint about his lonely labor puts the imagined neighbor in the position of both an accused parasite and a lamentably missing counterpart. The accusation of acoustically sponging off on the narrator is based on his understanding of the requirements of his own business. In the terms of understanding differentiated on the basis of Kafka's "Introductory Talk on Yiddish," the complaint about the neighbor lacks neither comprehension of, nor compassion with him. Yet the clearer both become in the course of the story, the clearer it is, too, that what subsides is the narrator's understanding for his own role, the reflection that the denounced offense might be his own, or at least his projection, and the sense that his neighbor might share his feelings about being eavesdropped. In spite of articulating plenty of statements, the complaint transcends the propositional order of speech inasmuch as the criterion for judging it is no verifiable truth or falsity but the concern for being heard, which is seminal to all plaintive speech. Therefore, the statements about the neighbor turn accusations against him, no matter whether he listens or not. What remains, in case the neighbor does, in fact, not listen at all, are clumsy, arduous conversations on the telephone, and lonesome failure on this side of the wall. In order not to have to acknowledge this—to rule out the possibility of remaining unanswered—the complaint about being listened to must not be audible next door.

The role of propositions in plaintive language as portrayed by Kafka is challenging to common approaches. In Schmidt's notion, for instance, the propositional content of complaining is limited to stating that the detrimental ought not to be, and due to this "penetrating lack of meaning" complainers are hardly well-liked.[21] Summing up the propositional structure of complaining to one basic judgment does justice neither to its function as phantasmagoria that is expounded in Kafka, nor to its insistence that is produced by way of a repetition and ostentation rather than on the semantic level. Lessing refers to this aspect complaining when commenting on sympathy:

---

[21] Schmidt, *Klage*, 119; my translation.

Sympathy [does] not endure throughout; at last we ... shrug our shoulders and recommend patience. Only when both cases are combined,—when the solitary one possesses no controul [sic] over his own body, when the sick man receives as little assistance from others, as he can render himself, and *his complaints are wasted away on the desert winds*; then, and only then, do we see every misery, that can afflict human nature, close over the head of the unfortunate one; and then only does every fleeting thought, in which we picture ourselves in this situation, excite our amazement and horror. We see nothing safe despair in the horrible form before us.[22]

Only complaints that evaporate into the empty air—that remain unheard and unanswered—arouse sympathy instead of impatient distaste. Lessing defines sympathy in terms of theater rather than interaction, as feeling of an audience that requires irreducible distance to a scene of suffering. This means, paradoxically, that complaining arouses sympathy and compassion only for those sufferers who are observed to be pitied by no one. In Kafka it seems that, consequently, no complaint arouses lasting sympathy beyond the stage. In the "Introductory Talk on Yiddish," the compassionate aspect of "understanding" subsides. Other texts by Kafka, therefore, seek to complain differently: inaudibly so as to complain without repelling the hearing and sympathetic response seminal to plaintive language. This is the second, as it were mirroring, reason as to why the neighbor does not entrust his complaint with Harras, the personified receiver, but keeps it silent in a text: to stir rather than prevent sympathy. The narrator of the 1924 "A Little Woman" spots a similar technique: "she keeps silent but betrays all the outward signs of a secret sorrow in order to draw public attention to the matter" (CS:318–319), signs like "the complaining lift of the eyes to Heaven, the planting of the hands on the hips, to fortify herself, and then the access of rage that brings pallor with it and trembling" (321). The gaze, not the mouth, is said to be complaining, and this attribution is, of course, itself result of a particular gaze: of a projection wherein the proposition is a means of defense and a (Freudian) negation of the complaint *about* the woman:

> From whatever standpoint I consider this small affair, it appears, and this I will stick to, that if I keep my hands over it, even quite lightly, I shall quietly continue to live my own live for a long time to come, untroubled by the world, despite all the outbursts of the woman. (CS:323–324)

In "A Little Woman" complaining is subdued so much it is not even a matter of speech or voice anymore, and potentially disturbing to the ears, but

---

[22]Lessing, *Laocoon*, 26–27; my italics.

pertains to the eyes and can easily be covered. In a 1920 letter to Brod, Kafka writes along the same lines: "Have I complained? I am not complaining. My appearance complains."[23]

Close examination, however, cannot fail at bringing out that the desperate attempts to fight off an attack that seems threatening exactly because its character and reality are uncertain transcend comic paranoia. The complaining in "The Neighbor" and "A Little Woman" gestures toward an understanding of how reciprocity is enabled prior to all specific (calls for) interaction—a concept alternative to that of juridical self-empowerment of the subject. This reading is permitted by Levinas's notion of the neighbor's face as constituting relationality:

> In a sense nothing is more burdensome than a neighbor. ... The neighbor strikes me before striking me, as though I heard before I spoke. ... In proximity is heard a command come as though from an immemorial past, which was never present, began in no freedom. This way of the neighbor is a face.
>
> The face of a neighbor signifies for me an unexceptionable responsibility, preceding every free consent, every pact, every contract.[24]

This phenomenological notion of addressed-ness preceding all speech and action is no primal scene of one specific, original face but, rather, an implication within speaking and acting, postulating a fundamental relationality without which both were impossible.[25] No concrete word or act can satisfy the demand placed upon the subject by the axiomatic face because what it installs is responsibility itself, an ethics that all speaking and acting implicitly answers to (or fails to answer, but that is a response, too).[26] Levinas illustrates the structural asymmetry that installs relationality with a paradigmatic lover's complaint, taken from the Song of Songs: "I opened to my beloved, but my beloved had turned and was gone."[27] This spells out, in Levinas's reading, that "my presence does not respond to the extreme urgency of the assignation."[28] The same asymmetry and urgency characterize the suspicion of being listened to in Kafka's "Neighbor": I "never got a good look at him yet" (CS:425), still, it seems to be clear

---

[23]Kafka, *Letters to Friends, Family, and Editors*, 238.
[24]Emmanuel Levinas, *Otherwise than Being or Beyond Essence*, 88.
[25]Ibid.: It is a "non-phenomenon" because it enables phenomenality.
[26]Ibid.: Levinas articulates this structure as temporality: "My reaction misses a present which is already the past of itself." This temporality corresponds to the puzzlingly void accusation in "A Little Woman" (ibid., 92): "It is the accusation by the other, my neighbor, accusing me of a fault which I have not committed freely, that reduces the ego to a self on the hither side of my identity, prior to all self-consciousness."
[27]Song 5:6, NRSV. Cf. Levinas, *Otherwise than Being*, 88.
[28]Levinas, *Otherwise than Being*, 88.

that the unseen one has a perfect grasp of the speaking protagonist. What is striking about Levinas's foundation of responsibility as having-been-seen by a neighbor who was here before I realized it is that it appears as an ethical correlate to the structural excess of plaintive language, which cannot be satisfied or appeased by any concrete response either—wherefore, in Kafka, complaining is the appropriate, or adequately inappropriate, response to the foundational gaze of the neighbor, to the imposition of having to act against the backdrop of ethical demands that are given, preceding the individual. With Kafka's insistence on hearing rather than seeing, however, it remains unclear whether the speaker has ever been seen by the neighbor (if ever an axiomatic face shone upon him) to install responsibility in an unattainable past. "The Neighbor" makes it seem as if the obligation of responsibility reigns, rather, in unattainable belatedness, letting the individual speak and act first, and following as threat of judgment. Yet the fullest understanding of the speaking neighbor's reason to complain might be provided by assuming that both temporalities apply, the phenomenological antecedence of an ethical demand that is as unanswerable in structure as complaining, and an ever-following assessment that is impossible to avert. This much pertains to the existential situation of plaints in Kafka.

With reference to the structure of plaintive language Kafka points out that it communicates by consuming conventional structures of language even with regard to their purpose: complaining makes the hearing, response, and understanding subside that it seeks to attain. Appealing to compassion in order to attain comprehension is obstructed by the cause and concern of lamenting and complaining: Plaintive language voices experiences of being overwhelmed by disorganizing conventional structures of language and the consequently hardly, or utterly in-comprehensible monotonous appeal exhausts all hearing and sympathy. The attempt to avoid this complication reduces complaining to a matter of appearance, of a theater-like distance that, rather than attaining sympathetic reciprocity, entwines sympathy and compassion into a circle of projections. In his 1917 essay on lament, Scholem, therefore, calls lament "language of the border" (LL:6) that either results in silence or turns to other modes of speech such as praise or calls for revenge: "There is no stability of lament" (LL:7). Kafka notes in 1918: "[It is] the old joke: We hold the world and lament that it holds us."[29] North comments: "A long-standing tendency is to lament this fact, to lament that we cannot start the world over one way or another, or thoroughly condemn it."[30] In complaining about not properly getting on, several of Kafka's narrators[31] fail to recognize that it is them who keep holding on by way of

---

[29] NSF2:90; translation North, *Yield*, 61.
[30] North, *Yield*, 61.
[31] This pertains to the stoker discussed below, too; A:14: "It must be sheer slander that keeps him back" (*in seinem Vorwärtskommen hindert* [DL:81]).

complaining—holding on to absurd ideas like continuous progress, steady growth, permanent happiness. "But lamenter is precisely not the role Kafka wants to occupy," North continues: "Lament is accusation; it throws the state of things away from the accuser. ... Lamenting the way the world plays with us, the way we are subordinated to it, is a self-deception; in fact we hold it."[32] Yet just as old jokes keep returning, that which is thrown away, projected somewhere else, and negated in lamenting, returns to the lamenter. Since propositions often function as projections in complaining, the attempt at reintroducing the excessive plaintive language into a propositional order of attribution, statements, and judgments hardly achieves a reorganization of language but, rather, effects a hermeneutic collapse. Kafka analyzes this dynamics in "The Stoker," the first chapter of the unfinished novel *Amerika*, published separately in 1913.

## Plaints, Vanishing into Juridical Action

"The Stoker" follows up the question suppressed in "Description of a Struggle": Of what help is complaining (*Was hilft die Klage* [NSF1:134])? Arrived in New York harbor, a "stoker" (A:6) of an emigration ship complains in his "wretched cubbyhole" (*klägliche Kabine* [A:4/DL:67]) about the lack of cheerful national concord aboard, addressing the young passenger Karl, who gives the cue:

> "I can hardly speak English at all. Anyhow, people here have a prejudice against foreigners, I think."—"So you've come up against this kind of thing too, have you? Well, that's all to the good. *You're the man for me.* See here, this is a German ship we're on, in belongs to the Hamburg-American Line; so why aren't the crew all Germans, I ask you? Why is the Chief Engineer a Romanian? A man called Schubal. It's hard to believe it. A measly hound like that slave-driving us Germans on a German shop! *You mustn't think"—here his voice failed him and he gesticulated with his hands—"that I am complaining for the sake of complaining.* I know you have no influence and that you're a poor lad yourself. But it's too much!" And he brought his fist several times down on the table. (A:7; my italics)

The stoker fuels not the steamer's engine but national and nationalist prejudice that provokes conflicts in Europe that are often reason to emigrate.

---

[32]North, *Yield*, 61–62. The same is true for a further 1918 note: "The lament about the monotony of life is actually the lament about not being sufficiently deep mixed with the world" (NSF2:104–105; my translation).

National prejudice is, still, regularly brought along across the Atlantic and—just as the lurking in "The Neighbor"—attributed to others encountered along the way.[33] The stoker can function as agitator all the better as Karl lacks not solely language skills but the very concept of foreignness, and foreign languages, such that to him their requirement seems like a prejudice against him.[34] Yet what the stoker cites as defense against the anticipated reproach of "complaining for the sake of complaining" is better suited to serve as evidence supporting the charge: Karl is incapable of changing anything about the chain of command aboard and has no financial or other means to exert any "influence." The stoker's negation of his complaints, which contradicts their obvious form and purpose so much that the negation cannot even be voiced but has to be gesticulated, amounts to a complaint about the futileness of complaining. Still, it finds what is crucial: hearing. The stoker's complaining finds a willing ear in Karl because the latter has no overview of the spatial or symbolical order aboard but lost his way (A:4) and, "following his own train of thought" (6), his suitcase in search for his umbrella. The stoker continues:

> "I have signed on in ever so many ships"—and he reeled off twenty names one after the other as if they were one word, which quite confused Karl—"... and here on this tub ..., here I am no good, here I'm just in Schubal's way, here I'm a slacker who should be kicked out and doesn't begin to earn his pay. Can you understand that? I can't." (A:7–8)

Nationally prejudiced and nautically ignorant, Karl does not discern the cause or course of events that gives Schubal and the stoker cause to complain about each other. Yet even without any comprehension of the two positions, Karl does reach some understanding, namely compassion with the complainer. Compassion makes him advise the stoker to look for a remedy: "'Have you seen the Captain about it? Have you asked him to give you your rights?'" (A:8) Karl understands the stoker's complaints as appeal to exercise his right as employee, and at least in terms of etymology, this is right. In German as in English, a complaint is primarily an "outcry against or because of injury."[35] There is, however, a deep fissure in between the law and understanding, as Kafka's texts keep pointing out. The stoker sees his complaint mistaken with Karl's response: "'Oh, get away with you, out you get, I don't want you here. You don't listen to what I say,

---

[33] Cf. A:4: "'Are you a German?' Karl asked to reassure himself further, for he had heard a great deal about the perils which threatened newcomers in America, particularly from the Irish."
[34] Cf. A:31: "... Harbour Official, who said two words in English, which made a ludicrous impression."
[35] *OED* 3:608, s.v. "complaint, n.3."

and then you give me advice. How could I go to the Captain[!]'" (A:8/ DL:72) Punctuation renders the last sentence an exclamation, while it is grammatically a question (and translated thus into English). This detail emphasizes that—unlike questions and lawsuits—the stoker's complaining demands no proposition, judgment, or action but hearing and attention. Yet Karl's response establishes, in Wittgenstein's terminology, the wrong language-game: counselling instead of complaining. The stoker's complaint seeks to initiate no juridical action and decision; it is, rather, concerned with finding a community—a national as much as a homoerotic community, both a "positively cheerful concord" with the same.[36]

Rather than with juridical action, the stoker's complaint is associated with the complaint as a genre in love poetry. It has been paradigmatically formed in Shakespeare's *A Lover's Complaint*, which expounds the relationality in the articulation of a (lyrical) "I." And just like a *Tagelied* (dawn song) of medieval poetry that laments the separation after a night spent together, the stoker's complaint and dispute with Karl takes place in bed. Even the reference to the law is based on the community in bed: "'Don't you put up with it!' said Karl excitedly. He had almost lost the feeling that he was on the uncertain boards of a ship, beside the coast of an unknown continent, so much at home did he feel here in the stoker's bunk" (A:8). The stoker's nationalist agitation comprises the ambiguous sentence: "You're the man for me" (A:7). Ambiguity is characteristic of the stoker, whose German name *Heizer* (DL:70) refers to "heating" the steam engine, yet in secondary connotation also to caressing and kissing.[37]

Karl, however, has no understanding of the subtext. He achieves a consultation on the captain's bridge where—just as anticipated—the stoker's complaints find no hearing: "''Clear out here at once!'/At this reply the stoker turned his eyes on Karl, as if Karl were his heart, to whom he was silently bewailing his grief [*Jammer klage*]" (A:13/DL:79). Yet again, Karl has no understanding of the—now silenced—complaint, hears it neither as a gesture of intimacy nor as an attempt to avoid the difficulty (mentioned in Lessing) that insistence prevents sympathy rather than arousing it. Karl certainly feels for the stoker but he shares no reciprocal passion. In a 1920 letter to Jesenská, Kafka explains the personal perspective in the story's opening statement that Karl "had been packed off to America by his [pitiable] parents" (A:3/DL:65): This testifies, Kafka writes, to "a sympathy without understanding [*unverstehendes Mitleid*] that Karl has with his parents as well."[38] Sympathy without understanding keeps Karl

---

[36]See George Mosse, *Nationalism and Sexuality*, 23–47 on institutionalized forms of homoeroticism in support of nationalism.
[37]*DW* 10:929, s.v. "heizen." By way of a bad pun, the stoker is also a "stroker."
[38]Kafka, *Letters to Milena*, 13/*Briefe 1918–1920*, 145.

from comprehending the cruelty of sending the son to America when a child springs from the advances of an older maidservant. Sympathy without understanding is also what Karl feels for the stoker and lets him ignore the longing in his complaints. "Without stopping to think" (A:13) Karl storms into the office from which the stoker is expelled, and brings about a "complete rightabout turn" (14)—a movement made by the Head Purser in his chair in order to turn to Karl and, consequently, by the plaintive discourse: It turns to the question of rights; *eine große Rechtswendung* (DL:79) suggests a turn toward, or of, the law. Karl transposes the stoker's complaint of love into juridical action: "an injustice has been done to … the stoker," Karl explains. "There's a certain Schubal aboard who bullies him" (A:14). Neither Karl nor the English translation has a grasp of the sexual imagery of the charge, which reads literally: There's a certain Schubal here who mounts him (*Es ist hier ein gewisser Schubal, der ihm aufsitzt* [DL:80]). The possible sexual background of the dispute is thus articulated but shortened by the possibly decisive "not"—just as Karl does not mount the stoker in his bed although Karl's last name is even Roßmann (steed-man). A possible understanding of the stoker's discourse as a lover's complaint is lost to the conventional imagery of a bully breathing down one's neck, and the scene is cleared for Karl to take juridical action, raising his voice and silencing the stoker.

"He can lay his specific complaints before you himself," Karl claims of the stoker. He "addressed all the gentlemen present, because in fact they were listening to him, and because it seemed much more likely that among so many at least one just man might be found, than that the one just man should be the Head Purser" (A:14). Not yet landed in New York and ignorant of the English language, Karl, nevertheless, already observes the US-American rules of legal discourse that differ profoundly from those of Continental Europe, as Kittler explains: In England and America, even preliminary investigations are organized like charges and carried out neither in secrecy nor in written from (as portrayed in Kafka's *Trial*) but publicly and orally.[39] Karl presents his notion of the stoker's complaints—shaped by sympathy without understanding—to the representatives of the public aboard as if they were a jury, and indeed obtains a hearing with the Captain: "'Better hear what the man has to say for himself. Schubal's getting a good deal too [independent] these days, but that doesn't mean [I'm talking in your favor].' The last words were addressed to the stoker" (A:15–16/DL:83). It is questionable, of course, whether this is the impartial stance a juridical hearing claims to take. Karl appears to see the transition of the stoker's complaint into legal action as what Menke calls a "self-empowerment of the subject": "The subject who says 'no' is the subject of the complaint—the

---

[39]Wolf Kittler, "Heimlichkeit und Schriftlichkeit," 196.

claim that things should change."⁴⁰ This complaint wields power, Menke holds, as the judgment about one's own suffering asserts and, at the same time, produces the right to consideration,⁴¹ thus instituting the rule by which it judges itself. What is problematic about this notion in general is that no utterance can produce the hearing or response it relies upon.⁴² Kafka's "Stoker" highlights a further issue in the concept of empowerment by way of the law: Representation sidelines and silences the subject is claims to serve justice.

Both Captain and stoker bear functional titles rather than individual names such as *Schubal* who, consequently, appears much too independent (*viel zu selbstständig* [DL:83]). The Captain judging him thus has no empowerment in mind but the annihilation of subjectivity. Listening to the stoker's complaining is a way of achieving this aim because, unlike Menke assumes, no complaint—neither a complaint of love nor a juridical accusation—"defines its relation to the Other is such a way that is being treated in a certain manner."⁴³ This notion skips over the fundamental relationality in plaintive language that depends on being heard in order to affect or move others. The claim to being treated differently cannot assert a subject parallel to others, what it can do is present the complainer as equal and capable of interaction. In case the claim remains unheard, and the presentation goes unnoticed, it fails to produce a self-empowered subject. This is what happens to the stoker's complaint that does not find a hearing but a transposition into juridical discourse. Making public what the stoker seeks to negotiate in bed only shows that "his specific complaints" (A:14) about not finding the right hearing, and not with the right one, comprise no propositional content that may be judged at all:

> All the same, nothing definite emerged from the stoker's out-pourings, and although the Captain still listened thoughtfully, his eyes expressing a resolution to hear the stoker this time to the end, the other gentlemen were growing impatient and the stoker's voice no longer dominated the room, which was a bad sign. (A:16)

Both aspects of Kafka's insight that "with every complaint understanding [subsides]" (IT:266/NSF1:193) apply to the stoker: the comprehension of his concern subsides as much as the compassion prerequisite to trying

---

⁴⁰Menke, "Sklavenaufstand," 115; my translation. Introduction, 10–11. A naïve reading of complaining as emancipation in Baggini, *Complaint*, 12: "Complaint is a secular, humanist act. It is resistance against the idea, promulgated by religion, that suffering is our divinely ordained lot and that we can do no more than put up with it piously."
⁴¹Menke, "Sklavenaufstand," 116.
⁴²Introduction, 11.
⁴³Menke, "Sklavenaufstand," 116; my translation.

to grasp it. There is no Schubal case, no "exact statement" (A:17) of a particular grievance, just querulous detail that makes the stoker's discourse appear pointless: "From all points of the compass complaints about Schubal streamed into his head, each of which, it seemed to him, should have been sufficient to dispose Schubal for good; but all he could produce for the Captain was a wretched farrago in which everything was lumped together" (17). The "end" (16) until which the Captain is determined to hear the stoker out turns out to be his end as plaintiff who deserves consideration. As the stoker's claim to consideration turns out legally void and the attention of the jury dissolves, his discourses is transposed, yet again, into a passion he endures. "From the general dispersion of interest the only one who seemed to be exempt was the attendant, who sympathized to some extent with this poor [*arm*] man confronting the great, and gravely nodded to Karl as though trying to explain something" (A:16–17/DL:84). This sentences is formed from Karl's point of view, he attributes sympathy to the attendant who had curtly turned away the stoker earlier. What indicates the personal perspective is particularly the adjective *arm* (poor, pitiable)—the same adjective that, as Kafka explains, expounds Karl's "sympathy without understanding" for his parents. The interpretation of the attendant's nodding displays a similar lack of interpersonal comprehension: Rather than displaying sympathy for the stoker, the nodding might underline in retrospect that the stoker had better not come in and lodged his complaint. The stereotypical differentiation between the "poor" and "the great," moreover, testifies to the condescension implicit in Karl's sympathy. For if the attendant is "the only one who seemed to be exempt" from the "dispersion of interest," then the one whose personal point of view informs the sentence—Karl—is not exempt. He reminds the stoker of the rhetoric of the *genus iudicale*:

> "Take your grievances in order, tell the most important ones first and the lesser ones afterwards; perhaps you'll find that it won't be necessary even to mention most of them." ...
> [If only this had helped!] Might it not already be too late? The stoker certainly stopped speaking at once when he heard the familiar voice, but his eyes were so blinded with tears of wounded [male] dignity, of dreadful memory, of extreme present grief, that he could hardly even recognize Karl. How could he at this stage—Karl silently realized this, facing the now silent stoker—how could he at this stage suddenly change his style of argument. (A:18/DL:86–87)

Lack of order is indeed what causes the stoker's complaints ever since his nationalist agitation: be it the, in his view, nationally disordered hierarchy aboard, the failing arrangement of desire in bed with Karl, or with Schubal who does (not) mount him, be it the disordered presentation of his complaints of love as juridical grievance. Exactly because the stoker complains about a general lack of order, urging him to order his complaints is futile. Calling on the ship's authorities, and finding hearing with the Captain, rather, silences the stoker—"a notorious grumbler," as the Head Purser warns (A:15). Lodging his complaint robs the stoker of the rest of his reputation and even of the possibility of "recogniz[ing]," or addressing, his advocate Karl. The voice and figure of the stoker is sidelined with this hermeneutic collapse, however, the juridical discourse of complaining continues. The more the stoker wears himself out in complaining, loses his voice and presence, the more the juridical discourses focuses onto Karl: Hitherto devoid of any attributes,[44] even his suitcase and umbrella, Karl is transferred into a propositional order that bestows him with background and status.[45] The stoker, on the other hand, who had no actionable charge to present, vanishes from the propositional order of juridical discourse.

## Representation and Betrayal

When finally facing Schubal, not even complaints that are, in Lessing's words, "wasted away on the desert winds" testify to the stoker any longer:

> Was the stoker even capable of saying a word by this time, of answering yes and no, as he must do if he were now to be cross-examined, although, to be sure, a cross-examination was almost too much to hope for? There he stood ..., his knees uncertain, his head thrown back, and the air flowed in and out of his open mouth as if the man had no lings to control the motion.

---

[44]Benjamin, "Franz Kafka." SW2.2:801: "Karl Rossmann is transparent, pure, without character, as it were."
[45]Complaints of love as well as juridical complaints are voiced where there is not solely necessity but just as well room for a decision, and thus also for a transposition into other genres of plaint. December 28, 1908, Kafka writes to Elsa Taussig: "You must consider that the necessary always happens, the superfluous just usually, the almost necessary rarely, at least in my case; with the result that, stripped of all context, it can easily become slightly pitiful [*leicht kläglich*], meaning entertaining" (Kafka, *Letters to Friends*, 49/*Briefe 1900–1912*, 93). Erica Weitzman shows how Kafka, the insurance expert, undermines the Kantian concept of necessity: "the business of risk assessment collapses Kantian ontology ... Kafka's professional duty—which in this sense is effectively a satanic one—is the almost unthinkable or (in the Kantian sense) undutiful duty of taking the laws of probability to task, to alter them or, in the case that they cannot be altered, to seek an often elusive source of accountability. ... The recognition of this position adds a further valence to Kafka's designation of the 'almost necessary' as 'slightly lamentable (*leicht kläglich*)': it is, also, literally the space of the *Klage*, the legal or professional grievance—with which, it should be recalled, in Karl's vain advocacy for the Stoker *Der Verschollene* effectively begins. The grievance—which, for Dr. Kafka, was more often than not a written document—also shapes the letter to Elsa Taussig, in the form of a parody of the genre of the lover's plaint" (*Irony's Antics*, 139).

> But Karl himself felt more strong and clear-headed [*bei Verstand*] than perhaps he had ever been at home. ...
> ... Why, for instance, had the first relevant word that occurred to him [Schubal] been "dishonesty"? Should he have been accused of that, perhaps, instead of nationalistic prejudice? ... Why had he allowed so much time to elapse ... [until] his arrival here? Simply in order to let the stoker weary the gentlemen, until they began to lose their powers of clear judgment, which Schubal feared most of all. (A:22–23/DL:91)

This turnaround of the juridical discourse, in the course of which Karl takes and the stoker loses shape, points out the diabolical versatility of the figure of the accuser: In the book of Revelations, the adversary is called "the accuser of our comrades ..., who accuses them day and night before our God" (Rev. 12:10, NRSV). The accuser (*katēgōr*, LXX) is a traitor rather than a righteous revealer of wrongdoing, as Benjamin's Kafka-inspired "Idea of a Mystery" expounds.[46] It does not matter in the book of Revelations whether the grievances are justified or not, the accusations are right or wrong—offense is taken at the very fact that the accuser raises his voice at all. Karl is diabolical in this way due to his sympathy without understanding: Acting as accuser against the stoker's will, he reveals the latter's "specific complaints" (A:14) to a public incapable of alleviating or even responding to it, and betrays the stoker as he leaves him behind in the process of "learn[ing] to understand" his newly acquired "position" (A:35) on the side of his uncle, a senator, who is unexpectedly revealed to Karl on the captain's bridge. This new understanding implies a comprehension of his changed social status as well as a change of heart about his compassion for the plaintiff on behalf of which he had raised his voice. The stoker suddenly appears only as "the figure of the stoker" (A:25) "and the other people here" as "[chaff]" (A:34/DL:106). What makes Karl diabolical is that he, still, insists—in spite of having turned the Schubal case into a mere slip, the *casus* into a *lapsus*, exposing the stoker to contempt—on acting "in a question of justice" (A:32). Yet not only are descend and desire no matters of justice, not even the public juridical discourse is, as Karl sees in the moment of the stoker's silent exhaustion. Schubal's objection to the complaint about "'dishonesty'" (22) applies (at least in Karl's eyes) a strategy of speech rather than relying on the propositional means of affirmation and negation. Schubal employs the complication Lessing notices as a rhetorical device, relying on his adversary's complaints to exhaust rather than address the jury's reason.[47]

---

[46]Chapter 4, 195–196.
[47]Karl notices this problem before; A:18: "The Captain might be a good man ...; but after all he wasn't a mere instrument to be recklessly played on, and that was exactly how the stoker was treating him in the boundless indignation of his heart."

The focus of the juridical discourses shifts onto Karl, who raised his voice in advocacy and instituted the legal proceedings instead of remaining with the plaintiff he portrayed as victim. This counter-representational shift reveals a similarity of complaints of love and juridical action: Just as complaints of love cannot accept the portrayal of what, and who, is missing as surrogate and consolation, thus refuting the very principle of symbolic substitution onto which they rely as linguistic structures, the substitution of a voice in Karl's advocacy is undermined. The "fundamental configuration of advocacy," Trüstedt sums up, is "speaking for someone, against someone in front of another."[48] Karl indeed does not only speak *himself* while claiming to speak up on behalf of the stoker, yet he also speaks primarily *for* himself rather than lending his voice to someone else, presenting his eloquence more than the stoker's case.[49] Unlike just speaking *oneself*, which the stoker does, too, speaking *for oneself* as Karl does by way of speaking up (or claiming to speak up) on behalf of the stoker requires skipping the difference between actual position and fiction: It requires the understanding that what is called a person in- and outside of the law springs from an ongoing negotiation between the needs of a living body and the opportunities provided by social roles by way of self-imagination and self-formation. Karl's discourse illustrates such an understanding of persons as "hybrids of living bodies and roles in systems of social differentiation," as Campe writes.[50] The nameless stoker, on the other hand, tells Karl in his cabin that his employment title "stoker" names him, as it were, only in catachresis because: "'My job's going to be free'" (A:6). Below deck, the release from a position that has taken up his whole self and replaced his name seems to give the (former) stoker the freedom to lie in bed with Karl.[51] On deck, however, the release appears as redundancy that allows Karl to withdraw from his advocacy for the stoker as the complaint is disregarded, and to replace him—not as stoker,

---

[48]Katrin Trüstedt, "Execution without Verdict," 136.
[49]In 1914 diary entry, Kafka comments on the imbalance between those who have reason to complain or lament, and the better rhetorical presentation of plaints by those who do not: "the best things I have written have their basis in this capacity of mine to meet death with contentment. All this fine and very convincing passages deal with the fact that someone is dying, that it is hard for him to do, that it seems unjust to him, or at least harsh, and the reader is moved by this ... But for me, ..., such scenes are secretly a game; indeed, in the death enacted I rejoice in my own death, hence calculatingly exploit the attention that the reader concentrates on death, *have a much clearer understanding of it than he, of whom I suppose that he will loudly lament on his deathbed, and for these reasons my lament is as perfect as can be*, nor does it suddenly break off, as is likely to be the case with a real lament, but dies beautifully and purely away" (Kafka, *Diaries 1914–1923*, 102; my italics).
[50]Rüdiger Campe, "Kafkas Fürsprache," 197; my translation.
[51]Cf. the quote continued: "to point his full consciousness of it, he stuck his hands into his trouser pockets and flung his legs in their baggy, leather-like trousers on the bunk to stretch them. Karl had to shift nearer to the wall" (A:6–7).

as initially planned,⁵² but as protagonist of the text. When at the end of the story, "Karl took a more careful look at his uncle, ... and doubts came in his mind whether this man would ever be able to take the stoker's place" (A:37), this is probably not about the same irreplaceability as voiced in a complaint of love. One trait that makes the stoker important, and irreplaceable, for Karl is, paradoxically, his replaceability that allows Karl to relinquish the role of the "poor lad" with "no influence" (A:7), and to get on by claiming to speak in the name of another—who, in fact, has no name at all.

In the course of undermining the principle of personal representation, however, the accusation further displays its diabolical versatility in turning even against the accuser: Once its focus has shifted onto Karl, the juridical action he initiated reveals "his transgression" (A:96), the encounter with the servant, which he would prefer to leave unmentioned, and which appears primarily as a chain of transgressions of others against Karl. The uncle/senator, however, representing both parental and legislative authority, declares: "his transgression was of a kind that merely need to be named to find indulgence ... for he was seduced by a maidservant, Johanna Brummer, a person of round about thirty-five" (A:26). This charge is diabolical insofar as it is brought while, at the same time, conceding its pointlessness—and, furthermore, admitting that "the word 'seduced'" might "offend" Karl, "but it is difficult to find another and equally suitable word" (26), while leaving hardly any doubt that the word is profoundly unsuitable. The presentation of Karl's "transgression" illustrates that accusations are diabolical not because they can be made against everyone but because while they claim to effect a distinction between just and unjust, they always need to leave out important aspects in order to present a case (Karl himself reminds the stoker of this), therefore, always misrepresent and, consequently, never attain a just judgment. The discourse of accusations is diabolical because while speaking in the name of justice, it serves neither to reveal truth nor to settle dispute but to install the authority of the judge. And the accuser is that judge inasmuch as his presentation of a case decides what "transgression" is judged.⁵³

The understanding seminal to juridical action is neither compassion nor comprehension of a subject matter, but more nuanced. What matters in the tribunal that leaves, as it were, his uncle's mark on Karl is not the "clear-headed" reason (*Verstand* [A:23/DL:91]) Karl senses to have attained earlier that would grant him comprehension and judgment. What matters in the tribunal is, rather, an understanding of rhetoric: "his uncle

---

⁵²"'I could be a stoker now too,' said Karl" (A:6).
⁵³Kafka analyzes this structure in the 1914/15 fragment *Der Unterstaatsanwalt* (Prosecuting Attorney): "Everything was so clear and so well thought out, it was as though all the people round about were interfering in a matter that belonged to him alone, a matter that he himself could carry through to its conclusion ... without any judge, any attorney, without any accused" (Translation Heinz Politzer, "The Puzzle of Kafka's Prosecuting Attorney," 436; NSF1:223).

had [understood] [*verstand*] to make a great song out of it" after the cook (not Karl's parents) "had informed [*verständigt*] his uncle of his arrival" (A: 30/DL:100–101). The Head Purser "was beginning to find the Captain's patience incomprehensible" (A:19), while the latter admonishes Karl: "[Do] understand your good fortune, young man[!]" (A:24/DL:94).

The claim to consideration seems to effect a "self-empowerment of the subject" not for the stoker but for Karl, who claims to speak on his behalf. Voicing the stoker's complaint supplies Karl with the very "influence" the lack of which the stoker had earlier attested—at the prize of public exposure, which renders Karl a "subject" of juridical discourse in the full sense of the word, so that he not only employs juridical terminology and rhetoric but is also subject to accusation and judgment.[54] It is remarkable, in view of the relation of the text's poetics to juridical discourse, that the senator/uncle's diabolical charge that Karl "was seduced by a maidservant" (A:26)—voiced although void and terminologically inappropriate—repeats the opening sentence of the story, where no personal speaker is easily identifiable yet: "As Karl Rossmann, a ... boy of sixteen who had been packed off to America by his [pitiable, *armen*] parents because a servant girl had seduced him and got herself a child by him" (A:3/DL:65). In an instance of interpolation akin to repression, Willa and Edwin Muir's translation of this sentence shifts the attribute "poor" onto Karl. He can certainly be read as a poor, deserted lad, yet relocating the adjective tears down the interrelation of views in which Karl fails to be seen. For if the view of the parents (rather than himself) as "pitiable" testifies, according to Kafka's letter to Jesenská, to Karl's "sympathy without understanding," what voices his sympathy is that he employs their wording of the scandal. Since its traumatic character becomes clear only later, the first sentence appears, upon initial reading, to take an authoritative stance. A retrospective comparison to the senator/ uncle's sentence proves that it is indeed authoritative, yet marked not by an anonymous author persona but by parental authority. The senator/uncle's charge can be read as targeting the authoritarian vocabulary that renders a "transgression" a "seduction," but the accusation diabolically uses the same terms. The revelation of Karl's "transgression" gives away his story as well as its own rhetorical instruments of power which, however, by no means reduces their effect but, in the contrary, exposes and affirms it. In Kafka's "Stoker," a "self-empowerment of the subject" instituting the rule by which

---

[54]Fort relates the ambivalence of the term to Karl's and the stoker's increasingly contrasting positions: "The story thus splits subjection in two directions: the stoker's submission into a crushing disciple, in a drive toward abjection and, ultimately, in his sacrificial expulsion from Karl's wayward symbolic economies, and on the other hand Karl's subject-formation, by which he is reinserted into the system of authority as newly legitimate, as having a recognizable status that invests him with a voice capable of speech, *as long as he no longer insists of speaking for the stoker*" (Jeff Fort, *The Imperative to Write*, 96).

it is judged is achieved solely by the highest-ranking officeholder who neither requires (further) empowerment nor has reason to complain—although his position as representative of the people suggests that he listens to, and takes care of, the complaints of others. In "The Stoker," the principle of personal representation, crucial both to (Karl's) juridical and (the senator's) political discourse, appears as none of assuming responsibility by way of hearing complaints and grievances of the represented and responding to them, but as one of raising above others and condescending onto them to silence their plaints.

Diabolically articulating his power, the senator's speech, furthermore, points out that no portrayal of events can desist from taking a stand. If it is articulated in the common form of propositions—in attributions, statements, and judgments—every portrayal either denounces (due to inappropriate attributions) or hurts (by failing to state detail). Yet if a portrayal is articulated otherwise than in clear statements, for instance because it testifies to ambivalent feelings, it remains incomprehensible such as the stoker's "specific complaints." Commonly considered the "normal form of human discourse," as Heidegger criticizes,[55] propositions appear as fundamentally juridical in Kafka's "Stoker": they are concerned with settling issues, silencing plaints, and sentencing subjects. The "Stoker" can be read as affirming what Agamben suspects: "the accusation is, perhaps, the juridical 'category' par excellence (*kategoria*, in Greek, means accusation), that without which the entire edifice of the law would crumble: the implication of being in the law. The law is …, in its essence, accusation."[56] Accusations constitute juridical subjects, Kafka points out. The accusations' propositional form, however, proves to be utterly unsuited to articulate or understand complaints about the fact that national, libidinal, economic, and other interrelations do not fit into the unambiguous order propositions establish. Complaints about the limitations of propositional speech cannot be negotiated by means of attribution (accusation) and statement (judgment). This is why the stoker is sidelined in what turns into Karl's negotiation with the Captain until he vanishes: "It was now as if there were really no stoker [any more]" (A: 37/DL:110).

There is one more reason why Karl, the advocate, soon replaces the stoker as protagonist of the negotiations on the Captain's bridge: While terminologically organized as juridical discourse, wherein advocacy is a seminal concept, some fundamental elements of juridical order are missing in these negotiations: Karl has an office neither aboard nor ashore, and while a civilian ship has an executive authority (the Captain), there is no judiciary aboard. Seven men (majorly) in uniform are, moreover, neither enough nor

---

[55] Heidegger, *Fundamental Concepts of Metaphysics* §72, 311; Introduction, 7.
[56] Giorgio Agamben, "K.," 15.

heterogeneous enough to form a Grand Jury—yet they are enough, and sufficiently uniform, to form a tragic chorus.[57] The presentation of the stoker's complaints in front of this committee meets the formal criteria of a tragic performance, of which plaints are a pivotal constituent and an important historical precursor. Unlike in juridical and political discourses based on advocacy and representation, in tragedy all figures speak for themselves, none on behalf of another one—except for the fact that all roles are played by actors, of course. And the *role* is a key historical link between tragic and juridical discourse as the modern notion of a juridical person derives from the adaption of the Greek theatrical mask (*prosōpon*) in Roman culture as *persona*, in the course of which it was widened to denote first the character on stage, later the roles played in social live as well as the grammatical position of the speaker in discourse. Yet there is a striking difference: On the tragic stage, the *persona* as hybrid of a living body and a role is defined by synchronic differentiation from other roles in the same temporally limited play, while the modern juridical fiction of a person responsible for their actions rests on the claim to diachronic stability in so-called identity. This claim testifies to a second tradition intertwined in the modern concept of personhood: After the end of Hellenistic theater in late antiquity, *persona* remains the Roman translation of *prosōpon*, which in turn becomes the Greek rendering of Hebrew *pā·nîm*, the "face" or "gaze" of God turned toward humans[58] as well as the "reputation" of humans, such as in the order: "You must not be partial in judging" (Deut. 1:17, NRSV) in the sense of "respect[ing] persons in judgment" (AV).[59] It is this notion of a stable countenance, transferrable even to God, upon which modern, institutionalized rather than rhetorical, juridical procedure is based that produces and prosecutes "the subject behind the person," as Trüstedt writes: "With the new figure of the prosecutor," the nation state institutionalization of the accuser, "a new procedure gradually takes over, shifting the attention from the *agon* and the technicality of the rhetorical procedure towards producing a (guilty) subject."[60] Against the backdrop of this institutionalized rather than rhetorically antagonistic understanding of juridical discourse, "instituting subjectivity"[61] always serves the purpose that, in Kafka's "Stoker," the Captain sees in hearing out a "notorious grumbler" (A:15): disciplining, controlling, exerting power.[62]

---

[57] *EA* 2:1142, s.v. "Chor": The number of chorus members varied, preferred numbers were 7, 9, 10, and 12.
[58] Num. 6:25–26, NRSV: "the Lord make his face to shine upon you, ...; the Lord lift up his countenance upon you."
[59] For the historical background Manfred Fuhrmann, "Person, 2," *HWRH* 7:269–283.
[60] Trüstedt, "Execution," 143; with reference to Kafka's *Trial*.
[61] Ibid., 139.
[62] Cf. ibid., 145: "the (main) trail re-quests and exposes the subject that it is supposed to protect."

The notion of the person-as-role is not the only link between juridical and tragic discourse. Juridical and tragic plaints are structurally related, as the court hearing concerning Orestes' matricide in the *Oresteia* demonstrates. Seremetakis finds the affinity in contemporary antiphonic laments of the Greek region Mani: "In Greek, the concept of *antifónisi* (antiphony) possesses a social and juridical sense in addition to its aesthetic, musical, and dramaturgical use."[63] Tragic stichomythia and ritual antiphony are concerned not with harmonious concord (as antiphons in church music) but with discord, with the communal negotiation of divergent complaints, opposing claims (to mourning and inheritance), ambivalent sentiments about the deceased, and even of skepticism about ritual dirges.[64] Seremetakis emphasizes that those who listen to plaints are as important to the ritual as those voicing them:

> "To hear" is to play an *active* role in the production of a juridical discourse. ... *Hearing is the doubling of the other's discourse*. Through the hearing of the chorus, the discourse is disseminated to the rest of society. The absence of hearing is equivalent to the "silent" death. The "silent" death is also the social death of the mourner without witness.[65]

In antiphonic ritual, the silent chorus functions as witness of lamenting, complaining, and suffering. The hearing it provides is essential because being heard is an interpersonal mark of the difference between life and death that becomes porous in mourning. Comprising dialogic exchange, articulate songs, wailing, sobbing, and crying,[66] antiphonic laments are a liminal means for achieving social reorganization (after shifts in social structures such as brought about by death or marriage) by way of linguistic disorganization. While the decomposition of those structures of language that commonly grant understanding, such as articulation and word reference, can be detrimental to listening comprehension, it is, nevertheless, concerned with the focal point of plaintive language: finding a hearing. In antiphony, the

---

[63]Seremetakis, *Last Word*, 102.
[64]Chapter 2, 122–127. German (§§395–402 StPO) and Austrian (§§46–51 StPO) criminal procedure has adopted an element of the dramaturgical form of ritual plaints with the option of *Nebenklage* to represent victims of major crimes not merely as witnesses but as permanent element of the trial with the right to hear witnesses, make objections, and ask questions, but excluded from prosecution and sentencing. I thank José Brunner, who brought the juridical uniqueness of this institution to my attention. The societal relevance of *Nebenklage* gained publicity during the 2015 trial against Oskar Gröning, SS-guard at the Auschwitz concentration camp, and the 2013–18 NSU-trial.
[65]Seremetakis, *The Last Word*, 104. For the "silent" death as punishment in tragedy, see Aeschylus, *Eumenides*, 565; Sophocles, *Antigone*, 548.
[66]Seremetakis, *Last Word*, 116–117.

muteness of the lamented deceased, who is often addressed in dirges but incapable of responding, is supplemented by the silence of those who listen to the lamenting and *are* capable of responding.

Karl and the stoker present a plaint that cannot refer to any conventionalized form of claiming attention. Therefore, their performance shifts from juridical to tragic form and even to that of a dirge, yet all of them are misplaced insofar as they fail to correspond to the (possible) ambivalent complaint of love which the stoker presents to Karl in bed, and because they find no conventionalized form of reciprocity with their audience. Antiphonic rituals, however, are no harmonious customs either but a form of communal dispute, of a controversial reformulation of an "I" in a community that includes criticism in social role models. Therefore, ritual plaints often articulate accusations. Transforming pain into charges is part of the passage ritual plaints are supposed to effect[67] by negotiating discord, that is by arousing mutual compassion for suffering and promoting comprehension for each one's plaint, such that a consent can be reached and the community continued. The stoker's complaints are incapable of reaching such consent with the captain's bridge. He does not even attain an understanding that there is a dispute to be resolved because the capitalist order aboard and ashore is not based on consent.

Karl's and the stoker's alternating speech as well as the latter's shift from articulation to crying, still, appear as antiphonic elements in the complaint they voice. And what matters is, just as in the ritual Seremetakis describes, not solely the Captain's hearing but the attention all of the officials gathering on the bridge devote to the turn-taking of dialogue between the changing role of protagonist and antagonist: the stoker and the Captain, the stoker and Schubal, Karl and the senator/uncle. These officials "function as a silent chorus" in Seremetakis's sense,[68] as listeners whose witnessing renders the failing transposition of the complaint of love into juridical action a public annihilation of the stoker's subjectivity, and the diabolic exposure of Karl's past a public testimony to the kinship between him and the senator/uncle. Adopting Karl as nephew is part of the social reorganization brought about by the discursive disorganization in the stoker's complaining: Shifting the role of the protagonist onto Karl correlates with sidelining the stoker, whose figure is exhausted as his complaint is voiced.

The stoker assumes his new role under the tragic protocol in hallucinatory adaption to a deceased over whom others lament in ritual dirges and tragic *kommos*—a transformation preformed by Karl's advocacy, which is also an instance of plaintive discourse voiced for someone else.

---

[67]Chapter 2, 122.
[68]Seremetakis, *Last Word*, 100.

> [Karl] was standing between his uncle and the Captain, and, perhaps influenced by his position, thought that he was holding the balance between them.
>
> And yet the stoker seemed to have abandoned hope. His hands were half stuck into the belt of his trousers, which together with a strip of checked shirt had come prominently into view during his excited tirade. That did not worry him in the least; he had displayed the misery of his heart, now they might as well see the rags the rags that covered his body, and then they could thrust him out. He had decided that the attendant and Schubal, as the two least important men in the room, should do him this last kindness. ...
>
> "Don't mistake the situation," said the Senator to Karl, "*this may be a question of justice, but at the same time it's a question of discipline.* On this ship both of these, and most especially the latter, are entirely within the discretion of the Captain."
>
> "That's right," muttered the stoker. Those who heard him and understood smiled uneasily. (A:32–33; my italics)

The distinction between justice and discipline apodictically introduced by the senator/uncle is no assessment of whether the stoker has been "unjustly treated" (A:34). Distinguishing "a question of justice" from "a question of discipline" is itself a question of power—the power to draw, and impose, distinctions. The distinction itself is neither just nor disciplined but arbitrary.[69] But why does the stoker agree, whose concern was (at least initially) not at all about an actionable case but about hearing for his complaint of love and nation? The stoker agrees because what he complains about is nothing else than the lack of power such as exercised by the senator or the Captain. That the claim to consideration for his "specific complaints" is not only "a question of justice, but at the same time ... a question of discipline" is indeed the insight that is to be gained from his humiliation on the captain's bridge: Calling upon justice is insufficient for making a complaint that can become an actionable case, mastery of the discipline of rhetoric—which makes up a large part of the discipline of law—is equally necessary. In Kafka's manuscript, the mentioning of "discipline" is followed by a sentence omitted in print: *Gerechtigkeit und Disciplin mischen sich aber nicht.*[70] (But justice and discipline do not mix.) In the printed version, the senator/uncle does not give away all that

---

[69]The distinction points out a difference between continental and transatlantic law; Arnold Heidsieck, *The Intellectual Contexts of Kafka's Fiction*, 105: "*Amerika* ... restricts the use of law to disputes between employer and employee that in Austria, for the most part, were not actionable in civil courts but seen as matters of discipline and contractual duties."
[70]Kafka, *DL:Apparatband*, 170.

clearly that in order to distinguish and judge, every discipline—the law included—must disregard "question[s] of justice." Brought to unease, or disconcerted (*befremdet* [DL:105]), by the stoker's agreement with the rigorous distinction between justice and discipline can only be who cannot grant him the wish to having the power to distinguish because he, or she, looks down upon the stoker, and ridicules him.

The insight into the irreconcilability of justice and discipline, however, again prompts the question bracketed as futile in "Description of a Struggle": "Of what help is complaining" actually? (NSF1:134)

## Politics of Outcry: Claiming Justice

In his 1934 essay on Kafka, Benjamin writes: "Kafka could understand things only in the form of *gestus*, and this *gestus* which he did not understand constitutes a cloudy part of the parables" (SW2.2:808). Elaborating on this remark, Müller-Schöll sees an implicit theory of theater in Kafka's writings: Suspending the clear distinction between appearance and essence, theatricality is, on the one hand, often the reason for a lack of understanding while, on the other hand, theater enables to grasp this lack of understanding as a gesture that cannot be reduced to a concept or statement.[71] The Brechtian *gestus* Benjamin discusses is, of course, more interpersonal habitus and attitude than conventional gesture, however, in Kafka, is often indeed a gesture that marks a decisive point of hermeneutical collapse. Such gestures are, for instance, in "A Little Woman," the narrator's resolution, "that if I keep my hands over it, even quite lightly, I shall quietly continue to live my own live for a long time to come" (CS:323–324), or the stoker's extension of vocal complaining by means of his hands: "You mustn't think—here his voice failed him and he gesticulated with his hands—that I am complaining for the sake of complaining" (A:7). What is more, Kafka's "Stoker" analyses a discursive *gestus*, the public outcry against social evils demanding that justice shall be served as a pivotal gesture of modernity in national(ist), capitalist, socialist, and other sociopolitical contexts. Kafka's text investigates this gesture of outcry and claim to bringing about justice that employs juridical, theatrical, religious, ritual, and other means yet belongs to none of these orders but to the practice of ordering communities, that is

---

[71]Nikolaus Müller-Schöll, "Lügen Tränen nicht?," 186: "der impliziten Theatertheorie in Kafkas Schriften: das Theatralische [ist] als Suspension der klaren Unterscheidung von Schein und Sein gewissermaßen die Ursache des Nicht-Verstehens. Zugleich aber erweist sich das Theatralische als der Ort, an dem sich dieses Nicht-Verstehen zumindest fassen lässt: Als nicht weiter reduzierbarer Gestus."

to say to politics. Kafka's investigation into the political gesture is theatrical (even though carried out in prose) insofar as the listening neighbor, father and son Bendemann, Karl, and the stoker can all be said to *make a scene*, and act out. It is not hard to see that the considerable difference in the success of Karl's and the stoker's performance results from their profoundly differing descend and education.[72] As Fort writes of the stoker, "He will have a much greater linguistic and social distance to traverse than Karl, who in effectively opening the space of power to the stoker's voice, also introduces this voice into an element of theatrical performance and groundless speech in which it will be unable to perform."[73] Kafka's text, however, is less interested in the details of their differing social backgrounds than in how these become manifest in speech and action. What makes the difference apparent is that Karl is capable of claiming the role of the advocate for himself by adopting the appropriate attitude and gestures (of storming into an office, urging to listen, reminding to speak up in the right manner) regardless of possible differences between claim and reality—while the stoker's complaint about Schubal is exactly about the divergence between claim and reality, wherefore he is unable to disregard it.

The stoker is incapable of fabricating the claim to a position. He has grievances rather than the means to self-imagination and self-formation—because unlike a position, the better treatment by others that he demands, the better hearing for his "specific complaints," and the better reciprocity aboard cannot be performed and thus formed by the complainer alone. The stoker's complaints all pertain to reciprocity. If, however, the public claim to consideration can succeed only by way of fabricating and performing the improvement as already attained, the status as already achieved—Karl's way of becoming-by-claiming-to-be an advocate—then the claim to better interaction and balanced reciprocity cannot succeed at all. Because the role of the other, whose hearing and response the complaint seeks to attain, cannot be fabricated by the complaint alone. Therefore, complaining is actually of no help to the stoker. In Kafka's "Stoker" it seems that a public outcry against injustice speaks not, in fact, for those in whose name it is raised—a subversion of representation mirrored in the story's (or chapter's) title that takes little heed of the fact that the stoker is already introduced as having been dismissed from this position, later becomes sidelined in the narrative, and is finally replaced as protagonist by Karl. Kafka suggests that a public complaint about injustice, and an outcry demanding that

---

[72]When entering the captain's bridge, Karl has already been identified as the senator's nephew (A:31), which makes it seem, in retrospect, as if the stoker's complaints had always been out of place.
[73]Fort, *Imperative to Write*, 90.

justice shall be served, speak only for those who already have the means for voicing the complaint and bringing it to an audience's attention.[74] Kafka's scenic presentation of the insight into the collapse of representation in the political gesture of claiming justice in "The Stoker" can be considered a plaint itself—one, however, that discloses all reasons for bracketing and silencing itself.

---

[74]This problem is analyzed in Jean-François Lyotard, *The Differend*, 8: "It is the nature of a victim not to be able to prove that one has been done a wrong. A plaintiff is someone who has incurred damages and who disposes of the means to prove it. One becomes a victim if one loses these means. ... In general, the plaintiff becomes a victim when no representation is possible of the wrong he or she says he or she has suffered. ... If there is nobody to adduce the proof, nobody to admit it, and/or if the argument which upholds it is judged to be absurd, then the plaintiff is dismissed, the wrong he or she complains of cannot be attested. He or she becomes a victim. If he or she persist in invoking this wrong as if it existed, the others (addressor, addressee, expert commentator on the testimony) will easily be able to make him or her pass for mad." Someone who cannot construct and present a case becomes a victim of a crime as well as the juridical apparatus claiming to sanction it. Lyotard's point is that in jurisdiction and public discourse, the burden of proof is more often than not imposed in the victim, most notably onto the victims of concentration and death camps (cf. 10). Written before the Shoa, Kafka's "Stoker" outlines that the stoker, the now jobless former worker at the lowest deck aboard, becomes a victim not solely of Karl's and of capitalism, but just as well of the nationalism he himself fuels, to which distinctions are proof enough.

# Conclusion: Transgenerational Trauma and the Inability to Lament

*The whole thing has nothing to do with mourning—it's all theater ...*[1]

The language of lamenting and complaining forms a speaking "I" in relation to others and situates the speaker within a social and hermeneutical context prerequisite to grasping pain, loss, and suffering as scandal or crisis. Plaintive language emphasizes the fundamental role of hearing, response, and reciprocity in speech, therefore, it features prominently in collective memory.[2] Plaints, however, do not simply guarantee intergenerational and interpersonal transmission of tradition. The insistence on hearing and the search for response in lamenting and complaining, rather, foreground *that* reciprocity is elementary yet not a given, but has to be established. In conclusion of the inquiry into plaintive language, the following pages highlight the precarious status of lamenting and complaining in the (post-)modern notion of history: Ritual plaints have become obsolete and left a void commonly negotiated in terms of individual or communal trauma. If lamenting and complaining are discussed in this paradigm at all, such utterances are taken to be masked accusations springing not from mourning but from the refusal to accept loss and the rejection of mourning. While this diagnosis is certainly right, it leaves the devastating gap of not being able to think a form of language capable of doing the work of mourning that renders traumata communicable history. An analysis of the structure of plaintive language in general and its discursive roles in modernity in particular would be incomplete without an attempt to understand how the lack of a language for lamenting history becomes manifest—a lack of a form

---

[1] Bernhard, *Extinction* [E], 389.
[2] For the construction of "collective memory" cf. Maurice Halbwachs, *On Collective Memory*, 46–51.

of speech that serves not to name genocides, attribute blame, and count victims but, when all of this is done, to mourn. What is at stake in looking at the present absence of lamenting and complaining is that living together is impossible if the task of lamenting cruelty and complaining about violence is shifted onto their victims alone while perpetrators, accomplices, and their descendants may carry on uncomplainingly.

Ritual laments often serve to form traditions that require reciprocity between members of a community and generations in order to attain repetition, reconstruction, and interpretation of the past. "Tradition," writes Giddens,

> is an orientation to the past, such that the past ... is made to have a heavy influence over the present. ... Yet ... tradition is also about the future, since established practices are used as a way of organising future time. ... Repetition ... reaches out to return the future to the past, while drawing on the past also to reconstruct the future. ... Memory is thus an active, social process, which cannot merely be identified with recall.[3]

In the retrospective construction of a tradition, ritual plaints often have a calendrical function, for instance in Christian Easter, the anniversary of the Passion and death of Jesus, in Jewish Tisha B'av, commemorating the destruction of the Jerusalem temple, as well as in Shiite Ashura, marking the death of the grandson of the prophet Muhammad in the battle of Kerbela.[4] The ritual laments essential to these occasions are performatives integrated in narratives, renewing the memory of an event that provides a basis for the comprehension of later events and a pattern to articulate the coherence that is called history. The rise of academic historiography in the nineteenth century, however, has resulted in "the elimination of every echo of 'lament' ['*Klage*'] from history" (SW4:401/GS1:1231), as Benjamin puts it.[5] This transformation of the concept of history entails the abolition of the relevance of mnemonic laments such as Tisha B'av, Easter, or Ashura, all devoted to the commemoration of defeats and their victims. Positivist historiography provides no place for those who succumbed to the formation of the Now. What remains for those who vanish in the course of the formation of a singular, teleological concept of (national) history is only: silence. But whence this drastic change in the historiographical role of plaints?

According to Benjamin, "the elimination of every echo of 'lament' from history ... marks history's final subjection to the modern concept of science" (SW4:401). This concept takes an inquiry as distanced, impartial contemplation and considers itself to be in no interrelation with the

---

[3] Giddens, "Living in a Post-Traditional Society," 62–66.
[4] Chapter 2, 80.
[5] Chapter 4, 199.

examined object, wherefore the asserted science of history fails to account for its point of view in the retinue of the victors of past conflicts.[6] Yet the concept of history as exact science is only one of many factors that resulted in the abolition of lamenting and complaining from the remembrance of the past; the concept is itself element of comprehensive changes in the wake of the industrialization and individualization of social life in modernity. These reorganizations changed the representation of the past, the view of ritual, and even the form of experience, as Benjamin's 1936 essay on the social role of narration discusses:

> It is as if a capability that seemed inalienable to us, the securest among our possessions, has been taken from us: the ability to share experiences.
> One reason for this phenomenon is obvious: experience has fallen in value. ... Beginning with the First World War, a process became apparent which continues to this day. Wasn't it noticeable at the end of the war that men who returned from the battlefield had grown silent—not richer but poorer in communicable experience? ... For never has experience been more thoroughly belied than strategic experience was belied by tactical warfare, economic experience by inflation, bodily experience by mechanical warfare, moral experience by those in power. A generation that had gone to school on horse-drawn streetcars now stood under the open sky in a landscape where nothing remained unchanged but the clouds ... (SW3:143–144)

Current research likewise assumes that the overwhelming numbers of victims in the First World War gave the decisive stimulus to the disappearance of ritual plaints from public life in the west.[7] And this is, still, "a process ... which continues to this day," as Leader points out in his 2009. *Mourning, Melancholia and Depression*:

> The erosion of public mourning rituals continues today in many parts of the world that had not experienced the mass slaughter of the great wars. In African societies, the toll of AIDS has meant that mourning and burial rituals that have been practised for hundreds of years are now being abandoned or abridged.[8]

Yet even though the First World War has proved that "experience has fallen in value," as Benjamin puts it, he hastens to qualify: "nothing would be more fatuous than to wish to see it as merely a 'symptom of decay',

---

[6]Benjamin, "On the Concept of History." SW4:391: "*even the dead* will not be safe from the enemy if he wins. And this enemy has not ceased to be victorious."
[7]Leader, *New Black*, 72.
[8]Ibid., 73.

let alone 'modern symptom'." (SW3:146) The disappearance is, rather, "only a concomitant of the secular productive forces of history ... that has gradually removed narrative from the realm of living speech and at the same is making it possible to find a new beauty in what is vanishing" (146). This beauty of vanishing narrative becomes manifest, Benjamin says, in the novel which does not present exemplary experience (any longer) but idiosyncratic individuals.[9] Benjamin has the formation of an individual in classic Bildungsroman in mind,[10] yet modern and postmodern novels often, rather, present a polyphony of voices and perspectives[11] as if to counter the notion of a monolithic, positivist history. Novels of (post)modernity thus examine the problem that continuity in perception, comprehension, and consequently representation is lost with traumatic experience—an issue that tends to be negated in positivist representations of history as (causal or successive) chain of actions and events. The novel thus adopts the narrator's function of forming a poetics of history as Benjamin describes it: The (oral) narrator presents memory, and "memory creates the chain of tradition which transmits an event from generation to generation" (SW3:154).

On the one hand, Benjamin sees the processes of capitalist reorganization of society, individualization, and media change from functional orality toward book culture—all of which contribute to the formation and development of the novel—active already at the outset of the modern era.[12] It is in the course of these reorganizations, too, that ritual forms such as dirges or wailing have been discredited as archaic, irrational, insincere, effeminate, or exotic, and were relegated from the status of widely shared communal practices into the arts, namely literature and opera.[13] On the other hand, even if Benjamin refuses to speak of "a 'symptom of decay', let alone 'modern symptom'" (SW3:146), he does note a significant change—or sudden culmination—in the loss of quotidian narration at the outset of the twentieth century. The sudden change becomes apparent in silent war veterans, later in the art of the so-called Modernity. Both point at now obsolete public laments and ritual plaints as an eminently lacking possibility of modern social interaction and negotiation of catastrophe. What remains is merely, as Benjamin writes, "to lament [the latest]: that even lamentation no longer exists." (SW4:227/ GS2:550) A number of Benjamin's writings from the late 1930s comment on this change in the capacity to make, share, and bemoan experience at

---

[9]SW3:146–147.
[10]Cf. ibid., referencing *Don Quichote* and *Wilhelm Meister*: "The birthplace of the novel is the individual in his isolation, the individual who can no longer speak of his concerns in exemplary fashion, who himself lacks counsel and can give none."
[11]For "polyphony" in the novel see Bakhtin, *Problems of Dostoevsky's Poetics*, 6.
[12]SW3:145–146.
[13]Chapter 2, 246.

## CONCLUSION: TRANSGENERATIONAL SILENCE    247

the outset of the twentieth century. A decisive comment, made only in a footnote, sees the experience of war continued in civilian life:

> *the pronounced threat to life in which people live today* ... corresponds to profound changes in the apparatus of apperception—changes that are experienced on the scale of private existence by each passerby in big-city traffic, and on the scale of world history by each fighter against the present social order. (SW3:132n33)

Freud says more explicitly than Benjamin that the introduction of the "national (conscript) army" during the First World War has served as "the precondition of the war neuroses" (SE17:208) as it enabled the spread of traumatization. What a majority of Europe's population encounters with the First World War as well as its political and financial aftermath was "shock." According to Freud, whom Benjamin quotes on this issue, the peculiar mode of non-experience called "shock" is a "traumatic neurosis ... caused by a lack of any preparedness for anxiety," a surprise, which results in "an extensive breach being made in the protective shield against stimuli."[14] Shock is no particular experience but a rupture in the very faculty for making experiences which, consequently, cannot become past but remains an ever-present stumbling block for psychic activity.[15] "Traumatic neurosis" obeys the "repetition compulsion" which endeavors, for instance in recurring nightmares, "to master the stimulus retrospectively, by developing the anxiety whose omission was the cause of the traumatic neurosis" (SE18:31). Benjamin regards the medium of film, which interrupts the beholders' association with ever-new images, as training for overcoming shock by way of "heightened attention."[16] Yet increasing attention comes at the prize of decreasing experience, and hence narratability: "The greater the shock factor in particular impressions, the more vigilant consciousness has to be in screening stimuli; the more efficiently it does so, the less these impressions enter long experience (*Erfahrung*)" (SW4:319). Fighting off surprise attacks prevents gathering experience. The "heightened attention" adequate to shock is an attention to nothing but ruptures. Hence there is nothing to tell. There would be plenty to lament with the First World War, of course: death, collapsed states, impoverishment, pain, belligerent repetition compulsion, and more. The once common forms of lamenting and complaining, however, have become obsolete in industrialized modernity

---

[14] Freud, SE18:30; quoted in Benjamin, "On Some Motifs in Baudelaire." SW4:317.
[15] This reading of shock connects to Freud's 1895 description of trauma as dysfunctional due to it inaccessibility for usage, "the normal wearing-away processes by means of abreaction and reproduction" (SE2:10); cf. Chapter 1, 32.
[16] Benjamin, "The Work of Art in the Age of Technological Reproducibility (Third Version)." SW4:267.

and its paradigm of authentic individuality. Psychoanalysis fills the void left by this disappearance by the outset of the twentieth century as a new form of listening to somatically uttered plaints and of paying attention to the glaringly lacking signs of sorrow in individual pathologies. The "process," however, which Benjamin says "became apparent" with the First World War, is the enfolding of a blatant contradiction: The omnipresent shocks of modern life interrupt and overwhelm everything individual and install the uniform pathology of trauma, however, the shocks result from exactly those processes of capitalism, industrialization, and media change that require and privilege individual action, or at least seem to require and privilege it. Moglen describes this contradicts in terms of a changing economy,

> as a shift from "competitive" or "market" to "monopoly capitalism." [...] The rise of monopoly capitalism produced unique cognitive difficulties, as the details of individual lived experience were less and less adequate to provide people with an accurate sense of the vast economic structures that were transforming their lives, palpably and often painfully.[17]

The discharge of the individual from social relevance by the very "secular productive forces of history" (SW3:146) which had produced individuality can be understood, Moglen suggests, as reason for a major experience of loss articulated in the literature of Modernity. In terms of economy, the psychoanalytical endeavor of reconstructing an individual's unique biographical continuity from incomprehensible complaints actually draws on a less-than-modern paradigm. This complication marks the relevance of the recent transgenerational turn in psychoanalytical research and trauma studies, "a kind of paradigm shift,"[18] as Salberg notes, that calls for contextualizing individual relationality in terms of community and history. For trauma—a rupture in experience due to a violent "breach in the protective shield against stimuli" (SE18:30)—may be caused in interaction with others as well as transmitted to others. Both, but especially the latter aspect, are highlighted in the concept of "relational trauma."[19] The term implies that traumatic non-experience is transmitted in speech by way of relation, however, in view of Benjamin's thesis that shock (the perceptional mode of trauma) undermines experience and thus narration (but installs

---

[17]Moglen, *Mourning Modernity*, 4.
[18]Salberg, "The Texture of Traumatic Attachment," 80.
[19]Ibid., 89: "Until recently, psychoanalytic focus had been on intrapsychic and interpersonal relationships, often evolving its ideas split off from the applied world of psychoanalysis – the world of cultural, political, historical, and trauma studies. ... We are now at a moment when theories of transgenerational transmission of traumas, formed through the epochs of great wars, famine, dislocation, the Shoa and other genocides, slavery, immigration, and now climate catastrophes, coincide with the volumes of scholarship within individual psychoanalysis, attachment research."

repetition compulsion, as Freud suggests), the role of silence and breaches in relations turns out to be at least as seminal as the choice of words. Relational trauma results, Salberg suggests, from a particular incapacity for interaction: In order to establish reciprocity with a traumatized attachment figure, usually a parent, children adapt to behavior that has been shaped by trauma even without knowing about, or undergoing, the original traumatization themselves. What is thus transmitted is no knowledge of traumatizing events but a particular disorganization of reciprocity, "the *texture of traumatic attachment*."[20] Transgenerational transmission of trauma is the backdrop of Freud's Dora case that expounds abusive patterns in sexual relations mirrored in the analytical setup (hence she stopped the treatment), and of his analysis of the "Wolf Man's" mother tongue of plaints that gives voice to an abusive family structure,[21] however, transgenerational transmission hardly come into Freud's theoretical focus. This focus is recent.

Relatively recent, or recently renewed, is also the inquiry into the transgenerational transmission of the aftermath of cruelty and its repression in perpetrators and their accomplices. In 1967, Alexander and Margarete Mitscherlich note on Hitler: "Absence of the work of mourning allows Hitler to continue to exist as an encapsulated psychic introject."[22] They put this in a footnote since their study on the *Inability to Mourn* focuses on the cultural specificity of family bonds that first provided the basis for the unconditional admiration of a leader, and later obstructed the admission to military and moral defeat prerequisite to mourning after the Second World War.[23] Abraham and Torok describe encapsulated objects that remain inaccessible to mourning as results not of regular introjection (according to Freud "the sole condition under which the id can give up its objects" [SE19:29]) but of incorporation that swallows in order to hide and silence the object. This results in "an intrapsychic secret" that Abraham and Torok call a "crypt" (MM:130) in which all pain, thoughts, and feelings linked to the loss as well as the very lost love object itself lay hidden from consciousness.[24] By the

---

[20]Ibid., 94.
[21]Chapter 1, 46–75.
[22]Alexander Mitscherlich and Margarete Mitscherlich, *The Inability to Mourn: Principles of Collective Behavior*, 46n\*.
[23]Although referencing the distinction, the Mitscherlichs see neither mourning nor melancholia at work in post-war Western Germany but, rather, the negation of all loss (ibid., 26): "The Federal Republic did not succumb to melancholia; instead, as a group, those who had lost their 'ideal leader', the representative of a commonly shared ego-ideal, managed to avoid self-devaluation by breaking all affective bridges to the immediate past." They see three stages of the breach (ibid., 28): first "emotional rigidity" in which "the past is de-realized," second a "shift of identification" onto the victorious US-Americans, and third "the manic undoing of the past, the huge collective effort of reconstruction." This negation and isolation of the past in a psychic capsule are largely congruent with Abraham and Torok's theory of melancholic incorporation (Chapter 1, 69).
[24]Chapter 1, 71.

'end of the 1990s, Gampel describes transgenerational lacunas as "psychic holes," Laub as an "empty circle."[25] In 2010, Schwab revisits Abraham and Torok's theory of mourning to explore the "collective crypts, communal crypts, and even national crypts" in the transgenerational transmission of repression, negation, and non-mourning to the descendants of perpetrators and their accomplices.[26] Literary and theoretical analyses of historical transmissions of trauma often focus on family settings without implying a separation between public and private; "the family is," rather, as Coates notes, "what might best be called a 'remembering context'"[27] fostering the transmission of individual attachment patterns as much as structures of collective memory.

What is striking, however, is the lacking account for the role of the language of lamenting and complaining in recent theoretical approaches to the transgenerational transmission of trauma—although Freud's *Mourning and Melancholia*, wherein the difficult hermeneutics of complaining features prominently, is still a reference point for many studies, and although there is a general agreement, even between otherwise-conflicting conceptions of trauma, that the process of "working through" in mourning and therapy is an "articulatory practice," as LaCapra writes,[28] that is to say a language-based process akin to witnessing which, according to Laub, has the effect of a "re-externalization—and thus historicization."[29] Against the background of the language of lamenting and complaining, which consumes conventional structures of language such as articulation, word reference, address, and even the distinction from silence, it does not seem necessary to break trauma theory down to a focus on either "gaps in the text" or "the text itself," as Pederson's criticism in Caruth's paradigm of silent trauma suggests.[30] In plaintive language, text and textual gaps are intertwined—not least in the lacking attention of (transgenerational) trauma theory to the lack of lamenting and complaining as a language to carry out the work of mourning. Schwab indeed focuses on discursive discontinuity and the disorganizing of speech: "The crypt becomes traceable, visible, or readable not only in cryptic or hieroglyphic verbs—such as in the Wolf Man's 'fetish

---

[25]Yolanda Gampel, "The Interminable Uncanny" (1996); Dori Laub, "The Empty Circle: Children of Survivors and the Limits of Reconstruction" (1998), discussed in Salberg, "Traumatic Attachment," 83–87.
[26]Schwab, *Haunting Legacies*, 46.
[27]Coates, "The Child as Traumatic Trigger," 123.
[28]LaCapra, *Writing History, Writing Trauma*, 21–22.
[29]Laub, "Bearing Witness," in Shoshana Felman and Laub, *Testimony: Crises of Witnessing*, 70.
[30]Pederson, "Speak, Trauma," 338; cf. ibid.: "As the first generation of trauma theorists subscribe to an understanding of trauma as unspeakable, they gravitate toward textual lacunae in their readings. ... a new generation of trauma theorists should emphasize both the accessibility of traumatic memory and the possibility that victims may construct reliable narrative accounts of it."

words'—but in other gaps in or deformations of language: incoherences, discontinuities, disruptions, and the disintegration of meaning or grammar or semantic and rhetorical coherence."[31] The language of lamenting and complaining, however, seems to have been eliminated from historiographical narrative and inquiry, as Benjamin notes (only to eliminate the note himself from his final manuscript). Speaking of a thorough "elimination of every echo of 'lament' from history" (SW4:401) is appropriate because not only have formulaic plaints like dirges come out of usage, as Rilke laments,[32] but lamenting, complaining, wailing, and other forms of plaints do not appear as possible practices of the "work of mourning" (SE14:245) in recent trauma theory at all. Plaintive language thus resembles the "storyteller" of oral narrative who "has council for his readers" but of whom Benjamin marks that he "has already become something remote from us and is moving ever further away" (SW3:143–145).[33]

What remains of the language of lamenting and complaining, under the paradigm of trauma, is solely the melancholic organization of masked accusations of others that springs from the refusal to accept loss and the rejection of mourning. The Mitscherlichs' *Inability to Mourn* still lists outright lamentations of loss next to melancholic self-reproach[34] but repeatedly adds that their analysis does not aim at making accusations,[35] which testifies to a general understating of plaintive language as melancholic. In Schwab, "complaints" and "lament[ing]" appear as signs of repression and negation in perpetrators, projecting their violence onto Holocaust victims and casting themselves as victims of wrongful persecution.[36] Schwab is, of course, far from misrepresenting the role of complaining in the transmission of the persecutors' repression. The restriction of plaintive language to a querulous means of repression and negation is, rather, a symptom of the historical crisis Benjamin detects already in the silence of the First World War veterans: The loss of the "ability to share experiences" in narrative (SW3:143) is brought about by the very disorganization of perception into a chain of shocks that also entails a profound inability to lament.

This is, however, the moment for drawing a distinction that might seem overdue: transgenerational transmission of trauma is, of course, broadly negotiated in literature, in particular in Holocaust literature, to which lament is not alien at all. First-generation writing often refers to traditional forms of such a lament, as Aarons and Berger note:

---

[31]Schwab, *Haunting Legacies*, 53.
[32]Chapter 2, 108–109.
[33]Cf. SW3:145: "But if today 'having counsel' is beginning to have an old-fashioned ring, this is because the communicability of experience is decreasing. In consequence, we have no counsel either for ourselves or for others."
[34]Mitscherlich and Mitscherlich, *Inability to Mourn*, 63, 42.
[35]Ibid., 13, 41.
[36]Schwab, *Haunting Legacies*, 73.

Survivor writing might be said to draw upon both midrash and lamentation, two defining traditions in Jewish literary expression. Midrash consists of stories that interpret and extend narratives and events in Jewish history. ... Such midrashic occasions for engagement and recognition ... take place alongside of lamentation ... In evoking the two ancient paradigms of lamentation and midrash, Holocaust narratives turn to these longstanding and defining literary and cultural conventions in response to the devastation of the Shoah as well as its aftermath. Both midrash and lamentation, through their literary invocation of trauma, invite the reader to participate in an act of consanguineous understanding and ethical engagement. Here midrash and lamentation give voice to memory, breathing life into absence.[37]

Aarons and Berger further point out that "the movement from survivor writing to second- and third-generation accounts of the Nazi genocide marks an important shift in the intergenerational transmission and expression of Holocaust memory, trauma, and representation"[38] as it cannot rely on personal testimony any longer. In post-Holocaust representation, absence takes center stage in a call to memory "in the face of silence":[39] "absence emerges as a marker of place, but also as a trope for those who perished or who no longer exist to tell their own stories. The third generation locates itself within and in defiance of such absence."[40] Third-generation Holocaust-writing is, Aarons and Berger conclude, "simultaneously a way of mourning relatives they never knew and an attempt to understand their own Jewish identity."[41] In witnessing the transgenerational transmission of trauma rather than traumatizing events, the reference to traditional forms such as the "literary convention of moral lament" originating in the *Eicha*, the biblical book of Lamentations,[42] is no longer an evident pattern but requires reconstruction. Unlike in transgenerational Holocaust writing, the reconstruction of plaintive language as traditional form for negotiating historical catastrophe is eminently lacking in narratives of the transmission of perpetrators', or accomplices', repression and negation, not least because tradition had been a keyword of fascist ideology and thus became an impossible frame of reference for its criticism. This debasement of tradition is far from exceptional but only a culmination of a long process of the marginalization of traditional forms such as ritual plaints in modernity.

---

[37]Aarons and Berger, *Third-Generation Holocaust Representation*, 48–49.
[38]Ibid., 41.
[39]Ibid., 145.
[40]Ibid., 64–65.
[41]Ibid., 144.
[42]Ibid., 49.

## CONCLUSION: TRANSGENERATIONAL SILENCE

In a postmodern context, under the paradigm of trauma, the language of lamenting and complaining is conceivable merely as melancholic refusal to mourn that intents to project guilt away from the speaker onto the listener at the price of destroying both reciprocal exchange and the present in the compulsive repetition of the past. What has become unthinkable with the abolition of ritual forms of plaint in favor of the paradigm of an authenticity of individual emotion is the language of lamenting and complaining as a way of doing the "work of mourning": of accepting loss and assimilating it to collective memory so as to form "a precipitate"—parallel to how, according to Freud's post–First World War theory of mourning, "the character of the ego is a precipitate of abandoned object-cathexes and ... contains the history of those object-choices" (SE19:29). What remains of the language of lamenting and complaining under the paradigm of authentic inwardness is the language of defense that Freud calls melancholic and that speaks in order *not* to lament, not to accept any loss, but to remain unmoved. Literature is one of the few discourses in which lamenting can be negotiated in modernity as it is a prominent realm into which plaintive language has been relegated from everyday practice. Embedded into the conditions of modernity, however, modern literature does not simply speak the obsolete language of lamenting and complaining, yet it may outline its lack.

A pivotal form of negotiating lack, especially in transgenerational transmission, is ghostliness and haunting. Chapter 2 has outlined that the ghostly presence of an absence is, notably, how the perceived anachronism of ritual forms such as plaints in modernity is often conceptualized: dirges, wailing, and other ritual forms are often cast as relics of antiquity that are vanishing just now when under scrutiny. This temporality employs the Christian model of superstition, of relics standing out of pagan pre-history into historical time Anno Domini, which was imported into art history and anthropology, Didi-Huberman explains as "the *phantasmic time of survivals*."[43] The temporality of phantoms can be applied to forms of ancient spirituality in modern-day life such as astrology[44] as well as to forms of lamenting and complaining. Survival introduces "the paradox of a residual energy, of a trace of past life"[45] effective as if even after the death, or end, of a practice, thus opening up history and, at the same time, anachronizing the present.[46] "It is the things which have long been dead, in fact, which haunt our memory the most effectively, and the most

---

[43] Didi-Huberman, *The Surviving Image*, 28.
[44] Ibid., 48.
[45] Ibid., 46.
[46] Cf. ibid., 48–49.

dangerously."[47] Didi-Huberman suggests a parallel between the notion of survival and the psychoanalysis of traumatic reminiscences. A supplemental concept that Abraham and Torok add to their notion of crypts may serve to support this parallel and to conceptualize how the lack of plaintive language can become apparent in modern literature, before turning to a concluding literary instance of such an articulation of lack.

Abraham and Torok assume that the individual "intrapsychic secret" they call a "crypt" (MM:130) is transmitted to the next generation, or generations, as "phantom":[48]

> Since the phantom is not related to the loss of an object of love, it cannot be considered the effect of unsuccessful mourning, as would be the case with melancholics or with all those who carry a tomb in themselves. It is the children's or descendants' lot to objectify these buries tombs through diverse species of ghosts. What comes back to haunt are the tombs of others. The phantoms of folklore merely objectify a metaphor active in the unconscious: the burial of an unspeakable fact *within the love-object*.[49]

An ancestor's crypt releases ghosts by which descendants are haunted without understanding what affects them because it results from no loss they have suffered, and could have mourned, themselves. The ancestral ghost is real, nevertheless, insofar as it informs the descendant's speech and psychic reality: traumatic phantoms bar introjection, prevent a regular usage of words,[50] and "point to a gap, ... refer to the unspeakable" that lays hidden in the other's crypt. The inherited phantom thus, paradoxically, appears as a lack, becomes present as an absence, when descendants cannot put into their mouths what lays buried in the ancestor's crypt. The exact manner in which crypts are transmitted as phantoms remains an open question "yet to be determined" in Abraham and Torok.[51] Recent approaches to

---

[47]Ibid., 48.
[48]Abraham and Torok, "Notes on the Phantom," 171.
[49]Ibid., 171–172.
[50]Cf. ibid., 174: "The phantom counteracts libidinal introjection; that is, it obstructs our perception of words as implicitly referring to their unconscious portion." This marks an important difference between Abraham and Torok's concepts and Derrida's "hauntology" (*Specters of Marx*, 9). What haunts ontology is the ambiguity of all words which philosophical language seeks to eradicate from terminology, most prominently in the concept of "spirit" (*Geist*) as supposed to designate nothing but rationality. While Derrida's approach is about the inevitable perspective in all thinking and knowing (the ghost that cannot be exorcised), the psychoanalytical concept applied here is about the destruction of comprehensibility and transmission due to repression and negation that (unlike Derrida's) cannot be accepted as a structural axiom because it destroys life and perpetuates genocide. For a detailed comparison, see Colin Davis, "*État présent*: Hauntology, Spectres and Phantoms."
[51]Abraham and Torok, "Notes on the Phantom," 173.

transgenerational trauma outlined above connect to this point, suggesting that it is the dependency on reciprocity with an attachment figure who keeps them alive what makes children form communicative patterns that complement their parents' traumatization so as to be able to address them in a way that invites response. "The child must do this in order to have an attachment relationship," Salberg explains, "thereby becoming attached to the parent's presence and absence."[52] Complementing the non-presence of repression, negation, and burial in a crypt requires a high intensity of repression that needs to be, Salberg adds, "transmitted to the child, who must not know what he/she actually does know."[53] This traumatic learning—an un-learning of individual perceptions to make room for traumatic heritage—comprises practice in disregarding one's feelings as much as repeating leaps in historical narratives. Hence, and although Abraham and Torok describe trauma within a family context, the theory of crypts and correlating phantoms is suited to describe transgenerational transmission in the larger context of communities and "collective traumatic histories," as Schwab notes.[54] For Abraham and Torok note that "the 'phantom effect' progressively fades during its transmission from one generation to the next and that, finally, it disappears"—except "when shared or complementary phantoms find a way of being established as social practices" associated with certain words, "staged words" that are meant to direct behavior and speech.[55] Bernhard's 1986 novel *Extinction* (Auslöschung: Ein Zerfall) portrays such an institutionalization of repression and refused mourning in the state of its decomposition (*Zerfall*), as the novel's subtitle specifies.

The extensive text of *Extinction* is a two-part soliloquy of the protagonist Franz-Josef Murau. In the novel's first part, he learns that he is the sole heir of his estranged parents' estate, Wolfsegg castle in upper Austria; in the second part, he returns to the castle to oversee the burial of his parents and late brother. The text is a negotiation of his ancestors' private and political violence, their complicity with Austro-fascism, German national socialism, and its continuities under the guises of both Catholicism and Socialism. Murau ruminates "the whole complex of our origins" (*unseren ganzen Herkunftskomplex*),[56] which is the architectural complex of the castle as much as the psychological complications caused by violence, repression, and refusal to acknowledge any loss and mourn. Confirming modernity's paradigm of authentic individuality that dismisses ritual as insincere performance, Murau denies the elaborately Baroque funeral preparations,

---

[52]Salberg, "Traumatic Attachment," 90.
[53]Ibid., 89.
[54]Schwab, *Haunting Legacies*, 78.
[55]Abraham and Torok, "Notes on the Phantom," 176.
[56]Bernhard, E:147/*Auslöschung: Ein Zerfall* [AL], 201.

pomp, and service[57] all meaning: "The whole thing has nothing to do with mourning—it's all theater, I said" (E:389) all the while, still, directing the performance. It culminates in a passage in which Muraus locates himself seventeen times "by the open grave," or more accurately: tomb (*an der offenen Gruft*)[58] in order to express everything he sees laying hidden within it: "the National Socialist criminals whose crimes are never mentioned today, having been hushed up for so many years" (E:334), or, rather about which dead silence is kept today while it had been profoundly repressed for so many decades[59]—thus remaining latent and incessantly ready to return. "The ghostly" (*das Gespenstische*)[60] aspect of National Socialism, according to Murau, is the subsequent silence about which his novel-within-the-novel *Extinction* shall extinguish: "It's the silence that's so [uncanny], I said. It's the nations silence that's so terrible" (E:334/AL:459). It seems adequate to link Bernhard's emphasis on the silence after the fact brought to light "at the open [tomb]" to Abraham and Torok's psychoanalytical concept of crypts and subsequent phantoms. Crypts are formed not by just any losses but by a "shameful secret" shared with the lost one which had also functioned as an ego ideal (MM:131). What needs to be swallowed and buried in the crypt, and bars from mourning, are the secret and the shame that would be brought upon the object if it was revealed as this would entail a retroactive loss, proving that the object had never been the ideal as which it has been loved. It is easy to understand the murders and other crimes of National Socialism as this secret, but what Bernhard's novel highlights just as much is the opportunism in which Murau's ancestors had embraced the respective rulers: the victorious US-Americans after the war just like, previously, the invading Germans—even paralleling both allegiances:

> While my parents dined with the Americans or toasted General Eisenhower at their champagne breakfasts, the Gauleiters sat just a few hundred yards away [in the Children's Villa], no doubt enjoying equal conviviality and an equal abundance of food and drink[, I think]. (E:323/AL:442)

Just like funeral pomp, luxurious entertainment is seminal to feudal culture. The connotation of these practices, however, changes in the context of modernity, and this changed connotation can be read in terms

---

[57]Cf. "funeral procession" (E:467), (missing) "laurel branches" (236), funeral "banner" (290), "catafalque" (238), "catafalque sheets" (246), golden "catafalque lamps" (412).
[58]E:468–473/AL:641–647.
[59]AL:458: *dessen Verbrechertum heute nur totgeschwiegen wird, nachdem es so viele Jahrzehnte gründlich verdrängt worden ist.*
[60]AL:458; original italics. MacLintock renders this "the full horror" (E:334), which is certainly correct but drops the notion of undead.

of psychoanalysis. A crypt, Abraham and Torok explain, results from the phantasmagoric incorporation of an unmourned loss, from literally swallowing it instead of putting it into one's mouth in order to speak about it.[61] This element of the psychoanalytical theory of transgenerational crypts and phantoms is suited to elucidate the relevance of entertainment and consumption in Bernhard's *Extinction*: Keeping the past alive while, at the same time, nourishing new alliances, they fill their own mouths and those of others in order not to talk. There is a particular secret not to tell, hidden from the US-Americans and from himself, as Murau finds out. After the war, Murau's parents hid wanted National Socialist criminals on their estates. "Our parents made themselves guilty, I said, by harboring and sheltering those loathsome people, who should have been tried and sentenced" (E:335). The parents' crime is structurally similar to psychic repression. They hide what shall not be seen; they prevent charges and secure their silence by not listening: "I later recalled that for years we were not allowed in the Children's Villa" (E:321).

> [W]hen we were suddenly allowed back in the Children's Villa in our middle teens, we naturally wanted to know why we had not been allowed in before ... <u>Our parents, as former party members, [answered] nothing</u>. But naturally they could not keep the secret forever, and one day it came out. One of the Gauleiters paid a visit to Wolfsegg, and no sooner had he entered the house than he began to talk, in my presence, of the time he had spent in the Children's Villa as *the best years of his life*. Standing next to him, I [had to take note of] how he and his comrades had lived in the Children's Villa for nearly four years. *How* they had eaten and *how* they had drunk! [How he could not be calmed down over being so] eternally grateful to my mother, who [did not want to hear any of it] because I was present. (E:324–325/AL:445–446; my underlining)

The Children's Villa, a piece of Baroque entertainment architecture, evokes the Romantic topos of a childhood in the countryside in midst of a fairy tale (that is to say: feudal) otherworld—in order to undermine this scenery. Just like the Mitscherlichs, Bernhard emphasizes that the tradition of teaching children unquestioning obedience had been the pivotal condition for the possibility of Fascism and National Socialism.[62] Using a scene to house

---

[61] Chapter 1, 71–73.
[62] "My parents didn't *bring* me up, they *dragged* me up ... [i]n their brutal Catholic National Socialist way" (E:103–104). The Mitscherlichs identify "the exploitation of obedience in ... social relationships," which leaves subjects in "inner helplessness" (*Inability to Mourn*, 39) as the education enabling the cult of an ideal leader because it results in "an unusually ambivalent attitude toward paternal authority" (ibid., 46). This ambivalence is expressed in "the inclination to desecrate authority (the reader may be reminded here of Luther's tone whenever he alluded to the Pope)" (ibid., 22).

children in order to hide National Socialist crimes and criminals appears like an architectonical adaption of Abraham and Torok's notion of the crypt that releases phantoms onto descendants: What the ancestors hide rather than mourn effects a deformation in discourse—a gap in speech and refusal to listen—that is transmitted to the next generation, which it haunts as dysfunctionality without cause. In Bernhard's text, the disclosure of the parents' secret results in an effect similar to trauma, namely a breach in experience that makes the personal past inaccessible.[63] Read in view of recent transgenerational trauma research, it is not the mere disclosure that entails, as it were, a childhood apocalypse but the lacking response by the mother, who "did not want to hear any of it" and reacted as if indeed she had not. Auestad notes on traumatization in children:

> The trauma is only completed ... when the adult acts towards the child as if nothing distressing or painful had happened, thus depriving the event that took place of its reality. Since what happened has not been acknowledged, not registered, it continues to exert an influence in the present.[64]

The lacking or refused acknowledgment of a loss or insult does not at all bar their effect on reality but, on the contrary, intensifies it. Even without acknowledgment, reciprocity is at the center of the "language game" thus installed,[65] yet due to the open denial of response it is traumatic rather than plaintive. Lacking reciprocity is at the center of *Extinction*, a soliloquy that constantly appeals to a rarely mentioned listener. Murau concedes: "The question of whether I had loved my parents and my brother was one that I at once fended off with the word *naturally*, [and it remained not only fundamentally but in fact unanswered]" (E:9/AL:12). Murau's hate of and resistance against Wolfsegg are, of course, formed by this architectonical and psychological "complex of ... origin" (E:147). Bernhard does not fail to expound the mimetic participation of resistance in that which it counters,[66] most notably the destructive impetus of fascist modernization that did not leave it at threatening to extinguish traditional institutions and established elites, which returns in Murau's book project entitled *Extinction*.[67] In

---

[63]Hückmann, "Topographie des Schweigens," 205–206.
[64]Auestad, *Shared Traumas, Silent Loss, Public and Private Mourning*, xix–xx.
[65]Chapter 3, 157–164.
[66]"I would not be the man I am if Wolfsegg had been different" (E:77).
[67]"The only thing that I have fixed in my head is the title, *Extinction*, for the sole purpose of my account will be to extinguish what it describes, to extinguish everything that Wolfsegg means to me, everything that Wolfsegg is, everything, you understand, ..., really and truly everything" (E:146).

## CONCLUSION: TRANSGENERATIONAL SILENCE

Bernhard, mimetic participation in, and even complicity with, a heritage of violence and repression appears as hardly avoidable consequence of a lacking response by, and responsibility in, the ancestors' generation.

A comprehensive practice of mortification and conservation takes the place of reciprocity in Wolfsegg:

> Canning jars I find a nightmare, and we had hundreds of them at Wolfsegg, not just in the larders but on the cupboards in the other rooms. At an early age the prospect of having to spend the next few decades consuming all the jam that was stored in these jars, carefully labelled by my mother and sisters, filled me with a permanent loathing for anything jarred, especially jam. The larders also contained hundreds of jars full of preserved chicken thighs, and pigeon thighs, which were of a dull yellow color that never failed to nauseate me. Although we ate less and less [preserves] at Wolfsegg, my mother and sister jammed and jarred increasing quantities; [they were indeed] obsessed with [a jamming and jarring mania]. (E:75/AL:101)

> The cooks and their assistants ... were kept busy most of the time canning and pickling, and even making sausages, because the slaughtering was done at Wolfsegg and we ate only the [self-slaughtered] meat [*das Selbergeschlachtete*]. (E:133/AL:182)

Practices of preserving are seminal to feudal subsistence economy; however, in the context of the silent and silencing repression of National Socialist crimes, they turn into practices of evasion accessible to a psychoanalytical reading: Busyness averts reflection,[68] preservation replaces mourning, catering and consumption replaces exchange and conversation, chewing and swallowing replaces talking and mourning. Whatever is fed into the economics of repression drastically changes its meaning. This is why Murau can be nauseated by preserved meat although "as small children we thought it natural for animals to be slaughtered and dressed" (E:134), or *processed* (*aufbereitet* [AL:182]), a word Bernhard puts in italics. The mortified and immortalized meat is nauseating because it appears as return of the bodies of the victims of National Socialism who remain invisible and unmentioned in Wolfsegg due to silent approval and active support. The preserves appear as a return of the bodies who had been refused a grave, or pompous tomb, and whose remains had been processed for reuse in concentration camps and other

---

[68]Mitscherlich and Mitscherlich, *Inability to Mourn*, 28, note a parallel busyness: "The very grimness with which the job of clearing away the ruins was immediately begun—which, in over-simplification, was taken as a sign of German efficiency—itself betrayed a manic element."

National Socialist institutions.[69] Nausea is fear of contact. For Murau it is fear of accepting his parents' complicity and guilt[70] and assimilating it as shared transgenerational secret—in psychoanalytical terms: fear of swallowing the ancestor's guilt and burying it within himself as an heritage in constant need of silencing that consumes the heir's psychic and linguistic integrity.

Like the language of lamenting and complaining, transgenerational trauma discourses center on hearing and response and entail a consumption of those structures of language that conventionally grant comprehension. Yet rather than stirring up disputes and inviting social reorganization by way of linguistic disorganization as plaints do, trauma silences conflict and disrupts social texture. Transmitting the fundamental structures of plaintive language to a very different effect, transgenerational trauma writing has a paradoxical effect: Lament survives in the outline of its lack.

---

[69] Bernhard's *Extinction* undermines the distinction between human and non-human corpses; the child's observation of a forestry practice is thus mirrored in thoughts about his parents' funeral: "We would then go through the woods and collect [*zusammenzuschleifen*] all the dead deer that hadn't survived and bury them" [*einzugraben*] (E:102/AL:136). "They're decomposing rapidly, I thought. They'll have to be buried [*eingegraben*] soon, otherwise they'll pollute the [air]" (E:329/AL:450). In humans, the verb is usually *begraben* (to bury) rather than *eingraben* (to dig in). Mimetically participating in the repression of National Socialist crimes, Murau, however, cuts the link between corpses and deceased: "Our parents no longer exist. There's nothing lying in the Orangery than *three bodies consigned to decay*, I said, which no longer have anything to do with the human beings they once were" (E:389). For the parallel on laying out corpses and storing food, cf. E:393.

[70] Cf. E:335 on receiving the parents' funeral guests: "And to think that I have to receive these murderers! I'll refuse to shake hands with them, I said. I can't exclude them from the funeral, but I won't shake their hands. If I did, I too would be guilty of a crime."

# BIBLIOGRAPHY

Aarons, Victoria, and Alan Berger. *Third-Generation Holocaust Representation: Trauma, History, and Memory*. Chicago: Northwestern University Press, 2017.
Abraham, Nicolas, and Maria Torok. *Cryptonymie: Le Verbier de l'homme aux loupes*. Paris: Aubier-Flammarion, 1976.
Abraham, Nicolas, and Maria Torok. [MM] "Mourning *or* Melancholia: Introjection *versus* Incorporation." In *The Shell and the Kernel: Renewals of Psychoanalysis*, translated by Nicholas Rand, 125–138. Chicago: University of Chicago Press, 1994.
Abraham, Nicolas, and Maria Torok. "Notes on the Phantom: A Complement to Freud's Metapsychology." In *The Shell and the Kernel: Renewals of Psychoanalysis*, translated by Nicholas Rand, 171–176. Chicago: University of Chicago Press, 1994.
Abraham, Nicolas, and Maria Torok. *The Wolf Man's Magic Word: A Cryptonymy*. Translated by Nicolas Rand. Minneapolis: University of Minnesota Press, 1986.
Abu-Lughod, Lila. "Islam and the Gendered Discourse of Death." *International Journal of Middle East Studies* 25, no. 2 (1993): 187–205.
Adorno, Theodor W. *Aesthetic Theory*. Translated and edited by Robert Hullor-Kentor. London: Athlone Press, 1997.
Adorno, Theodor W. *Negative Dialectics*. Translated by E.B. Ashton. New York: Continuum, 1997.
Aeschylus. *Agamemnon. Libation Bearers. Eumenides [Oresteia]*, with an English translation by Herbert Weir Smyth. London: Heinemann, 1926.
Aeschylus. *The Persian*, with an English translation by Herbert Weir Smyth. Vol. 1. London: Heinemann, 1926.
Agamben, Giorgio. "K." In *The Work of Giorgio Agamben*, edited by Nicholas Heron et al., 13–27. Edinburgh: Edinburgh University Press, 2008.
Alexiou, Margaret. *The Ritual Lament in Greek Tradition*. 2nd ed. Oxford: Rowman & Littlefield, 2002.
Amelang, James. "Mourning Becomes Eclectic: Ritual Lament and the Problem of Continuity." *Present & Past* 187 (2005): 3–31.
Amzallag, Nissim, and Mikhail Avriel. "Complex Antiphony in David's Lament and Its Literary Significance." *Vetus Testamentum* 60 (2010): 1–14.
Anderegg, Johannes. "Zum Ort der Klage. Literaturwissenschaftliche Erkundungen." In *Klage: Jahrbuch für Biblische Theologie* 16, edited by Martin Ebner et al., 185–208. Neukirchen-Vluyn: Neukirchener Verlag, 2001.
Arendt, Hannah. *The Human Condition*. Garden City: Doubleday, 1959.
Arendt, Hannah. *Origins of Totalitarianism*. New York: Schocken, 2004.

Ariès, Philippe. *The Hour of Our Death*. Translated by Helen Weaver. London: Boyars, 1976.
Aristotle. *The "Art" of Rhetoric*. Translated by John Henry Freese. London: Harvard University Press, 1947.
Aristotle. *The Categories. On Interpretation*. Translated by Harold Cooke and Hugh Tredennick. London: Harvard University Press, 1983.
Aristotle. *The Poetics*. Translated by Stephen Halliwell. London: Harvard University Press, 1953.
Aristotle. *Politics*. Translated by Harris Rackham. London: Harvard University Press, 1950.
Assmann, Jan. *Cultural Memory and Early Civilization: Writing, Remembrance, and Political Imagination*. Cambridge: Cambridge University Press, 2012.
Auestadt, Lene (ed.). *Shared Traumas, Silent Loss, Public and Private Mourning*. London: Routledge, 2017.
St. Augustine. *Confessions*. Translated by Benignus O'Rouke. London: Darton, Longman and Todd, 2013.
Austin, John Langshaw. *How to Do Things with Words*. 2nd ed. Cambridge: Harvard University Press, 1962.
Austin, Linda. "The Lament and the Rhetoric of the Sublime." *Nineteenth-Century Literature* 53, no. 3 (1998): 279–306.
[AV] *The Bible. Authorized King James Version with Apocrypha*. Edited by Robert Carroll and Stephen Prickett. Oxford: Oxford University Press, 1998.
Bachvarova, Mary R. "Sumerian 'Gala' Priests and Eastern Mediterranean Returning Gods: Tragic Lamentation in Cross-Cultural Perspective." In *Lament: Studies in the Ancient Mediterranean and Beyond*, edited by Ann Suter, 18–52. Oxford: Oxford University Press, 2008.
Baggini, Julian. *Complaint: From Minor Moans to Principled Protests*. London: Profile, 2008.
Bakhtin, Mikhail. "Discourse in the Novel." In *The Dialogic Imagination*, translated by Caryl Emerson and Michael Holquist, 259–422. Austin: University of Texas Press, 1981.
Bakhtin, Mikhail. *Problems of Dostoevsky's Poetics*. Translated by Caryl Emerson. Minneapolis: University of Minnesota Press, 1984.
Barley, Nigel. *Dancing on the Grave: Encounters with Death*. London: Penguin, 1995.
Barouch, Lina. *Between German and Hebrew: The Counterlanguages of Gershom Scholem, Werner Kraft and Ludwig Strauss*. Berlin: deGryuter, 2016.
Barouch, Lina. "The Erasure and Endurance of Lament: Gershom Scholem's Early Critique of Zionism and Its Language." *Jewish Studies Quarterly* 21 (2014): 13–26.
Barouch, Lina. "Lamenting Language Itself: Gershom Scholem on the Silent Language of Lamentation." *New German Critique* 37.3, no. 111 (2010): 1–26.
Benjamin, Walter. *The Correspondence of Walter Benjamin, 1910–1940*. Translated by Manfred Jacobson and Evelyn Jacobson. Chicago: University of Chicago Press, 1994.
Benjamin, Walter. [GS] *Gesammelte Schriften*. Edited by Rudolf Tiedemann and Herman Schweppenhäuser. 7 vols. Frankfurt am Main: Suhrkamp, 1974–1987.
Benjamin, Walter. *One Way Street and Other Writings*. Translated by Edmund Jephcott and Kingsley Shorter. London: NLB, 1979.

Benjamin, Walter. [O] *The Origin of German Tragic Drama*. Translated by John Osborne. London: Verso, 1998.
Benjamin, Walter. [SW] *Selected Writings*. Edited by Howard Eiland and Michal Jennings. 4 vols. Cambridge, MA: Belknap, 2002–2006.
Berges, Ulrich. *Herders Theologischer Kommentar zum Alten Testament [HThKAT]: Klagelieder*. Freiburg: Herder, 2002.
Berlant, Lauren. *The Female Complaint: The Unfinished Business of Sentimentality in American Culture*. Durham: Duke University Press, 2008.
Bernhard, Thomas. [A] *Auslöschung: Ein Zerfall*. Frankfurt am Main: Suhrkamp, 1986.
Bernhard, Thomas. [E] *Extinction*. Translated by David MacLintock. New ed. London: Faber & Faber, 2019.
Bielik-Robson, Agata. *Jewish Cryptotheologies of Late Modernity: Philosophical Marranos*. New York: Routledge, 2014.
Bielik-Robson, Agata. "The Unfallen Silence: Kinah and the Other Origin of Language." In *Lament in Jewish Thought*, edited by Ilit Ferber and Paula Schwebel, 133–152. Berlin: deGryuter, 2014.
Billings, Joshua. *Genealogy of the Tragic: Greek Tragedy and German Philosophy*. Princeton: Princeton University Press, 2014.
Blake, Fred. "The Feelings of Chinese Daughters towards Their Mothers as Revealed in Marriage Laments." *Folklore* 90, no. 1 (1979): 91–97.
Blok, Josine. "Solon's Funerary Laws: Questions of Authenticity and Function." In *Solon of Athens. New Historical and Philological Approaches*, edited by Josine Blok and André Lardinois, 167–247. Leiden: Brill, 2006.
Boehm, Fritz. *Die Neugriechische Totenklage*. Berlin: Minerva, 1947.
Braiterman, Zachary. "Review of *Lamentations of Youth: The Diaries of Gershom Scholem, 1913–1919*." *Religious Studies Review* 35, no. 3 (2009): 196.
Brueggemann, Walter. "The Costly Loss of Lament." In *The Psalms and the Life of Faith*, edited by Patrick Miller, 98–111. Minneapolis: Fortress, 1995.
Butler, Jenny. "Symbolic and Social Roles of Women in Death Ritual in Traditional Irish Society." In *Women, Pain, and Death: Rituals and Everyday Life on the Margins of Europe and Beyond*, edited by Evy Håland, 108–121. Newcastle upon Tyne: Cambridge Scholars, 2008.
Butler, Judith. *Antigone's Claim: Kinship between Life and Death*. New York: Columbia University Press, 2000.
Butler, Judith. *Bodies That Matter: On the Discursive Limits of "Sex."* New York: Routledge, 1993.
Butler, Judith. *Frames of War: When Is Life Grievable?* London: Verso, 2009.
Butler, Judith. *Precarious Life: The Powers of Mourning and Violence*. London: Verso, 2004.
Butler, Judith. *The Psychic Life of Power: Theories in Subjection*. Stanford: Stanford University Press, 1997.
Campe, Rüdiger. "Kafkas Fürsprache." In *Kafkas Institutionen*, edited by Arne Höcker and Oliver Simons, 189–212. Bielefeld: transcript, 2007.
Campe, Rüdiger, and Julia Weber. "Rethinking Emotion: Moving beyond Interiority." In *Rethinking Emotion: Interiority and Exteriority in Premodern, Modern, and Contemporary Thought*, edited by Rüdiger Campe and Julia Weber, 1–18. Berlin: deGryuter, 2014.
Canetti, Elias. *Crowds and Power*. Translated by Carol Stewart. New York: Continuum, 1981.

Caraveli-Chaves, Anna. "Bridge between Worlds: The Greek Women's Lament as Communicative Event." *Journal of American Folklore* 93, no. 368 (1980): 129–157.
Caruth, Cathy. *Unclaimed Experience: Trauma, Narrative, and History*. Baltimore: Johns Hopkins University Press, 1996.
Cavell, Marcia. *Becoming a Subject: Reflections in Philosophy and Psychoanalysis*. Oxford: Oxford University Press, 2006.
Cavell, Stanley. *Contesting Tears: The Hollywood Melodrama of the Unknown Woman*. Chicago: University of Chicago Press, 1996.
Cavell, Stanley. "Freud and Philosophy: A Fragment." *Critical Inquiry* 13, no. 2 (1987): 386–393.
Cavell, Stanley. "Knowing and Acknowledging." In *The Cavell Reader*, edited by Stephen Mulhall, 46–71. Cambridge: Blackwell, 1996.
[CEV] *Holy Bible: Contemporary English Version*. Edited by the American Bible Society. New York: ABS, 1995.
Chantraine, Pierre. *Dictionnaire étymologique de la langue grecque*. Paris: Klincksieck, 1999.
Cheng, Anne Anlin. *The Melancholy of Race: Psychoanalysis, Assimilation, and Hidden Grief*. Oxford: Oxford University Press, 2001.
Child, William. *Wittgenstein*. New York: Routledge, 2011.
Cicero, Marcus Tullius. *On the Republic. On the Laws*. Translated by David Fott. Ithaca: Cornell University Press, 2014.
Cioffi, Frank. *Wittgenstein on Freud and Frazer*. Cambridge: Cambridge University Press, 1998.
Claassens, Juliana. "Calling the Keeners: The Image of the Wailing Woman as a Symbol of Survival in a Traumatized World." *Journal of Feminist Studies in Religion* 26, no. 1 (2010): 63–77.
Clark-Decès, Isabella. *No One Cries for the Dead: Tamil Dirges, Rowdy Songs, and Graveyard Petitions*. Berkeley: UC Press, 2004
Clewell, Tammy. "Mourning beyond Melancholia: Freud's Psychoanalysis of Loss." *Journal of the American Psychoanalytic Association* 52 (2004): 43–67.
Coates, Susan. "The Child as Traumatic Trigger." *Psychoanalytic Dialogues* 22 (2012): 123–128.
Comay, Rebecca. "Paradoxes of Lament: Benjamin and Hamlet." In *Lament in Jewish Thought*, edited by Ilit Ferber and Paula Schwebel, 269–285. Berlin: deGryuter, 2014.
Craik, Katherine. "Shakespeare's *A Lover's Complaint* and Early Modern Criminal Confession." *Shakespeare Quarterly* 53, no. 4 (2002): 437–459.
Cunningham, Maurice P. "Ovid's Poetics." *The Classical Journal* 53, no. 6 (1958): 253–259.
Curtius, Ernst Robert. *European Literature and the Latin Middle Ages*. Translated by Willard Trask. Princeton: Princeton University Press, 2013.
Danforth, Loring M. *The Death Rituals of Rural Greece*. Princeton: Princeton University Press, 1982.
Daschke, Dereck. *City of Ruins: Mourning the Destruction of Jerusalem through Jewish Apocalypse*. Leiden: Brill, 2010.
Dassmann, Ernst. "Die Verstummte Klage bei den Kirchenvätern." In *Klage: Jahrbuch für Biblische Theologie* 16, edited by Martin Ebner et al., 135–151. Neukirchen-Vluyn: Neukirchener, 2001.

Davis, Colin. "*État present*: Hauntology, Spectres and Phantoms." *French Studies* LIX, no. 3 (2005): 373–379.
Deeb, Lara. "Living Ashura in Lebanon: Mourning Transformed to Sacrifice." *Comparative Studies of South Asia, Africa and the Middle East* 25, no. 1 (2005): 122–131.
Derrida, Jacques. *Aporias*. Translated by Thomas Dutoit. Stanford: Stanford University Press, 1993.
Derrida, Jacques. *Specters of Marx: The State of the Dept, the Work of Mourning and the New International*. Translated by Peggy Kamuf. New York: Routledge, 1994.
Descartes, Rene. OEuvres des Descartes. Edited by Charles Adam and Paul Tannery. Vol. 10, La Lumiere Naturelle. Paris: Vrien, 1996.
Descartes, René. *Discourse on Method and Related Writings*. Translated by Desmond Clarke. London: Penguin, 1999.
Deubner, Ludwig. "Ololyge und Verwandtes." *Abhandlungen der Preußischen Akademie der Wissenschaften 1941: Philologisch-historische Klasse* 1: 2–28.
Devi, Mahasweta. *Rudali: From Fiction to Performance*. Translated by Anjum Katyal. Calcutta: Seagull, 1997.
Díaz-Mas, Paloma. "Sephardic Songs of Mourning and Dirges." *European Judaism* 44, no. 1 (2011): 84–97.
Didi-Huberman, Georges. "Klagebilder, beklagenswerte Bilder?" *Trajekte* 15 (2007): 29–35.
Didi-Huberman, Georges. *Peuples en larmes, peuples en armes*. Paris: Minuit, 2016.
Didi-Huberman, Georges. *Survival of the Fireflies*. Translated by Lia Swope Mitchell. Minneapolis: University of Minnesota Press, 2018.
Didi-Huberman, Georges. *The Surviving Image. Phantoms of Time and Time of Phantoms: Aby Warburg's History of Art*. Translated by Harvey Mendelsohn. University Park: Pennsylvania State University Press, 2002.
Dobbs-Allsopp, F.W. *"Weep, O Daughter of Zion": A Study of the City-Lament Genre in the Hebrew Bible*. Rome: Biblical Institute Press, 1993.
Döring, Tobias. *Performance of Mourning in Shakespearean Theatre and Early Modern Culture*. Basingstoke: Palgrave Macmillan, 2006.
[DRB] *Douay-Rheims Bible*. London: Baronius, 2011.
Drügh, Heinz. "Warenästhetik." In *Warenästhetik. Neue Perspektiven auf Konsum, Kultur und Kunst*, edited by Heinz Drügh et al., 9–46. Frankfurt am Main: Suhrkamp, 2011.
Dué, Casey. *The Captive Women's Lament in Greek Tragedy*. Austin: UT Press, 2006.
Durkheim, Émile. *The Elementary Forms of Religious Life*. Translated by Joseph Ward Swain. London: Ellen & Unwin, 1915.
Durkheim, Émile. *Les formes élémentaires de la vie religieuse. Le système totémique en Australie*. Paris: Presses universitaires de France, 1991.
Dutsch, Dorota. "Nenia: Gender, Genre, and Lament in Ancient Rome." In *Lament: Studies in the Ancient Mediterranean and Beyond*, edited by Ann Suter, 258–279. Oxford: Oxford University Press, 2008.
Duttlinger, Carolin. "Kafkas Poetik der Aufmerksamkeit von *Betrachtung* bis *Der Bau*." In *Kafka und die kleine Prosa der Moderne*, edited by Manfred Engel and Ritchie Robertson, 79–97. Würzburg: Königshausen & Neumann, 2010.
[DW] Grimm, Jacob, and Wilhelm Grimm. *Deutsches Wörterbuch*. Repr. 1787ff. München: dtv, 1984.
[EA] *Der Neue Pauly. Enzyklopädie der Antike. Altertum*. Edited by Hubert Cancik and Helmut Schneider. Stuttgart: Metzler, 1996–2003.

Ehrenberg, Alain. *The Weariness of the Self: Diagnosing the History of Depression in the Contemporary Age*. Translated by Enrico Caouette et al., Montreal: McGill-Queen's University Press, 2010.

Ehrenberg, Hans. *Tragödie und Kreuz*. Würzburg: Patmos, 1920.

Eng, David, and Shinhee Han. "A Dialogue on Racial Melancholia." *Psychoanalytical Dialogues* 10, no. 4 (2000): 667–700.

Euripides. *Euripidis Fabulae*. Vol. 2. Edited by Gilbert Murray. Oxford: Clarendon, 1913.

Euripides. *Trojan Women*. In *The Plays of Euripides*, translated by Edward Coleridge. Vol. 1. London: George Bell, 1891.

Fabian, Johannes. *Time and the Other: How Anthropology Makes Its Objects*. New York: Columbia University Press, 1983.

Feld, Stephen. "Comments." *Current Anthropology* 47, no. 6 (2006): 904–905.

Feld, Stephen, and Aaron Fox. "Music and Language." *Annual Review of Anthropology* 23 (1994): 25–53.

Felman, Shoshana. "Benjamin's Silence." *Critical Inquiry* 25, no. 2 (1999): 201–234.

Felman, Shoshana, and Dori Laub. *Testimony: Crises of Witnessing in Literature, Psychoanalysis, and History*. New York: Routledge, 1992.

Fenves, Peter. *Arresting Language: From Leibnitz to Benjamin*. Stanford: Stanford University Press, 2001.

Ferber, Ilit. "'Incline thine ear unto me, and hear my speech': Scholem, Benjamin, and Cohen on Lament." In *Lament in Jewish Thought*, edited by Ilit Ferber and Paula Schwebel, 111–130. Berlin: deGryuter, 2014.

Ferber, Ilit. "A Language of the Border: On Scholem's Theory of Lament." *Journal of Jewish Thought & Philosophy* 21 (2013): 161–186.

Ferber, Ilit. *Philosophy and Melancholy: Benjamin's Early Reflections on Theater and Language*. Stanford: Stanford University Press, 2013.

Fögen, Marie Theres. *Das Lied vom Gesetz*. München: Siemens, 2007.

Foley, Helene. *Female Acts in Greek Tragedy*. Princeton: Princeton University Press, 2002.

Fort, Jeff. *The Imperative to Write: Destitutions of the Sublime in Kafka, Blanchot and Beckett*. New York: Fordham University Press, 2014.

Fortmann, Patrick. "Kafka's Literary Communities." *The Modern Language Review* 104, no. 4 (2009): 1038–1062.

Foucault, Michel. "What Is an Author?" In *Language, Counter-Memory, and Practice: Selected Essays and Interviews*, edited by Donald Bouchard et al., 113–138. Ithaca: Cornell University Press, 1977.

Freud, Sigmund. [GW] *Gesammelte Werke: Chronologisch geordnet*. Edited by Anna Freud et al., 19 vols. Frankfurt am Main: Fischer, 1968.

Freud, Sigmund. [SE] *The Standard Edition of the Complete Psychological Works of Sigmund Freud*. Translated from the German under the general editorship of James Strachey. 24 vols. New York: Vintage, 1999 [Reprint].

Friedlander, Eli. "On the Musical Gathering of Echoes of the Voice: Walter Benjamin on Opera and the *Trauerspiel*." *The Opera Quarterly* 21, no. 4 (2006): 631–646.

Fuchs, Ottmar. *Die Klage als Gebet*. München: Kösel, 1982.

Fuchs, Ottmar, and Bernd Janowski. "Vorwort." In *Klage: Jahrbuch für Biblische Theologie* 16, edited by Martin Ebner et al., v–vi. Neukirchen-Vluyn: Neukirchener, 2001.

Galas, Diamanda. *Diamanda Galas*. Berkeley: Metalanguage Records, 1984.

Gamliel, Toma. "'She Who Mourns Will Cry': Emotion and Expertise in Yemeni-Israeli Wailing." *Journal of Anthropological Research* 66, no. 4 (2010): 485–503.

Gana, Nouri. *Signifying Loss: Toward a Poetics of Narrative Mourning*. Lewisburg: Bucknell University Press, 2011.

Gardiner, Muriel (ed.). *The Wolf-Man by the Wolf-Man*. With *The Case of the Wolf-Man* by Sigmund Freud and *A Supplement* by Ruth Mack Brunswick. New York: Basic, 1971.

Garland, Robert. *The Greek Way of Death*. London: Duckworth, 1985.

Gebauer, Gunter, and Anna Stuhldreher. "Wittgenstein: Das Sprachspiel der Emotionen." In *Klassische Emotionstheorien*, edited by Hilge Landweer and Ursula Renz, 615–634. Berlin: deGruyter, 2008.

van Gennep, Arnold. *The Rites of Passage*. Translated by Monika Vizedom and Gabrielle Caffee. New York: Routledge, 2010.

Giddens, Anthony. "Living in a Post-Traditional Society." In *Reflexive Modernization: Politics, Tradition and Aesthetics in the Modern Social Order*, edited by Ulrich Beck et al., 56–109. Cambridge: Polity Press, 1994.

Goetz, Rainald. *Klage: Tagebuchessay*. Frankfurt am Main: Suhrkamp, 2008.

Goldhill, Simon. "The Ends of Tragedy: Schelling, Hegel, and Oedipus." *PMLA* 129, no. 4 (2014): 634–648.

Goldmann, Arthur (ed.). *Das Judenbuch der Scheffstraße zu Wien*. Wien: Braumüller, 1908.

Goody, Jeff. *Myth, Ritual, and the Oral*. Cambridge: Cambridge University Press, 2010.

Goppelsröder, Fabian. *Zwischen Sagen und Zeigen. Wittgensteins Weg von der literarischen zur dichtenden Philosophie*. Bielefeld: transcript, 2007.

Greenberg, Moshe. *HThKAT: Ezechiel 1–20*. Freiburg: Herder, 2001.

Gryphius, Andreas. *Catharina von Georgien*. Edited by Alois Haas. Stuttgart: Reclam, 1975.

Gurd, Sean Alexander. *Dissonance: Auditory Aesthetics in Ancient Greece*. New York: Fordham, 2016.

Haas, Volker. *Die hetitische Literatur: Texte, Stilistik, Motive*. Berlin: deGryuter, 2006.

Hacker, P. M. S. "Of Knowledge and of Knowing That Someone Is in Pain." In *Wittgenstein: The Philosopher and His Works*, edited by Alois Pichler and Simo Säätela, 244–276. Frankfurt am Main: Ontos, 2006.

Hacker, P. M. S. *Wittgenstein: Meaning and Mind. An Analytical Commentary on the Philosophical Investigations*. Vol. 3. Oxford: Blackwell, 1990.

Håland, Evy Johanne (ed.). *Women, Pain, and Death: Rituals and Everyday Life on the Margins of Europe and Beyond*. Newcastle upon Tyne: Cambridge Scholars, 2008.

Halbwachs, Maurice. *On Collective Memory*. Translated by Lewis Coser. Chicago: The University of Chicago Press, 1992.

Hall, Edith. *Inventing the Barbarian: Greek Self-Definition through Tragedy*. Oxford: Oxford University Press, 1989.

Hallett, Garth. *A Companion to Wittgenstein's Philosophical Investigations*. Ithaca: Cornell University Press, 1977.

Hamacher, Werner. "Bemerkungen zur Klage." In *Lament in Jewish Thought*, edited by Ilit Ferber and Paula Schwebel, 90–110. Berlin: deGryuter, 2014.

Hamacher, Werner. "The Right to Have Rights (Four-and-a-Half Remarks)." *South Atlantic Quarterly* 103, no. 2/3 (2004): 343–356.

Hamacher, Werner. "The Word *Wolke*—If It Is One." *Studies in 20th Century Literature* 11, no. 1 (1986): 133–161.
Hanfling, Oswald. *Wittgenstein and the Human Form of Life*. London: Routledge, 2002.
Hanssen, Beatrice. *Walter Benjamin's Other History: Of Stones, Animals, Human Beings, and Angels*. Berkeley: UC Press, 1998.
Hardwick, Lorna. "Philomel and Pericles: Silence in the Funeral Speech." *Greece & Rome* 11, no. 2 (1993): 147–162.
Hasebrink, Burkhard. "'Ich kann nicht ruhen, ich brenne.' Überlegungen zur Ästhetik der Klage im *Fließenden Licht der Gottheit*." In *Das fremde Schöne: Dimensionen des Ästhetischen in der Literatur des Mittelalters*, edited by Manuel Braun et al., 91–107. Berlin: deGruyter, 2007.
Havelock, Christine. "Mourners on Greek Vases: Remarks on the Social History of Women." In *Feminism and Art History: Questioning the Litany*, edited by Norma Broude and Mary Garrard, 44–61. Cambridge: Harper & Row, 1982.
Hegel, Georg Wilhelm Friedrich. *Hegel's Philosophy of Mind: Being Part Three of the Encyclopaedia of Philosophical Sciences*. Translated by William Wallace, Oxford: Clarendon, 1971.
Hegel, Georg Wilhelm Friedrich. *Phenomenology of Spirit*. Translated by A.V. Miller. Oxford: Oxford University Press, 1977.
Heidegger, Martin. *The Fundamental Concepts of Metaphysics: World, Finitude, Solitude*. Translated by William McNeill and Nicolaus Walker. Bloomington: Indiana University Press, 1995.
Heidsiek, Arnold. *The Intellectual Contexts of Kafka's Fiction: Philosophy, Law, Religion*. Columbia, SC: Camden, 1994.
Herder, Johann Gottfried. "Critical Forests ... First Grove." In *Selected Writings on Aesthetics*. Translated by Gregory Moore, 51–176. Princeton: Princeton University Press, 2006.
Herder, Johann Gottfried. *The Spirit of Hebrew Poetry*. Translated by James Marsh. 2 vols. Burlington: Smith, 1833.
Herder, Johann Gottfried. "Treatise on the Origin of Language." In *Philosophical Writings*, translated and edited by Michael N. Foster, 65–164. Cambridge: Cambridge University Press, 2002.
Herodotus. *Histories, with an English Translation by A.D. Godley*. Cambridge: Harvard University Press, 1920.
Heskett, Randall. *Reading the Book of Isaiah: Destruction and Lament in the Holy Cities*. Basingstoke: Palgrave Macmillan, 2011.
Hessel, Stéphane. *Time for Outrage: Indignez-vous!* New York: Twelve, 2011.
Hinterhuber, Hartmann. "Die psychiatrische Dimension der Klage." In *Der Mensch in seiner Klage: Anmerkungen aus Theologie und Psychiatrie*, edited by Hartmann Hinterhuber et al., 9–20. Innsbruck: Tyrolia, 2006.
Holst-Warhaft, Gail. *Dangerous Voices: Women's Laments and Greek Literature*. London: Routledge, 1992.
Holst-Warhaft, Gail. "No Consolation: The Lamenting Voice and Public Memory." In *Tradition, Translation, Trauma: The Classic and the Modern*, edited by Jan Parker and Timothy Mathews, 211–227. Oxford: Oxford University Press, 2011.
Homer. *The Iliad*. Translated by Peter Green. Oakland: University of California Press, 2015.

Honig, Bonnie. *Antigone, Interrupted.* Cambridge: Cambridge University Press, 2013.
Horn, Eva. *Trauer schreiben: Die Toten im Text der Goethezeit.* München: Fink, 1998.
Hoy, William. *Do Funerals Matter? The Purposes and Practices of Death Rituals in Global Perspective.* New York: Routledge, 2013.
Huber, Ingeborg. *Die Ikonographie der Trauer in der griechischen Kunst.* Möhnesee-Wamel: Bibliopolis, 2001.
Hückmann, Dania. "Topographie des Schweigens in Thomas Bernhards *Auslöschung. Ein Zerfall.*" In *Thomas Bernhard: Gesellschaftliche und politische Bedeutung der Literatur*, edited by Johann Georg Lughofer, 201–215. Wien: Böhlau, 2012.
Hughes, Richard. *Lament, Death, and Destiny.* New York: Lang, 2004.
Hussein, Ali. "The Mourning of History and the History of Mourning: The Evolution of Ritual Commemoration of the Battle of Karbala." *Comparative Studies of South Asia, Africa and the Middle East* 25, no. 1 (2005): 78–88.
[HWRH] *Historisches Wörterbuch der Rhetorik.* Edited by Gert Ueding. 12 vols. Tübingen: deGryuter, 1992–2015.
Jakobson, Roman. "Linguistics and Poetics." In *Style in Language*, edited by Thomas A. Sebeok, 350–377. New York: Wiley, 1960.
Jaques, Margaret. "Metaphern als Kommunikationsstrategie in den mesopotamischen Bußgebeten an den persönlichen Gott." In *Klagetraditionen: Form und Funktion der Klage in den Kulturen der Antike*, edited by Margaret Jaques, 3–19. Fribourg: Academic Press, 2011.
Kafka, Franz. [A] *Amerika.* Translated by Willa and Edwin Muir. New York: Schocken, 1974.
Kafka, Franz. *Briefe 1900–1912.* Edited by Hans-Gerd Koch. Frankfurt am Main: Fischer, 1999.
Kafka, Franz. *Briefe 1918–1920.* Edited by Hans-Gerd Koch. Frankfurt am Main: Fischer, 2013.
Kafka, Franz. [CS] *Complete Stories.* Edited by Nahum Glatzer. New York: Schocken, 1995.
Kafka, Franz. *The Diaries of Franz Kafka 1910–1913.* Translated by Joseph Kresh. New York: Schocken, 1948.
Kafka, Franz. *The Diaries of Franz Kafka 1914–1923.* Translated by Martin Greenberg. New York: Schocken, 1949.
Kafka, Franz. [DL] *Drucke zu Lebzeiten.* Edited by Wolf Kittler et al. 2 vols. Frankfurt am Main: Fischer, 1994.
Kafka, Franz. [IT] "An Introductory Talk on the Yiddish Language." In *Reading Kafka: Prague, Politics, and the Fin de Siècle*, edited by Mark Anderson, 263–266. New York: Schocken, 1989.
Kafka, Franz. *Letters to Friends, Family, and Editors.* Translated by Richard and Clara Winston. London: Calder, 1958.
Kafka, Franz. *Letters to Milena.* Translated by Philip Boehm. New York: Schocken, 1990.
Kafka, Franz. [NSF1] *Nachgelassene Schriften und Fragmente* 1. Edited by Malcom Pasley. Frankfurt am Main: Fischer, 1993.
Kaltwasser, Christóbal Rovira, and Cas Mudde. *Populism: A Very Short Introduction.* Oxford: Oxford University Press, 2017.
Kant, Immanuel. *Critique of Judgement.* Translated by J.H. Bernhard. 2nd ed. London: Macmillan, 1914.

Každan, Alexandar (ed.). *The Oxford Dictionary of Byzantium*. Oxford: Oxford University Press, 1991.
Kenny, Anthony. "Verification Principle and the Private Language Argument." In *Wittgenstein's Philosophical Investigations*, edited by Meredith Williams, 131–154. Lanham: Rowman & Littlefield, 2007.
Kenny, Michael. "Trauma, Memory, and Catharsis: Anthropological Observations on a Folk-Psychological Construct." In *Recollections of Trauma: Scientific Evidence and Clinic Praxis*, edited by Don Read and Steve Lindsay, 475–482. New York: Springer, 1997.
Kittler, Wolf. "Heimlichkeit und Schriftlichkeit: Das österreichische Strafprozessrecht in Franz Kafkas Roman Der Proceß." *The Germanic Review* 78, no. 3 (2003): 194–222.
Klein, Melanie. "A Contribution to the Psychogenesis of Manic-Depressive States." *The International Journal of Psycho-Analysis* 16 (1690): 145–174.
Kligman, Gail. *The Wedding of the Dead: Ritual, Poetics, and Popular Culture in Transylvania*. Berkeley: UC Press, 1988.
Kowalski, Robin. *Complaining, Teasing, and Other Annoying Behaviors*. New Haven: Yale University Press, 2003.
Krass, Samuel. *Die Wiener Geserah vom Jahre 1421*. Wien: Braumüller, 1920.
Kristeva, Julia. *Soleil Noir: Dépression et Mélancolie*. Paris: Gallimard, 1987.
Kutsch, Ernst. "'Trauerbräuche' und 'Selbstminderungsriten' im Alten Testament." *Theologische Studien* 78 (1965): 25–37.
Lacan, Jacques. "Desire and the Interpretation of Desire in *Hamlet*." Translated by James Hulbert. *Yale French Studies* 55, no. 56 (1977): 11–52.
Lacan, Jacques. *Écrits: The First Complete Edition in English*. Translated by Bruce Fink, 197–269. New York: W. W. Norton, 2006.
LaCapra, Dominick. *Writing History, Writing Trauma*. Baltimore: Johns Hopkins University Press, 2000.
Lagache, Daniel. "Le travail du deuil. Ethnologie et psychanalyse." In *Œuvres I: Les hallucinations verbales et travaux cliniques*, edited by Eva Rosenblum, 243–257. Paris: Presses universitaires de France, 1977.
Lagache, Daniel. "The Work of Mourning: Ethnology and Psychoanalysis." In *The Works of Daniel Lagache: Selected Papers 1938–1964*, translated by Elisabeth Holder, 15–29. London: Karnac, 1993.
Laplanche, Jean. *Essays on Otherness*. London: Routledge, 1999.
Lascaratou, Chryssoula. *The Language of Pain: Expression or Description?* Amsterdam: Benjamins, 2007.
Leader, Darian. *The New Black: Mourning, Melancholia and Depression*. Minneapolis: Graywolf Press, 2009.
Lee, Nancy. *Lyrics of Lament: From Tragedy to Transformation*. Minneapolis: Fortress, 2010.
Lee, Nancy. *The Singers of Lamentations: Cities under Siege, from Ur to Jerusalem to Sarajevo*. Leiden: Brill, 2002.
Lessing, Gotthold Ephraim. *Hamburg Dramaturgy. A New and Complete Translation*. Translated by Wendy Arons and Sara Figal. Routledge. http://mcpress.media-commons.org/hamburg/ (accessed November 5, 2019).
Lessing, Gotthold Ephraim. *Laocoon; or the Limits of Poetry and Painting*. Translated by William Ross. London: Ridgway, 1863.

Lessing, Gotthold Ephraim. *Laokoon, oder Über die Grenzen der Malerei und Poesie*. In *Werke und Briefe*. Vol. 5, edited by Wilfried Barner et al. Frankfurt am Main: Klassiker, 1990.
Levinas, Emmanuel. *Otherwise than Being or beyond Essence*. Translated by Alphonso Lingis. Pittsburgh: Duquesne University Press, 1998.
Leys, Ruth. *Trauma: A Genealogy*. Chicago: University of Chicago Press, 2000.
deLille, Alain. *De planctu naturae*. Edited by Johannes Köhler. Münster: Aschendorff, 2013.
Linafeld, Tod. *Surviving Lamentations: Catastrophe, Lament, and Protest in the Afterlife of a Biblical Book*. Chicago: University of Chicago Press, 2000.
Liska, Vivian. *When Kafka Says We: Uncommon Communities in German-Jewish Literature*. Bloomington: Indiana University Press, 2009.
Littré, Émile. *Dictionnaire de la langue française*. Édition intégrale. Paris: Gallimard, 1967 [Reprint].
Liu, Fei-wen. "Expressive Depths: Dialogic Performance of Bridal Lamentation in Rural South China." *American Folklore* 125, no. 496 (2012): 204–225.
Loraux, Nicole. *Mothers in Mourning*. Translated by Corinne Pache. Ithaca: Cornell University Press, 1998.
Loraux, Nicole. *The Mourning Voice*. Translated by Elizabeth Trapnell Rawlings. Ithaca: Cornell University Press, 2002.
[LSJ] *A Greek-English Lexicon*. Edited by Henry G. Liddell and Robert Scott. 9th ed. Oxford: Clarendon, 1996.
Lüddeckens, Erich. *Untersuchungen über religiösen Gehalt, Sprache und Form der ägyptischen Totenklagen*. Mitteilungen des Deutschen Instituts für Ägyptische Altertumskunde in Kairo 11. Berlin: Reichsverlagsamt, 1943.
Lupton, Julia Reinhard, and Kenneth Reinhard. *After Oedipus: Shakespeare in Psychoanalysis*. Ithaca: Cornell University Press, 1993.
Lyotard, Jean-François. *The Differend: Phrases in Dispute*. Translated by Georges Van den Abbeele. Minneapolis: University of Minnesota Press, 1988.
[LXX] *Septuaginta: id est Vetus Testamentum Graece iuxta LXX interpretes*. 2 vols. Edited by Alfred Rahlfs. Stuttgart: DBG, 1962.
Mahony, Patrick. *Freud's Dora: A Psychoanalytic, Historical, and Textual Study*. New Haven: Yale University Press, 1996.
Martin, Jochen. "Von Kleisthenes zu Ephialtes. Zur Entstehung der athenischen Demokratie." In *Demokratia. Der Weg zur Demokratie bei den Griechen*, edited by Konrad Kinzl, 160–212. Darmstadt: WBG, 1995.
de Martino, Ernesto. *Morte e pianto rituale nel mondo antico: Dal lamento pagano al pianto di Maria*. Turin: Einaudi, 1958.
de Martino, Ernesto. *The World of Magic*. Translated by P.S. White. Hong Kong: Pyramid, 1972.
Massumi, Brian. *Parables for the Virtual: Movement, Affect, Sensation*. Durham: Duke University Press, 2002.
Menke, Christoph. "Sklavenaufstand oder Warum Rechte? Eine Skizze." *Zeitschrift für Menschenrechte* 7, no. 2 (2013): 110–126.
Metcalf, Peter, and Richard Huntington. *Celebrations of Death: The Anthropology of the Mortuary Ritual*. 2nd ed. Cambridge: Cambridge University Press, 1991.
Mitscherlich, Alexander, and Margarete Mitscherlich. *The Inability to Mourn: Principles of Collective Behavior*. Translated by Beverley Placzek. New York: Grove Press, 1975.

Modersohn, Mechthild. *Natura als Göttin im Mittelalter: Ikonographische Studien zu Darstellungen der personifizierten Natur*. Berlin: Akademie, 1997.
Moglen, Seth. *Mourning Modernity: Literary Modernism and the Injuries of American Capitalism*. Stanford: Stanford University Press, 2007.
Mosse, George. *Nationalism and Sexuality: Respectability and Abnormal Sexuality in Modern Europe*. New York: Howard Fertig, 1997.
Mukta, Parita. "The 'Civilizing Mission': The Regulation and Control of Mourning in Colonial India." *Feminist Review* 63 (1999): 25–47.
Müller-Schöll, Nikolaus. "Lügen Tränen nicht? Ausdruck, Konvention und Körper in der Wooster-Group-Produktion To You the Birdie! (Phèdre)." In *Theater des Fragments: Performative Strategien im Theater zwischen Antike und Postmoderne*, edited by Anton Bierl et al., 183–205. Bielefeld: transcript, 2009.
Nägele, Rainer. *Reading After Freud: Essays on Goethe, Hölderlin, Habermas, Nietzsche, Brecht, Celan, and Freud*. New York: Columbia University Press, 1987.
Nägele, Rainer. *Theater, Theory, Speculation: Walter Benjamin and the Scenes of Modernity*. Baltimore: Johns Hopkins University Press, 1991.
Nenola-Kallio, Aili. *Studies in Ingrian Laments*. Helsinki: Academia Scientiarum Fennica, 1982.
Nietzsche, Friedrich. *Human, All-Too-Human*. Vol. 2. Translated by Paul Cohn. New York: Macmillan, 1913.
Nietzsche, Friedrich. [KSA] *Kritische Studienausgabe*. Edited by Giorgio Colli and Mazzino Montinari. New ed. München: dtv, 1999.
Nietzsche, Friedrich. *On the Genealogy of Morals. Ecce Homo*. Translated by Walter Kaufmann et al. New York: Vintage, 1989.
Nietzsche, Friedrich. *Thus Spake Zarathustra*. Translated by Thomas Common. New York: Random House, 1909.
Nilsson, Martin. "Der Ursprung der Tragödie." In *Opuscula Selecta*. Vol. 1, 61–145. Lund: Gleerup, 1951.
Ninoshvili, Lauren. "'Wailing in the Cities': Media, Modernity, and the Metamorphosis of Georgian Women's Expressive Labor." *Music and Politics* 6, no. 2 (2012): 1–15.
North, Paul. "Apparent Critique: Inferences from a Benjamin Sketch." *Diacritics* 40, no. 1 (2012): 70–99.
North, Paul. *The Yield: Kafka's Atheological Reformation*. Stanford: Stanford University Press, 2015.
[NRSV] *The New Oxford Annotated Bible. New Revised Standard Version with the Apocrypha*. Edited by Michael Coogan. 5th ed. Oxford: Oxford University Press, 2018.
[OED] *Oxford English Dictionary*. Edited by John A. Simpson and Edmund S.C. Weiner. 2nd ed. Oxford: Claredon, 1989.
[OJB] *The Orthodox Jewish Bible: Tanakh and Orthodox Jewish Brit Chadasha*. Edited by Phillip Goble. New York: AFII, 2010.
Orbell, Margaret. *Waiata: Maori Songs in History*. Rosedale: Raupa, 2009.
Ovidius Naso, Publius. *Amores, Epistulae, Medicamina faciei femineae, Ars amatoria, Remedia amoris*. Edited by Rudolph Merkel. Leupzig: Teubner, 1907.
Ovidius Naso, Publius. *Metamorphoses*. Translated Brooks More. Boston: Cornhill, 1922.

Pahl, Katrin. *Tropes of Transport: Hegel and Emotion*. Evanston: Northwestern University Press, 2012.
Parry, Ken et al. (ed.). *The Blackwell Dictionary of Eastern Christianity*. Oxford: Wiley-Blackwell, 1999.
Paul IV. *Constitution on the Sacred Liturgy*. http://www.vatican.va/archive/hist_councils/ii_vatican_council/documents/vat-ii_const_19631204_sacrosanctum-concilium_en.html (accessed August 15, 2019).
Pederson, Joshua. "Speak, Trauma: Toward a Revised Understanding of Literary Trauma Theory." *Narrative* 22, no. 3 (2014): 333–353.
Pinault, David. "Shia Lamentation Rituals and Reinterpretations of the Doctrine of Intercession: Two Cases from Modern India." *History of Religions* 38, no. 3 (1999): 285–305.
Pistrick, Eckehard. "Singing of Pain and Memory: Emotionalizing Mythistory of Migration in Epirus." *Zeitschrift für Balkanologie* 45, no. 1 (2009): 66–76.
Plato. *Laws*. Translated by Robert Gregg Bury. London: Heinemann, 1967–8.
Plato. *Phaidros*. Translated by Harold N. Fowler. Cambridge: Harvard University Press, 1925.
Plato. *Republic*. Translated by Paul Shorey. Cambridge: Harvard University Press, 1969.
Plöger, Otto. "Die Klagelieder." In *Die fünf Megilloth*, edited by Ernst Würthwein, 127–164. Tübingen: Mohr, 1969.
Plutarch. *Plutarch's Lives, with an English Translation by Bernadotte Perrin*. London: Heinemann, 1914.
Politzer, Heinz. "The Puzzle of Kafka's Prosecuting Attorney." *PMLA* 75, no. 4 (1960): 432–438.
Rappaport, Earnest. "The Ritual Murder Accusation: The Persistence of Doubt and the Repetition Compulsion." In *The Blood Libel Legend: A Casebook in Anti-Semitic Folklore*, edited by Alan Dundes, 304–335. Madison: University of Wisconsin Press, 1991.
Rasmussen, Susan. "Grief at Seeing a Daughter Leave Home: Weeping and Emotion in the Tuareg Techawait Postmarital Residence Ritual." *Journal of American Folklore* 113, no. 450 (2001): 391–421.
Reckwitz, Andreas. *The Invention of Creativity: Modern Society and the Culture of the New*. Translated by Steven Black. Cambridge: Polity, 2017.
Rehm, Rush. *Marriage to Death: The Conflation of Wedding and Funeral Rituals in Greek Tragedy*. Princeton: Princeton University Press, 1994.
Reiner, Eugen. *Die Rituelle Totenklage der Griechen*. Stuttgart-Berlin: Kohlhammer, 1938.
Richardson, Nicholas. *The Iliad: A Commentary*. Vol. VI: Books 21–24. Edited by Mark Edwards. Cambridge: Cambridge University Press, 1993.
Richter, Simon. *Laocoon's Body and the Aesthetics of Pain: Winckelmann, Lessing, Herder, Moritz, Goethe*. Detroit: Wayne State University Press, 1992.
Ricœur, Paul. *Freud and Philosophy: An Essay on Interpretation*. Translated by Denis Savage. New Haven: Yale University Press, 1970.
Ries, Nancy. *Russian Talk: Culture and Conversation during Perestroika*. Ithaca: Cornell University Press, 1997.
Rilke, Rainer Maria. *Duino Elegies and the Sonnets to Orpheus*. Translated by Stephen Mitchell. New York: Vintage, 1982.

Rilke, Rainer Maria. *Requiem for a Friend*, translated by Eric Torgersen. In *Dear Friend: Rainer Maria Rilke and Paula Modersohn-Becker*, edited by Eric Torgersen, 261–267. Evanston: Northwestern University Press, 1998.

Rilke, Rainer Maria. [RSW] *Sämtliche Werke*. Edited by Rilke-Archiv et al. Frankfurt am Main: Insel, 1955–1966.

Robertson Smith, William. *Religion of the Semites*, 2nd ed. London, 1984.

Robjant, David. "Learning of Pains: Wittgenstein's Own Cartesian Mistake at 246." *Wittgenstein-Studien* 3 (2012): 261–285.

Rosenzweig, Franz. *The Star of Redemption*. Translated by Barbara Galli. Madison: University of Wisconsin Press, 2005.

Rückert, Friedrich. *Kindertodtenlieder und andere Texte des Jahres 1834. Historisch-kritische Ausgabe ›Schweinfurter Edition‹*. Edited by Hans Wollschläger and Rudolf Kreutner. Göttingen: Wallstein, 2007.

Said, Edward. *Orientalism*. 25th anniversary edition. New York: Vintage, 1994.

Salberg, Jill. "The Texture of Traumatic Attachment: Presence and Ghostly Absence in Transgenerational Transmission." In *Wounds of History: Repair and Resilience in the Trans-Generational Transmission of Trauma*, edited by Jill Salberg and Sue Grand, 77–99. London: Routledge, 2017.

Santner, Eric. *On Creaturely Life: Rilke, Benjamin, Sebald*. Chicago: University of Chicago Press, 2006.

Saunders, Rebecca. *Lamentations and Modernity: Literature, Philosophy, and Culture*. New York: Palgrave Macmillan, 2007.

de Saussure, Ferdinand. *Course in General Linguistics*. Translated by Wade Baskin. New York: Columbia University Press, 2011.

Scarry, Elaine. *The Body in Pain: The Making and Unmaking of the World*. Oxford: Oxford University Press, 1985.

Schelling, Friedrich Wilhelm Joseph. *The Philosophy of Art*. Translated by Douglas Scott. Minneapolis: University of Minnesota Press, 1989.

Schmidt, Jochen. *Klage: Überlegungen zur Linderung reflexiven Leidens*. Tübingen: Mohr, 2011.

Scholem, Gershom. *Lamentations of Youth: The Diaries of Gershom Scholem, 1913–1919*. Edited and translated by Anthony David Skinner. London: Belknap, 2007.

Scholem, Gershom. [LL] "On Lament and Lamentation." Translated by Lina Barouch and Paula Schwebel. *Jewish Studies Quarterly* 21 (2014): 6–12.

Scholem, Gershom. *Tagebücher nebst Aufsätzen und Entwürfen bis 1923*. 2. Halbband. Edited by Karlfried Gründer et al. Frankfurt am Main: Jüdischer Verlag, 2000.

Schroer, Silvia. "Biblische Klagetraditionen zwischen Ritual und Literatur. Eine genderbezogene Skizze." In *Klagetraditionen: Form und Funktion der Klage in den Kulturen der Antike*, edited by Margaret Jaques, 83–101. Fribourg: academic, 2011.

Schwab, Gabriele. *Haunting Legacies: Violent Histories and Transgenerational Trauma*. New York: Columbia University Press, 2010.

Schüttpelz, Erhard. *Die Moderne im Spiegel des Primitiven. Weltliteratur und Ethnologie (1870–1960)*. München: Fink, 2005.

Schwebel, Paula. "The Tradition in Ruins: Walter Benjamin and Gershom Scholem on Language and Lament." In *Lament in Jewish Thought*, edited by Ilit Ferber and Paula Schwebel, 277–301. Berlin: deGryuter, 2014.

Seaford, Richard. *Reciprocity and Ritual: Homer and Tragedy in the Developing City-State*. Oxford: Claredon, 1995.
Searle, John. *Expression and Meaning: Studies in the Theory of Speech Acts*. Cambridge, 1979.
Searle, John, and Daniel Vanderveken. *Foundations of Illocutionary Logic*. Cambridge, UK: Cambridge University Press, 1985.
Sekher, Ayaj. "Gender, Caste, and Fiction: A Bahujan Reading of Mahasveta Devi's Rudali." *Economic & Political Weekly* 41, no. 42 (2006): 4422–4425.
Seremetakis, C. Nadia. *The Last Word: Women, Death, and Divination in Inner Mani*. Chicago: Chicago University Press, 1991.
Shapiro, H.A. "The Iconography of Mourning in Athenian Art." *American Journal of Archeology* 95 (1991): 629–656.
Singleton, Jermaine. *Cultural Melancholy: Readings of Race, Impossible Mourning, and African American Ritual*. Champaign: University of Illinois Press, 2015.
Solzhenitsyn, Aleksandr Isaevich. "Matryona's Home." In *The Solzhenitsyn Reader*, edited by Edward Ericson et al., 24–56. Wilmington, DE: ISI, 2006.
Solzhenitsyn, Aleksandr Isaevich. "Матрёнин Двор." In *Рассказыи и Крохотки. Собрание Сочинений*. Vol. 1, 116–148. Moscow: Vremya, 2006.
Sourvinou-Inwood, Christiane. Review of *Dangerous Voices*, by Gail Holst-Warhaft. *The Classical Review* 44, no. 1 (1994): 67–69.
Stears, Karen. "Death Becomes Her: Gender and Athenian Death Ritual." In *Lament: Studies in the Ancient Mediterranean and Beyond*, edited by Ann Suter, 139–155. Oxford: Oxford University Press, 2008.
Stow, Simon. *American Mourning: Tragedy, Democracy, Resilience*. Cambridge: Cambridge University Press, 2017.
Suchoff, David. *Kafka's Jewish Languages: The Hidden Openness of Tradition*. Philadelphia: University of Pennsylvania Press, 2012.
Susman, Margarate. "Das Hiob-Problem bei Franz Kafka." In *Franz Kafka: Wege der Forschung*, edited by Heinz Politzer, 48–68. Darmstadt: WBG, 1973.
Suter, Ann. "Male Lament in Greek Tragedy." In *Lament: Studies in the Ancient Mediterranean and Beyond*, edited by Ann Suter, 156–180. Oxford: Oxford University Press, 2008.
Temkin, Jack. "Wittgenstein on Epistemic Privacy." *Philosophical Quarterly* 31, no. 123 (1981): 97–109.
Thucydides. *The Peloponnesian War*. Translated by Richard Crawley. London: Dent, 1910.
Tolbert, Elizabeth. "Women Cry with Words: Symbolization of Affect in the Karelian Lament." *Yearbook for Traditional Music* 22 (1990): 80–105.
Torok, Maria. "Restes d'effacement entre Sigmund Freud at Emmy von N." *Cahiers Confrontation* 15 (1986): 121–136.
Trüstedt, Katrin. "Execution without Verdict: Kafka's (Non-)Person." *Law Critique* 26 (2015): 135–154.
Turner, Victor. "Betwixt and between: The Liminal Period in Rites des Passage." In *Reader in Comparative Religion*, edited by William Lessa and Evon Vogt, 234–243. 4th ed. New York: Harper & Row, 1979.
Urban, Greg. *Metaphysical Community: The Interplay of the Senses and the Intellect*. Austin: University of Texas Press, 1996.
Urban, Greg. "Ritual Wailing in the Amerindian Brazil." *American Anthropologist* 90, no. 2 (1988): 385–400.

Vasmer, Max. *Russisches Etymologisches Wörterbuch*. Heidelberg: Winter, 1967.
Veteranyi, Aglaja. *Das Regal der letzten Atemzüge*. Stuttgart: dtv, 2002.
Veteranyi, Aglaja. *Warum das Kind in der Polenta kocht*. Stuttgart: dtv, 1999.
Veteranyi, Aglaja. *Why the Child Is Cooking in the Polenta*. Translated by Vincent Kling. Champaign: Dalkey Archive, 2012.
Villanueva, Federico. *The "Uncertainty of a Hearing": A Study in the Sudden Change of Mood in the Psalms of Lament*. Leiden: Brill, 2008.
Wade, Cleo. *Heart Talk*. New York: 37ink, 2018.
Weber, Samuel. *Benjamin's – abilities*. Cambridge, MA: Harvard University Press, 2008.
Weber, Samuel. "Tragedy and *Trauerspiel*: Too Alike?" In *Tragedy and the Idea of Modernity*, edited by Joshua Billings and Miriam Leonard, 88–114. Oxford: Oxford University Press, 2015.
Weidner, Daniel. *Gershom Scholem. Politisches, esoterisches und historiographisches Schreiben*. München: Fink, 2003.
Weidner, Daniel. "'Movement of Language' and Transience: Lament, Mourning, and the Tradition of Elegy in Early Scholem." In *Lament in Jewish Thought*, edited by Ilit Ferber and Paula Schwebel, 237–254. Berlin: deGruyter, 2014.
Weigel, Sigrid. "Brünnhilde's Lament: The Mourning Play of the Gods." *The Opera Quarterly* 31 (2015): 1–18.
Weigel, Sigrid. "Lamento: Die Stimme von Klage und Oper." Lecture, Denkerei, Berlin, June 9, 2015.
Weigel, Sigrid. "'Public Crying': Zur Wiederkehr öffentlichen Trauerns auf den Straßen der öffentlichen Städte." In *Interkulturelle Schauplätze in der Großstadt*, edited by Kikuko Kashiwagi-Wetzel and Michael Wetzel, 43–57. Paderborn: Fink, 2015.
Weigel, Sigrid. "Télescopage im Unbewußten. Zum Verhältnis von Trauma, Geschichtsbegriff und Literatur." In *Trauma: Zwischen Psychoanalyse und kulturellem Deutungsmuster*, edited by Elisabeth Bronfen et al., 51–76. Köln: Böhlau, 1999.
Weiss, Naomi. "The Representation of Lament in Greek Tragedy." *American Journal of Philology* 138 (2017): 243–266.
Weissberg, Liliane. "Language's Wound: Herder, Philoctetes, and the Origin of Speech." *MLN* 104 (1989): 548–579.
Weitzman, Erica. *Irony's Antics: Walser, Kafka, Roth, and the German Comic Tradition*. Evanston: Northwestern University Press, 2014.
Wellbery, David. "The Pathos of Theory: Laokoon Revisited." In *Intertextuality: German Literature and Visual Art from the Renaissance to the Twentieth Century*, edited by Ingeborg Hoesterey and Ulrich Weisstein, 47–63. Columbia, SC: Camden, 1993.
Welz, Claudia. *Vertrauen und Versuchung*. Tübingen: Mohr, 2010.
Westermann, Claus. *Lob und Klage in den Psalmen*. Göttingen: Vandenhoeck & Ruprecht, 1977.
Whitman, Walt. *Poetry and Prose*. New York: Library of America, 1996.
Wickett, Elizabeth. *For the Living and the Dead: The Funerary Laments of Upper Egypt. Ancient and Modern*. London: I.B. Tauris, 2010.
Wilce, James M. *Crying Shame: Metaculture, Modernity, and the Exaggerated Death of Lament*. Chichester: Wiley-Blackwell, 2009.

Wittgenstein, Ludwig. [LW] *Last Writings on the Philosophy of Psychology.* Translated by C. G. Luckhardt und Maximilian A.E. Aue. Oxford: Basil Blackwell, 1982.
Wittgenstein, Ludwig. [LSPP] *Letzte Schriften über die Philosophie der Psychologie.* In *Werkausgabe.* Vol. 7. Frankfurt am Main: Suhrkamp, 1984.
Wittgenstein, Ludwig. [PI] *Philosophical Investigations.* Translated by G.E.M. Anscombe. 3rd ed. Oxford: Basil Blackwell, 1958.
Wittgenstein, Ludwig. [PR] *Philosophical Remarks.* Translated by Raymond Hargreaves and Roger White. Oxford: Basil Blackwell, 1975.
Wittgenstein, Ludwig. *Philosophische Bemerkungen.* In *Werkausgabe.* Vol. 2. Frankfurt am Main: Suhrkamp, 1984.
Wittgenstein, Ludwig. [PU] *Philosophische Untersuchungen.* In *Werkausgabe.* Vol. 1. Frankfurt am Main: Suhrkamp, 1984.
Wittgenstein, Ludwig. "Remarks on Frazer's *Golden Bough.*" In *Wittgenstein: Sources and Perspectives*, edited by C.G. Luckhardt, 61–81. Hassocks: Harvester, 1979.
Wittgenstein, Ludwig. [TLP] *Tractatus Logico-Philosophicus.* Translated by David Pears and Brian McGuinnes. New York: Routledge, 1961.
Wohlfarth, Irving. "On Some Jewish Motifs in Benjamin." In *Walter Benjamin: Critical Evaluations and Cultural Theory 3: Appropriations*, edited by Peter Osborne, 162–212. London: Routledge, 2005.
Worobec, Christine. "Death Ritual among Russian and Ukrainian Peasants: Linkages between the Living and the Dead." In *Letters from Heaven: Popular Religion in Russia and Ukraine*, edited by John-Paul Himka and Andriy Zayarnyuk, 13–45. Toronto: University of Toronto Press, 2006.
Young, Julian. *The Philosophy of Tragedy: From Plato to Žižek.* Cambridge: Cambridge University Press, 2013.

# INDEX

Abraham, Nicolas 2, 29, 53, 67, 69–75, 102, 171–2, 249–50, 254–8
Achilles 112, 117–18, 122, 127–8, 138
Adorno, Theodor 22, 148
Aeschylus
   *Oresteia* (*Agamemnon, Libation Bearers, Eumenides*) 24, 26, 37, 60–1, 77, 89–90, 124, 133–9, 171, 201, 236
   *The Persians* 24, 77, 88, 128–31, 138, 183, 201
affect theory 6, 29–35, 38–9, 43–4, 55, 60–7, 80, 96–7, 109, 126–7, 144, 205n.69, 214–16, 249n.23
Aristotle 7–10, 31, 112, 137, 144, 180, 201, 217
St. Augustine 84
Austin, John Langshaw 11, 13

Bakhtin, Mikhail 4–5, 246
Benjamin, Walter
   "Commentaries on Poems by Brecht" 198–99, 246
   "Franz Kafka" 196, 239
   "Idea of a Mystery" 195–8, 230
   "Karl Kraus" 195
   "On Language as Such and on The Language of Man" 165–6, 177–9, 188–200
   *The Origin of German Tragic Drama* 57, 179, 184–6, 194–5, 197–8, 200–7
   "The Role of Language in Trauerspiel and Tragedy" 179–84, 187, 198, 203
   "On the Concept of History" 176, 179, 186, 198–9, 245

Bernhard, Thomas 26, 255–60
Butler, Judith 13–14, 24, 55n.53

Canetti, Elias 62, 81
Caruth, Cathy 32, 52n.49, 256
Cavell, Stanley 28, 157–8, 161, 170, 173
chorus 8, 24, 90, 118, 120–1, 124, 129–31, 133, 138, 200–3, 235–7
civil war 25, 131–2, 134–5, 138

deferred action (see also *Nachträglichkeit*) 37, 51, 198, 207
Descartes, René 28, 151–3
dirge 9, 18–22, 24, 36–7, 46, 65, 75, 80, 83–93, 100, 105, 109–15, 118–24, 130–4, 137–9, 159–60, 168, 172, 236–7, 246, 251–3
"Dora" (Ida Bauer) 36n.19, 46–8, 50, 61, 215, 249
Durkheim, Émile 78–9, 91n.84, 133–4

*Eicha* (see also *book of Lamentations*) 11, 14, 18, 22–3, 142, 164–76, 252
elegy 14, 16–18, 28, 89, 95
emotion 3, 10, 79, 96–8, 109–10, 113, 120–6, 137, 149, 152–3, 214, 253
*epitaphios logos* 85, 132, 144
Euripides
   *Iphigenia in Tauris* 89
   *Trojan Women* 138, 183, 201
Book of Ezekiel 3–4, 13, 18n.67–8

Freud, Sigmund
   *Beyond the Pleasure Principle* 52n.49
   *The Ego and The Id* 64–6, 70, 128, 153n.36, 253

# INDEX

*Fragment of an Analysis of a Case of Hysteria* ("Dora") 36n.19, 46–8, 50, 61, 215, 249
*Interpretation of Dreams* 28n.5, 39–48
"Mourning and Melancholia" 13n.41, 55–64, 69, 74, 206–7, 250
*Studies on Hysteria* 27–39, 65–7
*From the History of an Infantile Neurosis* ("Wolf Man") 37, 48–56, 61–3, 67, 69–75, 102, 152–3, 249–50
*Totem and Taboo* 65–6, 78
funeral/funerary rites 17, 25, 67, 80, 84, 86–91, 95, 99–114, 117, 123–6, 130–4, 114–15, 255–60

gender 14, 16, 21, 24, 28, 37, 82, 85–8, 94, 113, 123–5, 130–3, 137, 178
Genesis 166 (1:19), 184, 188–91 (2:19-20)
genre 6, 9, 14–21, 25, 28, 80–2, 85, 89–91, 122, 143–5, 156, 160, 163–4, 171–2, 179, 182, 186, 204–5, 210, 225
Goetz, Rainald 18–19
*goos* 20, 85, 89–90, 117, 133
Gryphius, Andreas 188, 202

Hamacher, Werner 11, 190n.36, 193
Hegel, G.W.F. 88, 132, 134, 147, 181
Heidegger, Martin 7, 234
Herder, Johann Gottfried 23, 177–9, 188–94, 192, 194, 200–1
Homer 10n.28, 117–18, 123n.241, 132, 138

Jakobson, Roman 4
Book of Job 1 (13:17; 19:7), 22, 48, 54 (3:3), 161, 197 (3), 202n.63, 216

Kafka, Franz
 *Amerika* (*see also* "The Stoker") 223
 "Description of a Struggle" 216–17, 223, 239
 "An Introductory Talk on the Yiddish Language" 210–15
 "The Judgement" 217
 "A Little Woman" 220–1, 239
 "My Neighbor" 210, 218–22, 224
 "The Stoker" 210, 223–41
Kant, Immanuel 184–5, 189
*kommos* (see also *planctus*) 8, 20–1, 85, 90, 131, 180, 201, 237

Lacan, Jacques 5, 27, 60
Lagache, Daniel 67–9, 102
Book of Lamentations (see also *Eicha*) 11, 14, 18, 22–3, 142, 164–76, 252
law/legal action 10, 19–20, 58–60, 86, 130–2, 138, 180, 196–7, 210, 225–40
Lessing, Gotthold Ephraim 181, 200–2, 205, 219–20, 225, 229–30
Lévinas, Emmanuel 221–2
liturgy 17, 81, 105, 126
Loraux, Nicole 91, 130, 136–9
Luke 84 (23:27-8), 124 (7:32)

de Martino, Ernesto 91–2
melancholia/melancholy 47, 55–66, 69, 74, 92, 128, 206–7, 245, 249n.23, 250
Mitscherlich, Alexander and Margarete Mitscherlich 249–252, 257, 259n.68
mourning play ( see also *Trauerspiel*) 180–3, 186–8, 197–8, 200n.53, 202–6

*Nachträglichkeit* (*see also* deferred action) 37, 51, 198, 207
*nenia* (Roman dirge) 9, 86, 89–90
Nietzsche, Friedrich 10, 136, 181

Opitz, Martin 184, 202n.60
Ovid (Ovidius Naso, Publius) 16–17, 178n.4

St. Paul 104, 107–8, 200n.53
performativity 7, 11–13, 82, 94, 164n.53, 244

*planctus* (see also *kommos*) 20–1, 84, 89, 133
Plato 13n.43, 53, 89, 130–2, 143, 167
Plutarch 89, 130–4
politics 24–5, 122, 131–2, 136–40, 161, 210, 234–41
populism 24–5, 210
primal scene 51–2, 54, 61, 70, 131, 167, 179, 188, 207, 221
psalms 9, 15, 84, 110, 171
  Ps. 137:1 46
  Ps. 5:8 18

Revelations 230 (12:10)
revenge 13, 25, 28, 30–3, 37–8, 58–62, 66, 78–9, 85, 97, 127–40, 171, 197, 202n.61, 209, 214, 222
Rilke, Rainer Maria
  *Duino Elegies* X 16–19
  *Requiem For a Friend* 77n.1, 80, 100, 108–9, 115–16, 118, 127, 135–6, 160, 198
Rosenzweig, Franz 202–3
Rückert, Friedrich 8

Scholem, Gershom 26, 45, 141–3, 164–176, 177–80, 187, 194–5, 197–8, 200, 209, 216n.16, 222
Searle, John 11–13
Shakespeare, William
  *Hamlet* 38, 45n.36, 57, 60
  *A Lover's Complaint* 86, 225
Solon 89, 130–4
Solzhenitsyn, Aleksandr Isaevich 122
Song of Songs 221 (5:6)
Sophocles
  *Ajax* 88
  *Antigone* 13, 24, 132, 139, 236n.65
  *Philoctetes* 189, 191, 200–1
superstition 89, 92, 253

theory, criticism of 5–16, 23, 27–8, 34, 39, 47, 78, 95, 98, 141–4, 149, 157, 163–5, 176, 177–81, 184, 193–5, 199–207
*threnos* (see also *kommos*) 20, 85, 90, 131, 180

Thucydides 25, 131–2
Torok, Maria 2, 29, 53, 67, 69–75, 102, 171–2, 249–50, 254–8
tragedy 8, 13n.43, 17, 20–1, 28, 31, 35–7, 59–60, 81, 85, 87–8, 127–39, 161, 164, 169, 179–84, 197, 200–6, 235–6
*Trauerspiel* (*see also* mourning play) 180–4, 186–8, 197–8, 200n.53, 202–6
trauma 28–75, 90, 93–7, 108, 121, 133, 148n.22, 169, 199, 233, 243–60
Turner, Victor 83, 110–11

vendetta (*see* revenge)
Veteranyi, Aglaja 78, 99–108, 111, 118–120, 122, 127–8, 134

wailing 1–2, 14, 18, 20–1, 37, 44–5, 58, 60, 66, 75, 79–92, 97, 109, 113–14, 117, 127, 129, 138, 158–60, 200–2, 236, 246, 151–3
wailing-women 24, 79, 84–5, 88, 109, 117, 122–7, 166, 183
war (*see also* civil war) 25, 53, 56, 65, 86, 131–32, 142, 198–9, 211, 245–53
"war on terror" 24
Werfel, Franz 184
Winckelmann, Johann Joachim 200
Wittgenstein, Ludwig 166, 176, 179, 205
  *Last Writings on the Philosophy of Psychology* 158–9, 162
  *Philosophical Investigations* 12, 26, 141–65, 168–70, 174, 177, 183–4, 225
  *Philosophical Remarks* 147, 154
  *Tractatus Logico-Philosophicus* 143–4
"Wolf Man" (Sergei Constantinovitch Pankeiev) 37, 48–56, 61–3, 67, 69–75, 102, 152–3, 249–50